The Republic of Love

The Republic of Love

Opera and Political Freedom

MARTHA C. NUSSBAUM

OXFORD
UNIVERSITY PRESS

Oxford University Press is a department of the University of Oxford.
It furthers the University's objective of excellence in research, scholarship,
and education by publishing worldwide. Oxford is a registered trade mark of
Oxford University Press in the UK and certain other countries.

Published in the United States of America by Oxford University Press
198 Madison Avenue, New York, NY 10016, United States of America.

Library of Congress Cataloging-in-Publication Data
Names: Nussbaum, Martha C. (Martha Craven), 1947– author
Title: The republic of love : opera and political freedom /
Martha C. Nussbaum.
Description: [First edition]. | New York, NY : Oxford University Press, 2026. |
Includes bibliographical references and index. |
Identifiers: LCCN 2025041933 (print) | LCCN 2025041934 (ebook) |
ISBN 9780197812556 hardback | ISBN 9780197812587 | ISBN 9780197812563 epub
Subjects: LCSH: Opera—Political aspects
Classification: LCC ML3918.O64 N87 2026 (print) | LCC ML3918.O64 (ebook) |
DDC 782.109—dc23/eng/20250922
LC record available at https://lccn.loc.gov/2025041933
LC ebook record available at https://lccn.loc.gov/2025041934

DOI: 10.1093/oso/9780197812556.001.0001

Printed by Sheridan Books, Inc., United States of America

The manufacturer's authorized representative in the EU for product safety is
Oxford University Press España S.A. of Parque Empresarial San Fernando de Henares,
Avenida de Castilla, 2 – 28830 Madrid (www.oup.es/en or product.safety@oup.com).
OUP España S.A. also acts as importer into Spain of products made by the manufacturer.

For Gerd Wichert

O welche Lust in freier Luft
Den Athem einzuheben!
Nur hier, nur hier ist Leben.

Oh what delight to draw breath
In free air.
Only here, only here, is life.

—Beethoven, Fidelio, Prisoners' Chorus

Contents

Acknowledgments

This book draws on many years of work writing program essays for Lyric Opera of Chicago (also the Belgian National Opera), focusing initially on the Mozart operas, but then branching out; and also on more than ten years of teaching a class on opera jointly with Anthony Freud, general director and CEO of Lyric Opera of Chicago, now emeritus, where we have both explored a variety of works and interviewed outstanding guests, including especially singers Ana Maria Martinez, Lawrence Brownlee, and Eric Owens, composer Jake Heggie, conductor Enrique Mazzola, and many others, all of whom have been important to me in exploring Mozart further and in moving beyond Mozart into the nineteenth and twentieth centuries.

I have so far published essays for Lyric on Mozart's *Don Giovanni*, *The Marriage of Figaro*, *Idomeneo*, *The Magic Flute*, and *Così fan tutte*; on Beethoven's *Fidelio*, Verdi's *Don Carlos* and *Aida* (and one on Verdi's *Falstaff*, for the Chicago Shakespeare Theater); on Puccini's *Madama Butterfly*, Bizet's *Carmen*, Wagner's *Ring* cycle, and Janáček's *Jenůfa*. I have also written two longer articles: one on Mozart's *La Clemenza di Tito*, expanded from a program essay for Belgian National Opera, and published in a festschrift for the late David Konstan, but thoroughly recast, and a paper on *Idomeneo*, given at a conference in honor of the late Paul Woodruff, and unpublished. The *Figaro* program essay was based on an article that was published separately and also formed a chapter in my 2013 book *Political Emotions*; it is reproduced relatively intact as a chapter here. Finally, I have written a book on Britten's *War Requiem*, which appeared in November 2024; it contains much discussion of Britten's entire career, leaving the job of interpreting *Peter Grimes* and *Albert Herring* for this book.

The book does not simply reproduce the program essays as such (as philosopher Bernard Williams's widow did in his posthumous book *On Opera*, published by Yale University Press in 2016). Everything has been rethought, and in some cases my overall interpretation has shifted. This book is aimed at general readers who care about opera and are interested in its connections to political thought and political life. Throughout, I talk about the music, not simply the libretto (and frequently argue that the music goes beyond, or is even at times at odds with, the libretto), but I try to deal with music in an accessible manner and refer to the scholarship with a light hand, as it illuminates central themes.

I owe thanks to many people, and those thanks extend through almost my whole life, since I became hooked on opera at a very young age: so first, to my parents, who did not go to performances but were always playing records of arias and duets (my father favored Lily Pons and Joan Sutherland, my mother Mario Lanza, and both of them adored Kirsten Flagstad and Lauritz Melchior). My grandmother, who lived in New York, took me to the Metropolitan Opera one day when I was six and visiting her for the weekend. We had close-up orchestra seats for Verdi's *Rigoletto*, which shocked and profoundly moved me, so that for a long time after that I acted the story with my dolls, casting one as the ill-fated Gilda entering the sack. From that time on, I listened to the Metropolitan Opera Saturday afternoon broadcasts whenever I could. I remember staying in my room during a festive family gathering, in order to listen to *The Rake's Progress*, which did not interest my family. By the time I was thirteen, I began saving up to buy opera recordings, my earliest being Joan Sutherland's 1961 *Lucia*.

Then there was my best friend, Adrienne Child, who sang duets with me ("Sous le dôme épais" from *Lakmé* was a favorite), listened to recordings, and joined, with me, the Philadelphia Lyric Opera

Guild, where we heard both performances and dress rehearsals. (I remember especially a *Carmen* dress rehearsal in 1963 with Jon Vickers and Gloria Lane.) I began voice lessons in 1964, and from that time on I have learned from a long series of voice teachers, since one way I have tried to understand is by singing. Beyond these I have learned from the people with whom I have been fortunate to share musical experiences. Above all, these are the members of the Nussbaum family: my (now ex-) husband Alan Nussbaum, who preferred orchestral music but tolerated opera, especially the operas of Mozart; the rest of the Nussbaum family, especially Charles, Suzanne, and Miriam (Mimi); other family members, especially my sister Gail Craven, a professional organist and choir director; and, above all, my dear daughter the late Rachel Nussbaum, who delighted in opera from her first requests at the age of four (for the Toreador song from *Carmen*, under the name "Door," and the Gilda/Rigoletto vengeance duet from *Rigoletto*, under the name "Vendetta") and, later, her constant enacting of operas with her dolls and stuffed animals, once she got hold of a book of opera plots. (Because she chose her theatricals for the plot rather than the music, she sometimes chose operas rarely performed: a dramatic scene of a bandaged British soldier-doll being nursed by an exotic female doll depicted Delibes's *Lakmé*.) Our operatic companionship continued through hundreds of shared performances and recordings, until the day of her death in December 2019, when *The Marriage of Figaro* was playing in her hospital room. Fortunately that chapter of the present book had already been written, since I could not bear to listen to that opera until November 2024, when I lasted until the end of Act II. And finally her husband, Gerd Wichert, who now attends every opera with me, as well as many concerts, and has been a huge help with this book, since he has every program of every opera he has been to, and has been able to show me program essays of long-ago German productions, some of which I cite in my chapters. I dedicate this book to him, with affection and gratitude.

And of course I have learned from another type of opera "family": Anthony Freud and the many students in our opera class over the years.

I have had several generations of peerless Research Assistants, and give thanks to Miranda Bannister, Jonathan Jiang, Frances Mangina, Nima Mohammadi, and Teo Ruskov.

During the writing of this book I have presented numerous chapters at faculty Work-in-Progress workshops and received written comments from many colleagues and friends: especially Douglas Baird, Emily Buss, Frank Easterbrook, Philip Kitcher, Saul Levmore, Frances Mangina, Elise and Howard Masur, Charles Nussbaum, Suzanne Nussbaum, Eric Posner, and an anonymous referee. I am especially grateful to David Armitage, who commented on chapter 8 at a forum at Brown University in March 2025, and his insights have illuminated my final revisions.

For superb help with copy-edits and proofs, I am grateful to Dominic Sprigg.

Chapter 1 is based, with considerable revision, on the first chapter of my 2013 book *Political Emotions: Why Love Matters for Justice* (Cambridge, MA: Harvard University Press). Chapter 4 is a revised version of my contribution to *Hope, Joy, and Affection in the Classical World*, a festschrift for David Konstan, edited by Ruth R. Caston and Robert A. Kaster (New York: Oxford University Press, 2016), 226–40.

Opera and Political Thought

Opera is and does many wonderful things. To claim an essence or defining characteristic for opera is foolish bravado, and negates opera's marvelous many-sidedness. But one thing that opera most definitely does is to engage in political thought, entering a dialogue with other texts of political thought in other media. Political thought sometimes focuses on institutions and policies, but political thought in opera more often goes beneath these structures to ask what human beings have to be like to sustain political institutions of different types. What must their emotions be like? What rights and freedoms must they have? How should and do they relate to the surrounding institutional structures? How do and how should they conceive of gender, rank, and class? Composers of opera (aided but not bossed around by their librettists) express views on these matters not only in the plot and dialogue of their unfolding dramas, but also, and especially, in their music. This book is determined to show that, and how, music itself, often with a specificity underdetermined by the libretto, maps out a quasi-argument on these matters.

I attempt to honor the work of major musicologists, but my approach is, inevitably, that of a moral-political philosopher whose abiding interests combine the political thought of the Enlightenment and the emotions of the heart. The central contention of the book is that the development of a politics of emotion (and gender) in a group of operas makes a creative contribution to the imagining of a political culture in which equality and freedom are combined in a distinctive manner. The title of the book makes reference to my 2018 book, *The Monarchy of Fear: A Philosopher*

Looks at Our Political Crisis.[1] This book is an antidote, if you will, or a counterbalance, to the somewhat pessimistic reflections expressed there.

Opera engages in political reflection in a unique way. Its supreme contribution consists in mapping the contours of the emotions, both individual and corporate, which sustain or impede different types of political life. Unlike stage drama, it can use a chorus to give voice to group emotions. And music can show us more than the spoken word ever can about the trajectory and nuance of emotional lives, whether individual or group, showing how specific types of emotion fit or impede specific types of political structure.

Within the general project of working out political thought in opera, we find, naturally, more than one approach. Wagner's *Die Meistersinger*, for example, develops a picture of a conservative communitarian polity (albeit with no visible institutions), asking us to see a conservative xenophobic music-culture as a necessary condition for genuine musical art, and monophonic musical art (expressing a single artist's vision) for social health. I confront this antagonist in chapter 9, and investigate the underlying sense of human problems that leads to this repressive solution. In particular, I argue that this strand is driven by a despairing sense of the worthlessness of actual daily life and real human projects, a pessimism theorized by Schopenhauer, who persuaded many readers, who were already feeling a vertiginous sense of the instability of their real efforts, together with a belief that what is incomplete and imperfect is not worth loving.

One might, however, believe that real life, with all of its reversals and its lack of fruition, is worth loving for itself. And in that spirit one might embrace the realities of political life, even when they are messy and uncongenial. This love of the real is, I try to show, an essential part of achieving and maintaining a republic, in which each person—however incomplete and unsatisfactory—has a voice and

---

[1] Nussbaum (2018).

in which politics emerges from the reciprocal agreements of imperfect individuals. Mozart's instincts as a human being and a composer put him on the side of those who love the world as it is.

The Mozartean strand I follow is one associated with the liberal Enlightenment, for which the best institutional form is the republic and for which freedoms of expression and association are pivotal. Opera came of age in the eighteenth century, when the world was turning upside down and new revolutionary projects were springing up, with liberty, equality, and fraternity as their watchwords. Wagner's reactionary project is a reaction against this liberal tradition, and it is fair to say that liberal republicanism was long dominant in the opera world, perhaps more than in the world of political reality—with Enlightenment figures such as Mozart, Beethoven, and Verdi as leading contributors. My book concerns what I shall call a Mozartean tradition—of which living composers Jake Heggie and John Adams are heirs.

Mozart (1756–1791) was a committed man of the Enlightenment. He built that commitment into his life by becoming a Freemason in Vienna, but his liberal sympathies antecede that step. Music was central to the Freemasons, and Mozart wrote many works for his lodge. More generally, his operas are suffused with the radical Enlightenment spirit of the Freemasons and their sympathizers—with ideas of freedom, equality, and fraternal love. In spirit and in plot, quite a few of his operas express sentiments that place him in conversation with other political thinkers of the era, such as Jean-Jacques Rousseau (1712–1778), Immanuel Kant (1724–1804), and Johann Gottfried von Herder (1744–1803). There is, however, something distinctive about Mozart's republicanism: it is a republicanism of the heart. By this I mean that Mozart sees more deeply than many around him (Herder perhaps excepted) when he sees that the old order cannot be truly changed by simply changing outward institutional forms. Being a person and citizen supporting freedom, equality, and fraternity means becoming a new type of person, with new sentiments.

Before, during, and after the French Revolution, the age-old morality of feudal hierarchy and rigid class division was under siege, and, with it, the age-old morality of cringing fear, wounded honor, and mandatory revenge. The Enlightenment had a politics of both individual freedom and human brotherhood and equality. But it too often lacked a politics of the heart. Little attention was given in major theorists to a need for the reform of our sentiments, if we are really to live as free people and equals (see chapter 1). Feudalism had not just a politics but also an emotion map for its various actors. That map itself needed reform if people were not to be trapped in new hierarchies. To build the sort of community they sought, republicans would have to learn not to rely primarily on fear and retributive anger as their guides in human relations. They would need to cultivate an equality-based compassion. And they would need new forms of love. Love, under feudalism, was typically understood as a form of domination. The standard sentiment map for males, whether upper-class or lower-class, included domination over women. True human equality and fraternity couldn't just empower lower-class males: that would simply substitute one form of domination for another (as we are only beginning to comprehend, in the twenty-first century). It would also have to include a critique of gender domination and new models of love in which reciprocity and equal freedom are key. Mozart intuitively understood all this, with the result that his operas are so radical in their dismantling of hierarchies that their insights are far ahead of where we are today.

Mozart was the first great composer many of whose singers (after his earliest works) were actually women, not castrati. He took full advantage of this new freedom accorded to real women, giving them pivotal emotional roles everywhere, and even suggesting, in two "trouser" characters, the young men Cherubino and Sesto, both sung by mezzo-sopranos (although an impresario, assembling a cast without the permission of Mozart, then near death, assigned Sesto at the premiere to a castrato), that men would be a lot better off singing and behaving in ways more typical of the culture of women. Such men become teachers of love to their hardened and defective older counterparts—including, naturally, since we are speaking of cultural differences, not differences rooted in biological nature, women like Vitellia, who depart from their culture and emulate masculine domination. By showing men who heed the call of emotional reform (Figaro, Tito), Mozart indicates that the capacity for love lies deep in every person; it can be perverted by hierarchy, but it can also thrive in relationships of equality.

Mozart's Freemasonic belief that music itself is political, a space for brotherhood and reciprocity, introduces this book's subtheme: the connection of human freedom with breath. To sing with others is to express deep emotions, and the lodge was a space of freedom, where the breath of song was never stifled. So too, in *The Magic Flute*, the making of music—the flute and the magic bells—becomes a central emblem of human freedom and possibility. (Indeed, we should say "of animal freedom," since the bells inspire the nonhuman animals as well as humans.) At the end of *Figaro*, too, we find happiness represented by choral song: "Ah, we shall all be happy in this way," as they are singing freely together. But when the spirit of revenge prevails, people basically stifle themselves, as, finally, does Elettra in *Idomeneo*. As time goes on, this theme is taken up by one composer after another, as society locks people in airless prisons (*Fidelio*, *Aida*) or even death chambers (*Dead Man Walking*), as the obsession with revenge deforms the internal world, destroying operatic song (Strauss's *Elektra*), as people who defy the crowd are doomed to death by drowning (*Peter Grimes*). As Beethoven's chorus in *Fidelio* remarks, you can't breathe well in a prison, and to sing you have to breathe. Self-referentially, the work gestures to the political conditions that make its very existence possible. This sort of self-reference runs through the tradition. Opera in this way performs its own content: to sing it you must have escaped, at least temporarily, the worst assaults of unjust regimes.

Opera's largest contribution to political thought derives, I have said, from its power to delineate and excavate human emotions. In thinking about this it is valuable to turn to one Western philosopher who, whatever his perversities and shortcomings, has unsurpassed insight into the role of music in human life: Arthur Schopenhauer (1788–1860). Not surprisingly, composers have often turned to Schopenhauer to articulate in words their own projects: in particular Gustav Mahler and Richard Wagner were greatly influenced by his ideas (as we shall see in chapter 9). Schopenhauer attracted them, and many others, not only by the power of his overall view of life and suffering (which Mahler and many others rejected) but also because he gives music a special place in the understanding of life.[2]

In chapter 9 we will examine Schopenhauer's metaphysical framework of Will (*Wille*) and Representation (*Vorstellung*) and the normative view within which Schopenhauer puts these distinctions to work—his famous "pessimism." But his analysis of art is independent of pessimism and can be helpful even if we reject it, as I think we should. Schopenhauer argues that the arts—he discusses painting, sculpture, architecture, literature, and music (never dance)—are representations of human striving and failure. Engaged with a work of art, we are lifted out of our own personal projects for a time and can study the world dispassionately and see how it works, while being moved by generic emotions not related to any personal goal. This explains, for him, the large social and personal value of the arts.

Schopenhauer sees value in all the arts, and he has especially eloquent things to say about literary tragedy, which, he says, teaches us explicitly and repeatedly about the vanity of human endeavors. But there is one art to which he ascribes unique and paramount importance: music. Music, in his view, offers us a representation of the Will itself, uncluttered by any reference to specific objects. While poetry and other art forms approach Will only indirectly, through images, music depicts it directly, with a powerful and searing effect,

[2] The following paragraphs are closely related to my *The Tenderness of Silent Minds: Benjamin Britten and His "War Requiem,"* Nussbaum (2024).

showing us "the many different forms of the Will's efforts," especially the inner experience of our passions. Music does this through rhythm, accent, dynamics, and melody, all being forms of bodily movement that have, in turn, a direct effect on the listener's body.[3] Musical experience is detached but not dry, perceptual and not conceptual (we should say, instead, not only conceptual), and inexhaustibly rich.

Schopenhauer does not single out opera as a distinct genre, but since it is a blend of literary drama and music, it is not surprising that he takes a strong interest in it. (Rossini is a particular favorite of his, and he interestingly singles out Mozart's *Don Giovanni* as one of the world's greatest works of art.)

In what follows, it is useful for a reader to employ Schopenhauer's general idea of how music achieves its effects as a heuristic device, seeing music as representing strivings of many different types, their failures and successes. This is one way of looking at what my interpretations try to reveal. In opera we see striving sometimes from the point of view of particular characters, sometimes from that of a group, as enacted by a Chorus. But with caution and delicacy we may at times sense that the work as a whole has a spirit or stance—what literary scholars would call the "implied author." For example, Wagner and Verdi each depict a range of characters, but we cannot deny that the overall spirit of their works, the two "implied authors," are utterly different.

Part I. Mozart: Freemason and Architect of Love

The first half of the book is concerned with Mozart, in my view the deepest philosopher of the Enlightenment. Of course there was always a libretto. Some of his libretti basically served his purpose

---

[3] Schopenhauer (1958, vol. I, sec. 52).

but were poetically clunky (*Abduction, Idomeneo, Clemenza, Magic Flute*), while the three great Da Ponte libretti (*Figaro, Don Giovanni, Così*) were works of literary brilliance but in at least one case deeply at odds with Mozart's own insights and inclinations, or so I'll argue. Thus I am always talking primarily about the contribution made by Mozart's music to the delineation of characters and their journeys, and this contribution always goes beyond the libretto, giving delineation and precision to its sentiments. In one case, *Così*, Mozart's music goes rather firmly against Da Ponte's cynical rationalism, charting new roads of love and reciprocity for the characters.

Mozart, as I said, was a committed Freemason, active in his Lodge. Although *The Magic Flute* is among his operas the most programmatic and explicit expression of Freemasonic ideas of brotherhood, equality, and mercy—not without criticism of the realities of Masonic life—his entire career shows what can only be called an obsession with these ideas, and with the overcoming of a morality based upon honor and revenge toward a new morality based upon mercy, love, and even the equality of the sexes. There is reason to believe that Mozart (with his friend Schikaneder) was among those striving to include women as Freemason initiates in Vienna, as they were already included in lodges in other parts of Europe. *The Magic Flute* clearly represents this equality: Pamina is initiated alongside Tamino and even takes the lead at a crucial moment, while the chorus of initiates includes female voices. But there is no preaching, no dogmatic imposition of a Freemasonic creed. Indeed, as we'll see, Mozart is in some respects very critical of the Freemasons of his day. It is more accurate to say that an ongoing sense of what makes life worth living for both men and women both led Mozart to Freemasonry and finds expression in his operas, with Mozart's wholehearted and very original development of nuanced ideas of brotherhood, gender, and equality.

Chapter 1. Equality and Love at the End of *The Marriage of Figaro*: Forging Democratic Emotions

Mozart's mature view of reciprocity and its social role finds its fullest and most complete expression in *The Marriage of Figaro* (1786). Here Mozart, departing from the pure class politics of Beaumarchais, insists on a politics of love and reciprocity as the only way in which women and men can flourish. Da Ponte's libretto based on Beaumarchais greatly underdetermines the emotional trajectory of the characters; the arias of the pivotal character Cherubino could be musically set in many different ways. The libretto is not basically at odds with Mozart's design, but the music is essential in giving specificity and determinacy to the sentiments expressed.

Chapter 2. Mozart and the Freemasons: *Idomeneo* and *The Magic Flute*

I continue with a chapter on Mozart's Freemasonry and its influence on two works, one early and one late, in which the Freemasonic rejection of religious superstition is central, and in which the idea of a politics based on love and reason prevails: *Idomeneo* (1781) and *The Magic Flute* (1791). In *Idomeneo*, Mozart enters the world of ancient Greek tragedy. Like Homer's *Iliad*, the opera ends with reconciliation through the renunciation of hatred and revenge. Mozart always understood deeply what he warns against, and the character Elettra is just as searing as her twentieth-century counterpart in Strauss's opera—and with the same result: exhaustion, collapse, and death from the sheer weight of her own anger. Meanwhile religious superstition leads Idomeneo almost to the point of sacrificing his own son, in a pointed allusion to a key part of Judeo-Christian religion—until an unspecified Voice brings him to his senses and tells him not to do it. Instead he turns the kingdom over to a pair of lovers evenly matched, and determined to preside over a free people with both love and compassion.

In *The Magic Flute* Mozart lays out his own version of Freemasonry, controlling the detail of the libretto, written by a close friend and Masonic associate—not without criticism and even at times gentle satire of some failures of the movement to live up to its own ideals. Eventually the loving couple are initiated as equals, and a key role in their progress is played by music itself—the magic flute and the bells.

Both operas emphasize the rejection of superstition in favor of reason, of retribution in favor of love and mercy. Both assign a key role to the agency of women, but also show that a general capacity for love, in the case of some women (Elettra, the Queen of the Night), can be deformed by thwarted ambition.

Chapter 3. Two Problem Operas: *Don Giovanni* and *Così fan tutte*

A third chapter takes up two problem operas, *Don Giovanni* (1787) and *Così fan tutte* (1790), in the latter of which Mozart musically departs, or so I claim, from the spirit of Da Ponte's cynical libretto (an expression, perhaps, of Da Ponte's own career). Mozart is drawn inexorably toward a different type of journey: from superficial playfulness to genuine emotional depth. This journey cannot be happily completed in the social world of the libretto.

Don Giovanni is an enduring enigma, and I investigate a group of "Romantic" interpretations that see the work as glorifying the Don and his violence toward women as an expression of some type of life force. I reject those interpretations, and also, though more tentatively, the idea that here, too, Mozart's music is at odds with Da Ponte's libretto. Both libretto and, even more clearly, the music, I argue, focus on the journey of the three female characters from wounded honor and the quest for revenge to new emotions of delight, love, and forgiveness.

Chapter 4. "If You Could See This Heart": Mercy in *La Clemenza di Tito*

The final Mozart chapter concerns *La Clemenza di Tito* (1791), which, along with *The Magic Flute*, had its premiere in the month immediately preceding his death. Here Mozart returns once more to classical antiquity, in this case to the Roman Empire, in which one might have supposed an Enlightenment republic could not possibly flourish. And yet, in Tito's renunciation of imperial prerogative, his restoration of Senatorial autonomy, and Vitellia's choice for love over honor—all engineered by the compassionate youth Sesto, who tries to live in the old world but just cannot do it "right"—we see Mozart's final representation of the Republic of Love that, like an ideal form, encourages the aspirations and efforts of all those who would like to live by its laws. I show how Mozart's musical ideas extend and deepen ideas of mercy and human understanding already developed by the Roman philosopher Seneca, a well-known and influential figure in Mozart's time.

Part II. Mozart's Heirs and One Antagonist

Part II of the book is not a consecutive history of opera after Mozart. Such an effort would be both impossibly large in scope and too unfocused, since opera goes in many directions, not all of them Mozartean. I aim to follow a particular republican tradition within opera, the road mapped out by Mozart. Therefore I choose a group of works that, I claim, further develop Mozartean themes, with new musical tools in new contexts, confronting obstacles to Mozart's vision that he does not fully address. Mozart is in some ways naïve, ignorant about institutions and over-optimistic about people. The ensuing tradition reflects further on the prospects of Mozartean politics in a more profoundly flawed world. We need to ponder the warnings in these works, and to reflect about the emotions they inspire.

The chapters in this Part are often shorter, continuing Part I's themes in new times and places and with new obstacles, rather than offering exhaustive studies of the overall careers of later composers. The chapters are thematically organized, and represent my own illustrative choices of works that develop these themes. Many other works might have been discussed. Nor do I assume that these composers are directly inspired by Mozart, though quite a few are. My point is that they continue, in their own way, a tradition of thought about republican ideals and the obstacles to their realization. My choices are idiosyncratic and hardly exhaustive; but they should give at least a sense of what this art-form offers us as it develops. I had to omit for reasons of length two operas on which I have written essays and originally planned to include (Bizet's *Carmen* and Verdi's *Aida*), and others that make central contributions to the themes under discussion that I had also originally planned to include (Strauss's *Elektra*, Mussorgsky's *Boris Godunov*). I included two operas by living composers (Jake Heggie, John Adams), in order to show the tradition's evolving meditations on freedom and reciprocity—as Heggie extends Beethoven's meditations on punishment and Adams develops a Verdian idea of nationhood and a Mozartean idea of the embrace of flawed reality as the best basis for political reciprocity.

Chapter 5. Revenge and the Prison: Beethoven's *Fidelio*, Heggie's *Dead Man Walking*

Mozart has distinct limits in understanding political evil. His paradigm of the *ancien régime* is the unfaithful Count in *Figaro*, a man not profoundly bad, but simply weak and confused. His allegedly tyrannical rulers, Pasha Selim and Emperor Tito, turn out to be arch-exemplars of moderation, mercy, and even respect for women. *Fidelio* (1805, 1814), the only opera of Ludwig von Beethoven (1770–1827), develops a more embattled sense of the Enlightenment and the breath of freedom, reminding us that ours is a world in which airless prisons abound, taking away light and breath, and cruelty is not usually leavened by humanity or even softened by confusion. And yet, at least in opera, love can triumph even here. And if love's triumph is mythical (as the opera in many ways suggests), at least it is a virtual triumph, a triumph expressing the idea that love is better, more compelling, more resonant, than vengeance and hate.

Dead Man Walking (2000) by Jake Heggie (1961–) addresses contemporary capital punishment in today's United States, which has built retribution into the very foundation of its system of justice. In one of the most admired and widely performed among contemporary American operas, composer Heggie and librettist Terrence McNally depict the institutional face of retribution and the human distortions it creates. Based on Sister Helen Prejean's book of the same name, the opera does not take a definite stance on the death penalty, leaving that task to each member of the audience. Instead it investigates the deeper roots of the retributive system in people's unwillingness to deal with loss in constructive ways, as bereaved families are trapped by their own zeal for vengeance. Meanwhile, Sister Helen's journey requires her to stop living in the idealized world of the convent, learning to face, and love, a real world containing sexuality and lethal aggression.

Chapter 6. Liberty or the Inquisition? Authority and Fear in Verdi's *Don Carlos*

Giuseppe Verdi (1813–1901), among the composers this book considers, was the most politically involved in a practical way, a leading participant in the Italian *Risorgimento*, which sought to form a unified Republican Italy, dethroning neo-feudal power. Always in trouble with the censors, he displaced his real-life struggles onto many different times and places. For this reason my two Verdi chapters contain more historical context than other chapters: his operas are always written in the context of specific events in which he participated. Like Mozart, however, he explores republican struggles with a keen eye for the emotions that propel or, in some cases, doom them. He understands brotherly love like nobody else, and understands, too, how the whole project of a Republic of Love is threatened continually by clerical authority and the human weaknesses on which it feeds. A grave limitation in the optimistic Freemason Mozart is a failure to understand the human power of authoritarian religion. In *Magic Flute* the Queen of the Night, Freemasonry's enemy, is weak and ridiculous, albeit with some dazzling coloratura. Similarly, in *Idomeneo*, the cause of love wins the minute the Voice speaks, because Idomeneo all along rebelled inwardly against Neptune's command.

Verdi's *Don Carlos* (1867) depicting a republican movement in sixteenth-century Flanders, an uprising against the Spanish crown that was the real-life origin of the modern Netherlands, shows how monarchs endure and torment their people: by striking an alliance with the repressive force of the church and the Inquisition. And how does the Inquisition retain its power? By preying on human weakness, guilt, and fear. In King Philippe's guilty capitulation and in the ghastly auto-da-fé scene, we understand the way in which the "Republic of Love" is always pitted in a death struggle against the "monarchy of fear."

Chapter 7. Internal Exiles: Oppression and Reconciliation in Britten and Janáček

All republics have "internal exiles," people who are nominally citizens, whose breath is taken from them and who are not fully and meaningfully free, whether because of class or because of ethnicity, race, or sexuality—or simply because they are different in some unspecified way. This category is productive in opera, and I begin by discussing the many examples we might choose. Mozart is no good guide here, since his examples are made to seem grotesque and not worthy of our concern. To represent those voices is surely a huge task for the Republic of Love in our era.

Benjamin Britten (1913–1976), whose whole career focused on the struggles of outcasts in British society, was drawn to the topic through his own triple outcast identity—as an artist, a pacifist, and a gay man. From childhood on, he felt the weight of the social system and its cruel oppression of difference. Writing most of his works with key roles for his life partner, Peter Pears, he created a series of memorable portraits of the social outcast trying to breathe freely in stifling British society, and perhaps none more remarkable than *Peter Grimes* (1945). Britten understands deeply how being hated and bullied by others gets under the skin of the hated, rendering happiness impossible. He also knows that even people living in a republic and secure in their own liberties will almost gratuitously take it on themselves to hate and persecute others. People of the Enlightenment were too optimistic: although Mozart (nearly alone) saw that a radical change in sentiments would be needed to create a Republic of Love, he didn't imagine that once created, such a republic would find new victims to scapegoat. Why does this happen, and what can be done about it?

Although *Grimes* is a bleakly tragic work, offering not even a shred of hope, Britten elsewhere, albeit guardedly, shows a path forward for society, especially in the very Mozartean comic opera *Albert Herring* (1947), which shows a society learning its way beyond repression and persecution. I end the Britten section of this chapter with a study of this lovely opera.

A profoundly insightful engagement with society's oppression of women, tragic and yet allowing space for hope, is the opera *Jenůfa*

(1904), by Leoš Janáček (1854–1928), the first great success in a career obsessively focused on female freedom. The story depicts the heroine's premarital affair with an unreliable suitor, Števa, who then jilts her for a wealthy bride, leaving her pregnant. The stigma of unwed motherhood isolates her from the surrounding society, confining her to a virtual prison, and, initially, denying her even the kindness and concern of Števa's brother Laca, who has previously struck Jenůfa out of jealousy, scarring her face. Jenůfa's stepmother, the Kostelnička, believes that Jenůfa's future with Laca depends on getting rid of the infant, and in the night she carries the baby out and drowns it, telling Jenůfa that the baby died in its sleep. When, later, the body of the child is found beneath the ice, Jenůfa is suspected until the Kostelnička confesses. She is taken off to jail, and Laca insists on standing by Jenůfa, accepting, and loving, the real woman that she is. Despite this part-tragic and emotionally complex ending, the opera ends on a note of hopeful love, pointing forward toward a future in which sexual shame and inequality will less often deform human lives.

Chapter 8. War and the Search for Peace: John Adams's *Nixon in China*

War appears only around the edges of Mozart's operas: as a threatened destination for Cherubino and the antithesis of his entire world; as the backdrop to the comic antics of *Così fan tutte*, possibly more ominous than the jolly music lets on; as ended in *Idomeneo*, where Idamante takes up the job of postwar reconstruction. But war in Mozart's time and in the entirety of subsequent opera-time is a huge threat to lives of liberty, love, and brotherhood, and its meaning for the liberal tradition and its prospects remains to be assessed and reassessed. I open this chapter with a general discussion of different ways in which opera might approach these issues.

Since I have just published, in 2024, a book on war and music focused on Benjamin Britten's *War Requiem*,[4] I turn, in the remainder of the chapter, to a remarkable opera that portrays a search for international understanding and détente, using diplomacy as a prelude to peace: *Nixon in China* (1987) by John C. Adams (1945–) another much-performed and justly admired opera by a living composer. Adams and his librettist Alice Goodman, remaining close to the historical details of Nixon's 1972 visit to China, show how the search for future peace depends, inevitably, on flawed human beings who, despite their flaws, dare to make a bold effort to communicate across divisions.

Chapter 9: Ahasuerus "Redeemed": Wagner from Despair to the Closed Community

So far, all the voices in this Part have been Mozartean: musical thinkers for whom the idea of a Republic of Love is deeply attractive, and who wrestle with obstacles in its way. Now, however, Mozart's chief antagonist appears on the scene, clarifying the options before us. For Richard Wagner (1813–1883), the open multicolored craziness of a Mozartean Republic of Love was anathema. His political norm and goal was that of a closed community, governed by the insights of an artist who could revivify dead German traditions. The society of *Die Meistersinger* (1867), in which all "foreign influences" are kept at bay, has, I argue, a source: in the profound anomie and alienation that modernity brought to some of its citizens. I begin with *The Flying Dutchman* (1843), an indelible expression of the pain of alienation that makes some people wanderers on this earth, hoping for redemption by love but finding only despair. This despair is altogether unknown to Mozart, and perhaps unknown in his world.

[4] Nussbaum (2024).

For that pain, a Republic of Love offers no solace: the Republic is too open, too crazy, too prone to flights of boyish or womanish fancy. The only answer seems to lie in a very different political ordering, one in which tradition and ethnic identity rule, difference is countenanced only within strict bounds, and the comedy that is permitted has happy endings without the unpredictability of humor. *Die Meistersinger*, and the sinister events that it presages, is Mozart's deepest antagonist, showing us that a realm of love must be built by people who have understood how to live with themselves on this earth as fragile beings with grace and wit. Understanding the antagonist leads us back to Mozart and his heirs with new insight and new resolution.

Chapter 10: A "Pandemonium as Bright as the Sun and as Crazy as a Madhouse": Verdi's *Falstaff*

It seems fitting to allow a powerful Mozartean voice the final word.

Mozart died so young that he never pondered aging, though he was certainly preoccupied with death. Aging poses obstacles to each individual citizen of any republic, and it also challenges the modern liberal state, as their populations are rapidly growing older. How can such a state support human frailty, while at the same time respecting the resilience and strength of its aging citizens?

At the end of his life, Verdi's final statement, and his only comedy (with one disastrous early exception) gives the nod to love—and to music. In *Falstaff* (1893), he represents love and joy defeating every obstacle, with zest, fizzy musical complexity, and humor. It is a profoundly Mozartean work, but also, because it was written by an octogenarian, while Mozart didn't get to forty, it expresses a sense of the joyful possibility that love can defeat age itself, and, in a very secular sense, perhaps also death. I've said that Mozart was in awe of death, despite his Freemasonic preparation. Verdi thumbed his nose at death, and showed a way forward for all of us who choose life.

This is a political idea in the largest sense, since a politics of love can prevail only if it thinks well about aging and finitude.

PART I

1

Equality and Love at the End of *The Marriage of Figaro*

Forging Democratic Emotions

I have no idea to this day what those two Italian ladies were singing about. Truth is, I don't want to know. Some things are best left unsaid. I'd like to think they were singing about something so beautiful, it can't be expressed in words, and it makes your heart ache because of it . . . , and for the briefest of moments, every last man in Shawshank felt free.
—Morgan Freeman ("Red"), in *The Shawshank Redemption*, of the "Canzonetta sull'aria" from Act 3 of *The Marriage of Figaro*

My great *peace woman* has only a single name: she is called *universal justice, humaneness, active reason.* . . . Her function, in accordance with her name and her nature, is to inculcate *dispositions of peace.*
—Johann Gottfried Herder, *Letters for the Advancement of Humanity* (1793–1797)

"Happy in That Way"

The *ancien régime* sings in a loud and authoritarian voice, saying, "No, no, no, no, no, no." So, just before the end of Mozart's opera, the Count, as yet secure in his status, rejects the urgings of the other characters to mercy and sympathy, as they kneel, one by one, before him. To Almaviva, revenge for insulted honor is all-important ("the only thing that consoles my heart and makes me rejoice"[1]). To display kindness to the imploring, as they humbly kneel, is a noble prerogative, not a general human virtue. He can give it, or withhold it. If he chooses the latter course, putting slighted honor ahead of generous condescension, nobody can say he is wrong. That's how the *ancien régime* operates, animated by a morality of status, shame, and kingly prerogative.

But suddenly the Countess, removing her disguise as Susanna, reveals herself—revealing, at the same time, the stratagem that has trapped her husband in both error and hypocrisy. (Having boasted of ending the *droit du seigneur*, he has all the while been scheming to enjoy it.) Everyone present exclaims in hushed voices that they don't know what is going to happen next: "Oh heavens, what do I see! Madness! A hallucination! I don't know what to believe!" The strings, coursing rapidly up and down, express agitation and uncertainty. It is the uncertainty of transition between two political regimes.

And now the Count, kneeling before the Countess, sings—in a voice newly softened by confusion—a phrase of a type, lyrical and legato, hushed, almost gentle—that we have never heard from this man before: "Excuse me, Countess, excuse me, excuse me." There is a long pause.[2]

The Countess then sings softly out of the silence: "I am nicer, and I say yes" (*più docile io sono, e dico di sì*).[3] The musical phrase

---

[1] "Già la speranza sola / Delle vendette mie / Quest'anima consola, / E giubilar mì fa," the end of his third-act Aria. Throughout I rely on the edition of the libretto in *Wolfgang Amadeus Mozart: Three Mozart Libretti* (Da Ponte [1961] 1993).

[2] The length of the pause is interpreted variously by different conductors, but both Solti and Karajan hold it for 4 seconds, which feels very long. In the score, the pause is designated by a quarter-note rest with a fermata. (See Da Ponte [1941] 1979, p. 422.)

[3] *Docile* is difficult to translate: one could also say "gentler," or "kinder." I've chosen "nicer," in order to convey the fact that this is a very everyday word, not an exalted moral or philosophical one. It also connotes (to some extent in Da Ponte's time, even more so today) tractability and yielding, perhaps even submission. However, one cannot

arcs gently upward, and then bends down as if, almost, to touch the kneeling husband. And now, in hushed and solemn tones, the entire assembled company repeats the Countess's phrase, this time to the words, "Ah, all of us will be happy in that way" (*tutti contenti saremo così*). The choral version of the phrase is reminiscent of the solemn simplicity of a chorale (which, in this mostly Catholic musical context, denotes a sudden absence of hierarchy).[4] A hesitant orchestral interlude follows.

The group now bursts out, a sudden eruption of dizzy elation:[5] "This day of torment, of craziness, of foolishness—only love can make it end in happiness and joy." Love, it seems, is the key not only to the personal happiness of the central characters, but to the happiness of "all," of the whole community, as they sing: "Let us all rush off to celebrate" (*corriam tutti a festeggiar*).

The usual story about Mozart's *Le Nozze di Figaro* (1786) is that it is a cop-out. Taking the radical Beaumarchais drama of 1778, whose essential point and emphasis are political, a denunciation of the *ancien régime* and the hierarchies it imposes, Mozart and his librettist Lorenzo Da Ponte have fashioned an innocuous drama of personal love, defanging the text by omitting, for example, Figaro's long fifth-act monologue denouncing feudal hierarchy and substituting a more extensive treatment of women and their private desires. The Beaumarchais play, which is usually understood

read even the libretto as saying that the Countess simply acquiesces in her subordinate role: for she says not "I am *docile*," but, rather, "I am more docile," suggesting that being *docile* is a virtue that all should possess, and that the Count possesses to a deficient degree. I would think of it, then, as denoting yielding to life's complexities and imperfections, being pliant rather than rigid.

[4] The chorale, involving many voices singing together, all contributing equally, suggests Protestant more than Catholic worship, but it also fits well with the Freemasons' love of choral singing and equal participation (see chapter 2). See also Joseph Kerman's "half hymn-like" in *Opera as Drama* (Kerman 1988, p. 87). For related observations about Mahler's use of Bach in the Second Symphony, see my *Upheavals of Thought: The Intelligence of Emotions* (Nussbaum 2001, ch. 15).

[5] At this point the key changes from G major to D major, and the tempo is marked *Allegro assai*.

to be a major harbinger of the French Revolution, was refused production for many years, and even in 1784, when it was allowed production in France, becoming wildly popular, it remained controversial.[6] Mozart and Da Ponte, by contrast, decided (so the story goes) to escape controversy. The relatively progressive Joseph II had forbidden the Beaumarchais play to be performed in theaters within his realm. Da Ponte, however, persuaded the Emperor that an acceptable opera could be written on the basis of the play.[7] In the process, however, says the received story,[8] he and Mozart, despite producing a wonderful love-drama, sold out the radicalism of the original.

I shall argue, by contrast, that the opera is as political and as radical as the play, and more deeply so: for it investigates the human sentiments that are the necessary foundation for a public culture of liberty, equality, and fraternity. This construction of sentiment is accomplished more clearly in Mozart's music than in the libretto, so making my argument will require going into considerable musical detail.[9] I shall argue that Mozart agrees (in effect)[10] with Rousseau in understanding that a political culture requires a new shaping of human attitudes in the realm of love, but that he disagrees with Rousseau about the specific shape

[6] For the Beaumarchais play, I use the edition by Malcolm Cook, *Beaumarchais: Le Mariage de Figaro* (Cook 1992).

[7] For an excellent treatment of the historical background of the opera, see Tim Carter, *W. A. Mozart: "Le Nozze di Figaro,"* an excellent treatment of the opera covering a wide range of issues (Carter 1987).

[8] The received story has some foundation in Da Ponte's *Memoirs* (on which see further in chapter 3), which tell us what he said to try to persuade Joseph II. That hardly shows that the libretto's real intent was apolitical, however; and even if Da Ponte's intent had been utterly apolitical, that would hardly show us that the music that animates the libretto is apolitical.

[9] See Kerman (1988, pp. 90–91), who emphasizes Mozart's transformation of his material, especially at the end of the opera.

[10] I see no reason to suppose that Mozart read Rousseau, but these ideas about civic sentiment were widely disseminated in the 1780s. Mozart's primary source was the culture of the Freemasons (see chapter 2), but of course he had similar ideas before he joined any lodge.

of the new attitudes. Whereas Rousseau emphasizes the need for civic homogeneity and solidarity, a patriotic love based on manly honor and the willingness to die for the nation, Mozart envisages the new public love as something gentler, more reciprocal, more feminine—"nicer," to use the Countess's everyday word—connected more to the page Cherubino's horror of warlike exploits (on which see below) than to Rousseauesque ideas of nationalistic valor. In the process, Mozart also eschews Rousseauian homogeneity, emphasizing that the new fraternity must protect spaces for the free play of mischief, craziness, humor, and individuality—all of which are connected, in the opera, to the women's world.

In arguing that the culture of the Enlightenment requires a new form of subjectivity, one that the music of this period explores and in part creates, I am agreeing with the central thesis of Michael P. Steinberg's book *Listening to Reason*[11]—though not at all with the content of his argument. I shall argue that Steinberg's more or less total neglect of the politics of gender in *Figaro* means that he cannot offer us a deep or precise enough account of what needs to change if the revolution is to be humanly possible (see also chapter 3). Symptomatic of the difficulty in Steinberg's reading (which also neglects the Countess and her "yes") is its total neglect of the male/female character Cherubino (a teenage boy sung by an adult woman); but Cherubino, I shall argue, is in many ways the opera's pivotal character, a male who can be both delightful and loving, capable of empathy and reciprocity, only because he has been educated by women and by music, and thus has grown to love jokes instead of put-downs, singing rather than marching, mischief rather than revenge.

[11] Steinberg (2004).

The *Ancien Régime* and the Male
Voice: Honor, Shame, Disgust

According to the received view, Beaumarchais dramatizes the opposition between an *ancien régime* based on hierarchy and subordination (personified by the Count) and a new democratic politics, based on equality and liberty (personified by Figaro). The key moment of the Beaumarchais play is thus Figaro's Act 5 monologue, in which he denounces the Count's hereditary privilege. Mozart, omitting this political speech, has depoliticized the opera, turning the conflict between the Count and Figaro into a merely personal competition over a woman.

This view contains a tacit premise: that the contrast that should hold our interest, as political thinkers, is the opposition between the Count and Figaro. It is because Mozart does not locate the center of the political conflict here that his version is felt not to be political at all, but merely domestic. Let us, however, keep an open mind. Let us not assume that Figaro represents the new citizenship (as the Count so clearly represents the old).

If we do keep an open mind, we are likely to notice very soon that Figaro and the Count are very similar, both musically and thematically. What do they sing about when they are alone? Outraged honor, the desire for revenge, the pleasure of domination. The energies that drive these two men are not alien, but deeply akin. (Indeed, the two roles are set in such a way that one and the same singer might, in principle, sing either role, and their musical idioms are so alike that it is easy to confuse them.[12]) Figaro's initial aria, "*Se vuol ballare,*" follows his discovery that the Count has plans to sleep with Susanna. But if we simply look at what Figaro says in the aria, we would not discover that any such creature as Susanna ever existed. All his thoughts are about his rivalry with the Count, and

[12] Bryn Terfel, for example, well known in performance for his Figaro, has also recorded the Count.

his insistent negatives (*non sarà, non sarà*) anticipate the Count's peremptory negations at the opera's end (as well as those in the Count's Act 3 aria). What energizes Figaro? The thought of paying the Count back in kind, teaching him to dance in Figaro's dancing school.

Similarly, two acts later, the Count imagines Susanna, his own future property, being possessed by Figaro (*ei posseder dovrà*), whom the Count sees as "a base *thing*" (*un vil oggetto*), a mere object.[13] This thought torments him—not because he is filled with any love or even any particularly intense desire for Susanna, but because the idea of being bested by a mere "thing" is intolerable. To this competitive loss he, like Figaro, has to say "no": "Ah no, I am not willing to allow you to enjoy this happiness in peace. Brazen one,[14] you were not born to give me torment, and perhaps even to laugh at my unhappiness." Figaro, not Susanna, is the person whom he addresses in the second person. Like Figaro, his head is filled with the picture of another man, laughing at him, insulting his honor. In return for that tormenting picture, he proposes (like Figaro) to substitute the image of a tamed enemy dancing to his tune, in this case the picture of Figaro forced to marry Marcellina and separated forever from Susanna, whom the Count can then enjoy: "Now only the hope of revenge consoles my heart and makes me rejoice."[15] Figaro's "*Se vuol ballare*" is closely based upon the Beaumarchais text; this aria of the Count's, however, is a complete innovation of Da Ponte, since Beaumarchais gives us only what forms the recitative before the aria, not the aria's extended development of sentiments of humiliation and reactive rage.

---

[13] The Countess understands that she too is a thing to him: Later, when he addresses her as "Rosina," she replies, "I am no longer she, but the wretched *oggetto* of your abandonment."

[14] I translate *audace* in this awkward way because to supply "man" or "person" would constitute an acknowledgment that Figaro is human, which is what the Count has just been denying.

[15] Literally, the Count speaks of "revenges" in the plural—thinking, presumably, of the way in which he will both force Figaro to marry Marcellina and then humiliate him further by sleeping, himself, with Susanna.

Musically as well as textually, the Count's aria is a cousin of Figaro's: full of an ill-governed fury that bursts out as the voice reaches the words *felice un servo mio*, and then again at *ah no, lasciarti in pace*; anger, in the music, is complemented by sneering irony (the downturning phrase accompanying *un vil oggetto*). The libretto gives us some indication of the kinship between the two men, but the expressive range of the music goes much further to emphasize their rhythmic and accentual similarity, as both express attitudes that range from snide contempt to furious rage.[16] What emotions are absent? Love, wonder, delight—even grief and longing.

According to the conventional political reading of Beaumarchais, Figaro becomes, by Act 5, the apostle of a new type of citizenship, free from hierarchy. Mozart's Figaro makes no such progress. As Michael Steinberg aptly notes, throughout the opera (or, at least, until late in Act 4), Figaro dances, musically, to the Count's tune: "[H]e hasn't found a musical idiom of his own; his political and emotional vocabulary suggests a similarly unfortunate mimetic duplication of the Count's"[17]—both in "*Non più andrai*," at the end of Act 1, where he reenacts "the authority with which [the Count] has just dispatched Cherubino to serve in one of his regiments, forming his phrases from the relevant military march,"[18] and even at the opening of Act 4, when, waiting to catch Susanna in infidelity, he sings, once again, of slighted honor, asking all males to "open your eyes" to the way in which women function as agents of humiliation. Again, it is men, not women, far less a particular woman, whom he addresses in the second person.

Now maybe this means that Mozart has failed to understand the opposition between Figaro and the Count that Beaumarchais has depicted. But let's not pass judgment so quickly. Perhaps, instead,

---

[16] For a general account of emotional expression in music, on which I rely here, see my *Upheavals of Thought* (2001, see the Appendix).

[17] Steinberg (2004, p. 43).

[18] Ibid.

Mozart sees something that Beaumarchais does not see: that the *ancien régime* has formed men in a certain way, making them utterly preoccupied with rank, status, and shame, and that both high and low partake of this social shaping. What one does not wish to lose, the other wishes to enjoy. For neither, given their obsession, does any space open out in the world for reciprocity or, indeed, for love.

The suspicion that Mozart is deliberately subjecting the male morality of status to critical scrutiny is confirmed when we see what Mozart puts in the mouths of two males who have little to do with the plot of this opera, though they are central to *The Barber of Seville*, Beaumarchais's predecessor play and the origin of operas by Rossini and others: Bartolo and Basilio. Perhaps, someone might argue, the sentiments of Figaro and the Count are not to be read as serious political thought: after all, the plot requires them to compete in this way. We have seen that even so, Da Ponte constructs a parallel that is not so plain in the original text, and that Mozart takes this similarity much further by giving the two men a similar expressive musical range. Nonetheless, someone might still argue that Mozart and Da Ponte are simply amplifying the suggestions of the Beaumarchais plot. This, however, cannot be said of the treatment of Bartolo and Basilio, whose role in this opera's story line is minimal. Each sings an aria—Bartolo in Act 1, Basilio in Act 4 (though typically cut in performance)—both of which supply crucial commentary on the morality of maleness. Neither of these arias is based on anything in Beaumarchais's text.

Bartolo is an emotional first cousin of Figaro and the Count. Vocally distinguishable, since he is a basso, he nonetheless sings from the same expressive palate: similar outbursts of rage, tempered by a type of sneering already known to us from Figaro's "Se vuol ballare." Textually, his role appears to be to offer a general theory of what Figaro and the Count both exemplify: "Revenge, oh revenge! It is a pleasure reserved for the wise. To forget humiliations and outrages is baseness, is utter lowness."[19] So, life is more or less utterly occupied by competition for status and the avoidance of shame between males, and the smart thing to do is to play that game to the hilt. The recommended attitude not only causes outrage and humiliation to eclipse love and longing (Bartolo, like Figaro and the Count, has no thought at all for Rosina, whom he has lost to the Count through Figaro's scheming in the backstory to this opera), it also precludes any kind of mercy or reconciliation. It is this attitude that leads to the Count's six consecutive "no's" at the opera's end.

Bartolo also shows us something else pertinent to citizenship: for he is very interested in reason and law. His attitude is that the law is an instrument of male revenge, and someone who knows the law will be ahead of someone who does not, because he can find the little weaknesses and loopholes that will allow him to do down his enemy. At this point the aria becomes rapid, joyful, with a kind of sneering playfulness, a patter song of legal one-upmanship: "If I have to search through the whole legal code, if I have to read all the statutes, with an equivocation, with a synonym, I will find some obstacle there. All Seville will know Bartolo! The rascal Figaro will be defeated!"[20] (Here the music, once again, goes well beyond the text, expressing the sly joy of legal cleverness dragooned into the service of humiliation.) The aria ends four-square and martial as it began (though with a little sneer accompanying the words *il birbo Figaro*). Bartolo announces that "he" will be known to all—showing us that he takes his practical identity to be utterly encompassed in his revenge project. His joy at the thought is unqualified—despite the fact that the revenge in question would never return Rosina to him—or even her money. She is simply not on his mind at all.

[19] *La vendetta, oh la vendetta è un piacer serbato ai saggi. L'obliar l'onte, gli oltraggi, è bassezza, è ognor viltà.*

[20] *Se tutto il codice dovessi volgere, se tutto l'indice dovessi leggere, Con unequivoco, con un sinonimo, qualche garbuglio si troverà. Tutta Siviglia conosce Bartolo: il birbo Figaro vinto sarà.*

At the opening of Act 4, another minor character has his say, and he both inverts and ultimately reinforces the morality of Bartolo. Basilio, a music-master, is a less powerful character than Bartolo, and it was he who, in the predecessor play, discoursed enthusiastically on the crushing humiliation that gossip and slander can offer someone who wants to defeat an enemy. (Here he is sung by a tenor rather than a bass-baritone, for reasons of musical balance.) Da Ponte portrays him throughout as both spiteful and weak, lacking the resources to compete on an equal footing with the nobles, lacking the cleverness to compete on an equal footing with Figaro. His Act 4 aria offers advice to men who are in this weakened position.[21] He begins by telling the audience that it is always risky to enter a competition with the *grandi*: they almost always win. So, what should one do? A story from his youth offers guidance. He used to be impulsive, and didn't listen to reason; then, however, Lady Prudence made her appearance before him, and handed him the skin of an ass. He had no idea what it was for, but when, shortly after that, a thunderstorm began, he covered himself in that ass's skin. When the storm abated he looked up—and found a fearful beast before him, almost touching him with his mouth. He could never have defended himself from a terrible death. But: the disgusting smell of the ass's skin scared the beast away. "Thus fate taught me that shame, danger, disgrace, and death can be escaped under an ass's skin."[22]

This aria offers advice diametrically opposed to the advice in Bartolo's, which told us to use reason and law to hound the person who has caused one's humiliation. It's obvious, however, that the difference is slight. Both men see the world in the same way, as a zero-sum game for honor and status. The only difference is that Basilio is aware that some are bound to be losers, and he wants to

---

[21] Because this aria is so commonly cut, it is not in the Dover edition of the libretto, and so I use the text from the libretto accompanying the 1983 Solti recording of the opera.

[22] *Così conoscere me fè'la sorte ch'onte, pericoli, vergogna e morte col cuoio d'asino fuggir si può.*

give those losers advice about damage control. If you are perceived as smelly and low anyway, use that spoiled identity to protect yourself from yet further outrage. Sung in a sneering reedy tenor, the aria, like Bartolo's, complements Figaro and the Count from the other direction. It shares with them a view of what the world is really about. If women figure in the aria at all, it is only in the way Basilio confesses to a kind of "fire" and "craziness" in his youth—a false direction soon put right by the counsels of Lady Prudence. The *ancien régime* does not like low-class people who allow their fire free rein.

Females: Fraternity, Equality, Liberty

The females of the opera inhabit a musical and textual world that is from the beginning utterly unlike that of the men. First of all, it contains friendship. Susanna and the Countess might have seen one another as rivals: after all, the Count is trying to seduce Susanna. However, the thought does not occur to them: they understand that they share a common set of purposes, and that the desired outcome for both is that both men, Figaro and the Count, become loving and faithful husbands focused on affection and pleasure, rather than revenge and jealousy. (The Count is as dominated by jealousy as is Figaro, despite his apparent loss of his earlier love for his wife.) Like the two men, the two women share a musical idiom—so much so that they can be mistaken for one another even by the men who ostensibly love them (until, interestingly, Figaro does at least recognize Susanna by her voice, "the voice that I love"—a reference, unusual in opera, to the connection between voice and a person's identity).

Unlike the men, however, the women use their similarity for cooperation, not combat, and, in particular, for the complex masquerade that ends up revealing the Count's hypocrisy. When we focus on their teamwork, we notice, as well, that there is absolutely nothing like cooperation and reciprocity among the men. The women's partnership, moreover, despite their class difference, appears to be quite unhierarchical, as they benefit one another with genuine mutual friendliness. (Susanna, for example, is surprised that it is she—presumably not all that well educated—who is to write the letter to the Count suggesting the rendezvous: "I should write? But madame...." The Countess will have nothing of her deference: "Write, I say, and I will take the consequences"—another sign of their equal agency.) One way we see their reciprocity is in the nature of their jokes: for here there are no sneering put-downs, no snide spitefulness, only mutual solidarity and the equal love of a good scheme.

Let's pause to reflect about playfulness. Both the men and the women like a good joke—but how differently they express this general human capacity: for the men, sneering competitive put-downs, for the women, equality and reciprocity. Mozart subtly suggests that the men's attitude is a deformed version of a tendency that the women develop in a more healthy direction. (Could men, bad by custom rather than by nature, be reformed by learning a new experience of games and humor? Certainly Act 4 invites this reading.)

Once again, all this is in the libretto: but the music takes the suggestion of reciprocity and equality much further. As Countess dictates the letter and Susanna writes it down, the women take inspiration from one another's musical phrases, exchanging ideas with a sinuous capacity for response and a heightened awareness of the other's pitch, rhythm, and even timbre. They begin by exchanging phrases, as in a conversation. As the duet continues, however, their reciprocity becomes more intimate and more complex, as they wind around one another, ultimately achieving closely knit harmony. Their musical partnership expresses a kind of friendly attunement that is, we might say, an image of mutual respect, but also a reciprocal affection that is deeper than respect. Neither runs roughshod over the utterance of the other, and yet each contributes something distinctive of her own, which in turn is recognized by the other, and carried forward.[23]

This duet has acquired fame in American popular culture because of its use in the film version of Stephen King's *The Shawshank Redemption*,[24] when Andy Dufresne (Tim Robbins), the convict who has become the prison's librarian, figures out a way to play it for all the prisoners over the PA system, and, locking the door, stops the prison hierarchy from interfering until the duet is done. The men of Shawshank certainly are not fans of classical music, but they hear something in this music, and stop in their tracks, transfixed by a promise of happiness. As Red (Morgan Freeman) expresses it, looking back:

> I have no idea to this day what those two Italian ladies were singing about. Truth is, I don't want to know. Some things are best left unsaid. I'd like to think they were singing about something so beautiful, it can't be expressed in words, and it makes your heart ache because of it . . . , and for the briefest of moments, every last man in Shawshank felt free.

What do the prisoners hear in the duet? Freedom, they say. But why, and how? First, they cannot help hearing an absence of hierarchy in the evenly matched voices, and a partnership based on responsiveness rather than dictatorial power. This, in the context of Shawshank, is already freedom. But, as the voices soar out over the squalor of the prison yard, I think there is more to be heard in it: the idea of a kind of internal freedom, a freedom of the spirit that consists precisely in not caring about hierarchy, neither seeking to avoid being controlled by others nor seeking to control them. Suppose we imagine Tim Robbins playing the Count's "Vedrò

---

[23] For discussion of a similar moment in the final movement of Mahler's Second Symphony, the contralto and soprano voices wrapping around one another, see *Upheavals* (Nussbaum 2001, ch. 15).
[24] Darabont, dir. (1994).

mentr'io sospiro," or Bartolo's "La vendetta." Well, those two powerful men express, in their own way, an idea of freedom: freedom as power to dominate, escaping the shame of being dominated. But we know that the men of Shawshank would not have been transfixed by that image of freedom: after all, it is what they live every day. The promise of the duet is not simply a promise of freedom as reversal, freedom as getting your turn to humiliate the one who has humiliated you. It is a freedom that takes us beyond that anxious and always unsettled picture of what liberty, for men, might consist in. It is freedom as being happy to have an equal beside you, freedom as not caring who is above or beneath. And that's a freedom that does take the mind away from Shawshank, and from the American society of which that institution is the apt mirror.

In other words, this music has constructed democratic reciprocity. Whatever the faults of the film—which is in many ways sentimental—this moment contains a correct insight into Mozart's Freemasonic politics and into the politics of equality more generally. You don't get the right kind of liberty, the idea is, without also having this type of fraternity and this type of equality. To shoot for liberty without fraternity, as Beaumarchais's Figaro does, is simply to turn the hierarchy upside down, not to replace it with something fundamentally different. If there is to be a new regime, if there is ever to be something like a politics of equal respect in this world, the suggestion is, it must start by singing like those two women, and this means becoming a fundamentally different type of man.[25] Freemasons understood that music plays a central role in cultivating dispositions of reciprocity (see chapter 2).

---

[25] Where, if ever in opera, do men sing like that (in close-knit interweaving harmonies, each taking cues from the other)? The duet in Bizet's *The Pearl Fishers* comes to mind, but it is not nearly as complex: the men simply sing together in close harmony. Similar is the wonderful liberty duet (*Dio, che nell'alma infondere*) sung by Carlos and Roderigo in Verdi's *Don Carlo*—close harmony and, we might say, solidarity, but without responsiveness to the separate moves of the other. So it would seem that men, in opera, can on occasion attain solidarity and unanimity, but perhaps not this level of responsiveness or attunement. One might also study the Otello–Iago duet in Verdi's *Othello*, where they both swear vengeance together. Here there is an appearance of attunement, but it is only

To put it a different way: the male world of *Figaro* is its own prison, as each man goes through life dominated by rank-anxiety. What those prisoners heard in the duet was the promise of a world without that tension, a world in which one would then really be free to engage in the pursuit of happiness. The new regime, as it never has been realized in any nation in the world.[26]

Both the Countess and Susanna exemplify reciprocity and internal freedom. Susanna, however, emerges as the more complete person. While the Countess remains preoccupied with her own sadness and eventual hope, Susanna displays enormous empathy with the Countess's situation (as well as that of her beloved Figaro), and has a mischievous quick-wittedness that makes her the primary driver of the plot. She exemplifies what a whole person can be: both clever and compassionate, decisive and loving, and all of this combined with humor and delight.

Creating a Man: "Mischievous Looks," a "Good Outside Myself"

The headings of the last two sections referred to "females," but to "the male voice," and it is the male *voice*, not maleness itself, that the opera associates with the endless and exhausting fight against

superficial, since at a deeper level the two are profoundly at odds; such attunement as there is is profoundly unhealthy. I welcome other examples and counter-examples.
As for men and women singing together with the responsiveness of the Countess and Susanna, we shall shortly see a Mozartean example in chapter 2's analysis of *Idomeneo*.

[26] This new world surely involves transformation on the part of real-life women as well—for although the world of males has its distinctive pathologies, it would be absurd to claim that the world of real-life women is a stranger to jealousy and rivalry. (We should not forget Susanna's sniping at Marcellina, and vice versa, in that Act I duet—although that rivalry is harmoniously resolved soon enough.) I return to this issue in chapter 4. Marcellina's Act 4 aria, *Il capro e la capretta*, tells us that the new world will also require change in the position of real-life women: men and women, she says, are at war with one another in a way unknown in the rest of nature—because "we poor women" are treated cruelly and subjected to all sorts of suspicions.

the "lowness" of shame. There is, however, a male in the opera who does not sing in a male voice: the teenage boy Cherubino, performed by a female mezzo-soprano. This already seems significant: and Cherubino's education, it shortly emerges, is the focal point of the opera's depiction of the new egalitarian citizenship. And it is clearly a point about education, not natural tendencies.[27]

Cherubino is usually treated superficially, as a running joke throughout the opera, and this is, more or less, the way Beaumarchais treats him. His preoccupation with women and sex is indeed the source of much of the plot, as he turns up repeatedly in places where he should not be, to the consternation of the possessive males around him. In many productions he is treated as a person with no sentiments, but only very intense bodily desires. Let us, however, pay closer attention to what he says and what he does.

Cherubino is clearly, in crucial ways, masculine. He is reasonably tall (Susanna has to ask him to kneel down so that she can put on his bonnet), good looking (Figaro and the Count are both jealous of him), and sexually active (with his teenage girlfriend Barbarina)—indeed, very likely, the only male who is actually having sex with anyone during the time span of the opera.[28] On the other hand, the fact that he is sung by a female voice forces us to pay attention to the ways in which that voice, and the sentiments it expresses, differs from all the male voices in the opera. So, what does Cherubino talk about?

He talks about love. He is the only male in the opera who has the slightest interest in that emotion. Certainly, the breathlessness of his first aria, "Non so più," expresses the promiscuous quality, as well as the confusion, of adolescent infatuation: "Every woman

---

[27] Women elsewhere in Mozart can be just as overweening and hierarchical—if they are badly brought up and given too much regal power: Elettra, Vitellia, the Queen of the Night.

[28] The Countess is eloquent about her husband's neglect and indifference. So much is made of the idea of Susanna's virginity at the time of marriage that it seems plausible to think that she and Figaro have not yet occupied the bed that he is so anxiously measuring at the opera's opening.

makes me blush, every woman makes my heart leap." Still, even when he is reporting his state of sexual obsession, he is talking about love: "I talk about love when I'm awake, I talk about love in my dreams, I talk about it to the water, to the shadow, to the mountains, to the flowers, to the grass, to the fountains, to the echo, to the air, to the winds."[29] He shows, here, a romantic and poetic conception of what he is after that is quite unlike the ideas of all the other males in the opera, who all see sex as a means of asserting domination over a key piece of property in the male world. The musical idiom, breathless and yet tender, is utterly unlike the tense accents of the adult males. Indeed, it is the musical idiom, far more than the Beaumarchais-inspired text, which makes us see that Cherubino's sensibility is poetic and romantic, rather than simply energetic.

When we reach the Countess's chamber, Cherubino's difference from other males becomes even more evident. Deeply infatuated with the Countess, he has decided to make her a present. What sort of present? What naturally occurs to him is to write a poem, set it to music, and sing it himself. Thus, accompanying himself on the guitar, Cherubino becomes the only leading character in the opera who sings a solo, that is, whose solo singing represents singing.[30] Growing up in a world of sentiment and musicality, he naturally gives his passion a musical shape.[31]

---

[29] Da Ponte has altered Beaumarchais here in an interesting way: in Beaumarchais, the passage goes, "Finally, the need to say 'I love you' to someone has become so urgent for me that I say it when I'm all alone, when I'm running in the park, I say it to your mistress, to you, to the trees, to the clouds, to the wind that carries the clouds and my lost words away together." This comically confused utterance—he can hardly tell the difference between one woman and another, or between a woman and a tree—is subtly altered by Da Ponte into something much more delicate, a mood that the musical idea brings out more vividly still.

[30] I say "leading character," because the various choruses saluting the Count for his wisdom and virtue—"Giovani liete," "Ricevete, o padroncina," and "Amanti costanti"—are presumably to be imagined as real-life singing inside the plot: Figaro at one point says, "the music-makers are already here." I say "solo" because of the duet between Susanna and the Countess, the "canzonetta sull'aria," already discussed.

[31] In Beaumarchais he simply takes a traditional folk melody and writes his own words to it. The words themselves express love for the Countess, though they are far less interesting than the Da Ponte text; the music, however, is utterly banal, the tune of "Malbrough s'en va-t-en guerre," a bouncy somewhat aggressive war song.

The content of that passion (in the beautiful aria "Voi che sapete") is remarkable for its utter difference from the arias of all the other males. First of all, Cherubino simply talks about his feeling of love, and about its beautiful female object. He has nothing to say about other men, and he seems utterly impervious to all questions of honor, shame, and competition. Second, he is eager to learn something, and he is eager to learn it from women: "You who know what sort of thing love is, women, tell me whether that is what I have in my heart." All the other men are eager to teach rather than to learn; what they are eager to teach is a lesson in competitive one-upmanship, and they are eager to teach it to other males. (Figaro imagines himself as the dance-master running a school that will teach the Count to dance to his tune; Bartolo is eager to show "all Seville" that he can defeat Figaro; the Count is eager to show Figaro that his "cause" is not, as Figaro believes, "won," but, rather, lost.) Third, Cherubino, unlike all the other males, is utterly vulnerable, and he makes no attempt to conceal his vulnerability, which is emotional more than bodily: "I feel my soul in flames, and then it turns to ice in a moment." He describes an intense longing that leaves him no peace. Finally, and most remarkably, he locates what he is pursuing in a place outside of his own ego: "I seek a good that is outside myself" (*ricerco un bene fuori di me*). Hearing these words, we realize that no other male in the opera *does* seek a good outside himself: all are preoccupied with winning a competitive victory, or shielding the ego from shame.

The music of the aria would tell us all this without the words, and indeed it communicates, well beyond the words, the young man's delicacy, vulnerability, and sheer kindness. Indeed it is hardly by accident that audiences who have utterly no idea what Cherubino is saying should have found in this aria (as in the duet between Susanna and the Countess) an image of emotional integrity. Here if anywhere, Mozart's music moves well beyond Da Ponte's text.[32]

---

[32] Indeed, it is formally very different. The text is a repetitious strophic song, and each strophe is like the preceding, rather like a simple folk ditty. It is Mozart who supplies

How did Cherubino get to be this way, a way that promises real reciprocity in passion? Answer: he was brought up by women and kept a stranger to the men's world. Indeed, we've already seen that the prospect of military service utterly confuses and appalls him. In the scene, at the end of Act 1, in which Figaro tells him what to expect when he goes off to the army ("Non più andrai"), Figaro's joke to Cherubino is that he has lived in the women's world of sentiment, music, tenderness, and delicacy—and now, suddenly, he will have to enter a world of drunken men (they swear by Bacchus) with inflexible necks (*collo dritto*), tough faces (*muso franco*), long mustaches (*gran mustacchi*), and "lots of honor" (*molto onor*). Now, in Act 2, we see more fully how much the young man will have to unlearn in order to enter this male world: in particular, lovely, sensuous music. "What a beautiful voice," says the Countess when Cherubino finishes his aria—drawing attention, again, to the fact that this is *singing* singing. Figaro has already told Cherubino, however, that the world of male honor knows nothing of beautiful music: Its only music is "the concerto of trumpets, of shells and cannons, whose shots, on all pitches, make your ears whistle."[33] The aria itself, with its boringly four-square military rhythm, now, in retrospect, contrasts sadly with the grace and elegance of Cherubino's composition.

By singing so beautifully, Cherubino shows himself to be a candidate for fraternity, equality, and the women's-world type of liberty. But before he can be finally confirmed as lovable-with-good reason, one thing more must happen to him: he must put on women's clothes. The plot requires the disguise, but Mozart connects this moment to the deeper sentiments of the heart.

the contrasting middle section, with its more complex expressions of longing, fear, and delight.

[33] *...al concerto di tromboni, / Di bombarde, di cannoni, / Che le palle in tutti i tuoni / All'orecchio fan fischiar.*

It has often been sensed that Susanna's tender aria, "Come, kneel down," *Venite, inginocchiatevi,* is a pivotal moment in the opera, that something profound is going on when Susanna, first perfecting Cherubino's female disguise, then takes a look at him and sings, "If women fall in love with him, they certainly have their good reasons" (*se l'amano le femmine, han certo il lor perchè*). The music is perhaps the most sensuous and tender in the opera, as Susanna, asking him to turn around, adjusts his collar and his hands, shows him how to walk like a woman—and then notices how the guise complements the young man's mischievous eyes and graceful bearing: *che furba guardatura, che vezzo, che figura!* What Mozart slyly suggests, by making this aria so riveting, and, at the same time, so playful, is that it is here, in an intimate moment of tenderness, that the seeds of overthrow for the *ancien régime* are decisively sown.

To begin with, the aria concerns kneeling. There is lots of kneeling in this opera, and in every other place (until the very final moments) kneeling is a symbol of feudal hierarchy: exalted status on the one side, obedience on the other. In the women's democratic world, however, kneeling is just kneeling. You kneel in front of your dressmaker so that she can fix your bonnet and collar. Kneeling has no symbolism; it is just a useful action. Hierarchy is simply out the window, irrelevant, a non-issue. The music itself expresses this thought: instead of the thumping accents of the quest for honor, we hear little trill-like bursts from the violins, playful jumpings, like muffled outbursts of laughter, that not only betray no hierarchy, but that positively subvert the whole idea.[34] Bit by bit, the woman's costume is assembled, the woman's walk learned—until, at the end, Susanna surveys, with wonder and amazement, the result she has produced. "Admire (*mirate,* wonder at) the little devil, admire how beautiful he is. What mischievous looks (*che furba*

---

[34] A possible allusion in the text is to the popular eighteenth-century Christmas carol *Adeste fideles,* with its chorus *venite adoremus,* O come let us adore him (which would often be a prelude to kneeling). Here, Susanna says, "Come, kneel down"—but it is not adoration of the transcendent that she seeks; it is fun and play.

guardatura), what charm, what allure. If women love him, they certainly have their good reasons." Cherubino is alluring, it seems, precisely because, while manly and drawn to women, he is not drawn to controlling them or using them as pawns in games with other men: instead of domination, charm and grace; instead of plots to conceal shame or avenge insult, "mischievous looks," as he joins the women in their love of jokes and gossip.[35]

All of this is in the libretto—after a fashion. We can, however, imagine musical settings of the text that would have signaled irony, or skepticism, or bitterness (certainly an emotion that we could imagine Susanna feeling at this time). Instead, the music expresses both tender sensuousness and, as I have said, with the playful movements of the strings, laughter, suggesting that these two attitudes go well together, and that both are key parts of the woman's world. We are now led to recall a feature of the Overture whose significance we might have missed before: the same type of muffled laughter from the violins is present there, suggesting that subversive play is a major theme of the opera as a whole.

This reading of the aria is shortly confirmed by the duet "Aprite, presto, aprite," as Susanna and Cherubino plot together about getting him safely out of his compromising hiding place. The two sing, extremely rapidly, in hushed conspiratorial voices that show a rare degree of attunement—foreshadowing the more developed duet between Susanna and the Countess in Act 3. Cherubino shows that he has now, in effect, become a woman: a co-conspirator, a voice of fraternity and equality, and therefore, as if we didn't know it already, a person internally free from the bonds of status.

---

[35] Here Da Ponte has made major alterations to Beaumarchais. Beaumarchais's stage direction says that Cherubino kneels, but Susanna does not ask him to kneel, so the inversion of feudal kneeling is not emphasized. Far more important, when Cherubino becomes a woman Susanna says that she, as a woman, is jealous of him. This not only puts rivalry and jealousy into the women's world, whereas Mozart and Da Ponte represent that world as a world of reciprocity; it also fails to state that a man is more attractive *as a man* for behaving in ways that we have heretofore associated with that world.

As we look at Cherubino, we realize afresh how un-radical Figaro's apparent radicalism is. It's not only that he takes over from the *ancien régime* its proprietary attitude to women; it's something more global than that. Figaro simply sees the world the way the Count sees it: in terms of the quest for honor and the avoidance of shame. He doesn't understand reciprocity, and he really doesn't understand humor. (His idea of a joke is a mean-spirited put-down.[36]) If the new world has citizens like that, its commitment to equality and fraternity will be bound to be problematic. New hierarchies will be thrown up to replace the old, like ramparts defending the male ego. Could there, however, be citizens who simply like to laugh and to sing?

In her fascinating reflections on eighteenth-century pornography, Lynn Hunt has argued that the pornographic idea of the interchangeability of bodies is closely linked to the revolutionary call for democratic equality.[37] Legal theorist Lior Barschack argues that the new subjectivity created by Mozart's operas is just this hedonistic idea of sexual freedom.[38] No doubt such ideas were prominent in the eighteenth century, as people (meaning men) tried to make sense of the new world they inhabited.

---

[36] In a fascinating survey of the use of diminutives in the libretto (sent to me as a personal communication), scholar Marco Segala finds definite patterns in the use of different types of diminutives. The diminutives ending in *-etto/a* typically connote tenderness and playfulness, almost never sarcasm or irony; diminutives ending *-ino/a* often have an ironic or sarcastic meaning. When diminutives (usually ending in *-etto/a*) connote affection or play, the speaker is always feminine—with the exception of Cherubino, who has learned to speak the women's language. The men of the opera mainly use diminutives (usually ending in *-ino/a*) to express sneering or sarcasm.

[37] Hunt (1993, p. 44). Robert Darnton's earlier study of eighteenth-century pornography (and, in particular, of the anonymous novel *Thérèse Philosophe*) comes to a subtly different conclusion: the new idea is not one of intersubstitutability of bodies, but rather the idea of women's control and autonomy: thus the relationships that are prized are personal and long-lasting, but include contraception. See his *The Forbidden Best-Sellers of Pre-Revolutionary France* (Darnton 1996).

[38] Barshack (2008, pp. 47–67). Later, Barshack seems to arrive at a more nuanced view: "as Mozart saw, the libertine account of humaneness is as one-sided as the sentimental" (63); but I'm not sure I have fully understood his argument at that point, or how it is related to his earlier contention.

If I am right, however, Mozart sees the world rather differently, and more radically. The objectification of bodies as interchangeable physical units is itself, the opera suggests, just one aspect of the *ancien régime*, which invented and depends upon the idea that some classes of people, including, prominently, women, are just *oggetti*, and thus can be used at will in one's quest for personal gratification. Seeing bodies as interchangeable is, indeed, a clever route to what the *ancien régime* wanted all along: male control and invulnerability. What would be truly opposed to the *ancien régime* would be, not the democratization of bodies as interchangeable machines, but—love. Which, as Cherubino understands, means seeking a good outside oneself, a scary idea. It is, nonetheless, an idea that Figaro must learn before he can be the kind of citizen Mozart (not Beaumarchais) demands—and learn it he does, as, in the recitative before his still-defensive aria in Act 4, he acknowledges both longing and pain. Saying "O Susanna, what suffering you cost me," he, like Cherubino, seeks a good outside himself.

What's suggested here, then, is that democratic reciprocity needs love. Why? Why wouldn't respect be enough? Well, first of all, respect is unstable unless love can be reinvented in a way that does not make people obsessed all the time with hierarchy and status. That private obsession, unchallenged, threatens to disrupt the public culture of equality. But, more deeply, the public culture needs to be nourished and sustained by something that lies deep in the human heart and taps its most powerful sentiments, including both passion and humor. Without these, the public culture remains wafer-thin and passionless, without the ability to motivate people to make any sacrifice of their personal self-interest for the sake of the common good.[39]

---

[39] See Nussbaum (2013).

Cherubino, Rousseau, Herder: Spaces for Craziness, "Dispositions of Peace"

Now that I have given a general idea of what I believe Mozart is attempting, let me make it more precise by comparing the opera's insights about citizenship in the new era to those of two of Mozart's philosophical contemporaries, Jean-Jacques Rousseau (1712–1778) and Johann Gottfried Herder (1744–1803). Both share with Mozart the view that a new political culture needs to be sustained by new sentiments, and both also share with him the view that these sentiments must be not only the calm sentiments of respect and civic friendship, but must include, and be sustained by, something more like love, directed at the nation and its moral goals. We shall now see, however, that Rousseau takes this idea in an utterly different direction, whereas Herder and Mozart share many ideas.

In the important final section of *On the Social Contract* entitled "On Civil Religion," Rousseau makes it clear that intense love-like bonds of patriotic sentiment are needed to bring citizens together, rendering egalitarian institutions stable over time.[40] Early in human history, he observes, people "had no kings but the gods," and needed to believe that their leaders were indeed gods. Both paganism and feudalism were sustained by some such fiction. "A lengthy alteration of feelings and ideas is necessary before men can be resolved to accept a fellow man as a master, in the hope that things will turn out well for having done so" (220). These new sentiments must have the intensity of the religious sentiments they replace, or they will not succeed in holding the new political order together.

Christianity looks at first blush as if it might be that "civil religion," since it does teach the brotherhood of all human beings (224).

---

[40] I am citing the work in the translation by Donald A. Cress in *Jean-Jacques Rousseau: The Basic Political Writings* (Indianapolis: Hackett, 1987), original publication of *On the Social Contract* 1762; page numbers are from that edition.

On further inspection, however, Christianity has a number of fatal flaws from the point of view of the political order. First, it teaches people to hope for a salvation that is other-worldly and spiritual, rather than political; thus "it leaves laws with only the force the laws derive from themselves, without adding any other force to them" (224). Second, Christianity turns people's thoughts inward, as each is urged to examine his own heart; this teaching produces indifference to political events. Third and finally, Christianity teaches nonviolence and even martyrdom, thus teaching people to be slaves. "Its spirit is too favorable to tyranny for tyranny not to take advantage of it at all times" (225). Christian emperors, Rousseau argues, ruined the Roman empire: "when the cross expelled the eagle, all Roman valor disappeared" (225).

The civil religion we need must inculcate "sentiments of sociability, without which it is impossible to be a good citizen or a faithful subject" (226). These sentiments are based on some quasi-religious dogmas, including "the sanctity of the social contract and the laws" (226). But what are the sentiments themselves like? It is clear that they involve an intense love of the nation and its laws. They also involve a type of fraternity grounded in unanimity and homogeneity: the person who dissents from the "civil religion" is to be banished "for being unsociable, for being incapable of sincerely loving the laws and justice" (226). Civic love, then, is incompatible with active critical thought about the political order, and with a sense of the separateness of the individual from the group. The test for sincerity is unanimity. Furthermore, one thing that citizens must be unanimous about is the willingness to die for the nation—presumably without thinking critically about the plan for war, and whenever the sovereign body of citizens so decrees. The sentiment of civil love has, then, a strong commitment to the suspension of both individuality and reasoning. Indeed, we might say, more generally, that the person-to-person dimension is missing, since the approved sentiments of communal bonding do not lead to or rest upon any sentiments directed at individuals, even sentiments of concern and respect.[41]

Notice, then, that despite Rousseau's intense hatred of the feudal order, he has not been able to think his way very far beyond it. Civic love, like feudal love, is obedient, hierarchical. (Even if "the general will" is sovereign, not an individual, it nonetheless bears to the wayward individual a strongly hierarchical relationship.) There is no room for the sort of reciprocity exemplified by Mozart's women, a reciprocity based on plotting, joking, a sense of the free space within which people can live and be themselves. Moreover, despite Rousseau's attempt, in Book IV of *Emile*, to substitute the egalitarian sentiment of *pitié* for sentiments based upon feudal inequality, that experiment remains deeply unrealized in his idea of the civil religion, since the civil religion counters the allegedly excessive meekness of Christianity by relying, it would seem, on the very ideas of manly courage, assertiveness, and honor that sustained the *ancien régime*. There is a shift, in that the object of civic shame, civic anger, and civic assertiveness is now the nation, seen as embodiment of the general will. The sentiments themselves, however, feel very much the same, as the nation seeks to establish itself in the world's hierarchy of nations. It's still true, in this new world as in the old, that "to forget shame and insult is baseness, complete lowness of status."

Mozart, by contrast, proposes a radical alteration of the very content of civic love. No longer should love revolve in any way around ideas of hierarchy and status. Instead, it must be aspirational: like Cherubino, it must "seek a good outside myself."

To sustain truly egalitarian institutions, moreover, this aspirational love must remain multivocal and inclusive of diverse voices, given that each individual has a quirky mind that is not exactly the

---

[41] I owe this point to Daniel Brudney, who also points out that the *Letter to d'Alembert on the Theater* contains a rather different picture of the preferred types of social interaction.

same as any other. (Indeed, although I speak of "civic love," it is crucial to the new conception that there is a family of types of love that play a role, interwoven, sharing some features but differing in other respects, as do the people these loves connect.) Rather than Rousseau's homogeneity, the Mozartean regime seeks real-life heterogeneity, gives it space to unfold, and takes delight in its oddness. That is what I mean by "craziness," mentioned in crucial parts of the libretto: following your idiosyncratic passion, so long as it does no harm to others. The fondness of the women's world for plotting, joking, every subversion of tradition and obedience, is the sign of something that ultimately becomes crucial to the Enlightenment, in its Kantian and especially Millian forms: the idea of the mind of the individual as containing an untouched free space, a funny unevenness that is both erotic and precious. What the women's world knows is that those "mischievous looks" are precisely what make Cherubino worth loving (so that, if women love him, they "certainly have their good reasons"). They also know that the aspirational nature of his love is deeply interwoven with his capacity for subversion. Civic love, then, also has a downward movement: it can aspire in a healthy way only if it is also capable of poking fun at itself, noticing the everyday messiness and heterogeneity of real people.[42]

How do we imagine this civic love expressing itself? We connect Rousseau's love with solemn public ceremonies, with anthems, with the drumbeat of the call to arms. Mozart's love, by contrast, is expressed—well, through many different types of artistic and musical performance, but, crucially, through comedy, including comedy that pokes fun at the call to arms (as in "Non più andrai") and points out some of the unpleasant realities of what passes in some quarters for warlike glory: "instead of the fandango, a march

---

[42] This idea of the two aspects of decent patriotism is a central theme in Jeffrey Israel's *Living with Hate in American Politics and Religion* (2019), with a foreword by Martha C. Nussbaum.

through the mud (*il fango*)."[43] (In chapters 2 and 3 I shall criticize Romantic Mozarteans who underrate comic characters and laughter-inflected love.)

At this point, we notice that Mozart has an eighteenth-century ally: Johann Gottfried Herder, whose *Letters for the Advancement of Humanity* (1793–1797) develops a remarkably similar conception of a reformed patriotism that would need to be inculcated if the world were ever to become a world of peace. Herder begins by making the point that if patriotism is an attitude toward an entity called "Fatherland," it had better figure out what is valuable in the relationship of a child to its father.[44] If we ask this question seriously, he argues, we will see that we want this love to contain aspiration to genuine merit, but also a love of peace, since we all remember with greatest longing and love the peaceful times of our childhood. Moreover, what delighted us in those peaceful times was "*games of youth*": so, the new patriotism must at the same time be something playful. Above all, it would never involve blood lust and revenge: "*Fatherlands against fatherlands* in a combat of blood [*Blutkampf*] is the worst barbarism in the human language."

Later in the collection, Herder returns to this theme, making it clear that he imagines the animating spirit of the new patriotism as less paternal than feminine, and requiring a profound gender transformation on the part of males. Here he alludes to what he has managed to learn about Native American Iroquois customs, which, he argues, involve casting one of the potentially warring tribes in the role of "the woman," and then requiring all the others to listen to what "she" says:[45]

---

[43] Here I echo ideas already developed by Israel, in writing about the wartime cartoons of Bill Mauldin.

[44] *Letters*, extracted and translated by Michael N. Forster in *Herder: Philosophical Writings* (2002, p. 378).

[45] Here Herder is apparently paraphrasing a writer named G. H. Loskiel (1740–1814), a priest of the United Brethren, who published an extensive account of Iroquois customs in 1794.

Hence if at some time the *men* around her are at blows with each other and the war threatens to become severe, then the *woman* should have the power to address them and say to them: "You men, what are you doing that you belabor each other about with blows in this way? Just remember that your wives and children are bound to die if you do not stop. Do you, then, want to be responsible for your own annihilation from the face of the earth?" And the *men* should then pay heed to the *woman* and obey her. (401)

By dressing the (members of the) chosen nation in women's skirts and women's jewelry, they express the thought that "from now on they should no longer occupy themselves with weapons" (401). Herder now notes that the members of the Iroquois nation address one another as "sister-children" and "fellow female playmates."

Now to Europe. Herder observes that feudal hierarchy once played, after a fashion, the role of this "woman," making people keep the peace. Now that we have rejected feudalism, however, we have to put the women's clothes on all of us, in effect, and this means inculcating in all citizens "dispositions of peace." His "great peace woman" (whom he equates with "universal justice, humaneness, active reason") will seek to produce seven (emotional) "dispositions" in the citizens of the future. First is a "horror of war": citizens should learn that any war not limited to self-defense is mad and ignoble, causing endless practical pain and deep moral degeneration. Second, they will learn "reduced respect for heroic glory." They should "unite to blow away the false sparkle that dances around a *Marius, Sulla, Attila, Genghis Khan, Tamerlane*"—until citizens have no more awe for these mythic "heroes" than they do for common thugs. Herder does not say how this "blowing away" should be accomplished, but comedy is clearly a useful technique. Third, the peace-woman will teach a "horror of false statecraft." It's not enough to unmask warlike heroics: we must also teach disobedience and disrespect to the sort of political authority that likes to whip up war to advance its own power-interests. To produce this result we must teach active critical citizenship: "The universal voice-vote must be victorious over the value of mere *state rank* and of its *emblems*, even over the most seductive tricks of vanity, even over early-imbibed prejudices" (406). Of course this critical spirit must be taught in conjunction with an admiration for and aspiration to what is really fine.

Fourth, peace will teach patriotism, but a patriotic love that is "purified" of "dross," above all purified of the need to define the lovable qualities of one's nation in terms of competition with other nations, and even war against them. "Every nation must learn to feel that it becomes great, beautiful, noble, rich, well ordered, active, and happy, not in the eyes of others, not in the mouth of posterity, but only in itself, in its own self" (406). The fifth, closely related, disposition is that of "feelings of justice towards other nations." The sixth is a disposition to fair principles for trade relations, involving a ban on monopoly of the seas and a determination to make sure that poorer nations are not sacrificed to the greedy interests of the richer. Finally, citizens will learn to delight in useful activity: "the *maize stalk* in the *Indian woman's* hand is itself a weapon against the sword." All of these, concludes Herder, are the principles "of the great peace goddess *Reason* from whose language no one can in the end escape" (408).

Herder and Mozart are in harmony. Each sees the need to follow aspects of the (culturally) women's world,[46] criticizing the culture of male one-upmanship, if civic love is to be productive of true happiness. The Countess, we might say, is Herder's great peace-woman Reason, whose gentleness and whose refusal to focus on insulted pride show a way in which "all" can be happy. And Cherubino, her pupil, has learned from her a horror of war, a horror of false statecraft, and a love of mischievous subversion of the countless

---

[46] Once again, this is about culture, not innate tendencies; indeed, males could not be reformed did they not share similar basic capacities.

ways in which men try to make the world a world of war. Herder emphasizes the negative side more than does Mozart: the decent society must teach appropriate fear and even *horror*, not just appropriate *love*. And he rightly emphasizes the fact that critical Reason plays a crucial role in the new approach, thus echoing Kant's call for an approach to world peace that rests on the Enlightenment value of a critical public culture. In essence, however, he and Mozart are on the same page. The adult men are led, in the end, to put on those long skirts and think about daily life in a reasonable way, rather than a way informed solely by the insatiable greed of honor run amok.

But Herder's imaginary Native Americans are just his fantasy. He seems to have no interest in real communities of women. Here Mozart goes beyond him, examining the cultural creation of reciprocity and peace in the (wrongly devalued) women's world of his place and time.

What we have in the end of the opera is something that would appall Rousseau (or at least the Rousseau of this particular text), a world of craziness, foolishness, joking, idiosyncratic individuality—and, inseparably, a world of peace.[47] It's the world that Kant and Mill would have depicted, if either of them had had a sense of humor.

Transcending the Everyday? Nussbaum
contra Nussbaum

What, then, happens at the opera's close? Temporarily, at least, the men's world yields before the women's world, asking for pardon. And then there is a pause. As Steinberg nicely says, "[F]rom Mozart to Mahler, the rest, the musical pause, the moment of silence is the

---

[47] Is the new temper sufficient for peace? Clearly not, since external dangers may still threaten. But it seems to be his view that it is necessary.

indicator of a first-person musical voice taking stock of itself. Music stops to think."[48] And what, in this silence, might the Countess be thinking, before she says "Yes"?

If she has any sense—and we know that she has a great deal—she will be thinking, What on earth does this promise of renewed love really mean? Has this man, who has behaved badly for years, really become a new person just because our joke succeeded and he is publicly embarrassed? And when, like the sensible woman she is, she gives herself the answer, "Surely not," then she must think again, asking herself, "But then, shall I accept him as he is, with his arrogance, his status-consciousness, his anxiety-driven infidelities? Shall I agree to live with just the hope or promise, and the occasional reality, of reciprocal love, rather than its assured stability?

When, then, after that pause, she answers "I am nicer, and I say yes," with that downward-leaning phrase, she is saying yes to the imperfection in all their lives, accepting the fact that love between these men and these women, if frequently real, will always be uneven and far from blissful; that people will never get the entirety of what they long for; that even if men are capable of learning from women—and Steinberg has nicely shown how Figaro learns from Susanna a newly tender musical idiom[49]—nonetheless we hardly have reason to expect these achievements to be stable, given the pressures culture and upbringing exert on human development. Indeed, it seems far more likely that Cherubino will be corrupted by the male world around him than that the other men will drop their quest for honor and status and learn to sing like Cherubino. Even in the best of cultures, the aversion to shame and the narcissistic desire for control are profound human desires; they are unlikely to go away, yielding a world in which all lovers get everything they want. (And wouldn't the image of such a world itself be a

---

[48] Steinberg (2004, p. 45). He is talking about a pause in Susanna's aria *Deh vieni, non tardar*, which he discusses so nicely that I refrain from adding anything further.

[49] Steinberg (2004, pp. 45–46): "In his emotional maturity, Figaro is awarded by Mozart with a musical sensuality that departs from his earlier, metronomic ditties."

narcissistic fantasy that might inhibit the real perception of another individual reality?)

So, when she says that "yes," she is agreeing to love, and even trust, in a world of inconstancy and imperfection—an affirmation requiring more courage than any of the battlefield exploits mentioned by Figaro in "Non più andrai."

And what she agrees to, here, is what the ensemble also agrees to. The new public world is a world of happiness "*in that way.*" What that seems to mean is that all present say yes to a world that seeks and aims at reciprocity, respect, and attunement without being starry-eyed about perfection, a world in which people commit themselves to liberty, fraternity, and equality, while understanding that these transcendent ideals are not to be attained by exiting from the real world into a pristine world, but rather by pursuing them in this one, in episodes of love and craziness. (We shall see in chapter 2 that this is also the world of Freemasonry, at least as Mozart understands it.) The new regime will fail if it demands perfection. It will succeed only on the basis of a realistic conception of men and women, and what they are capable of. But sustaining the hope of fraternity without being starry-eyed (and therefore, in due course, disillusioned and cynical) requires something like an unjaundiced trust in the possibility of love (at least sometimes and for a while), and, perhaps above all, a sense of humor about the world as it is.[50]

These ideas of trust, acceptance, and reconciliation are not in the text, but only in the music.[51] As has long been felt by interpreters, Mozart's sensibility is, at the very least, more determinate than

[50] Here I think Barshack is perceptive: "Affective intensity" (in Mozart) "does not result in a retreat from the play of variations and ambiguities which make up everyday existence. . . . In the height of passion, Mozart often invokes the frivolous and the commonplace."

[51] See Kerman (1988, p. 91) and Carter (1987, pp. 120–21), who writes that the text is "perfunctory to an extreme" and that the musical setting is "magnificent in its serenity and translucence."

Da Ponte's, and at times, even at odds with it (see chapter 3). But Mozart's music is not in some unattainable heaven, it is in the middle of our world, and in the bodies of those who sing it; it reshapes the world by reshaping breath itself.

In his outstanding book *The Musical Representation: Meaning, Ontology, and Emotion*,[52] Charles O. Nussbaum gives us the best picture we have in philosophy to date of the experience of musical listening, the nature of the virtual space it creates and the mental representations it evokes. At the end of the book, he adds a chapter that is in many ways underdetermined by the book's overall argument, in which he argues that the great interest we take in (Western, tonal) music derives from our horror of the merely contingent, our desire for an experience of transcendence and unity that is akin to religious experience. This chapter contains fascinating material on quite a few philosophers, including Kant, Hegel, Schopenhauer, Nietzsche, and Sartre—all of whom supply arguments that harmonize with Nussbaum's contentions in a variety of ways. It also contains material on mystical experience that convinces one that the religion/music parallel Nussbaum investigates is real, and illuminating for at least some music.

And yet. Why should we be so inclined to suppose that music offers one particular type of good to human life, rather than many types of good? Charles Nussbaum is far too subtle to claim such a thing outright; but in his insistence on this one function of music, he at least suggests the primacy and centrality of this type of good. Like, and continuous with, philosophy, however, music would appear to assume different argumentative positions, seeing the world from different and contrasting points of view. (Indeed, religion itself contains many types of experience—including the mystical impression of transcendence, but including, as well, the passion for

---

[52] (2007).

earthly justice and the acceptance of an imperfection in earthly striving.[53])

I have given a reading of Mozart's opera that maintains that it offers a different sort of happiness, a happiness that is comic, uneven, uncertain, wary of grandiose claims of transcendence. Indeed, the music itself laughs up its sleeve at pretensions of that sort (as in those little muffled bursts of laughter in the Overture and in "Venite, inginocchiatevi"[54]). Charles Nussbaum may well respond that opera, that impure mixed art form, which relies on real bodies and real sights, is not the musical medium that his argument (based on music's disembodied and invisible nature) addresses. Even the human voice itself appears an anomaly within the Nussbaum conception of a musical art without bounded spatiotemporal existence. All musical instruments refer in some way to the human body, but the voice, alone among the instruments, is a part of the body, and always expresses bodily frailty as well as potentiality.[55]

Just as there is a love that seeks transcendence and a love that repudiates that aspiration as immature and a precursor of disillusionment, so too, I think there are both sorts of music. It is no accident that Beethoven is on the cover of Charles Nussbaum's book,[56] and a major source of his musical examples. But the yearning for the transcendent that is embodied in Beethoven's version of the Enlightenment can be first cousin to cynicism: realizing that the

[53] Indeed, C. Nussbaum's characterization of religious experience is more at home in Christianity than in Judaism, with its emphasis on the earthly nature of our ethical duties.

[54] And if I am right about the allusion to *venite adoremus* (see above), the aria quite directly pokes fun at the search for transcendence.

[55] Here a comment made by Mollie Stone, then Assistant Conductor of the Chicago Children's Choir, is illuminating. Describing the contribution the Choir makes to the political and social development of children from a wide range of ethnic and racial backgrounds, she commented that the children become close to each other because they actually share their breath with one another, a kind of physical reciprocity that is much more intimate than anything that would be involved in orchestral performance, (Nussbaum 2016b).

[56] A cover chosen by the author.

world embodied in the Ninth Symphony and *Fidelio* doesn't really exist, what can one do but make a sour face at the real world? In Part II we shall pursue that question, and ask how far from Mozart Beethoven really is.

If, however, one follows Mozart's version of Enlightenment politics, one will still see that the world as it is needs a great deal of work, and one will not stop aspiring to get that work done, making the world of the male voice somewhat more like the world of the female voice, with its commitment to fraternity, equality, and liberty. One will not stop seeking to educate young men to love music rather than the concerto of shells and cannons. One will, however, also at the same time embrace real people—even men!—as they are, and one won't stop loving them because they are (no doubt like oneself) a mess. That, suggests the pause within the music, is a more hopeful direction, if not the only possible direction, for a workable conception of democratic political love.

2

Mozart and the Freemasons

Idomeneo and *The Magic Flute*

Though it is proper to recall his achievements as an artist, let us not forget to honor his noble heart. He was a zealous member of our order. His love for his brothers, his cooperative and affirmative nature, his charity, his deep joy when he could serve one of his brethren with his special talents, these were his great qualities. He was husband and father, a friend to his friends and a brother to his brothers.

—Oration, Memorial meeting for Mozart at the
lodge "New-Crowned Hope," December 1791

Love yourselves, love your brothers. . . .
Hold out to one another the brotherly hand of eternal
friendship.
Only delusion, not truth, withheld it for so long.
Break the grip of that delusion, tear the veil of prejudice.

—Franz Heinrich Ziegenhagen, text for Mozart's
cantata "You who honor the Creator of the
immeasurable Universe," K. 619, one of
Mozart's last works

Mozart the Freemason

In chapter 1 I situated Mozart among great political thinkers of the Enlightenment, defending my claim that he is one of them and articulating key aspects of a "Mozartean" ethos: cultivation of powerful sentiments of brotherhood and compassion; rejection of the old ideology of class privilege, honor, and revenge; the idea that males have much to learn from the world of women. Now we need to place him more narrowly in the Viennese world that was so crucial for his overall musical and philosophical development, visualizing him in a time of dynamic political reform and high aspiration.

These aspirations took a particular form: Mozart's affiliation with a lodge of Freemasons and his heartfelt belief in the ideals of that movement, which included detailed thought about how music could help humanity realize them. He joined officially only in 1784, but he was drawn to the ideas of the movement long before—at least from 1773, when he began working with Freemason playwright Tobias Philips, Baron von Gebler, to compose incidental music for Gebler's play *Thamos, King of Egypt*, which expressed key Masonic ideas and used many Masonic symbols.[1] Already in 1776, he had expressed his own goals, in a letter, in terms highly congenial to the Freemasons: "We live in this world in order to learn industriously and, by interchanging our ideas, to enlighten one another and thus endeavor to promote the sciences and the fine arts."[2]

From that time on, and especially after his move to Vienna in 1781, he was surrounded by Masons, and counted them among his closest friends. When he formally joined the lodge Beneficence (*Zur Wohltätigkeit*)—later merged with another lodge and renamed New-Crowned Hope (*Zur neugekrönten Hoffnung*)—this step deepened commitments already dear to him, and in the fellowship of the lodge he developed them further, becoming the lodge's quasi-official composer and writing many works for lodge occasions. His father, Leopold, joined at around the same time, and seems to have

---

[1] See, in addition to the sources for Mozart's Freemasonic connections listed below, Edward Joseph Dent, *Mozart's Operas* (1913, pp. 55–56).
[2] Letter to Padre Martini cited in Waldoff (2019, p. 51).

held in some respects more radical views than his son (rejecting as superstition many tenets of conventional Catholicism).

This chapter will place Mozart in his Freemasonic context, studying the general beliefs of the movement and the particular flavor of Freemasonry chosen by Mozart—as a prelude to examining in detail two operas in which Masonic ideals are especially prominent: *Idomeneo*, K 366 (1781) and *The Magic Flute* (*Die Zauberflöte*, K 620, 1791). One is the earliest Mozart opera now considered among his best and regularly performed; the other is one of his two last operas, and the last to be premiered, only two months before his death. (*La Clemenza di Tito*, K 621, had its premiere only a few weeks earlier.) Both denounce religious superstition and announce a personal and political reign of love in which males and females are coequal partners. Both also in different ways make room for human fallibility and the imperfection of the idealists themselves, suggesting the need for flexibility and (above all in the latter work) a sense of humor.

Mozart's Vienna

In Salzburg, Mozart's life had been difficult on account of a fraught relationship with his employer Archbishop Colloredo. The Archbishop treated Mozart and his father like servants and cramped their style with austere musical ideas (limiting the length of choral works), requirements to provide incidental music for courtly entertainments, and just a general lack of respect for their freedom. After this, Vienna was a breath of fresh air. Although the manner of his dismissal stung—the famous "kick in the ass" described by Mozart as given him by the Archbishop's Chamberlain, Count Arco—he quickly made himself at home in the greater freedom and diversity of the larger city.

Mozart rented lodgings in the only house in the city freely selected (i.e., with no restrictions to a Jewish quarter) and rented by a family of Jews.[3] The Arnsteins were unconverted Jews; the elder Arnstein was strictly observant and wore a long black beard. Meanwhile the younger members of the household took advantage of the gradual process of Jewish emancipation to establish themselves in polite society. Mozart had many other Jewish friends and acquaintances, most of them converts, who were treated as equals in bourgeois circles, but who also shared with non-converts the experience of an oppressed minority.

He also encountered racial diversity.[4] Angelo Soliman, a Black African apparently originally named Mmadi Make, had been abducted as a child by a rival tribe and taken from his native land (location unclear). He was then sold to Christians and baptized, and later brought up and educated in Messina and given as a gift to a Bohemian prince. This prince, in turn, bequeathed him to the Prince of Liechtenstein, where he served as a major-domo and accompanied the Prince when, as Austrian envoy, he went to Frankfurt to vote in the election of Joseph II as Holy Roman Emperor. He was treated by the Prince as a paid employee, and became independently wealthy, thanks to his skill at card games. Eventually he established an independent life in Vienna, and even married a white woman and had a child with her—although when the Prince learned of this he fired and disinherited him (before that he had been amply provided for in the Prince's will). So he lived independently but modestly, gaining a salary as a tutor to the Prince's nephew's children. He was known to be immensely dashing and glamorous—as a surviving portrait shows—spoke three languages fluently and understood three more. And in 1783 he joined, as an equal brother, the Masonic lodge True Concord (*Zur wahren Eintracht*), where lodge records show that on several occasions he met Mozart, who often visited there. He rose to become Grand

---

[3] Volkmar Braunbehrens, *Mozart in Vienna: 1781–1791*, translated by Timothy Bell ([1986] 1991, pp. 66 ff.). This superb book will be cited so often that I shall subsequently cite by the letter B and the page number.

[4] See B 80–87.

Master of that lodge. After his death in 1786, however, he was vilely abused, and his body was later stuffed like a human specimen.

It was, then, a time of halting steps toward greater inclusion, together with constant dangers of cruelty and backsliding. Such was the reign of Joseph II (1741–1790), who was Holy Roman Emperor beginning in 1765 and sole ruler from 1780. Joseph was a man of the Enlightenment, with high ideals and firm beliefs. He was also, however, an autocratic ruler, whose basic idea was that a state led by a one-man ruler should produce the enlightening on the ruler's own terms. He was also the son of Maria Theresa and the brother of French queen Marie Antoinette (1755–1793). So as the French Revolution progressed, imperiling the very idea of monarchy, he drew in his sails to some extent, especially where the Freemasons were concerned.

Joseph's reforms were sweeping.[5] He had sincere beliefs in human dignity and equality, and made real efforts to realize them, albeit within the context of autocratic monarchy. He modernized the economy, made many improvements in industry, agriculture, and travel, and upgraded education at all levels (including instituting compulsory elementary education for all boys and girls). More radically, he abolished serfdom and the special privileges of the nobility under the criminal law. He reorganized the entire legal system, abolishing the death penalty, introducing a code of civil law, and liberalizing the censorship to permit wider freedoms of speech and publication. (For example, he permitted the staging of Mozart's *The Marriage of Figaro* and at least the publication of the Beaumarchais play.) Criticism of the monarch was also permitted, and many such pamphlets saw the light of day.

Joseph's ideas in religious matters were progressive. He proclaimed total religious freedom and forbade curtailing basic civil liberties on religious grounds. (Elsewhere too, ideas of toleration burgeoned: the play *Nathan der* Weise by G. E. F. Lessing,

---

[5] A good summary is in B, 215–25.

perhaps European literature's most famous statement on religious freedom and equality, was written in Hamburg in 1783.) Joseph still treated Jews as a special case and restricted them in some ways, making them pay a special tax and use the German language in all official communications. But they could now wear clothing of their choice, circulate freely in society, and engage in trade with no restriction. The Catholic Church fared less well: Joseph simply dissolved all the monasteries and convents, devoting the proceeds of their sale to the support of their former members. Needless to say, Catholic leaders were not happy with his policies, although Catholics too enjoyed religious freedom within the bounds of Enlightenment rationalism.

In matters of health Joseph intervened paternalistically—for example banning the wearing of corsets because they were unhealthy. He even banned coffins on hygienic grounds, insisting on burial outside the city in a plain linen sack—another incursion that displeased the Church.

Thus the ideas Mozart embraced as a Freemason were squarely in his society's mainstream, although he chose to pursue these within a nominally secret society, always a somewhat uncertain undertaking.

Mozart Joins a Lodge

On December 5, 1784, Mozart joined the lodge Beneficence; he was initiated on December 14, promoted to the second degree on January 7, and became a Master shortly after that. The ceremonies for these rituals are well known and described in contemporary sources.[6] If Freemasonry was a secret society, the secret was not about who attended or, in general outline, what happened—these facts were entirely public—but only, perhaps, about details of the

---

[6] See the extensive citations in B 226–31.

ceremonies, and the inner transformation of the self that the ceremonies were supposed to produce.

Beneficence was a small lodge, with thirty-two members, only two being from the nobility—quite unlike the larger True Concord, which enrolled quite a few nobles and many luminaries, including the scientist Ignaz von Born and the composer Franz Joseph Haydn. Both Beneficence and True Concord were moderate Enlightenment rationalist lodges, not extremely anti-clerical like the Illuminati and also not mystical like the Rosicrucians. Since Mozart often attended events at True Concord and even wrote a composition celebrating an honor given to Born (*Maurerfreude* or *Masonic Joy*, K 471), historians wonder why he chose the smaller lodge with its lower profile. It seems likely that it was because Beneficence was middle-class, not full of show-off nobles, and it was dedicated to practical acts of charity, for example, taking up a collection for flood victims that brought in the equivalent of $80,000 today.[7] Mozart quickly became the lodge's *de facto* resident composer.

But what exactly was Freemasonry in Vienna?[8] The Masonic movement, which had enormous influence in late eighteenth-century Europe and North America, was a form of humanist rationalism that favored brotherhood, the equal dignity of all people, and an end to blind superstition. It was primarily a bourgeois movement, though some of its members were nobles and others favored a more radical egalitarianism. Masonry was compatible with some form of Christian (and, indeed, Jewish) affiliation, but some Masons tended to be anti-Catholic, linking that church to

---

[7] See B 240.

[8] Other valuable sources include: Paul Nettl, *Mozart and Masonry* (1952), which cites the entire speech about Mozart from his memorial meeting; Katherine Thomson, *The Masonic Thread in Mozart* (1977), a comprehensive survey of dozens of works that show Masonic links; H. C. Robbins Landon, *Mozart and the Masons* (1982 and 1991), which reproduces and discusses a remarkable painting depicting a meeting at the lodge Crowned Hope in 1790, in which Mozart seems to be depicted; and Jessica Waldoff, "Mozart and Freemasonry," in *Mozart in Context*, ed. Simon P. Keefe (2019, pp. 50–58).

superstition and priestly authority. In Vienna, however, lodges enrolled many practicing Catholics and even priests. Mozart was always a practicing Catholic.

Freemasonry was a quasi-religion, a fraternity based upon ethical commitments, whose members aimed to cultivate their ethical capacities and ethical sentiments by joining together in a club with shared rituals and strong fraternal bonds.

Like a church, Freemasonry was concerned with matters of life and death, and a central tenet was that death was not to be an object of terror, but should be faced with calm determination. This teaching was much emphasized in lodge meetings, and was no doubt one thing that drew members to the group. Mozart's last letter to his father, when Leopold was near death, described these familiar Masonic views, which Leopold could be expected to share:

> As death, when we come to consider it closely, is the true goal of our existence, I have formed during the last few years such close relations with this best and truest friend of mankind, that his image is not only no longer terrifying to me, but is indeed very soothing and consoling! And I thank my God for graciously granting me the opportunity (you know what I mean) of learning that death is the *key* which unlocks the door to our true happiness. I never lie down at night without reflecting that—young as I am—I may not live to see another day. Yet no one of all my acquaintances could say that in company I am morose or disgruntled. For this blessing I daily thank my Creator and wish with all my heart that all my fellow creatures could enjoy it.[9]

In many ways, Freemasonry was like somewhat later groups such as Unitarian/Universalism, Reform Judaism, and Reform Judaism's offshoot the Ethical Culture Society. Some Masons were Deists; others, like Mozart, were more traditional theists, though denying

---

[9] The letter is dated April 4, 1787.

the church's authority over reason; still others were believers in the oneness of all religions (the view espoused by Ziegenhagen, whose libretto for Mozart's "Die ihr" speaks of a god whom different people call "Jehovah or Brahma or Fu"). And some were atheists. They were held together by a shared commitment to human dignity and equality and by the goal of self-cultivation, in democratic fraternity with others. Each Masonic lodge was a self-governing democratic community, an image of what a larger polity might be.

Unlike the other movements I have named, Freemasonry in Vienna was all-male. This was a topic of controversy, and in France women could join some lodges. We shall see that Mozart later took women's side in this discussion. Meanwhile, women in Vienna wore Masonic jewelry and knew quite a lot about the movement, which, as I have said, was only quasi-secret.

It may help Americans here to think about American Freemasons of the same era, of whom George Washington was the most ardent and famous. Washington was a pious man in his own way, but his piety had a distinctly egalitarian flavor, and the choice of the simple abstract Masonic obelisk for his monument was appropriate to the man: it eschews traditional religious and heroic symbols. Nobody would have called Washington a radical, but the ceremony of laying the foundation for the Capitol, at which Washington used the traditional Masonic apron and trowel—its three corners representing the Masonic triad of Wisdom, Beauty, and Strength—expressed an idea of equality and the dignity of human fellowship.

Joseph II was permissive about Freemasonry—at first. But as the revolution in France heated up, the very idea of secret societies worried him more and more: so in December 1785 he issued the Freemason Decree, which spoke in surprisingly harsh terms about the danger of secret societies, and reduced the number of lodges, suspending some of the more extreme and leading others to merge. Mozart's lodge survived, but consolidated with two others into the lodge New-Crowned Hope (*Zur Neugekrönten Hoffnung*), where he remained until his death.

Freemasonry had a profound commitment to the centrality of music in ethical culture, feeling that suitable music fostered brotherhood and stirred members to good work. It also had a specific set of views about music—including a preference for sequences of three everywhere, and hence for the key of E-flat major, with its three flats. Dotted rhythms were also favored. Mozart absorbed and used all these Masonic ideas, imbuing them with greater depth and emotional power. In keeping with Freemasonry, but even more with his distinguished and subtle heart, he understood that music can express emotional ideas with a precision that needs no words. In Masonic contexts, and often elsewhere, he developed what critics have called a "humanist style," characterized by simple, lofty, hymnlike melodies. The presence of this style contrasts his more evidently Masonic works with works in what is known as the *galant* style, popular in his time, characterized by elegance and brilliance, rather than profundity.[10]

Mozart's directly Masonic compositions were all written for some specific lodge occasion. The earliest of these was the song "Gesellenreise" (Comrade Journey), K. 468, March 26, 1785, probably written for Leopold's promotion to the second degree. The cantata honoring Born followed: *Die Maurerfreude* (*Masonic Joy*, K. 471). There were quite a few other songs; the well-known *Mauerische Trauermusik* (*Masonic Funeral Music*, K. 477/479a), written for the memorial service honoring two brothers; and the *Kleine Freimaurer-Kantate* (*Little Masonic Cantata*, K. 623), with words by Schikaneder, written for the consecration of the temple of Mozart's lodge in November 1791.[11] Not performed at a lodge but closely related was the cantata to Ziegenhagen's words, "Die ihr des unermesslichen Weltalls Schöpfer ehrt" ("You who honor the Creator of the immeasurable Universe," K. 619), written for a

---

[10] See Thomson (1977, p. 45).

[11] See Nettl (1952, pp. 52–53): Schikaneder was not a member of that lodge, and it is unclear how he came to write the words.

meeting of the Masonic-related group, "Colony of the Friends of Nature."

Masonic ideas and commitments were deep in Mozart's heart and mind, and, as many scholars have shown, wove themselves into his non-lodge works in many ways.[12] It is now time to investigate two operas that I believe to be especially Masonic in both substance and style—although one precedes his formal initiation and has not been explicitly linked to Freemasonry in the literature.

Idomeneo: The Reign of Love

Idomeneo is Mozart's first mature opera, and it remains one of his most profound and musically satisfying. Although its premiere took place on January 27, 1781, just after the composer's twenty-fifth birthday, the opera provides one of Mozart's most searching explorations of some cherished Mozartean themes: the triumph of love over hatred, and of reconciliation and mercy over revenge and rigidity.[13]

Unlike most of his best-loved works, it is an *opera seria*, with no admixture of comedy; and although it contains haunting stories of romantic and familial love, it is also a political opera, whose three acts all end with choral singing and with a statement about how the choices of the characters affect the political community. In both of these respects, it has strong links to *La Clemenza di Tito*, one of Mozart's last two operas; but *Idomeneo*'s libretto is far better written, and Mozart got a chance to write all of its music, including

---

[12] See especially Nettl (1952) and Thomson (1977).

[13] Julian Rushton's *W. A. Mozart, Idomeneo*, Cambridge Opera Handbooks (Cambridge: Cambridge University Press, 1993), is an excellent account of the work on both the historical and the musical planes. (All chapters not attributed to another author are written by Rushton.) See also the fine account of the opera in Dent, *Mozart's Operas* (1913, pp. 55–108).

the recitatives, which time pressure prevented him from writing himself in the later work.

In 1780 Mozart and librettist Giambattista Varesco were commissioned by Karl Theodor, Elector of Bavaria, to write an opera for a court performance. Mozart seems to have had a key role in the choice of the subject. Varesco's libretto was based on a French drama by Antoine Danchet, which had already been turned into an opera by another composer in 1712. Many letters between Mozart and his father Leopold inform us about the opera's development. But this was all Mozart: the first work he composed without his father's direct supervision.[14] (Perhaps this turning point helps explain the opera's emphasis on the idea of freedom from authority.) We learn from the letters that key roles were fitted to singers whom Mozart preferred, and that the libretto and music required, ultimately, many cuts in order to be suitable for the court performance.

The work premiered at the Cuvilliés Theater in Munich. Mozart was not happy with many of the cuts, and today the opera is typically performed virtually uncut. A second performance in Vienna in 1786 occasioned a major rewrite of some scenes, the restoration of many cuts, and a total recasting of the role of Idomeneo's son Idamante: sung by a castrato soprano at the premier, the role was adapted for a tenor in the Vienna version. Today most productions return to the original scoring, giving the role to a female mezzo-soprano. This permits the close harmonies in the Ilia–Idamante duet that are among the opera's most moving musical effects, and a full exploration of Idamante's gender-atypical gentleness. Like Cherubino in *The Marriage of Figaro* (see chapter 1) and like Sesto in *La Clemenza di Tito* (see chapter 4)—the former written directly for a female mezzo-soprano and the latter assigned to a castrato without the dying Mozart's permission—Idamante is a tender, loving type of male who eschews the common male competition for honor and domination. Although his heroic dragon-slaying links

---

[14] See Rice (2009).

him to traditional castrato roles, it seems fitting, both dramatically and musically, to cast the role today with a female mezzo-soprano, thus contrasting him musically with his (heroic tenor) father.

Idomeneo is set in ancient Greece and loosely based on tales of the aftermath of the Trojan War. Its target, however, is the Hebrew Bible itself. The central plot idea is that Idomeneo, to be rescued from a storm at sea that almost destroys him, promises the god Neptune (the Roman name for Poseidon) that if he is saved, he will offer up as a human sacrifice to the god the first person he meets when he comes ashore. But the person who meets him is his own son, Idamante. We see already, then, that the realm of the gods is depicted (as in ancient Greece) as amoral, non-deliberative, and securing allegiance by fear and asymmetrical groveling. The sea-god's rigid authority is depicted already in the heavy thumping chords of the overture—along, however, with a chromatic theme working against it, which we come to associate with human initiatives against cruel fate.[15] After vain attempts to avoid the requirements of this promise, Idomeneo prepares to obey, and Idamante is willing for the murder to be carried out (although Idamante's fiancée, Ilia, offers herself as a substitute).

Greek tragedies sometimes have happy endings—Aristotle, we know, preferred this sort—but typically the good ending is produced by sheer luck, some intervening *deus ex machina*. In *Idomeneo*, by contrast, it is the evolving story of the power of human love that prepares the way for the final scene. Idomeneo insists that his inner human *natura* rebels against the deed commanded by impersonal Nature (*natura* in its other meaning, the realm of the gods and fate). Ilia volunteers herself as a substitute sacrifice. And even the priests join in chorus to criticize the sea-god's behavior: "Abate your anger, your rigidity!" Then, in a very un-Greek and rather Masonic denouement, the gods yield to the power of love and reason. Suddenly a Voice—unnamed, specified in the libretto only

---

[15] See Rushton (1993, pp. 5–6).

as *Voce*—breaks in, in the Masonic key of E-flat major, announcing that "Love has triumphed!" and that Idomeneo must make way for new rulers of the political community: the loving male–female duo, Ilia and Idamante (prefiguring the dual initiation of Pamina and Tamino at the end of *The Magic Flute*). The Voice not only solves the sacrifice problem, it also announces that this regime change will bring peace to the whole people. Instead of a monarchy based upon fear, we have a new regime (albeit of unspecified institutional shape), based on freedom, flexibility, reciprocity, and love. In his parting gesture, Idomeneo announces a new law: peace. And the Chorus, celebrating the marriage of the young couple, wishes them "peace of spirit" (*d'alma pace*).

It is worth contrasting this ending with the famous happy ending of Gluck's *Orfeo ed Euridice* (1762), also engineered by Love. In *Orfeo*, Amor is part of the divine superstition-apparatus; here the Voice, unlinked with any anthropomorphic deity, undoes the order of the gods. There the loving couple end up together, but not exactly as equals: it is Orfeo's steadfast love that is rewarded, and there is little sense of equality and reciprocity. Finally, the ending of *Idomeneo* is explicitly political: the Voice inaugurates a new type of rulership, in which the loving couple will rule as equals for the good of the people.

To appreciate the opera's radicalism further, we must understand its ending against its familiar biblical background. The opera's sea serpent story alludes unmistakably to two Biblical stories of human obedience to a bad divine command. The closest is the story of Jephthah in *Judges* 11. Going into battle against the Ammonites, Jephthah promises God that if he wins he will sacrifice the first person he meets after the battle. (God apparently has not expressed any opposition to human sacrifice.) The first person he sees is his own daughter, his only child. He is devastated, but prepares to obey. She too submits to the promise, asking only for a period of time to roam in the mountains and weep with her friends. He gives her two months. At the end of that time he fulfills his promise.

Another even more famous, and equally troubling, story also lies in the background: the sacrifice of Isaac, or Akedah, one of the central ethical tales of Judeo-Christian religion. As narrated in the Bible, God tests Abraham, commanding him to sacrifice his son Isaac. Abraham prepares the sacrifice and binds his son. However, at this point an Angel intervenes, stopping the sacrifice—but apparently praising Abraham for his obedient willingness to offer his only son. From antiquity on, this tale has been interpreted in contradictory ways. Some have seen the test as a legitimate expression of divine authority and praised Abraham for his obedience. Others, feeling that God could not really have ordered such a heinous act, hold that God intended to intervene all along, and within this group there are many who hold that Abraham fails the test: it was a test of ethical maturity and judgment, and his slavish obedience shows his ethical inadequacy. Still others hold that the tale derives from an immature time in human history and contains an archaic picture of God that we ought to reject. However, the first (approving) sort were in the vast majority in Mozart's time, especially within standard Roman Catholicism, with its strong role for religious authority over human reason.

What Mozart and Varesco have done is therefore shocking—or would have seemed so had the story not been set in ancient Greece, where the gods are not expected to act morally. Mozart clearly found in Greek antiquity the opportunity to create a political universe in which the gods are not moral and in which human beings must take upon themselves the task of creating a decent political community. But in keeping with his Masonic optimism about the power of human freedom and reason, the world of *Idomeneo* is (unlike the world of many Greek tragedies) an ultimately untragic place in which people really can chart their own course, and human reason and love prove capable of surmounting and replacing both divine harshness and communal superstition.

Joseph Kerman claims that *Idomeneo* is "static," and that the happy ending is produced by "passivity." Indeed, he calls the entire opera a "drama of passivity.[16] This seems to me completely wrong: Idomeneo's obedience to Neptune was passive, but both Ilia and Idamante manage to break free from Neptune's sway before the Voice declares the happy ending: it is because their active love has shown what unfettered human choice can do that the Voice puts them in charge. Already in the overture we have heard freedom and flexibility asserting themselves against authority. Nor are the subordinate religious figures passive: the Priests protest against the sacrifice, demanding mercy and flexibility, becoming important catalysts of the solution.[17]

The great nineteenth-century musicologist and critic Eduard Hanslick judged *Idomeneo* inferior to Mozart's more "Shakespearean" operas (his comparison), which, like Shakespeare's tragedies, contain a mixture of tragedy and comedy. Hanslick was short-sighted. Although it is true that *Idomeneo* has no comic scenes or characters, it is its own remarkable mixture— of tragedy with happy love story—and indeed a story that ends up subverting and rewriting the world of tragedy, bringing about peace and reconciliation on the political plane as well.

But how did we reach this point? Mozart always insisted that music took priority over the words: "I would say that in an opera the poetry must be altogether the obedient daughter of the music."[18] In *Idomeneo* his subtle and original musical language accomplishes what the libretto itself could not, showing us what good judgment, tenderness, and flexibility can be and do. Let us turn, then, to the opera, tracing two threads that run through it: the ethical growth of Ilia, and the emotional and ethical character of Idamante.

---

[16] Kerman (1988, pp. 83, 85). My critique is in agreement with Rushton's interpretation.

[17] See also Dent (1913, p. 79): "Nor is *Idomeneo* a cold and stately succession of formal movements.... We feel that the characters ... [are] individuals with wills and passions of their own."

[18] Letter quoted in B, p. 61.

The opera is set in the aftermath of the bitter Trojan War, which, as Homer tells us, brought "thousandfold pains" even on the victorious Greeks, and more or less wiped out the Trojans. Ilia, daughter of Priam, one of the last of the Trojan royal family, is a captive along with other prisoners, "bereft of father and brothers." Stateless, homeless, she stands alone on the shore, and sings a lament filled with emotional conflict.[19] Able at first to see the world only in terms of war and enmity, she feels at first a terrible tension—depicted in the turbulent music in G minor—between her loyalty to her family and her love for the Greek prince Idamante.[20]

Operas rarely depict ethical and emotional growth, but this one clearly does. Ilia's views at the start of the opera, focused on vengeance and blood relations, are characteristic of the old morality of the Greek gods. But, in her growing love for Idamante, she is already open to seeing the world differently. Idamante now begins to reshape Ilia's world: he has what we might call a more Mozartean view of loyalties, insisting that reconciliation can bring warring sides together in harmony and love. His opening aria, "Non ho colpa" ("The blame is not mine"), shifts into the major key, B-flat major, corresponding to Ilia's minor key, as he insists that he is not to blame for her distress, the tyrannical gods are to blame, but he intends to rectify their wrong and relieve her suffering. B-flat major, though not a special Masonic favorite, has been associated by many composers through the ages with ideas of peace and reconciliation.[21] (Benjamin Britten, for example, chooses that key repeatedly to express sentiments of pacifism.) In this peaceful key Idamante declares his decision to undo the gods' wrong by freeing the Trojan prisoners. Already, then, he is exerting an independent will and challenging the old order of the gods. He then continues, in the subsequent recitative, "Now I will break their bonds and give

---

[19] See the analysis in Patrick Mackie, *Mozart in Motion* (London: Granta, 2023).
[20] See Rushton (1993, pp. 106–13).
[21] On the musical contrast between Ilia and Idamante, see Dent (1913, pp. 80–81).

them consolation." Idamante's music is resolute and decisive, but centered and not tormented. As we soon see, the gods do nothing to impede his autonomous action, suggesting that they have no real power, except in weak humans' minds.

Later, proclaiming his love for his father, he chooses another serene key, F major ("Il padre adorato," "Beloved father"). (Again, there is a long history of linking this key with ideas of peace and calm, Beethoven's Pastorale Symphony being just one outstanding example.) Now his serene and solid music draws Ilia into his world, as, calming herself, she begins to see that the world does not consist simply of tyrannical chance and implacable enmity.

As the opera progresses, it is Idamante's capacity for love (soon more hesitantly joined by his father's) that propels the plot, bringing it ultimately to its happy conclusion. But Ilia, through his love, quickly learns to see the world in new terms, and perhaps contributes something of her own through her experience of suffering.[22] In each act she has an aria, and each aria marks her growth. Her beautiful Act 2 aria, "Se il padre perdei" ("If I have lost my father"), sung to Idomeneo, is in the Masonic key of E-flat major, as, in ascending arcs of aspiration and trust, she serenely expresses her love for her adoptive father.[23] And at the opening of Act 3, in the beautiful "Zeffiretti lusinghieri" ("Gently caressing breezes"), her long, delicate phrases are musical caresses sent through the breeze to her lover, showing that she no longer harbors conflict or suspicion and has learned a kind of trust that is a prelude to a successful and happy union. She now finds her solitude not agony but a pleasant friend ("solitudini amiche"), since she is able to fill the solitude with thoughts of him.

Right after this her lover arrives. It is remarkable that in all of Mozart's other major works there are almost no happy duets

---

[22] See also Dent (1913, p. 94).

[23] On Mozart's love of the key of E-flat major, see Dent, though he does not mention the Masonic associations of that key (1913, p. 87).

between two truly loving lovers. Either the lovers are at cross purposes (Susanna and Figaro in the opera's opening scene, the Count and Countess in Act 2), or they are ill-matched (Sesto and Vitellia), or the love is based upon deception (Don Giovanni and Zerlina, the two pairs of lovers in *Così fan tutte*). Ilia and Idamante are an exception—along, interestingly, with Papageno and Papagena in *The Magic Flute*. Idamante has been a tender peace-loving lover from the beginning, and now Ilia joins him.

When Idamante arrives, they sing the remarkable duet "S'io non moro a questi accenti" ("If I do not die at these words"), in which the two voices, in close-knit harmony, express the joy of trusting reciprocity looking forward to happiness: "Ah, our happiness overcomes the cruel anguish we have suffered. Our passion conquers all." (The key is A major, with its Masonic three sharps.) Although this unique duet precedes the displacement of the gods, it prefigures it, and its exemplary beauty causes it: the strength of their love makes them confident, and they simply act on love and choice. It turns out that this is all they need. Superstition rules only as long as people grovel. People were free all along, they simply didn't act on their freedom. The Allegretto section in 3/8 time that concludes the duet is a sprightly dance of freedom from superstition's severe bonds. The lovers have the reciprocity of Susanna and the Countess in the letter duet, but they are actually (supposed to be) male and female, a remarkable achievement in Mozart's world.

Moreover, in the face of death, Idamante strikes a defiantly Masonic note. Refusing to tremble before the gods, he sings a soaring aria, "No, la morte io non pavento" ("No, I do not fear death"), whose calm sentiments in the face of life's end are orthodox Freemasonry and might have been taken directly from Mozart's letter to Leopold—showing that these ideas of steadfastness were already in the now-mature Mozart long before he joined the lodge, and long before his father's final illness led him to put them on paper. Many critics think that this aria retards the action,[24] and in fact it was often cut in performance. But for Mozart's subtle psychology it is central, and the culmination of one strand in the action. It turns out that the gods rule only because mortals slavishly defer to them out of fear and superstition. When people take their lives into their own hands, following what we might call the Voice of Reason, their power simply ceases.

What of the other characters? Idomeneo is the opera's title character, and he is depicted as a military hero, a loving father, and a decent ruler. His role is written for a powerful tenor (a particular singer, Anton Raaff, whom Mozart admired as a singer, though his acting was rigid and unimpressive, and he was sixty-six when he undertook the role).[25] And yet, in the end he is not the opera's hero. At the end the Voice says that he must step aside and give the kingdom to Idamante and Ilia. Why? It seems that Idomeneo is a bridge figure between the old and the new worlds. He is loving and courageous, but also a dupe of religious superstition. At the beginning, he says that he wants to free Ilia—but he does nothing about it, and it is Idamante who actually takes action. He makes a foolish promise to irrational forces, and that promise dooms him to kill what he loves. Again, he does nothing. Passively collaborating, he sees no way to extricate himself from that predicament—while Idamante charts a new course, exerting his autonomy from the very start of the opera, with his merciful freeing of the prisoners and his desire to rule by love. Well-intentioned but ineffectual, Idomeneo gracefully steps aside at the opera's end.

So far we have left out one of the major characters: Elettra, rejected lover of Idamante, who has some of the opera's most dramatic and dazzling music, in the two towering revenge arias "Tutte nel cor vi sento" ("In my heart I feel you all"), addressing the

---

[24] See, for example, Dent (1913, p. 102).

[25] On Raaff and the other singers, see Mark Everist's chapter in Rushton (1993, pp. 48–61).

Furies, goddesses of revenge,[26] and, near the opera's end, "D'Oreste d'Aiace" ("I have in my breast the torments of Orestes and Ajax"), again referring to the Furies she feels within. And it was fitting to leave her isolated, because she isolates herself. She never changes, nor does she respond to any other character. In her single-minded dedication to vengeance and the Furies, in her renunciation of "love, mercy, pity," she belongs to the old cruel world and refuses the lure of the new world. She begins in Ilia's position—an exile, wanting revenge. But whereas Ilia, already activated by unselfish motives (concern for her family), soon finds a lover who helps her see the world differently, Elettra, self-preoccupied through and through, proves unable to find love, and blames this disappointment on everyone else but herself. As she finishes her first aria, the ensuing music of the storm outside is very similar to the music she has just been singing about her insides—Mozart's way of showing that she embodies the older world of cruelty and rigidity, untampered by tenderness or gentleness. We notice that she has no supportive community around her. Isolated by her power and her egoism, she fails to learn reciprocity.

Elettra's music is spectacular but ultimately solipsistic and hard, even ugly. Her arias, both the early and the late, have a breathless character that a good singer will mimic (with, of course, supreme breath control!). Revenge, after all, takes your breath away. Retributive anger operates as the opposite of Ilia's tender love, which extends itself in long breeze-like phrases. And in her final aria, sung after the Voice has announced the triumph of Love, Elettra simply sings herself to death. Singing of suicide ("Alecto's torch brings me death . . . or a sword shall end my pain"), she verges on vocal collapse, with the cackling pyrotechnics of the aria's end, rapidly ascending to high C, and then descending in very rapid staccatos that are simply not written to be beautiful. And then, done with the aria,

---

[26] See Craig Ayrey in Rushton (1993, pp. 137–44).

she simply collapses in most productions—killed, apparently, by her own exhausting emotions of anger and hatred.

Elettra's collapse is sad, because Mozart lets us see that she does have a softer side. In her first aria we encounter a more delicate theme as she bids farewell to her former emotions of "love, mercy, and compassion." And in Act 2, briefly, she sings an aria, "Idol mio," expressing love of Idamante, acknowledging that he does not love her in return, but saying that she will accept him even so. But she fails to express any tenderness, or wish for his happiness, concluding that an unwilling and "austere love attracts me more."

Joseph Kerman, in *Opera as Drama*, says that Elettra is far from the center of the work, a peripheral character[27]—and in a way this is true, but it does not show that she is irrelevant. Like the Queen of the Night in *The Magic Flute*, she is an antitype, the exemplar of an older realm with no reciprocity and a self-centered refusal of compassion. What Mozart shows us is that this way of being in the world leads ultimately to exhaustion and burnout. Ilia and Idamante, by contrast, lead forward to personal and political regeneration and to happiness, both personal and communal.

And what of the Chorus, the people of Crete? As Rushton rightly observes, they are pivotal to the opera's overall organization: all three acts begin with solitary reflection and end with public scenes.[28] On the whole, the operatic chorus is not Mozart's forte. Often his use of it is perfunctory, more decorative than (as in Verdi) key to the action. In *Idomeneo*, however, the Chorus is much more prominent than usual—suggesting that this opera is about the people and the inauguration of a new regime. For the most part the Chorus is reactive to the action as it unfolds. Unlike the Priests they do not protest; they simply recoil in horror. And yet in the end they seem to understand their new fortune and the change it portends. In the confident key of D major, they exclaim: "Descend,

---

[27] (1990, p. 85).
[28] See Rushton (1993, p. 95).

Love and Hymen, descend Juno to the royal spouses. May the god of marriage instill peace of spirit forever in their breasts." They understand that something decisively new has been accomplished, and they celebrate it.

Idomeneo does not really create a democratic republic, something that would have been impossible in the fictional world of Homeric antiquity. It is reminiscent of Joseph II's reforms: enlightened autocracy, with a larger space for human choice than was previously available. The new world of the opera's end, however, represents a huge advance beyond the world of religious submission within which its characters lived, and within which most of its intended audience was still living. Once again: Mozart's idea seems to be that if the sentiments are right, other good things will follow. This idea is insufficient, and surely naïve; but it is profound, and perhaps necessary.

The Magic Flute: Noble Ideals, Imperfect People

The Magic Flute is an enchanting fairy tale that also contains some of Mozart's most serious ideas about reason, mercy, and human brotherhood. It owes its enduring popularity to the way in which it expresses these ideas in radiant music and through captivating fantasy. (Nor should we suggest that Mozart had conceptual ideas first and only afterward embodied them in music. No doubt they took a musical form from the start: as Mozart said, the music always comes first.) Although the overcoming of resentment by love is a recurrent theme in virtually all of Mozart's operas, *The Magic Flute* gives this idea particular depth and detail, connecting it to Freemasonic commitments and to many details vaguely suggestive of Freemasonic ritual.

The opera was commissioned by Emanuel Schikaneder, impresario of a very successful theater in Vienna that performed both plays and also lighter operas. Schikaneder wrote most of the libretto and sang the role of Papageno. The intended audience was the general bourgeois public, rather than the more elite audiences of some of Mozart's other works. As was common in Vienna, the opera has the form of a traditional *Singspiel,* or opera with spoken dialogue. A savvy man of the theater, Schikaneder insisted on a work that would use all theatrical media to please the public, and Mozart eagerly agreed. The two men collaborated closely on the opera's fairy tale elements and spectacular effects. Mozart conducted at the premiere on September 30, 1791, and when he became ill he continued, friends said, to think constantly and lovingly about the opera. He died on December 5.

Although the somewhat clumsy libretto has many sources (the Egyptian elements drawing on Jean Terrasson's 1731 novel *Sethos* and a related article by Ignaz Born in the *Journal für Freymaurer*),[29] there can be no doubt that Schikaneder and Mozart set out to write what is essentially a Masonic opera. This has been publicly acknowledged since the nineteenth century,[30] but at the time, given ongoing attacks on Freemasons, it was merely implicit. But no Freemason (or the many non-initiates who attended Masonic social events) could have denied it. *The Magic Flute,* as we shall see, is by no means a straightforward portrait of Masonic activities, nor is it uncritical. But its core ideals (reason, steadfastness, wisdom, brotherhood, and love) are those of the Masons (shared, of course, by many Enlightenment non-Masons). Above all the transformative power of music—displayed in the ability of the magic bells to change aggression to harmonious dancing, and that of the flute to make animals dance and, later, to guide the lovers through their ordeals—is an idea that sets Masons apart from other more prosaic defenders of Enlightenment. Musically the opera is full of

---

[29] See Nettl (1952, pp. 72–78).

[30] See Leopold von Sonnleithner, essay of 1857, reprinted in *Mozarteums-Mitteilungen,* 1919; and the full discussion in B 255–65 and Nettl (1952, pp. 82–87).

Freemasonic ingredients, including the use of groups of three everywhere. Already in the overture, the pounding rhythms suggest the Masonic idea of working the rough stone,[31] and one might say that a major subtheme of the opera as a whole is the need for patient work with the sometimes unpromisingly rough material of humanity.

The opera was written at a time when the Freemasons were under especially harsh attack, especially by Count Pergen,[32] who had written to the Emperor (now Leopold II, Joseph II's successor) a very harsh memo decrying the influence of "such secret and deceptive organizations," referring to Masons and to Mozart's lodge in particular. This letter was sent to the lodge as well, inviting a response, but the members eventually sent it back saying that they had no intention of responding.[33] The lodge went on meeting, but its response was to keep a low profile and to make no inflammatory public statements.

Mozart and Schikaneder, it seems, took on the job of public defense in their own indirect way, showing the movement's ideals in an attractive light. The original libretto even contained a passage, later cut, apparently referring to the Pergen controversy: "Let prejudice find fault with us initiates. It affects wisdom and reason like a spider web attacking a column. But malicious prejudice must go; and it will go as soon as Tamino himself grasps the greatness of our art."[34] Given the aim of defending Masonic practice, they might have produced a prettified and idealized portrait of Masonic life. This they do not do: instead, they ask the audience to see Masons as incomplete human beings with attractive ideals and many human weaknesses.

As we saw in chapter 1, it is characteristic of Mozart to ask us to embrace the real in all its imperfection, cherishing high aspirations

---

[31] See Nettl (1952, p. 91).
[32] Johann Anton Graf von Pergen (1724–1814), a leading diplomat and statesman.
[33] See B, 253–55.
[34] See Nettl (1952, p. 144).

while frankly acknowledging the frailty and the sometimes contradictory nature of the people who embody them. If we can love the real, then, and only then, will we be able to continue striving for the ideal, avoiding a despair that all too often besets idealists who come belatedly and resentfully to the conclusion that people are uneven and imperfect.

The fairy tale plot charms the audience and sweeps it along. And yet it has puzzling and even apparently contradictory elements. Prince Tamino has encountered a terrible serpent—who is actually killed, after he faints, by three Ladies, sent by the Queen of the Night. Through these rather vain and flirtatious emissaries, the Queen has conveyed a portrait of her daughter Pamina, who, they tell him, has been kidnapped by an evil magician Sarastro, and is being held as a prisoner in his dwelling. The Queen appears in all her glory, imploring his aid. Enchanted by the picture and moved by the Queen's tale, he takes on the task of rescuing Pamina. However, things look very different when Tamino, accompanied by his new partner, the bird-catcher Papageno, arrives at the academy where Sarastro presides, guided by three child-spirits. For instead of an evil wizard, Sarastro is a sage presiding over a rather democratic priesthood who express noble thoughts. Tamino is urged to seek initiation into their number. Meanwhile Pamina, escaping rape by Monostatos, an enslaved man whose task is to oppress and bully other enslaved men, meets Papageno, and they eventually contrive an escape. Pamina, told of Tamino's love, is delighted, and encourages Papageno to persist in his search for a life partner. Greeted by a solemn Priest, Tamino is told that Sarastro is actually good and that the Queen is not to be trusted. He plays his magic flute, delighting animals, who appear and begin to dance.

Meanwhile, Pamina and Papageno are recaptured, although Monostatos and the other enslaved men change their demeanor and begin to dance when Papageno plays his magic bells. Sarastro now enters, in a chariot drawn by lions. He listens with sympathy to Pamina's story, blaming Monostatos and ordering him to be whipped. But Sarastro refuses to let her go back to her mother, saying that the Queen is not to be trusted, and that in any case a man must guide the young woman. The two lovers meet for the first time, and are enchanted by one another. They agree to undergo many trials in order to achieve initiation.

In the second act, they undergo a variety of painful ordeals, as does Papageno, whose longing for a bird-woman of his own is toyed with by a woman who appears to be elderly and who says that she is his future mate. The Queen of the Night appears before Pamina, asking her to kill Sarastro. Pamina refuses and asks Sarastro to forgive her mother. He replies that revenge has no place in his domain. Somewhat later, Pamina is on the brink of despair because Tamino, in accordance with his ordeal of silence, refuses to speak to her. The child-spirits restrain her and assure her of Tamino's love. Tamino, having completed his trial, is freed to speak to Pamina. She gives him the magic flute, and together they enter the temple to be initiated. Meanwhile Papageno, despairing of finding the wife for whom he longs, prepares to hang himself, but he too is deterred by the child-spirits, who tell him to play his magic bells. As he does so, his bird-wife Papagena appears, and they sing happily of the many children they will have. After this another conspiracy by the Queen and Monostatos is foiled. Sarastro announces that the sun has vanquished the night, and the two lovers, now both initiates, are united.

This plot is bound to confuse anyone who expects simple polarities, good and evil, light and dark. Is the Queen really bad, despite her obvious love for her daughter and her sincere desire to bring two lovers together? Is Sarastro really all good, despite his despotic behavior? The story that Mozart and Schikaneder changed plots mid-course was an attempt to solve these problems, but it solves nothing, and there is no evidence for it. Let us provisionally begin with the idea that perhaps the opera presents complex characters, who are not all good or all bad.

The worst way to read the opera as a Masonic opera is to read it as a kind of Bible, in which Sarastro is flawless and exemplary.[35] If we read it that way, we can only conclude that Mozart and Schikaneder are incompetent. Sarastro does indeed express some noble sentiments. When one of the Priests says of Tamino, "He is a prince," Sarastro replies, "He is more: he is a human being (Mensch)," thus exemplifying Masonic egalitarianism. Particularly impressive is his second aria, "In these sacred halls" ("In diesen heil'gen Hallen"):

> Within these sacred halls,
> Revenge is unknown.
> And when a man has fallen,
> Love shows him his duty.
> A friend's hand then guides him,
> Happy and satisfied, to a better land.
>
> Within these sacred walls,
> Where mankind lives by love,
> There can lurk no betrayer,
> For we forgive our enemies.
> Whoever is not gladdened by such teaching
> Is unworthy to be called human.

Mozart's music for this aria is also profoundly moving: simple, transparent, hymnlike.

However, all this is fine talk. Sarastro's conduct is very different. To begin with, the Queen is right: he did kidnap Pamina, and is holding her against her will. He also simply decides that Tamino ought to be initiated: the request does not come from Tamino. As for mercy, when Pamina asks why she can't love her mother and also follow Sarastro, he curtly says that women are untrustworthy.

---

[35] Thomson, for example, reads it that way.

Still worse, he is portrayed as a despotic autocrat. He makes his first appearance in a chariot drawn by six lions. Nor is he a benevolent reformer like Joseph II: for he is a slaveholder, who treats the enslaved men very harshly and sets them under Monostatos, a harsh and physically abusive steward-slave. The libretto has dialogue scenes among three enslaved men, typically cut in performance, in which they complain of their harsh treatment and express sympathy with Pamina, who seems to them another victim of tyranny. In short, as Braunbehrens says: "Sarastro's weak point is that the wise pronouncements made in his sonorous bass voice often have little to do with his conduct."[36] Especially noteworthy is his cruelty to Monostatos, a Black man, already disadvantaged by his color along with other enslaved men. Monostatos, enslaved by Sarastro, executes Sarastro's orders, and is then beaten with seventy-seven lashes for simply doing his job. Furthermore, the misogynistic remarks that make modern audiences cringe are put above all in Sarastro's mouth. In Act 2, the trials he concocts for the two lovers are sadistic and not admirable as tests of character.

Mozart and Schikaneder, then, if not hopelessly incompetent, and let us venture to assert that they are not, must be making a point: Masons can have high ideals and yet behave in an autocratic and hierarchical way, and also, at times in a way unacceptably tinged with racism and misogyny. (Let me venture to add ageism, in the humor surrounding Papageno's bride, although the critique of ageism was surely not on the authors' agenda.) Mozart's acquaintance with the two-faced treatment of Angelo Soliman showed him plenty of racism in the ranks, and the continued refusal of Viennese lodges to admit women as full members, despite years of discussion, showed him recalcitrant misogyny.

The redeeming feature of Sarastro's realm, however, is that in fact Sarastro is a despot only in his own household: the priests are organized democratically, as are Masonic lodges, and he cannot

---

[36] B 258.

simply impose his way on them. Tamino's initiation has to be put to a vote, and the priests discuss it as an open matter. The opera shows them as a diverse group, apparently with heterogeneous views and many questions. At times, Mozart's music appears to show them even parodying or mocking Sarastro. At any rate the duet between the two priests has a definite parodic tone—though whether they are parodying Sarastro or Mozart is parodying this particular group of priests is unclear.[37]

In general the opera's message is that one must follow one's own path and question claims to authority. Presenting Freemasonry this way actually contributes to the defense of Freemasonry, showing it not as a closed cabal but as a club peopled by striving and uncertain individuals.[38]

As for Monostatos, he is indeed a repellent figure, attempting to rape Pamina because (he says) his black skin prevents him from finding love. But the opera shows that things are more complex: Monostatos is cruel above all in his tyranny over the other enslaved men, and it is one of those same men who first objects to his "pitiless" cruelty to Pamina: "To have to see such a thing is the torture of hell." So Monostatos, far from standing for all Black Africans, is portrayed as an individual warped by envy and resentment, and indeed by enforced domination over others of his race. In his egoism he is a kindred spirit of the Queen of the Night, whose side he ultimately takes. And we see, further, that any suggestion of biological racism is totally repudiated by Mozart in his demonstration that all human beings respond similarly to the influence of the magic bells, ceasing retribution and cultivating brotherhood. All the enslaved men, including even Monostatos, are amazed and transformed by these sounds that surprise them, since they

---

[37] B 264.

[38] A similar interpretation is in Eberhard Schmidt, "Sinnspiel *Zauberflöte*," program essay for a production of the opera at Komische Oper Berlin, July 6, 1997. I am grateful to my son-in-law, Gerd Wichert, for preserving all his opera programs and lending me these two remarkable examples of the program essay.

have never heard such things before. The defective culture they are forced to live in, including its racism, has produced envy and bad conduct; but even these settled habits can be overcome and transformed by the power of music.

A different way of understanding Monostatos has been current since the nineteenth century: he is meant to be a Jesuit priest. Indeed, by that time "a black" was a slang expression for a priest, denoting his habit, and this association with an order that Joseph II thought particularly hostile to reform (unlike today's Jesuits, who are the Catholic Church's strongest rationalists) would help explain his alliance with the Queen of the Night, who in some way represents religious superstition.[39] Tales of sexual corruption in the priestly orders were current then, and no doubt partly true, just as such tales are current, and partly true, today. So even though I am not convinced that this is what Mozart and Schikaneder had in mind in 1791, it is not impossible, and it would certainly deepen the critique of Sarastro: unlike Joseph II, who banned and defunded the Jesuit order, Sarastro is using it to reinforce his domination.

As for women, Sarastro makes his suspicious and condescending views amply evident, and he conveys the impression that Pamina had to be rescued from a matriarchy in order to learn from a patriarchal ruler. However, if we look more closely—and in particular if we listen to Mozart's music—this reading of the opera as a whole cannot survive. The Queen of the Night is not "Woman": she is a basically loving mother whose love has been deformed by the power of superstition, the power of egoistic eroticism, and, above all, the power of revenge. Mozart gives her music that is glorious, and a love of her daughter that is genuine. But her fervor is distorted by possessive egoism (like the Three Ladies, she is all about "Me," "Me," "Me"). She plots revenge not just against Sarastro, but

---

[39] On the history of this interpretation, see Gerhard Müller, "Die Stadt als Schauplatz," in the same program of the Komische Oper Berlin. Müller does think the interpretation plausible for 1791.

"against humanity." And her aria "The revenge of Hell" makes it clear to the listener that, dazzling though her ornamentation is, there is no tenderness left in her, no human sympathy. Rather than bringing "death and despair" to others, she herself, in her inability to understand love, exemplifies death and despair. So she is another example (like the Count in *Figaro* and Elettra in *Idomeneo*) of a person initially good by nature whom tyrannical power deforms and spoils, so that she even seeks to destroy what she loves.

By contrast Pamina, even before she exchanges a word with Sarastro, is shown to have love that is not distorted—indeed. to have the true spirit of Freemasonry. In the duet with Papageno ("All people who can feel love"), in which she takes the lead, she announces that love must be built—not on superficial romance (as Tamino thinks, rapturously loving her portrait)—but on the goodness of the heart, and a spirit of friendship that opens onto universal brotherhood. Only in that way could a partnership of two people possibly "reach toward to the divine." By contrasting her approach to love with Tamino's initially more superficial vision, Mozart even suggests that young men are unfortunately prone to equate love with romantic attraction to beauty, responding to a picture rather than a whole person, whereas women more easily understand that lasting love must be grounded in sympathy. A little later, it is Pamina who introduces the opera's other key Masonic theme: the overcoming of enmity through the spirit of brotherhood, promoted by music. "Without this sympathy, there is no happiness on earth." In Act 2, she asks her mother why she cannot continue to love Tamino even if he is initiated: her father, after all, she says, associated with these wise men and always spoke well of them. And even when she believes Tamino has abandoned her, she announces that she "cannot hate" him. She is definitely not her mother's daughter.

Thinking of *The Marriage of Figaro*, we notice the absence of a supportive women's community in the Queen's realm: although she dwells with the three Ladies, her own ill treatment at Sarastro's hands, and her unlimited royal power, have made her obsessed with revenge, and what could have been reciprocity degenerates into tyranny. Pamina is lucky to have escaped.

In short, Pamina tells us everything we need to know about the opera's key themes, for the most part even before Sarastro gets around to singing "In these sacred halls"; and later her commitment to her views only deepens. A 1794 essay on the opera by another Viennese Mason said that Pamina represents Enlightenment, which ought to be understood as the child of Superstition and Patriarchal Reason. Although Mozart writes complicated people, not allegories, there is something basically on-target in this idea.

Furthermore, Mozart and Schikaneder emphasize very strongly that at the key ritual moment within the initiation, Pamina, not Tamino, must take the lead. We have had earlier indications that women are fully equal parts of the Masonic community. The Chorus at the end of Act 1 is clearly scored for both male and female voices, and when Tamino appears before the priests to face initiation he is in the company not of another man, as was the custom in the Masonic lodges of Vienna, but in the company of Pamina. Moreover, even the Act 2 "Chorus of Priests," which is traditionally sung by an all-male chorus, may actually be scored for both women and men, as some musicologists hold. Mozart uses the treble clef for the two top voices, not the tenor clef, but this is not decisive, since that was one common way of scoring a four-part male chorus. Braunbehrens, however, argues that female voices are meant. He notes that drawings of the original production may show women among the men.

At any rate, during the initiation itself, at its most difficult moment, it is Pamina who advises Tamino to play the magic flute, saying: "I shall be at your side everywhere. I myself will lead you, and love leads me." The text is unambiguous—and so, even more, is the glorious music Mozart gives Pamina to sing at this point. Braunbehrens remarks, "It is as if Mozart and Schikaneder wrote a private memorandum to Freemasons, admonishing them to replace self-righteousness with modesty, fight authoritarianism in their own ranks, pursue freedom, equality, and brotherhood, and maintain their goal of 'enlightenment,' which brings with it reason, justice, and humanity."[40] Tamino acquires a new courage and decisiveness through her influence, shaking off the excessive obedience that has characterized his relationship to authority. He no longer understands courage in male terms, and grants: "A woman who does not shrink from night and death is worthy, and will be initiated.

At the opera's conclusion, the stage directions tell us that both Tamino and Pamina are "dressed in priestly garments." And both are hailed by the (mixed-sex) Chorus as "initiates."

So far we have left out a major part of the opera: Papageno the bird-catcher, who supplies a lot of the fun and some of the best musical moments of the opera. Sometimes he is taken to be a lesser being than Tamino, and put in only for comic effect. But this would be an odd way to write an egalitarian drama about a group that defends the worth of manual labor. The fact that Papageno was Schikaneder's own role and that the character has always been an audience favorite suggests that this condescending reading is wrong. Jokes in Mozart are never just jokes: they are an essential part of life's zestful quirkiness. In the reactions, aspirations, even fears of Papageno we have a surrogate for the non-elite audience, and, indeed, for Mozart himself, whose letters irrepressibly contain outrageous, often joyfully obscene, humor. As Eberhard Schmidt writes, we see in Papageno "the reactions of a healthy human understanding," as Mozart with all his high spirits knows humanity.[41] Moreover, his eventual duet with Papagena shows intimate attunement and mutuality. Pamina and Tamino have no such moment.

---

[40] B 265.
[41] Schmidt, program essay.

As we shall see again in discussing *Così fan tutte*, Mozart is fond of putting his most serious thoughts about love into the jokey banter of lovers. In this opera (perhaps because Tamino has already been established as deficient in the humor department—perhaps because being a prince leads to a bad moral education), Mozart's serious statements about love and friendship are set out in the playful duet between Pamina and Papageno, "All people who can feel love." The duet praises friendship and the kind heart as love's only good basis and boldly claims, "We live by love, by love alone." The music is down to earth rather than lofty; it is not Tamino's musical idiom, though we feel that he must eventually become capable of it. The fact that Pamina can understand and share Papageno's jokey earthiness is yet another reason why she must lead Tamino along the path of initiation. Although the fact that Papageno is not initiated could be taken as a sign of class-based contempt, I'd rather see it as another way in which Mozart and Schikaneder take their own Masonic seriousness lightly. Papageno doesn't want to join that stuffy academy. He wants what he gets: a bird-wife, and many children to come. Mozart expresses respect for non-Masons: it is a club that you may join if it suits you, but it is far from the only way to practical wisdom or a flourishing life.

And what, finally, of the three child-spirits, who appear when things are going badly and guide the plot toward its happy end? Typically sung by boy sopranos, they strike an earthy note through the unprofessional sound of their voices, and the music they sing is transparent and non-ornate, reminding us of a kind of simple goodness that is not so often seen in the opera house. Twice, as I noted, we see them intervene when characters (first Pamina, then Papageno) are about to commit suicide out of despair. According to Eberhard Schmidt, the three boys are the childlike aspect of Mozart's personality, the artist inserting his own hand to make things end well. And in their music, even more than in the words, we also hear "our own hopes and life-wishes . . . and also the impatience of those who not only long for a better world-order but would like to enjoy it sooner than the laborious developmental process of humanity permits."[42]

I think this is partly right. But I would also see the child-spirits as the voices of a hope that we must sustain in our encounters with the awkwardness of reality, especially when reversals tempt us to despair and hatred of a life that is merely human. We must recover in ourselves those childlike voices, whenever real life seems impossible. Music and the musical imagination assist us powerfully in this task. The Masons knew what they were doing when they made music integral to a politics of brotherhood and equality, and Mozart knew what he was doing when he looked at death itself with hope for love's triumph over hatred.

The opera had immediate and lasting success. Among its admirers, Goethe (who joined a Masonic lodge in 1780) was inspired first to produce it at Weimar in 1794 and then to compose a sequel—which he never completed, not finding a suitable composer, though a fragmentary libretto was published in 1807.[43] We will no doubt continue to debate its meaning. But all our difficulties and quarrels are always overcome by the glorious spirit of its music—thus proving Mozart's point.

---

[42] Schmidt, program essay, my translation from the German.

[43] It seems to have a lot of metaphysics and little humor; even Papageno and Papagena are depicted as sad (because of childlessness). See references to the literature on Goethe's libretto in Nettl (1952, p. 144).

3

Two Problem Operas

Don Giovanni and *Così fan tutte*

Don Giovanni

The earth is truly beautiful, and no one can be blamed for
wanting to remain on it as long as possible. Thank God,
I feel as fit and well as ever and prepared for a thousand
deeds, all to be performed immediately one after another
as soon as my new work is completed and performed.[1]

—Mozart, in Eduard Mörike's *Mozart auf der Reise
nach Prague* (*Mozart on the Way to Prague*)

he says your soul you have no soul inside only grey matter
because he doesn't know what it is to have one … of course
hes right enough in his way to pass the time as a joke sure
you might as well be in bed with what with a lion God Im
sure hed have something better to say for himself an old
Lion would.[2]

—Molly Bloom in James Joyce's *Ulysses*, thinking of
her lover Blazes Boylan, whom her husband,
Leopold, associates in his mind with Don Giovanni,
Molly being a singer who sings the role of Zerlina

---

[1] Translation by Michael Fleming, in *Eight German Novellas* (1997).
[2] Joyce (1992).

Don Giovanni is a glorious enigma. Its music is so enthralling, and yet its sentiments are confusing, perhaps also confused. Is the listener to be captivated by the Don, and to feel a sense of loss when he leaves the world—as many "romantic" interpreters have believed? If so, there is one sort of problem: for this Don is a really horrible person, who, despite a certain boyish energy and charm, has no sympathy at all for anyone else and who uses a combination of class dazzle and sheer force to make his conquests. If nineteenth-century audiences (or, at any rate, their male members) viewed this behavior indulgently, surely audiences today cannot. And already in the nineteenth century, there were leading thinkers—among them the philosopher Friedrich Nietzsche and the novelist Eduard Mörike—who felt that the pro-Don interpretation was, as Nietzsche put it, a "sin against Mozart," whose whole attitude to life is characterized by "courtesy of the heart" (*die Höflichkeit des Herzens*).[3]

Mozart typically portrays the Don's sort of domineering masculinity in a very negative light (think of the Count in *Figaro*). From *Idomeneo* to *La Clemenza di Tito*, he prefers men who approach women with gentle and tender sentiments (even when, like the lovers we shall meet in *Così fan tutte*, their emotions aren't going to last very long). Could it be, then, that the Don is a scoundrel for whose punishment we should be rooting all the time, as librettist Lorenzo Da Ponte's subtitle, "The Profligate Punished" (*Il dissoluto punito*) suggests?

Such a reading, though promising, raises another sort of problem. Mozart is virtually obsessed with the repudiation of a morality based upon revenge, especially revenge for outraged honor. Again and again, in *Idomeneo, The Marriage of Figaro, The Magic*

---

[3] Nietzsche, *The Wanderer and His Shadow* in *Human All Too Human* ([1886] 1996, Section 160), *Beyond Good and Evil* ([1886] 1966, Section 245). The "sin" may refer especially to those who believe that the D minor chords of the opening are superior to Mozart's tender and serene moments.

Flute, and, as we shall see in chapter 4, *La Clemenza di Tito,* mercy and gentleness win out over vindictiveness and hate—not just in the libretti, but also, and more powerfully, in the music.

Where, then, in *Don Giovanni,* is the Mozart whose gentle humanity we love? It's tempting to agree with the great opera critic Joseph Kerman: Da Ponte gave Mozart a libretto that was in some ways a bad fit for the composer's own emotional preoccupations, and Mozart did the best he could.[4]

However, there is a much longer road to be traveled before we can draw any conclusions. I shall first situate the opera in Mozart's life, then investigate the "Romantic" interpretation carefully, and only then turn to the musical and dramatic reasons why we must reject it.

Mozart Goes to Prague

Don Giovanni had its premiere in Prague on October 29, 1787. On May 28 of that year, Mozart's father, Leopold, had died suddenly, after a very brief period of serious illness, though a much longer period of fatigue and miscellaneous complaints. Mozart wrote little about this event, but in one letter to a friend he added the postscript, "I inform you that on returning home today I received the sad news of my most beloved father's death. You can imagine the state I am in."[5]

Mozart traveled to Prague in September with his wife, Constanze, to supervise rehearsals and to work further on the opera. He was joined there by librettist Lorenzo Da Ponte. Mozart

---

[4] Kerman wrote about the opera twice: in the Mozart chapter of *Opera as Drama* (1988), which I shall henceforth call Kerman (1988), and in "Reading *Don Giovanni,*" in *Myths of Seduction and Betrayal,* ed. Jonathan Miller (1990, pp. 108–25), henceforth Kerman (1990). The interpretation I describe above is in Kerman (1988).

[5] B (1991, p. 292).

conducted the premiere himself. Prague was a backwater by comparison to Vienna, much poorer and less influential, but it had a dedicated musical public for whom Mozart was a celebrity. On a previous visit in January 1787, just to enjoy the popularity of his own *The Marriage of Figaro*, Mozart and Constanze had been lavishly entertained and shown the sights; they stayed at Count Thun's palace. This second visit was for work, and evidently the opera needed a lot of it, especially since theatrical personnel were not at the Vienna level of professionalism. But everyone still treated Mozart like a great figure, showing gratitude that he had written an opera for them. When he entered the orchestra pit, before a note was played, he was greeted with enthusiastic applause and had to bow three times.

The opera was a brilliant success, "received with thundering applause," as Mozart wrote back to Viennese associates.[6] And yet the opera sparked controversy elsewhere from the very beginning. Most critics agreed that the music was outstanding, but the plot occasioned debate. The character of the Don was a familiar stock figure in low popular entertainments, and some critics took Mozart to task for making him the hero of an opera, even a comic opera. (For *Don Giovanni* was clearly so classified, and attempts to say that the phrase *dramma giocoso* means something new and different, a middle way between *opera seria* and *opera buffa*, have by and large been rejected by today's critics.) The story of the "stone guest" was also accused of low taste.[7]

Controversy, it seems, is never far from this admittedly glorious work. Let me now return to my two puzzles, tracing the origin of the "Romantic" interpretation that turns the Don into a hero, and the reasons why this interpretation should not be accepted.

---

[6] B 302.

[7] On early reviews in different cities, see B 308–10.

The "Romantic" Interpretation: Kierkegaard, Steinberg, Williams

Here and henceforth, I place quotes around the word "Romantic," because, although the interpreters I shall discuss are influenced by Romanticism, the Don, even in their positive view, is very different from paradigmatic heroes of Romantic literature, such as Goethe's Werther and Faust. The "Romantic" interpretation has many supporters—all those many, decried by Nietzsche, who see in the D minor chords of Mozart's overture an exhilarating dramatic and musical departure. They also include many members of contemporary audiences.

The "Romantic" interpretation is at least as old as E. T. A. Hoffmann's story "Don Juan" (1813), largely based upon Hoffmann's response to Mozart's opera, rather than on other versions of the Don Juan legend. For our purposes, however, its main source is the interpretation of the opera offered in the *Either-Or* (1843) of Danish philosopher Søren Kierkegaard (1813–1855). In what follows I focus on Kierkegaard, but supplement his account with those of two contemporary interpreters: music historian Michael P. Steinberg (c. 1965–), in his 2004 book *Listening to Reason: Culture. Subjectivity, and Nineteenth Century Music,*[8] and the marvelous philosopher Bernard Williams (1929–2003), in his 1988 article "Don Giovanni as an Idea."[9] I choose Steinberg because his overall project—to study the way in which Enlightenment ideas were developed in music—is closely related to my own (see chapter 1). I choose Williams because he is always a superb

---

[8] Steinberg (2004).

[9] This article was first published in Julian Rushton's Cambridge Opera Handbook (1988), but I consult and cite it in the posthumous edition prepared by Patricia Williams, who edited the collection *On Opera* (2006, pp. 31–42), since P. Williams stated that her husband went on revising the articles right up to his death, and one would need to do a word-by-word comparison to find out what revisions he did or did not make in this article. This version, at any rate, is the latest one approved by its author.

philosophical writer about opera, even though in this case I find his interpretation somewhat bizarre.

Either-Or is a pseudonymous work. Kierkegaard does not make any claims in his own name. Instead, he introduces two characters, A and B, one of whom describes what is called the "aesthetic" life, and the other of whom describes what is called the "ethical life." A puzzle immediately arises: art concerns so many things, and eroticism is hardly its only topic, so it is very unclear why a life devoted to the erotic, as A understands it, should count as the (essence of the) aesthetic life. It would seem that what is meant is not a life of artistic creativity or contemplation, but simply a life of detachment from ethical values. But this is not what Kierkegaard actually says. Even then, one can think of many lives divorced from ethical values that are not "aesthetic": lives of scientific inquiry, of historical understanding, of religious insight, of political power. So his classification is at best murky.

A begins his investigation of the erotic (for A is clearly male) by observing that sensuality as a principle of life is the creation of Christianity. In ancient Greece, sexual desire was "not an enemy to be subdued," and therefore was not even under control, but just "given freedom of life and joy in the beautiful individual" (73). Music is sensuality's quintessential medium, and therefore music, too, is developed fully only under Christianity. I shall not discuss these claims here, beyond saying that there is some truth to the idea that Christianity attached special problems to sexual desire, which the Greeks considered one of the appetites, like thirst and hunger, that could be both controlled and moderated.

A now divides the erotic into three stages. Each stage is represented by a Mozart character. The first stage, when desire is first awakened, is typified by Cherubino in *The Marriage of Figaro*, who, says A, is characterized by stasis and "profound melancholy" (85), a very peculiar claim that I shall contest later. The second stage is that of searching for a suitable object, and it is typified by Papageno in *The Magic Flute*. While not as flat-out absurd as the claim about Cherubino, this claim seems to miss most important things about Papageno: his humor, his gentleness, his love of marriage and family. (A admits that he is speaking not about the character in the opera, who utters "all sorts of dubious gibberish" [88] but of a "mythical Papageno," whatever that means.)

The third stage is represented by Don Giovanni. He represents desire as a principle, desire "as that which the spirit excludes." Because we are in a post-Christian world, erotic bodily desire is also "the realm of sin" (97), a realm that has nothing to do with thought or language. The Don seduces not by words but by representing carnal desire and manifesting desire as his entire being. He is a seducer, but what seduces is simply desire itself, with nothing of the soul about it. He has no soul, and therefore no love from the soul, so what attracts women to him is the bare energy of bodily desire for another's body, a desire seen as totally lacking in particularity: every woman has what he desires. "In every woman he desires the whole of femininity" (105). For this same reason, he is also "absolutely musical" (107): words have nothing to do with him, because words would make him a reflective individual, as he is in Molière's version. (A oddly thinks that because music does not use words it is inarticulate and unintelligent, a mistake often made, but what a terrible mistake.)

In the opera, A continues, the Don is like the sun in the solar system: the planet (other characters) derive their light (energy, life) from him (121, 125). Every character (except the Commendatore) stands in some erotic relation to the Don (127). A now praises the D minor section of the Overture as containing the essential energy and weight of the entire opera. "It is powerful as the thought of a god, stirring as the life of a world, trembling in its earnest, quivering in its passion, crushing in its terrible anger, inspiring in its zestful joy" (128). There is dread here, and dread too in the Don, but it is not a spiritual dread: it is "the full might of sensuality, which is born in dread, and Don Giovanni is himself this dread, but this dread is precisely the demonic joy of life" (130). This conclusion is hard to understand, given that the Don is presumably unaware that his realm is the realm of sin. What ought to be said is that his life inspires dread in pious Christians.

Steinberg does not refer often to Kierkegaard, but he sets himself in that general tradition by arguing that the Don is the source of life and energy in the opera. By associating the Don with Enlightenment ideas of autonomy and subjective freedom, he does appear to take issue with Kierkegaard's claim that the Don has no intellect or self-consciousness, though he does concede that the Don has a spirit of negativity that is "not highly self-conscious," then muddies the waters by comparing him to Mephistopheles in Goethe's Faust, surely a highly self-conscious character.[10] At any rate, he makes the very Kierkegaardian assertion that the Don's "powers, sensuous energy and affective manipulations are musical powers as well.... He exerts power from beginning to end over the world around him through an erotic power musically defined."[11] Steinberg grants to Kerman that the Don's music is the opera's least innovative (we'll see more of that in the following section), but replies that "he is at least *simultaneous* to the opera's musical and emotional energy.... After his demise, the surviving characters sag and droop."[12]

New in Steinberg is the idea that the goal of the opera is the overthrow of a "patriarchal order"—although precisely how this is accomplished by the rape and humiliation of women is difficult to understand. Of course the Commendatore is a patriarch, but he is defending his daughter, as all too many patriarchs fail to do, so it would seem that he is an agent of women's choice to refuse consent to sex, an idea that is quite far from patriarchal. However, Steinberg addresses that concern by saying that the three women represent

---

[10] Steinberg (2004, p. 27).
[11] Steinberg (2004, p. 26).
[12] Ibid.

a sexuality that has made compromises with the social order. As contrasted with what, one might ask? With a sexuality subject to the pressures of force and coercion? It was already clear long before 2004 that women themselves, given a chance to speak, did not want a sexuality free from norms and laws, but rather better and more laws against rape and sexual harassment. Certainly the Don refuses such constraints, as have men from ancient times to such recent paradigms of Donnishness as Bill Cosby and Harvey Weinstein, and if he is saying that the Don is similar to those men, I would agree. But he does seem to think that the Don resembles something more attractive. I am not sure what that something is.

Steinberg's most significant addition to the literature is a political one: the opera as a whole is Mozart's protest against the Habsburg political and moral order, which he understands as highly Catholic, conservative, and oppressive. According to his reading, Mozart's trip to Prague, a place not ruled by the Habsburgs, sets him free from this domination: he "could look back on Habsburg culture and, with the opening chords of *Don Giovanni*, hurl modernist thunder at Habsburg society."[13] He adds that the opening chords represent "a Reformation and Old Testament idea of divine authority, musically prefiguring and opposing a Catholic representational world."[14]

Let me enumerate the problems in this set of claims. Prague, first of all, was ruled indirectly by the Habsburgs, and it was a Catholic city. Furthermore, when Mozart had the option of staying there, he chose to return to Vienna. Most commentators attribute his choice to the fact that Prague, though culturally attractive and very enthusiastic about Mozart's music, was still a backwater, and Vienna was the capital. Second, nowhere does Steinberg mention Mozart's devoted Freemasonic affiliations, which clearly shaped his views of freedom and of which people were his true brothers

---

[13] Ibid.
[14] Steinberg (2004, p. 28).

and sisters. (Not the Don!). Third, the opening chords are music associated later on with the Commendatore, the emblem, according to Steinberg, of a negated patriarchal order. How, then, can they exemplify "modernist fury" hurled against that order? Fourth, the sentence about prefiguring the Reformation is simply bizarre: the Reformation had taken place already in 1517, the year of Luther's Ninety-Five Theses, and it was going strong in northern Germany, which in fact gave *Don Giovanni* shocked and negative reviews.[15] Finally, the Catholic world Mozart actually lived in was one in which the powers of the Church were highly constrained by the Enlightenment reforms of Joseph II (see chapter 2), some of them directly serving the cause of women's freedom (e.g., the ban on corsets).

Steinberg's book shows how much nonsense one can utter by forgetting to examine Mozart's real views in his actual world, an Enlightenment world being prodded in an even more Enlightenment direction by Mozart and his Masonic lodgemates—some of them, Mozart included, being genuine feminists, favoring women's membership and women's voices, rather than espousing a bogus feminism of *force majeur* masquerading as pleasure.

It is, then, a relief to turn to Williams, an altogether subtler mind, and one with meticulous attention to accuracy. His essay is the best thing to read on the Kierkegaard interpretation, since it gives a very clear and concise summary of Kierkegaard's argument—including its denial to the Don of any articulate subjectivity or inner life. The Don is the life of the opera, yet he seems to have no life of his own. "We are not given any insight into what he really is, or what drives him on. We could not have been: it is not that there is something hidden in his soul. It is notable that he has no self-reflective aria—he never sings about himself, as Mozart's other central characters do."[16] And yet, we must grapple with the fact that "the opera is of

---

[15] See B 306–9, imputing the negative reviews to severe Protestant moralism (1991).
[16] B. Williams (1988, p. 32).

great and unsettling power, that a seducer is at the centre of it, and that the seducer is virtually characterless"—though he adds that Kierkegaard underestimates the Don's "nastiness."[17]

Williams then notes that Kierkegaard ignores the way in which his idea of the erotic "suffocates both the individuality and the desires of women." If we are to make something meaningful of the view today, he argues, we must recast it in a more general sense, according to which the Don represents "a principle of vitality," or Kierkegaard's "exuberant joy of life." His freedom is not exactly that of the existentialist hero, because he lacks the idea that freedom as something all should share.[18] It is, then, the bare idea of life energy, of a life lived "at the fullest energy, at the extreme edge of desire." "Mozart has . . . shown us that life without Giovanni will be life that has lost a very single-minded embodiment of qualities which are indeed human. Because he was *just* those qualities, he himself lacked humanity—he was without love, compassion, and fairness, to mention only a few of the things he lacked." The end of the opera affirms that "there is no actual human life that could be lived as un-conditionally as his."[19]

This is progress, for Williams gives us a very lucid account of the "Romantic" interpretation, shorn of absurdity, and in a form that at least tries to show what might make it attractive. Doubts remain: is there no intense desire that has an articulate content? Are no extreme desires moral desires, or desires for political justice? Does imposing conditionality on sexual desire always make it weaker, rather than better? (And who would think this way?) Doesn't the Don, seen correctly, seem terribly limited, rather than boundless, in what he can desire and be? But at least we know what we are talking about, and we can now look in the opera to see what it has to say about this picture of the erotic.

---

[17] B. Williams (1988, p. 36).
[18] B. Williams (1988, p. 37).
[19] B. Williams (1988, pp. 40–41).

Rejecting the "Romantic" Interpretation: Nietzsche, Mörike, Dent, Kerman, Allanbrook, Nussbaum

Before we reach the musical and dramatic problems with Kierkegaard's view as an interpretation of the opera, we have to observe that Kierkegaard and his followers have a very bizarre picture of "sensuality" and "the erotic."[20] First and most obviously, they are talking only about men and men's desires (as Williams concedes). But even with that limitation their view is highly peculiar. Kierkegaard already shows a good deal of tone-deafness when he depicts Cherubino as sad and depressed in his erotic longing. Surely, instead, he is a high-spirited and eager adolescent, full of *joie de vivre*, though confused by the gusts of desire he feels. The song he composes for the Countess exhibits tenderness and respectful longing. Significantly, throughout he asks women to speak to him, saying what they want and think. His statement "I search for a good outside myself" summarizes his non-narcissistic attitude to his potential partners. We know that he does satisfy his desire later with Barbarina, and we are encouraged to imagine that relationship as playful, mutually eager, and fully consensual and reciprocal. So even the example Kierkegaard mentions as leading up to the Don, sensuality's crowning exemplar, is misread bizarrely.

When he later claims that the Don is the paradigm of sensuality, what can this mean? A man who refuses to listen to any woman, who uses force when consent is not forthcoming—who could possibly think this the epitome of "the erotic"? Kierkegaard seems utterly unaware of erotic relationships characterized by mutual delight, reciprocity, and mutual respect for consent. It is odd and a little sad that his experience and imagination have

---

[20] Here I refer to the two Nietzsche passages already cited; to Eduard Mörike's novella *Mozart auf der Reise nach Prag* (*Mozart on the Way to Prague*, [1855] 1997); to Dent's *Mozart's Operas* (2013, chs. 8, 9, and 10); to Kerman (1988) and Kerman (1990); and to Wye Jamison Allanbrook, *Rhythmic Gesture in Mozart: "Le Nozze di Figaro" and "Don Giovanni"* (1983).

such narrow bounds. The Don's spirit, as Joseph Kerman says, is that of the Erlkönig (Elf King) in Goethe's poem: "Bist du nicht willig, so brauch'ich Gewalt" ("If you aren't willing, then I'll use force."). How strange that anyone would think that this character exemplifies the essence of eroticism! The character A seems to be such a captive of Christian anti-sex ideas that he thinks that all erotic relationships, being transgressive according to that order, are the same, and all equally bad. And A imputes to Christianity a power that it surely never had: that of wiping the slate of possibility clean so that sexual energy can appear only through the distorting lens of the idea of sin.

Even if Kierkegaard was hoodwinked in this way, this can hardly be true of Steinberg and Williams, both of whom I know or knew personally, and know to be people both ardent and highly respectful of women. Williams's first wife, Shirley (1930–2021), was one of the nation's most powerful Labor Party politicians. I know from their daughter Becky that both parents took an equal part in her care (including bathing and diapering a young child, a very rare activity for a powerful man in the 1950s). His second wife, Patricia, whom he adored, carried on a career as lead Philosophy editor at the Cambridge University Press throughout their marriage, while they raised two children together. In sexual matters Williams was way ahead of his time, encouraging his students to complain about sexual harassment—before there was any tribunal to complain to. I remember vividly a walk on the "backs" in Cambridge in 1973 during which he said (of a harasser colleague), "You don't have to put up with this." So it does puzzle me greatly that this exemplary man, who was clearly made happy by a respectful mutuality in love, seems so captivated by the Don, though highly critical of him. Again, maybe it is a holdover from the iron hand of Christian puritanism, which Williams always railed against, that he finds this rebel character in some respects impressive, rather than merely ugly and empty, the way that Harvey Weinstein and Bill Cosby seem—to women and men both—to be ugly and empty.

At the very best, the soulless seducer the "Romantics" describe is exactly as interesting as Molly Bloom's lover Blazes Boylan—tirelessly energetic, but dreadfully dull. As Molly says: a lion would no doubt have more to say for himself.

But quite apart from life—and perhaps philosophers are often clumsy about life and what it offers, or, more oddly, may fail to look in opera for the genuine delights their own lives actually possess—Kierkegaard and his heirs could have been disabused not only by listening attentively to Mozart's operas, starting with *Idomeneo* and ending with *Clemenza*, but also by studying the history of opera more generally. For lest we think that the Don is an innovator, at least in opera—as Steinberg's remarks often suggest—the history of the genre rebuts that fantasy. Kierkegaard's knowledge of opera may be narrow, but Steinberg and Williams are ardent connoisseurs of the entire genre, and must be aware that it has a history focused on the erotic and its allure, but not so much on the Don's special force-laden version.

One of the first successful operas was Claudio Monteverdi's *L'Incoronazione di Poppea*, *The Coronation of Poppea* (1643), based on historical Roman sources, concerning the passion of the emperor Nero for the courtesan Poppea. Their mutually obsessive erotic love has in the opera, and had in history, some very unpleasant consequences, including the forced exile of Nero's wife Octavia and the forced suicide of the philosopher Seneca, Nero's tutor. Internally, too, the relationship is not ethically exemplary—Poppea is probably feigning love and using Nero to become Empress—and yet the sensuality the lovers display is reciprocal and fully mutual, focused on thoroughly shared bodily delights. At the opera's end, after Poppea is crowned, the retinue of attendants and trumpeters all leave the stage, and the two are left alone, to sing, as if in an improvised sexual act, what may be the most thoroughly sensuous music in all opera. "Pur ti miro, pur ti godo" ("Let me wonder at you, let me delight in you")—as the two vocal lines snake round one another, very slowly, on and on. This is not exactly Mozart's style: his ecstatic duet in *Idomeneo* fuses erotic desire with deep love, whereas Nero and Poppea are all about naked erotic obsession. We could, however, at least imagine Mozart writing this way, since sensuousness without deep love is at least one part of his personal repertory. Both modes are very far from the Don/Erlkönig, and as we shall see, both are far more musically interesting.

Let us begin by dispensing with the "Romantics'" overreliance on the opening chords of the overture. Nietzsche is correct that this is a "sin against Mozart," which turns a subtle drama into a melodrama. And since these interpreters typically link the exhilaration they feel at those D minor chords with the Don's energy as seducer, we must immediately point out that the music of the opening is later linked not with the Don but with the Commendatore, defender of conservative morality. So Mozart cannot possibly have intended that music to signal some exciting new departure. Its gravity signifies the gravity of the Don's violations.

The Don is described by the "Romantics" as a "seducer." We must immediately qualify this by saying that he is a seducer the way the Erlkönig seduces. I am less troubled than Dent by the absence of genuine consummated seductions during the opera.[21] A more serious problem is that so often the Don needs force to achieve his ends—even with Zerlina, initially interested though she is. And lest we try to reply that rape was not viewed in such a negative light in Mozart's time, we should remember that even the not-very-moral Leporello protests: "But Donna Anna didn't ask to be raped."

As a seducer, moreover, the Don conspicuously lacks characteristics that Mozart elsewhere associates with the ability to inspire love in and in that sense to seduce a woman—such as tenderness, humor, playfulness, an inner life. Susanna (in *Figaro*) says of Cherubino, "If women love him, they surely have good reason." Could anyone say this with a straight face about the Don? Rather, we should say, "If women love him, they are bewitched by wealth,

---

[21] See Dent (1913).

class, and false promises." He certainly doesn't have the appealing playfulness of the Don in Tirso de Molina's *The Prankster of Seville* (*El Burlador de Sevilla*, 1630), probably the first literary example of the Don Juan legend. He doesn't have ideas either, as Molière's Don Juan, another of Da Ponte's sources, conspicuously does. Taking these characteristics away, Da Ponte leaves only hollowness in their place. He is little more than a series of elegant poses: truly a "No-Man," as Wye Jamison Allanbrook puts it in her subtle and important study.[22]

So far, there appears to be no clash between Da Ponte's libretto and Mozart's musical interpretation of it.[23] But Mozart further emphasizes the Don's hollowness—as Williams himself points out—by refusing him a real aria, in which inner thoughts and feelings could be explored. Moreover, almost every extended solo he does sing is "a conscious performance or disguise."[24] Nor is the Don's music (as opposed to the opera's) at all innovative or romantic. The serenade is banal, if pleasing. The wine aria ("Fin ch'han dal vino"), perhaps his sole undisguised utterance, is manic, a fevered contredanse lasting a mere ninety seconds. As Allanbrook justly notes, "The contredanse had no place in the hierarchy of eighteenth-century social dance; it was a new dance, a 'danceless dance,' and hence the true dance of 'No-Man.'" In the text (*senz'alcun ordine / La danza sia*), the Don commands "the very anarchy that the contredanse had introduced into the cosmos of the social dances."[25]

As for what is perhaps his most appealing musical utterance, the duet with Zerlina "La ci darem la mano," it borrows a spurious

[22] Allanbrook (1983, pp. 207–8 and following pages). She notes his graceful gentlemanly behavior during the duel.

[23] Commentators have sometimes been misled by Da Ponte's self-proclaimed profligacy in his *Memoirs* into thinking that he must have written a pro-Don libretto; but he didn't. He was clearly capable of creating characters of many different types.

[24] Allanbrook (1983, p. 219).

[25] Allanbrook (1983, p. 220). In the contredanse there is no leading pair as in the minuet; each couple takes the lead role at some point.

tenderness (the Don is disguised as a wooing nobleman) in the service of violence to come. Moreover, as Kerman astutely notes, all the real musical invention is supplied by Zerlina.[26] We have only to compare this "hero" with genuine romantic heroes such as the Werther of Goethe and Massenet in order to see that he is not that sort of thing at all: no boundless inner world, no surging love, no subjectivity at all, musical or verbal.

I fear that these romantic men have been duped by the evident power of Mozart's music in this opera into locating this "demonic" power in the person of the Don, where it surely does not reside. Perhaps the idea of boundless sexual energy without love or tenderness has appeal for men of a certain age—but that doesn't license projecting those sentiments onto Mozart, who associated music of enormous power and gravity with the critique of the Don and his actions.

So far as my first enigma is concerned, then, the opera—both libretto and music—gives a clear answer: the Don is a horrible and empty person, whose passing we should not lament, and who surely is not the source of the vitality of all the other characters. Kerman's idea that there is a dissonance between libretto and music seems unfounded, and is probably based upon his view of Da Ponte's life and personality, which was certainly promiscuous for some years, although there is no evidence of force. (I'll discuss him further in the next section, arguing that he is not at all like the Don, despite the fact that Da Ponte records in his *Memoirs* that *Don Giovanni* is his favorite of Mozart's operas.[27]) The sense Mozart gives us musically that the Don is going through a much-repeated and rather tired routine actually conduces to the opposite conclusion: he has nothing new to do or say. We feel no energy emanating from him.

---

[26] Kerman (1990).

[27] Da Ponte, *Memoirs*, trans. Elizabeth Abbott with an Introduction by Charles Rosen (2000). See especially his account of using "his" *Don Giovanni* to inaugurate his New York opera house: 429, 436. Carlos Sauri made a movie about Da Ponte's life boldly titled *Io Don Giovanni* (2009), but the similarity, as we'll see, is slight.

(We are not told how old he is, but given his batting average here, getting to the total of 1,003 seductions just in Spain, and his far larger total overall, probably took a long time.) As in Ivo van Hove's 2023 Metropolitan Opera production, he is tired of himself, one step from being a No-Man in fact.

We are still left with a problem: why do so many women say "yes" to No-Man? Why are the other characters preoccupied with him in a way that he clearly does not deserve? The answer, however, must be (as it is with Harvey Weinstein and Bill Cosby and other celebrities who cause great harm) that these characters, like us, live in a corrupt culture in which power, status, and wealth have been sexualized and women have been brought up on these unpromising ideas—until they experience the harm such a character can do.

The Journey of Three Women

My second puzzle—the one about revenge—is far more difficult. The desire for revenge motivates all the other characters in the opera much of the time, and it surely gives the plot its structure. Here Kerman's idea of a misfit between Da Ponte's libretto and Mozart's sensibilities is far more convincing. The libretto requires revenge, but Mozart evidently has a hard time subscribing wholeheartedly to the cruel punishment of anyone—a reason why the final ensemble has always been felt unconvincing and flat, and has sometimes been cut in performance, including by Gustav Mahler (although this practice is seldom encountered today). Does Mozart, then, find any way to extricate himself from the trap set for him by Da Ponte? The trap of making revenge look fitting and mercy inappropriate?

Searching for an alternative and more typically Mozartean emotional statement, one might first try turning to Don Ottavio, who surely does express sentiments of sympathy and altruism that are highly Mozartean, and closely linked to Mozart's rejections of revenge in other operas—especially in his beautiful aria in Act 1, "Dalla sua pace," in which he wishes peace for Anna's traumatized spirit and says that his own peace depends on hers. This aria was added for the Vienna performance at the request of a singer who had trouble with the florid runs of the Act 2 aria, "Il mio tesoro" (which was cut on that occasion), so it was not an original part of Mozart's conception, but it does fit the character. His Act 2 aria expresses a similar desire to comfort Anna. And yet: the way he proposes to do so is by avenging her. Though sensitive and in many ways appealing, Don Ottavio is a thoroughly conventional figure, and throughout the opera he pursues revenge as much as anyone else.

The answer, then, must be found by turning to the opera's trio of remarkable women, surely the prime sources of its extraordinary vitality and musical glory. Though required by the plot to approve of the final heavenly punishment of the Don, each of them has a moment in which she turns away from the morality of revenge to embrace a richer conception of love and life. For Zerlina, access to tenderness is easy, since, as a young peasant woman, she has no outsized attachment to honor (for Mozart always a trap) to stand in her way. In the sensuous and tender "Vedrai carino," she says that sexual love can heal the wounds created by a vain competition be-tween men: the body affirms what hierarchical culture so often denies. The melody is simple, straightforward, and very sensuous. I am inclined to say that it refers to the Monteverdi example I have discussed, but for uncertainty about whether Mozart knew that opera. As Zerlina calms her wounded husband she places his hand on her breast, and in dotted rhythms that mimic heartbeats, says, repeatedly, "Sentilo battere, toccami qua" ("Hear it beating, touch me there"). Having already said that nature provides a cure for his wounds, she now proceeds to administer the cure. This is real sensuousness, with musical imagination and quasi-improvisatory musical creativity, all of which the Don and his music utterly lack. James Joyce knew what he was doing in *Ulysses* when he imagined the earthy Molly Bloom (a professional singer) playing this role, and Molly in the novel, like Zerlina in the opera, epitomizes a sexuality free from all vindictiveness. Joyce also knew what he was doing when he, or, rather, his protagonist Leopold Bloom, mentally casts the Don as Blazes Boylan—the only major character in the novel whose inner life is never shown us, presumably because, as Molly says, he lacks one.

The two aristocratic ladies have a more difficult time with tenderness since, in an honor culture, outraged honor seems to demand steely revenge. Donna Anna even puts this honor culture in its best possible light in her splendid aria, "Or sai chi l'onore," which makes the demand for bloodshed sound almost like a high-minded assertion of human dignity with no downside. The soaring musical lines sound like aspiration rather than a call to violence. Still, as many commentators note, she really is metallic at this point, and seems imprisoned by cultural norms and demands. She has no room in her heart for love of Don Ottavio.

By the opera's end, however, Donna Anna sings a different tune, literally: the lyrical, flowing first half of her aria, "Non mi dir," in which she expresses tenderness to Ottavio, insisting that she is not indifferent and unfeeling, and its vigorous second section, with its excited hope for a future of love with him, expressed in coloratura runs whose flexibility is utterly unprecedented for her. Both sections sound so unlike her earlier stern self that they puzzle many interpreters. Few singers can have equal success in both arias, a serious casting problem. And staging is equally difficult: how to portray the change? (Peter Sellars even staged the later aria with Donna Anna high on drugs, to explain the sudden shifts of mood.) Some, including Kerman, describe her as "diminished" and exhausted. (Perhaps this is because he likes her demand for revenge—but that is hardly Mozart's attitude.) To me, she seems just the opposite of exhausted: she is relieved of a heavy cultural burden and freed to become herself. Could one not say that Anna, who knew how to be a lady, has now discovered how to be human?

Donna Elvira is all along, in a sense, the opera's emotional center, since it is through her distress and distraction that we see what this Don is worth and what his vaunted glory comes to. Culturally she is a liminal figure—with a lady's title but free to travel on her own with a degree of freedom impossible for a high aristocrat. She is clearly a proto-bourgeois, which opens choices for her that Anna lacks. She is also another character who undergoes change. For the first half of the opera she pursues the Don, seeking revenge and vindication. Then, surprisingly, with a recitative reporting on her inner conflict, followed by a glorious aria "Mi tradi quell'alma ingrata," she opts for compassion and abandons the quest for punishment. As with Anna, the music she sings expresses a new freedom—phrases surging upward, with graceful arcing lines and none of the percussive combativeness of her earlier arias. It is surely not very satisfactory that the way in which she departs from the revenge mentality and embraces compassion ("pietà") is through a renewed love for the Don! It would have been nicer, one feels, if she could have found a new love interest—but the plot does not provide one for her. Still, her emotional shift is the focus, and its unsatisfactory object is less important.

"Mi tradì quell'alma ingrata" is another aria added at the Vienna premiere and so was not an original part of the score or libretto. But in this case the opera's overall plan appears to require the addition. The plan is really not about the Don at all—it is about the emotional journey of these three women, each wronged, each tempted by revenge, but each, in the end, overcome by love. And it is also about how each, through that change, awakens to a life that is less exhausted (for revenge is very fatiguing), less strained, more capable of genuine delight and happiness.

The Shadow of Death

In the end, however, the opera's happy ending is not fully convincing, and the Don's descent to Hell leaves negative emotions in its wake. There remains a sense of darkness, and of loss, that hangs over Da Ponte and Mozart's *dramma giocoso*. If it is not a sense that the Don has taken life's energy out of the world with him, what is it, and where does it come from?

Recall that Mozart was mourning his father, who had been dead less than four months when Mozart went to Prague. Thus the entire time of composition took place in the interval just after Mozart's bereavement. Complicated though their relationship always was, Leopold was the person closest in the world to him, closer even than his wife. And Mozart himself seems to have had a heightened sense of life's fragility. The shadow of his own imminent death always followed him. In his delicate and beautiful novella *Mozart auf der Reise nach Prag, Mozart on the Way to Prague*, Eduard Mörike imagines the journey of Mozart and Constanze to Prague for the opening of *Don Giovanni*.[28] They stop in a wood, and Mozart is overwhelmed by a sense of life's beauty—mingled with an awareness of how little he has managed to enjoy among the beauties there to be enjoyed, how little he has done among the things he wants to do. Delight, a looming sense of death, and guilt for misspent time mingle together. Mörike then (accurately, so far as we know) describes Mozart's usual daily pattern as a frenetic combination of blazing creativity and casual pleasures, drinking, eating, gambling, playing billiards, hanging out in bars—and then composing through the night—"high" and "low" strangely run together, leaving him often with a sense of wasted life. Sex is mentioned by Mörike, in connection with Constanze's jealousy over a flirtation; we believe that Mozart had some casual affairs. But we should agree with the novelist that sex is not the main issue (and Erlkönig force is nowhere in the picture: we know from his

---

[28] A fine study of the novella and its relation to the opera is Hans Vaget, "Mörike's Mozart and the Scent of a Woman," in *The Don Giovanni Moment: Essays on the Legacy of the Opera*, ed. Lydia Goehr and Daniel Herwitz (2006, pp. 61–74). I am grateful to Vaget for correspondence. (The conclusions expressed here diverge in some respects from his, but we are in basic agreement.)

sexually explicit letters to his cousin that this is not his sexual profile at all). The problem that inspires guilt is prodigality and waste of his great gifts, and that guilt, Mörike plausibly contends, is thoroughly interwoven with Mozart's joy and Mozart's genius, like its dark shadow.

The couple arrive in a park belonging to a noble house. Struck by the beauty of a rare type of orange tree, Mozart picks an orange and is in the middle of eating it, while composing a melody in his head, when a servant of the owner reprimands him: this is private property, and the fruit is forbidden. Although Mozart is subsequently invited to the Countess's home and warmly received, along with his wife, this pivotal event is a paradigm of original sin. Mozart draws attention to this idea in his initial letter of apology to the Countess, comparing himself to "Adam of old after he had tasted the apple." The idea of judgment for idle pleasure is a real idea in Mozart's life, albeit not a judgment about raping anyone or even about sex in particular—just about a dark sense that his life will be short and he has wasted lots of it. Mozart, received at the Countess's home, delights the company by playing extracts from his new opera. Not surprisingly, the story ends (after the Mozarts depart for Prague) as the Countess, alone, is overtaken by a vivid presentiment that Mozart will shortly die.

I think Mörike has it right: the bond between Mozart and the solemn ending of *Don Giovanni* is not really about the Don, who is far from Mozart and even from Mozart's particular sense of guilt: it is about impending death. (Of course he did die just four years later, and his health was already compromised.) The punishment feared is not heavenly punishment—Mozart didn't believe in Hell—but rather the punishment of being ended before he could create all he had it in him to create. Think of the final banquet before the Don is snatched down to Hell. The on-stage entertainers play a cheerful march from *The Marriage of Figaro*, as, naturally, the Prague orchestra did at the performance of his own opera that Mozart attended on his first visit to that city. That music now becomes a death-march—not only for the Don, but also for Leopold Mozart and for Mozart himself.

Don Giovanni remains a glorious if puzzling work, its insights not diminished but enriched by a nebulous sense of life's brevity and the looming shadow of death.

Così fan tutte

To take *Così fan tutte* seriously is not, as people sometimes impatiently insist, to refuse to treat it as a comedy. On the contrary, it is to take it seriously as a comedy, something we are certainly prepared to do with other comedies, and with Mozart's other great Italian operas. Since one is dealing with an opera, that involves attending at once to the music and to the meaning of the action, and when one does that a problem certainly arises.

—Bernard Williams, "Passion and Cynicism: Remarks on *Così fan tutte*"[29]

People of noble birth must never marry from inclination or love, but only from interest and all kinds of secondary considerations. . . . But we poor humble people can not only choose a wife whom we love and who loves us, but we may, can, and do take such a one, because we are neither noble, nor highly born, nor aristocratic, nor rich, but on the contrary, lowly born, humble, and poor; so we do not need a wealthy wife, for our riches, being in our brains, die with us.

—Mozart, letter to his father, February 7, 1778 (trying to prepare his father to accept his own marital choice)

---

[29] In Bernard (1998, pp. 43–48).

Così fan tutte (Thus do all women), subtitled *La scuola degli amanti* (The school for lovers), has entered the operatic canon. Once banished or rewritten because it was thought offensive and immoral,[30] it has now become popular. Its music is adored, its comedy found delightful—and yet, for listeners who take the comedy seriously, there is a problem, a bitter aftertaste. Joseph Kerman goes so far as to write, "Even the most devout Mozartian will have to admit that there is something unsatisfactory about *Così*"—which he calls "Mozart's most problematic work."[31] Bernard Williams, similarly, says that when we take it seriously as a comedy, "a problem arises."

What is the problem? In essence, it is a felt dissonance between what Williams calls the "heartless" spirit of Lorenzo Da Ponte's libretto and the remarkable emotional expressivity and tender sensuousness of the music, especially in the second act. This dissonance is then rendered more problematic still by the neat cookie-cutter ending in which everything snaps back to the way it was before Act 2. Kerman imagines the cynical character Don Alfonso, a spokesperson for Da Ponte, being progressively upstaged by the very different sensibility of one Don Wolfgango—and yet, of course, it was Da Ponte, not Mozart, who wrote the final scene and determined how things would end up for the characters. So the different sensibility has, basically, nowhere to go.

Compounding this problem is another: the libretto's treatment of women. From the title onward, the piece announces itself as an unmasking of women's pretenses of fidelity and nobility. They are all cheats, and dupes into the bargain, ready to fall for the first set of false mustaches that come their way. This becomes especially clear when we consider the subtitle alongside the title. Whereas *tutte* is

---

[30] On the various attempts to rewrite the opera to make it less shocking, see Bruce Alan Brown, *W. A. Mozart: "Così fan tutte"* (1995). During the nineteenth and early twentieth centuries it endured a long eclipse, being considered offensive and immoral. Sometimes, loving the music, people attempted to provide it with a totally different libretto: in one version, the text was that of Shakespeare's *Love's Labours Lost* in French!

[31] Kerman (1988), pp. 91–98, at 92.

unambiguously feminine, *amanti* could refer to the male lovers only, or to all lovers, male or female. However, in Don Alfonso's world, it is men who do the learning, women who exhibit an unchanging nature, the *necessità del core* mentioned by Don Alfonso as responsible for women's fickle behavior. So apparently the purpose of the game is to make the men learn something about a female nature that is fixed and incapable of growth, so they will grow from naïve dupes to wise and tolerant husbands.

This denigrating portrayal of all women is simply alien to Mozart's sensibility, though perhaps less so to Da Ponte's (at least at this time). Mozart's respect and admiration for women is not incompatible with gentle comedy of the *Magic Flute* type, which mocks human frailty very generally; but it certainly does not fit with this cynical damning of one entire sex and the implicit glorification of the other. Figaro uttered such sentiments in Act 4 of *The Marriage of Figaro*, but later repented; and that opera as a whole shows enormous respect for women.

The people Williams implicitly criticizes presumably would say, "Why are you getting so upset? This is just a comedy." Edward Dent appears to be one such person. He says that the libretto "is as perfect a libretto as any composer could desire,"[32] and concludes that at the end of the opera it does not matter at all who is paired with whom: "it will not make any difference to speak of"[33]—presumably because we, like Don Alfonso, are delighted by the comedy of it all. But Williams is right: to take the opera seriously *as a comedy*, listening to Mozart's increasingly tender and emotional music—in the service of a portrayal of women as learning and growing, alongside their partners—is to encounter the problems.

These are indeed problems, but they seem to me somewhat simpler than the *Don Giovanni* problem, because Kerman and Williams—though in somewhat different ways—are basically on

---

[32] Dent (1913, p. 288).
[33] Dent (1913, p. 306).

the right track. Both agree that the libretto is a perfect creation on its own terms, and it ends the game in a Da Ponteish way—but this turns out to be a way that is at odds with what has happened in the music. In *Figaro* the libretto left open possibilities, especially for Cherubino, that Mozart filled out in his own way. Here, by contrast, Mozart fills things out in ways that go seriously *against* the sense of the libretto as a whole, giving characters drawn like superficial pawns in a clever game unexpected depth, and thus creating an altogether different sort of work and turning the game into what seems almost like a tragedy. In short, both Williams and Kerman identify the problem correctly, and diagnose it as involving a dissonance between Mozart and his librettist, which increases as the opera goes on and Don Wolfgango increasingly rewrites the emotional plot. This is the trajectory we need to study.

The Libretto and Its Author

Così was first performed on January 26, 1790, at the Burgtheater in Vienna. It was initially well received, but had only five performances during Mozart's lifetime, on account of the death of the emperor Joseph II only a month later, and the ensuing mourning period. (Recall that Mozart himself died on December 5, 1791.) We know very little about the origins of the plot. The story that it is based on a real local incident that amused Joseph II—and which he therefore expressed the wish that an opera be made of it—is probably false, because the emperor was then too ill to have had any such thoughts. The opera has an air of lively realism that made people believe that it could have a basis in life, but we cannot go further. No single literary source suggests itself: instead, it alludes to many.[34]

---

[34] See Brown (1995, ch. 4 and Introduction).

Da Ponte's libretto is polished, well-constructed, witty, and cynical. Don Alfonso, the opera's resident philosopher/observer/cynic, who creates the plan to test the fidelity of the young women, opines that emotions are short-lived and fickle, but the libretto ultimately goes yet further, suggesting that they are altogether unreal and factitious. Much of the work's humor, in Act 1, derives from the fact that the women take their own emotions seriously, but we are urged to see that they are only play-acting, imitating literary—and operatic—expressions of passion. (Singer-actresses have a challenge: while acting they must create the impression of mere play-acting, and later on show how different that is from genuine feeling.) One of the most impressive aspects of the libretto is its enormous range of literary reference. As Bruce Alan Brown shows in enormous detail, Da Ponte ranges widely through both epic and lyric works in several languages, so that often the heroines are in effect presenting a parody of serious and famous works of literature that the audience could be expected to recognize.[35] Especially striking is its constant reference to other operas,[36] mostly serious operas. Even the title is a quotation: from *The Marriage of Figaro.* When the Count discovers Cherubino hiding in a chair in the Countess's room, Basilio, the cynical music-master, says, "Così fan tutte le belle, / Non c'è alcun novità": "that's how all women behave, there's nothing new about that." (Mozart even weaves the musical setting of this line in *Figaro* into the overture he writes for *Così.*) The sisters in their Act 1 declamations of high-tragic emotion are constantly alluding to the conventions of *opera seria,* and the audience is supposed to recognize this, therefore seeing their passion as fictive. There are also historical allusions: to Mesmer and his theory of "animal magnetism," to the war Joseph II was currently waging against the Turks.

[35] See Brown (1995, Introduction).
[36] See Brown (1995, Introduction and ch. 4).

We know that sometimes Mozart and Da Ponte worked closely together—as with *Don Giovanni,* for which Da Ponte went to Prague to help with rewriting. With *Così,* however, things were a little different. Da Ponte had a finished libretto that he offered first to Salieri, his constant patron and supporter; and Salieri even began writing some of the music. Pieces of his setting appear to survive in the Austrian National Library, discovered by musicologist John Rice.[37] Salieri then abandoned the project—apparently because he was not making much progress with it—so Da Ponte brought it to Mozart. This history, however, implies that it was basically a done deal, and Da Ponte's creation rather than a thorough co-creation, though one to which Mozart agreed, and to which he contributed in local and specific ways (rewriting this or that line).

The libretto has an air of worldly wisdom. We see in it a kind of hard realistic rationalism characteristic of some of the Enlightenment *philosophes,* for whom emotions were of little import. It also has the misogyny of the *philosophes,* for whom women's inferiority was shown in the fact that they live by emotions. Don Alfonso urges the young men not to set women on a pedestal, but to accept them as they (allegedly) are: without rational control, without fidelity, without a stable self. The fact that they fail to measure up to the young men's exalted standard should not be held against them: they can't do anything but be who they are:

> Take them as they are; Nature couldn't make an exception or grant you a privilege by creating two women of different clay just for your handsome faces. You must see everything philosophically. . . . All men accuse women, but I excuse them—even if they change their affections a thousand times each day. Some call it a vice, others a habit, but I believe it to be a necessity of the heart. The lover who is disillusioned at the end should not condemn the folly of others, but his own.

[37] See Brown (1995, p. 10).

This acceptance of the ways of the world fits reasonably well with what we know about Da Ponte, at this stage in his strange and remarkable career—although Da Ponte is considerably less misogynistic (most of his cynicism in the *Memoirs* being directed at male authority figures who disappoint him).

Lorenzo Da Ponte (1749–1848) was born into an Italian Jewish family; his birth name was Emanuele Conegliano.[38] When he was fourteen his father, a widower, converted the entire family to Roman Catholicism so that he, a man of forty, could marry a Catholic woman only seventeen years old. Emanuele was given the name Lorenzo Da Ponte, the name of the Bishop of Ceneda, who became his patron. Da Ponte pursued his studies at the seminary, focusing on literature, and was eventually ordained as a priest in 1773. He then earned a living in Venice teaching literature and languages, and led a promiscuous and indulgent life. He became a close friend of Casanova starting in 1777; the friendship endured for twenty years. His lifestyle got him into trouble with the law for allegedly organizing the entertainments in a brothel, and in 1779 he was convicted of "public concubinage" and banished from Venice. That's when he moved to Austria—where, with an introduction from Salieri, who befriended him, he became librettist to the Italian Theater and court poet to Joseph II. From these posts it was but a short step to Mozart.

This was but chapter two in a very long life with many vicissitudes that Da Ponte turns into entertainment for the reader. His aim, explicitly avowed, is to tell a good story. (He once remarks that the more placid parts of his later life in New York afford less to amuse readers.) At the deaths of Joseph and Mozart, he had no strong protectors (Leopold was unfriendly), so he simply moved on—meeting in Trieste in 1792 the half-Jewish woman Nancy Grahl (1771–1831) a chemist's daughter, who would be with him until her death and bear him four children—though he and Nancy

---

[38] Da Ponte (2000).

were unable to marry legally, since he was still a Catholic priest! He expresses profound love for her, and speaks of no infidelities during their long marriage. The French Revolution drove the couple to London, and, by 1805, to the United States, where he reinvented himself yet again, becoming the first professor of Italian literature at Columbia University, a well-connected—if intermittently impecunious—member of New York high society, and an opera producer. In 1825 he produced the first full version of *Don Giovanni* ever given in the United States. In 1833, aged eighty-four, he founded the Italian Opera Theater, probably the first specialized opera house in the country and the ancestor of the Metropolitan Opera. He never stopped complaining about New Yorkers' indifference to Italian culture—despite their love for Italian olive oil. His children with Nancy married into the highest ranks of society, with names such as Yale, Ogden, and Chauncey.

This is the man of unquenchable joie de vivre and endless vitality whom some like to compare to Don Giovanni—forgetting that Da Ponte had a soul, a deep love of his wife and children, an almost obsessive love of poetry and the Italian language, and a sophisticated and fecund creativity, all traits utterly absent from the Don. (His description of his grief at the death of his oldest son is especially moving.)

He is not the Don. Is he Don Alfonso? He certainly has a world-weary cynicism about powerful people's intentions, and tells readers often that he should not have trusted the many people who betrayed him (in financial and professional, not romantic, dealings). The two also share a love of a good story. Don Alfonso is highly lettered, though without evidence of creativity, and his genial role as advisor to the two young men is isomorphic to Da Ponte's role as wise advisor to his readers. However, Don Alfonso fails to exhibit Da Ponte's indomitable love of life. In that sense Da Ponte is more like the plot's primary agent, the servant Despina, whose energy and imagination drive the action forward.

Act 1: The Game Begins

The libretto as a whole is funny, sophisticated, beautifully constructed, full of ingenious twists and hilarious masquerades. Throughout Act 1, Mozart's music serves Da Ponte's cynical purpose quite well, creating an artificial comedy with characters who are essentially cardboard cutouts and objects of knowing laughter (by Don Alfonso and the knowing Despina, and by us). The setting is a bourgeois house, and all four lovers are indisputably bourgeois, servants being common in bourgeois houses. Don Alfonso strikes a bet with the two hopelessly romantic young men, to test the fidelity of their sweethearts. As Braunbehrens remarks, Mozart "debases the character of Don Alfonso by underlining his acerbic and skeptical rationality with dry string accompaniments and denying him support from the wind instruments" (340). His accomplice Despina is far more lively, and we see that her unwillingness to trust love has a practical origin: servants are typically used by the sentiments of others, so she has learned to manipulate in her turn. The two young men, meanwhile, are not distinct at all, apart from the fact that one is a tenor and the other a baritone.

The two young women whom Despina serves are naïve, and given to substituting literary/operatic sentiment for genuine introspection. They often sing together in thirds, and are very sketchily characterized—largely, we come to feel, because they don't yet have definite characters at all. Both theatricalize their passion in mock-heroic terms, in the arias "Smanie implacabili" ("Unabating torments") and "Come scoglio" ("Like a rock"). And the funny disguises of the men and Despina's masquerade as the Mesmeric doctor are delightful comedy.

Two moments of purely musical passion, however, begin to show us that there is more to these young people than their play-acting suggests. As the men prepare to leave, the four sing in broken phrases, "Write me every day," etc. One soaring phrase sung by

Fiordiligi, on "Be true to me alone," has such simple beauty that it seems to come from the heart, and then, as Brown observes, "the music embarks on a rapturous development, whose culmination anticipates a chromatic cadential phrase in Mozart's *Ave verum corpus* of 1791."[39] Where is this beauty coming from?

A later moment that also heralds Act 2's serious musical turn is Ferrando's aria "Un' aura amorosa" ("A loving breath"). The libretto's poetry here is thoroughly conventional. Mozart's music, however, reveals a surprising and quite sincere depth of feeling. At that point we are prepared for new developments.

Act 2: Love Upsets the Game

Act 2, as the libretto intends it, simply plays out the game. The women fall for their new suitors—so grotesquely attired, and so utterly different from their betrothed lovers. First Dorabella yields, then, after more difficulty, Fiordiligi. The trick is then revealed, to the women's consternation. At this point, however, a spirit of patronizing toleration and reconciliation takes over. The men pardon their erring fiancées, given the frailty of the female nature, and the women quickly rejoin the relationships they had temporarily abandoned. The spirit is not exactly heartless; it is, however, a kind of patronizing rationalism that treats emotions as female and not to be respected. The worldly spirit of Don Alfonso tells us that it basically doesn't matter who is united with whom: all relationships are imperfect, all contain the ongoing possibility of deceit and infidelity, given women's nature, but let's get on with life. Emotions are not important enough to be taken very seriously.

Mozart, however, cannot help taking emotions seriously, nor can he accept Don Alfonso's patronizing view of women as interchangeable automata propelled by natural necessity without

---

[39] Brown (1995, p. 31).

choice or reason. (Both Kerman and Williams represent this attitude as a generalized cynicism and do not notice how condescending and asymmetrically diminishing of women it is.) By Act 2, Mozart's genius for emotional insight, range, and particularity takes over, breaking the clever mold and subverting its purpose—in effect writing a different plot. In the other Da Ponte operas, it is also true that Mozart supplies emotional depth to texts that might have been set otherwise. (In chapter 1, for example, we considered in how many ways the text of Cherubino's aria "Voi che sapete" in *The Marriage of Figaro* might have been set, and how completely it might have lacked the tender longing that it in fact expresses.) In *Così*, however, the music doesn't just render emotionally determinate texts that are indeterminate; it actually subverts the entire point of the libretto. No, Don Alfonso, emotions are not just a game, they are real, and people—men and women equally—have deep, interesting, and highly individual emotional lives.

In Act 1, the young women, we saw, were not very different from one another, both being very young and inexperienced, and lacking knowledge of their own hearts and their own tastes. Both play-acted at emotions with a grandiosity that signaled an absence of authentic self-knowledge and real erotic experience—although glimpses of more mature emotions appeared here and there. Mozart's music underlined this aspect of play-acting. In Act 2, both—now exploring life on their own, without the shelter of their early betrothals—gradually discover depths of emotional response in themselves—in highly particular ways.

The Act begins in an Act 1 mode, with another duet mainly in thirds, in which the women, discussing their new suitors, sound rather alike—but less so than before. Dorabella opts, she says, for the brunette: "he seems more amusing to me." We realize, of course, that Ferrando is anything but amusing, so she is discovering in herself a taste that the old pairing did not satisfy. At this point Fiordiligi simply parrots her sister: "I'll laugh and joke with the nice blond one"—although she has never shown a taste for joking, nor does Ferrando offer anything in that department. But she will soon discover her own emotions in new ways,

Both Kerman and Williams focus on the duet between Fiordiligi and Ferrando, "Fra gli amplessi" ("In the embraces"), which shows Fiordiligi discovering love along with Ferrando, and so discovering new capacities in herself. Emotions strike both of these lovers as mysterious, but also as totally real and urgent, as real as anything in the world can be. (And this is so, whether the emotions actually last or not: so long as they exist, they are both real and at the core of the person's humanity.) The contrast between Fiordiligi's Act 1 aria, where she is playing around with ideas of constancy like a would-be drama heroine, and this duet, with its soaring phrases and tremulous expression of passion, could not be more striking—and moving, too, as if we are seeing a mature woman being born. We now see how implausible and unsuitable her early pairing with the jokey Guglielmo was; Ferrando's ardent romantic sentiments suit her far better.

Kerman seems to prefer the emotions of the serious pair to those of the comic pair simply because they *are* serious. Williams's preference for the serious pair must be understood in connection with his often-expressed preference for Wagner's *Tristan und Isolde* as *the* operatic paradigm of genuine love. (In introducing the posthumous collection in which his article on *Così* appears, Williams's widow Patricia notes that he tested their budding relationship by taking her to a performance of *Tristan*, to see how much she liked it. She loved it, and realized later that this had been a test. I am reminded of the common pop-quiz question, "Which locations for a first date would be deal-breakers for you?," and I have to state unequivocally that, despite my intense admiration for Williams, I would surely have flunked the *Tristan* test.)

But this is Mozart, the same Mozart who shows again and again, in his letters as in his works, that playfulness and humor can be a supreme expression of love's reciprocity, and a key to his type of happy sexuality.[40] (And isn't this an important truth in real life?) So I propose, *contra* Williams and Kerman, that we also do justice to the other pair. (After all, it was Dorabella who first discovered her own individual taste for humor and play.) The moment in all opera that most unfailingly makes me weep for sheer joy at the precariousness and lovability of the world is Dorabella and Guglielmo's Act 2 duet, "Il core vi dono" ("I give you a heart"). The usual staging has him give her a heart-shaped locket as a token of love. She accepts it, and they then joke that the heart that was in one breast is now beating in the other's: his heart (the locket) is now on her breast, and (she says) hers has now gone over there and is beating in his. The music first expresses tender playful alternation, and then, with the delicate staccatos of the line "E batte così" ("And beats just so"), they are suddenly together. (That's where I cry, invariably.) "O cambio felice" ("O happy exchange"). We have become painfully aware that Ferrando, her original fiancé, was utterly wrong for her (and right for Fiordiligi), since he is all lofty sentiment and no play. And now, with Guglielmo, she suddenly finds what she wanted all along: in the intimacy of joking and play she emerges into her full self and finds love's reality, as the hearts change places and then somehow beat in harmony, though from the opposite place. Nobody but Mozart understands so fully how jokes and play can elicit deep emotion and real vulnerability from a previously self-defensive person. It's too bad that critics usually don't get this point, assuming that jokes are low. That's a further problem with the "Romantic" interpretation: it can't include one key element of Mozart's character.

In effect, as Kerman wittily puts it, the second act belongs not to Don Alfonso but to "Don Wolfgango,"[41] who, being himself,

---

[40] Especially striking in this respect are his letters to his cousin Maria Anna Thekla Mozart, his first great love, in which tender professions of love are sandwiched between games and excremental jokes: see Maynard Solomon, *Mozart: A Life* (1995, pp. 164–67).

[41] Actually the coinage is originally that of Dent (1913, p. 289), but it is Kerman who makes something apt and interesting of it.

took emotion very seriously—including its soaring heights but including, as well, its capacity for tender play—and probed the characters' depths with varied and aching effect, meanwhile showing women to be indisputably capable of change, growth, and real individuality. As Kerman says: "Mozart's music clarifies and damns Da Ponte's cynicism."[42]

How Do Things End?

Act 2 belongs to Mozart, but it must end as Da Ponte wrote it. Although the work has been staged in multiple ways, according to the libretto we are evidently supposed to think that the girls go back to their original partners. Alfonso tells the lovers to marry the girls *in spite of* their fickleness, which implies that they take their original partners back. This is also the "correct" or conventional thing. Finally, this is also the "lesson" intended from start to finish—in the "School for Lovers" that is Da Ponte's libretto. That is to say, the women have to be taught a lesson, or the whole finale will seem pointless.[43] According to the libretto, there is no loss, because all is convention and emotions are factitious anyway. As I suggested earlier, this need not be read as utterly heartless: it is a kind of eighteenth-century rationalism that denigrates emotion and urges toleration of such human frailties. It is also misogynistic, suggesting that men can learn to free themselves from dependence on emotion, whereas women are stuck with their "necessities."

Given the music of Act 2, however, the ending is deeply disturbing, and the message finally conveyed a very unpleasant one: as Williams puts it, "the idea that emotions are indeed deep, indeed based on reality, but the world will go on as though they were not,

[42] Kerman (1988, p. 97).
[43] See Kerman (1988, p. 94 and footnote).

and the social order, which looks to things other than those emotional forces, will win out."[44] Surely, if the emotions of Act 2 are taken seriously, for the women to go back to their original partners with any hope of love and happiness would require a lot of time and change, a kind of dramatic development that the libretto does not offer.[45] We must, then, view the return to the original pairings as one that negates the possibilities of love and happiness that have been revealed. We might even see in the work a critique of the institution of marriage, as inimical to genuine love, at least for women.

Kerman thinks the work broken and unconvincing in its duality. I think Williams is right, however: the new work written by "Don Wolfgango" "is upsetting not because it is a failure, or broken-backed, or the product of a misunderstanding, but because it succeeds in being upsetting.... [I]t is a deep and unsettling masterpiece," not like any other work of Mozart's, or of anyone else.

One might try to argue that Mozart and Da Ponte collaboratively create this dark and disturbing insight. I find more persuasive the suggestion of Kerman and Williams that the libretto is one thing, the music in some respects quite another, and Mozart is trapped by the contrivance of the libretto, creating an ending that turns out jarring and unsatisfying. I prefer the conundrum, which provokes thought, to the increasingly common practice of solving the problem by directorial fiat, pairing the lovers with their new partners, which simply papers over the problem Mozart and Williams have identified.

Is there any way out of this problem? Braunbehrens suggests that there is. Act 2's music has indeed revealed new emotional depths, he says, but the result is that the characters end up confused, and yet free from their former exaggerated self-assurance and prepared to "begin the search for true self-knowledge, happiness, and

---

[44] B. Williams (1988, p. 45).
[45] See Kerman (1988, p. 95).

wisdom."[46] This is indeed a Mozartean solution, if it is really available. But to believe it available we need to be convinced that the women are not legally and socially bound to their former (unsatisfactory) lovers and are really free to search. Even though these are bourgeois women who have a good deal of freedom, and even though the ending could be (and sometimes is) staged this way, there are definite indications in the libretto that the women go back to their former partners. They are well-off, so a betrothal contract means something, and they are not as free as Mozart himself, bohemian and impoverished.

I believe that the libretto forecloses this middle way—but that Mozart, once again, gestures emphatically toward it. Mozart was a poor bourgeois man who viewed marital choice as essential, and who changed partners at least twice. First, he abandoned his beloved cousin for the attractions of Aloysia Weber, who really did not suit him emotionally (their letters are rather cold and formal), and whose plan was clearly to use Mozart to advance her own musical career. When she realized that he was poorer and less influential than she had thought, she rudely dismissed him—to which he responded by sitting down at the piano in their house and singing, "Let the one who doesn't want me lick my ass."[47] Before long he turned his attentions to the middle Weber sister, Constanze, who became his wife and a true partner, the two being bound by a joyful and totally reciprocal love.[48] Mozart, in short, had lived the plot of Da Ponte's libretto, and he knew well that in real life it could end happily in his own not-wealthy bourgeois world.

---

[46] B 339. Braunbehrens does not feel tension between the libretto and the music; he concludes that the two together have created a new type of drama—realistic, complex, and profound.

[47] Solomon (1995, p. 169); Solomon contrasts this angry use of obscenity with its tender use in letters to his cousin. The story is told in a biography by Constanze's second husband, Georg Nikolaus von Nissen, and clearly derives from her memory. (The published form is more polite, but the manuscript contains the real vulgarity.) Constanze outlived both husbands, dying at the age of eighty in 1842.

[48] Braunbehrens gives the best account of Constanze, refuting many misplaced critiques of her contribution to Mozart's life (1991).

I would say, then, that the opera itself, given the clash between libretto and music, ends in the dark and unsatisfying way that Williams depicts, but that hope nonetheless gleams out around the edges through the power of the music and the indomitable optimism of Don Wolfgango about love.

And what of the war to which the men march off to cheerful choral song in praise of the military life, and from which they return unscathed? Is that part of the comic contrivance, or is it all too real? Might war not be another way in which the conventions of the world treat human emotions as if they do not matter? Some modern productions suggest that the reality of war lies behind the comedy, and that this reality, leaving nothing as it was before, renders the ending yet darker. The audience of the original production knew that Joseph II was carrying on a war against the Turks that was no joke. In *The Marriage of Figaro*, Figaro's dark depiction of war to Cherubino in the aria "Non più andrai" shows that, in that opera at least, Mozart is well aware of the cannons that negate music, the whizzing bullets that make your ears deaf. John Cox, director of a fine production of *Così* for which I wrote a program essay in October 2017, writes me that, as he sees it, the entire comedy "is played out on the edge of this abyss," and that the darkness of the ending derives from this background reality. This suggestion is certainly absent from the libretto, and it is not easy to see it in the music, but to develop this idea in production seems to me not to undermine the music's human depth and may even enhance it. *Figaro* shows that serious ideas about war can be explored by Mozart within a comedy.

⋆ ⋆ ⋆

These two "problem operas" both show Mozart affirming ideas of love and reciprocity against cynicism, misogyny, and glorification of the domination of others. Musically at least, they are consistent with ideas of a "Republic of Love" depicted in *Idomeneo*,

The Marriage of Figaro, and *The Magic Flute.* But the two operas also have a dark side, showing us limits to all our human projects—limits imposed by social rigidity and above all, by the looming prospect of death, a reality for which Freemasonry was supposed to prepare the Mason's heart, but for which no heart is truly ready.

4

"If You Could See This Heart"

Mercy in *La Clemenza di Tito*

Soon we shall breathe our last. Meanwhile, while we live, while we are among human beings, let us cultivate our humanity. Let us cause no one fear or danger. Let us show disdain for losses, wrongs, abuses, and insults. Let us bear our short-lived ills with a generous spirit. While we look over our shoulder, as they say, and turn around—death will be upon us.

—Seneca, *On Anger* (*De Ira*), III.43

A Final Statement

Mozart's *La clemenza di Tito*, which had its premiere in Prague on September 6, 1791, was written after most of *The Magic Flute* (which opened on September 30) had already been completed. One could, then, call it Mozart's final opera. The commission was for the celebrations surrounding the coronation of Leopold II, Holy Roman Emperor, as King of Bohemia. Domenico Guardasoni was charged by the Estate of Bohemia with arranging an opera. The subject of good leadership seemed appropriate to the occasion— preferably good leadership at a distance from present tensions and controversies. Since it was June already, haste was essential, and Guardasoni decided to use an existing libretto by Metastasio, written some forty years before, which had already been set by Caldara, Gluck, Myslivicek, and others. Mozart had attended at least one performance of such a setting, so he knew the libretto. Guardasoni approached Mozart after Antonio Salieri turned him down. The poet Caterino Mazzolà edited the libretto (ultimately based on Seneca's philosophical essays *De Clementia* and *De Ira* and on ideas from French classical tragedy, especially Corneille's *Tite et Bérénice*), artfully condensing it to two acts and streamlining the action. Mozart worked feverishly to meet the deadline, having received the revised libretto only on August 19–20. He met the deadline—then died on December 5, less than three months after the premiere.

Guardasoni had assembled most of the cast himself, without consulting Mozart—including hiring a leading castrato, Domenico Bedini, to sing the role of Sesto. This was not Mozart's usual modus operandi: he liked to write for specific voices he knew. Furthermore he had not used a castrato since *Idomeneo*, preferring female mezzo-sopranos for roles like Cherubino (and Sesto). Having failed to control casting, Mozart at least was able to engage his good friend Anton Stadler (1753–1812), for whom he had written so much wonderful clarinet music, including the Clarinet Quintet and the Clarinet Concerto: he invited Stadler to play basset clarinet, rewarding him with wonderful emotionally expressive solo obbligatos in two key arias, as we shall see.

It remains unclear whether all the music was written by Mozart. Handwriting suggests that the *secco* recitatives were the work of someone else. But the main musical structure of the opera shows such striking thematic unity that no doubts should be raised about that.

From its beginning, the opera has had its hostile critics, from the new Empress Maria Luisa, who proclaimed it "German swill" (*una porcheria tedesca*), and Count Zinzendorf, usually friendly to Mozart, who wrote in his diary, "They regaled us with the dullest of spectacles, *The Clemency of Titus*,"[1] to the great twentieth-century

---

[1] Badol-Bertrand (2006), Introductory essay to the 2006 recording of the opera under the direction of René Jacobs.

musicologist Charles Rosen (1927–2012), who opines that it is "difficult to convey how unmemorable it is."[2]

The circumstances of the premiere—Mozart's ill health, the rush to get it ready in time for the coronation, and the lack of a composer-chosen cast for whose idiosyncrasies Mozart could write—certainly prevented the fertile close collaboration between composer and librettist that make the Da Ponte operas such thrillingly integrated works. The libretto is in some ways awkward and wooden, often lacking the emotional nuance and variety of the music. Nonetheless, in the end the opera is a profound statement about mercy and the sympathetic imagination—a statement merely outlined in the libretto itself, but to which Mozart's music gives flesh and blood, with a gentle and humane spirit all his own. Many aspects of the libretto suggest Masonic themes—especially preparation for death and the overcoming of hostility and rage— and Mozart fully took advantage of this Masonic connection in composing, starting with the three dotted-rhythm orchestral flourishes, accompanied by tympani, at the start of the overture.[3]

Mozart is repeatedly, almost obsessively, drawn to the topic of retributive anger. Again and again he shows, both musically and dramatically, its hollow uselessness as a response to injury and its poisonous effect on the person who allows its spirit to determine her course. Ilia quickly abandons her thoughts of retribution under the influence of Idamante's forward-looking and generous love. Donna Anna eventually turns around from her single-minded rage to productive future-oriented love. Less happy are Elettra in *Idomeneo* and, later, the Queen of the Night in *The Magic Flute*, both of whom are essentially consumed by their anger and who fail, therefore, to create for themselves any productive future, sealed off as they are, or become, from all human love. Although this book has

---

[2] Rosen (1976, p. 141).
[3] See Badol-Bertrand (2006, p. 34), corrected by Charles Nussbaum in correspondence.

not devoted close attention to *Die Entführung aus dem Serail* (*The Abduction from the Seraglio*, 1782, K 384), it is worth mentioning that this opera includes one example of each type. Pasha Selim, initially punitive, and particularly enraged to discover that Belmonte is the son of his old enemy, decides to forgo his anger and send the loving couple on their way—although, since his is a spoken part, Mozart wrote no music expressive of the change. Osmin, meanwhile, expresses futile and unchanging rage in a manner that is comic, and yet in a sense also tragic, since his future is as bleak as Elettra's.

In the personal life, retributive anger can give way to love. What of the political life? Mercy is generally understood as the mind's swerving from harshness to leniency in considering punishment (Seneca's definition, as we shall see). So a political actor's tendency to retributive severity might be curbed by a turning to mercy, and it is often considered a judicial virtue, pertaining especially to the sentencing phase of a trial. Mozart portrays merciful politics in other operas: Idamante's freeing of the Trojan prisoners, Pasha Selim's release of his captives. But in these operas the political context is only vaguely sketched. In *Clemenza* we have a real historical story. The story is pertinent to Mozart's struggles with anger: for he chafed under imperial authority just as he did, personally, under the authority of his father. His final opera, I shall argue, illuminates both levels at once, portraying a just and merciful ruler, quasi-republican, and two lovers who are just and merciful toward one another.

We can appreciate Mozart's project more fully if we understand, first, a little more about the historical sources behind the libretto and then, even more important, the tradition of thought about mercy and human vulnerability on which the opera is drawing. Mozart probably had not read Seneca, but the historical accounts of Titus he knew are suffused with Seneca's spirit, and Mozart's stance in life already embodied it. Seneca's *De Clementia* (*On Mercy*) and *De Ira* (*On Anger*) were widely read and discussed in his lifetime, so he probably knew their overall ideas, as would many in the audience.

Who, then, was Tito? What was his mercy? And what did Roman philosophy think about mercy as a human and, especially, a political virtue?

Titus in History

Titus (full name Titus Flavius Caesar Vespasianus Augustus) lived from 39 to 81 CE and reigned as Emperor for a mere two years, from the death of his father Vespasian in 79 until his premature death in 81. His life is narrated in two main sources: Suetonius's *Lives of the Caesars*, and Cassius Dio's *Roman History* (books 65 and 66). In addition, we learn a lot about his early life from *The Jewish Wars* by the Hellenized Jew Flavius Josephus. His life story would have been well known to Mozart's audience, who would have associated him with Seneca's *De Clementia* of which more shortly.

Titus's early career gave reasons for skepticism about his likely character as ruler. He was clearly very gifted, both mentally and physically. He was a skilled horseman, wrote poetry in both Latin and Greek, and sang and played the harp skillfully. He was also very good-looking, as both literary reports and visual art attest. As a military officer he showed energy and some distinction. His father, who became emperor in the year 69 (the "year of the four emperors" after Nero's death), put him in charge of subduing the Jewish rebellion, and in 70 CE he besieged and conquered Jerusalem, destroying the Second Temple. (The Arch of Titus in Rome commemorates this victory.) Because of his role in destroying the temple, rabbinic Jewish sources depict him in an extremely negative light.

Titus then served as prefect of the Pretorian Guard, gaining a reputation for arrogance and cruelty. He used his office to murder his enemies—including one whom he ordered to be stabbed at a dinner party to which he had himself invited him. "Thus," concludes the Roman biographer Suetonius, "he incurred a great deal of ill will, and hardly anyone ever assumed the principate with so negative a reputation, and so much against the will of all."

In addition to his reputation for cruelty, Titus was known as a profligate, with a fondness for all-night parties. He did obey conventional norms to some extent. He was married twice in his youth: first to Arrecina Tertulla, a woman of modest background, and then, after her death, to the wealthy and distinguished Marcia Furnilla, whom he relatively quickly divorced, perhaps because her family was suspected of involvement in the conspiracy against Nero. He had several daughters from these two marriages, but no sons, and never married again. However, his love affairs outside of marriage (during and after) were notorious. He had a very public and controversial affair (before assuming the throne) with the Jewish queen Berenice, daughter of Herod Agrippa. At one point she actually moved into the palace. Because of her Jewishness and her foreign origins, this affair was very unpopular.

At the same time, like most Roman men of his class, Titus also pursued sexual relations with men, going around with a group of male prostitutes, including some well-known dancers and actors. Craig Williams's monumental work of scholarship, *Roman Homosexuality*, gives a fine account of the sexual customs of the time, showing that sex between men was regarded as fine for a Roman gentleman, so long as the sex object was of lower social status (and, as we shall see later, in a narrower range of cases with a younger man of good social status).[4] In Titus's case, what was objected to, apparently, was not the fact of such relations but the intemperance and lack of judgment with which they were conducted—including both his promiscuity and revelry and his decision to give so much power to a non-Roman, not to mention Jewish, queen. People were fond of predicting that Titus would be

---

[4] C. A. Williams (2010).

a second Nero, meaning a ruler whose genuine gifts would become harmful on account of his vices.

He surprised them all—becoming a famous example of moral reform. As soon as he ascended the throne, he changed his ways. He sent Berenice packing immediately ("against her will and against his own," says Suetonius), and also repudiated his low-life male lovers, refusing even to attend their theatrical performances henceforth. He replaced riotous revels with modest restrained dinner parties, and chose prudent sober friends. Frugal himself from that time forward, he showed a generous and kindly disposition to all. He never seized property from anyone, and he gave generously to all who implored him. Once at dinner, remembering that he had done no act of philanthropy all day, he remarked, "Friends, I have lost a day."

One of his most famous acts of beneficence was public: after the eruption of Mt. Vesuvius in 79, when thousands were homeless and destitute, Titus both offered emotional support through edicts of consolation and supervised the restoration of the region, giving the surviving inhabitants generous financial subsidies and also bequeathing to them the property of people who had died and left no heirs. This famous act of public subsidy receives attention in the opera. In Act 1 scene 4, the senators bring Titus the tribute payments from the provinces, intended for a temple dedicated to the cult of the emperor. He thanks them, but says he would rather not use the money for personal glorification. Describing the eruption, he says that "poverty oppresses those spared by the fire. Let this gold serve to repair the havoc suffered by so many afflicted people. This, O Romans, is the temple you should build for me." (Not surprisingly, the details of property law are omitted.)

And he did indeed show mercy to personal opponents. He often said that he would rather be killed than kill, and Dio tells us that he did not put anyone at all to death during his rule, a fact extraordinary by Roman imperial standards, even over such a brief period. Once, when two conspirators against him were discovered, he let them off with a warning, telling them that the principate was a gift of fate, but he would gladly give them anything else they wanted. He even invited them to dinner the next day—and sent an express messenger to the mother of one of them to let her know that her son was all right. He discouraged the widespread public practice of informing on others, initiated the concept of double jeopardy (one can't be tried twice for the same offense), and did away with the crime of insult to the emperor. He said, "It is impossible for me to be insulted or abused in any way, since I do nothing that deserves reproach, and I don't care about what is reported falsely."[5]

In this way he gained unprecedented popularity. Suetonius calls him "the delight and darling of the human race." Dio remarks, more cautiously, that it is hard to say what might have happened had he lived longer: for a short time he "ruled with mildness and died at the height of his glory, whereas, if he had lived a long time, it might have been shown that he owed his present reputation more to good fortune than to merit."[6]

In one way Titus was too merciful for his own good. His brother Domitian was always plotting against him, rather openly, and Titus took no steps to banish or otherwise restrain him. Indeed, it was said that in private he begged Domitian to reciprocate his love. Some said that Domitian's hostility was based on a long-ago affair Titus had with Domitian's wife Domitia. She, however, always insisted that there was no such affair, and people felt that she would not have denied it if it had occurred, since in general she liked to boast of her scandalous conquests. In any case, Domitian needed no provocation, for he later revealed a savage and intemperate character.

Titus died while traveling in the Sabine territory—apparently of a fever. However, Domitian is suspected of complicity in his death. He is said to have ordered Titus to be packed into a chest filled

---

[5] Dio, book 66, chapter 19, Loeb translation by Earnest Cary (1925, vol. VIII).
[6] Book 66, chapter 18.

with snow, saying it would help the fever—but really intending to do him in.[7] Dying, Titus remarked that there was only one act in his entire life for which he was sorry.[8] Some thought this a reference to the Domitia story. Others, including Dio, thought he meant not doing something to restrain his brother—and, in addition to his personal peril, thereby turning Rome over to a man who would prove a disastrous ruler.

Mozart's opera is a mixture of history and utter fiction. Titus's generosity and restraint are historical, as is his relief work after the eruption of Vesuvius, a central part of Act I.[9] The affair with Berenice and her repudiation, mentioned early on, is also historical. And the conspiracy of Sesto is at least suggested by the tale of the two unnamed conspirators whom Tito (for we must use that name in dealing with the opera) treats mercifully. However, the main lines of the plot are fictional. Vitellius, who was emperor for a brief few months prior to Vespasian's ascent to the throne, did have a daughter—but nothing is known of her, and there is certainly no evidence that Tito considered marrying her. Indeed, there is no evidence that he considered marrying anyone after ascending the throne.

As for Sesto, he appears to be utterly fictional. What we know about Tito suggests that he very much enjoyed sex with men, and in the Roman world it would not be considered inappropriate for a man of good class. If the younger man were also of good class, such an affair would be approved only during the period after he grew tall and before the complete adulthood marked by the full growth of his beard. So Sesto, were he a real young Roman, would likely have been Tito's lover at one time, and the "primo amor" to which he alludes would have been both mentorship and erotic involvement. Like most such young men, Sesto would now be moving on

---

[7] See Dio 66, chapter 26.
[8] Ibid.
[9] See Dio 66, chapters 21–22.

toward marriage. Since, however, Sesto is an eighteenth-century fiction, we can hardly say with confidence what relationship is meant to be depicted in the libretto. Surely it is a strong love of some sort, but we cannot go further.

At this point, although it is interesting to compare the libretto to the historical sources, we had better approach the opera on its own, and see what these characters do as fictional characters. Antiquity has something more to offer us, however: for thinking about the classical tradition of mercy does help us understand what we shall find.

Roman Mercy

What is mercy (Ital. *clemenza*, Lat. *clementia*) in the Greco-Roman tradition? The canonical work is *On Mercy* (*De Clementia*) by the Roman Stoic philosopher Seneca (4 BCE–69 CE), though key points are also made in his *De Ira* (*On Anger*). Seneca was no mere ivory-tower academic: he was himself a ruler, serving as regent of the Roman Empire for five years (along with a colleague, the Pretorian prefect Burrus) during the youth of the emperor Nero (who later ordered his death). This period was later famous as a time of good governance and called honorifically the *quinquennium Neronis* (the five-year regency of Nero). The *De Clementia* was written during this period, probably in 55 or 56. He addresses this work to Nero as a piece of advice on how to govern well.[10]

At this early time, Seneca seems to have had unjustified optimism about Nero's moral and intellectual qualities. His odd satire *Apocolocyntosis Divi Claudi* (*The Pumpkinification of Claudius the*

---

[10] I have discussed Seneca's ideas about mercy earlier in "Equity and Mercy," *Philosophy and Public Affairs* 22 (1993, pp. 83–125), and a revised version in my book *Sex and Social Justice* (1999, pp. 134–83). But I have in significant ways altered my view: I did not recognize there the two traditions I describe here, but focused only on the Greco-Roman one.

God), written shortly after the death of the emperor Claudius in 54 CE, includes a lengthy poem of praise to Nero, the new emperor, that at least seems to be utterly sincere.[11]

In *De Clementia*, Seneca defines mercy as "An inclination of the mind toward leniency in exacting punishment." Mercy, then, is an attribute of the good judge. It is not the same thing as compassion (Lat. *misericordia*, Ital. *pietà*), although, as we'll see, the opera traces a close and fascinating connection between the two concepts. Mercy is a mental inclination but not necessarily an emotion; compassion is an emotional reaction to the plight of another person. This difference means that mercy is compatible with Stoic refusal of emotions and the high valuation of life's accidents that they display, whereas in compassion, allowing oneself to get upset at the person's plight, one shares that person's high valuation of the significance of the chance events that caused the plight.

Mercy recognizes that the person is at fault: it belongs, so to speak, at the penalty phase of a trial, after conviction. Compassion, by contrast, need have nothing at all to do with fault: indeed, as typically understood, it recognizes a large role for uncontrolled events in getting people into the bad situation that inspires the painful emotion.[12] Sometimes the people for whom we have compassion are guiltless, like those poor people who lost all their property in the eruption of Vesuvius. Sometimes they did something bad, but with mitigating circumstances: they didn't know what they were doing, or they were overwhelmed by a situation that put tremendous pressure upon them. In such cases our two concepts,

---

[11] I translated the *Apocolocyntosis*, with a lengthy introduction and copious notes, for the University of Chicago Press Seneca series, edited by Elizabeth Asmis, Shadi Bartsch, and Martha C. Nussbaum, in the volume titled *Seneca: Anger, Mercy, Revenge* (2010). See also my "Stoic Laughter: A Reading of Seneca's *Apocolocyntosis*," in *Seneca and the Self*, ed. Shadi Bartsch and David Wray (2009, pp. 84–112).

[12] See my *The Therapy of Desire* (1994, ch. 10). For more extensive discussions of compassion's structure, see Nussbaum, *Upheavals of Thought: The Intelligence of Emotions* (2001, chs. 6–8) (ch. 8 also includes a discussion of mercy), and Nussbaum, *Political Emotions* (2013, chs. 6, 9, 11).

compassion and mercy, draw close. But there is one further link necessary to connect them: the sympathetic imagination.

Let us, however, step back. For we cannot move forward until we recognize that there are actually two different modern conceptions of mercy, with very different consequences for the understanding of both mercy and compassion.[13] Seneca's view is opposed, it turns out, to a view that has considerable influence in the Judeo-Christian tradition. And yet it is itself so influential that it has strongly influenced that tradition in its own way.

When we think of mercy, at least in Anglophone nations, we are likely to think, first, of this famous speech from Shakespeare's *The Merchant of Venice*:

> The quality of mercy is not strain'd,
> It droppeth as the gentle rain from heaven
> Upon the place beneath: it is twice blest;
> It blesseth him that gives and him that takes:
> 'Tis mightiest in the mightiest: it becomes
> The throned monarch better than his crown;
> . . . .
> But mercy is above this sceptred sway;
> It is enthroned in the hearts of kings,
> It is an attribute to God himself;
> And earthly power doth then show likest God's
> When mercy seasons justice.

This is what we might call monarchical mercy, the free gift of an all-powerful ruler to those way down below. It is modeled on the mercy of an omnipotent and fault-free God, and its starting point is a huge gulf: between God and mortals, perfection and guilt, the (godlike) king and mere erring mortals. The monarch can bestow mercy not because of his recognition of common humanity, but

---

[13] See also my *Anger and Forgiveness* (2016a, ch.6).

because of his secure knowledge of permanent difference and hierarchy. Nor does monarchical mercy require any effort of sympathy or imagination: for all of mercy's objects are alike low, base, and sinful, so imagining the heart of another will show us no particular reasons for mitigation and would thus be a waste of time. It is notorious that Portia makes absolutely no effort to imagine what a Jew in Venice might feel, what experiences of stigma and hatred might have led to his obdurate insistence on his bond.

Since the opera's Tito is a monarch, we might hastily suppose that his mercy is of this monarchical sort. And since the origins of this concept of mercy are Judeo-Christian, and since Mozart and his librettist are operating within a Judeo-Christian universe, that concept of mercy is surely available to him. Before concluding anything, however, we need to realize that the Greco-Roman concept of mercy, the sort of mercy historically imputed to Titus, is significantly different. This concept of mercy is the subject of a long philosophical tradition that includes not only Greco-Roman authors but many moderns influenced by them—including Shakespeare himself, in *Measure for Measure*: Thus, Isabella asks Angelo to have mercy on her brother by asking him to scrutinize his own heart and see whether he does not find similar desires there. There is no suggestion that as ruler he is infallible or above others; indeed, just the opposite. He is assumed to be human and similar. As we'll see, this is the Senecan conception. It is fully alive in the eighteenth century, and a fitting candidate, as well, for depiction in Mozart's Roman opera. Indeed, I think we'll soon see that it is this conception, and not the monarchical conception, that figures in the opera.

Greco-Roman mercy begins from a simple insight: there are many obstacles to acting well. Thus, when people do bad things, it is sometimes fully their own fault, but often we want to say that they have been tripped up by the circumstances and pressures of human life. Thus, close inspection of particular circumstances often leads to a downward deviation in assessing punishment.

Already in classical Greek tragedy, motive and intention—what the criminal law calls *mens rea*—are recognized as relevant to criminal convictions. Thus, a morality based upon pollution, according to which a person utterly innocent of bad motives could bear blood guilt, was rejected. If they didn't intend the bad deed, they are innocent: so people can't inherit guilt from a parent or otherwise be polluted without a wrongful act. And even when an act appears wrongful, we need to ask about the state of mind in which it is done. Oedipus—who, in the ancient understanding, killed an aggressor in self-defense without realizing that the victim was his father, indeed after having made the most elaborate efforts to avoid proximity to his father—is regarded as trapped by life and not personally culpable, since, as he insists in the *Oedipus at Colonus*, his act was "non-voluntary."[14]

The new interest in *mens rea* gave rise to a picture of the good judge as the one who can imagine the particular circumstances in which a criminal defendant acted. Aristotle concludes that particularism or "equity" is essential to the justice of such a judge, and that a sympathetic attitude to "human things" is essential for equity. Recognizing the burden that human life imposes on action, the equitable judge is inclined not to be "zealous for strict judgment in the direction of the worse," but to prefer merciful mitigation.[15]

Greco-Roman mercy is not monarchical, but egalitarian: it says that we are all in it together, we understand human life because we are in its midst and burdened by its difficulties. Nobody is secure, and the judge no more than the offender.

We are not all the way to a doctrine of mercy: for Aristotle simply recommends asking whether offenders acted fully intentionally; if they did, no mitigation is recommended. The Roman Stoics and Seneca take things one step further. In *On Mercy* and *On Anger*,

---

[14] *Akôn*, 987.
[15] See *EN* 1137 34-1138a3, *Rhetoric* 1374b2-10, further discussed in my "Equity and Mercy" (1999).

Seneca, after defining mercy, insists that "it is a fault to punish a fault in full" (*Clem.* II.7). This is true, he says, even if the fault is fully intentional—because people form bad intentions under the great pressures of human life. In a crucial passage, Seneca says that the wise person is not surprised at the omnipresence of aggression and wrongdoing, "since he has examined thoroughly the circumstances of human life" (*Ir.* II.10). Circumstances, then, and not innate evil propensities, are at the origins of vice. And when a wise person looks at these circumstances clearly, he finds that they make it extremely difficult not to go wrong. The world into which human beings are born is a rough place, one that confronts them with obstacles of many types: scarce resources, competition, the aggression of others, the pressure of the passions. Being so vulnerable and needy, we are likely to go wrong in some way, being too grasping, or too angry, or too jealous, or too acquiescent to someone we love. And given the omnipresence of these errors, he now argues, if we look at the lives of others with unsympathetic hardness or self-complacency, then we will be punishing everyone all the time—ourselves too, if we are honest. But this retributive attitude, even when strict justice seems to demand it, is not without its consequences for the human spirit. We become hard, rigid, closed to others. His proposal: "Give a pardon to the human species" (*Ir.* II.10).

Senecan mercy includes the categories Aristotle already mapped out, but, as I've said, it extends to people who commit bad acts intentionally. For how did they get there? They learned the wrong values, or they fell in love with the wrong person, or they were terribly confused, or all of the above.[16] Such flaws are common to us all.

In *On Anger*, therefore, Seneca describes his practice of mercy as based on a new attitude to himself. Like everyone else, despite his long-term commitment to Stoicism, he gets a lot of things wrong,

---

[16] See the more extended discussion in "Equity and Mercy" (1999).

he admits, and every night, after dark, he examines himself to sort things out. He has been too upset at an insult, too angry at an incompetent employee, and so forth. At the end of all this, he tells himself: "See that you don't do this again: This time I pardon you" (*Ir.* III.36). Seeing his own faults helps him understand others; and learning not to be punitive to himself helps him learn how to be gentle to others.

Senecan mercy is built on sympathetic imagining: for when you look into the heart of the offender, you don't find pure evil, you find a human being. Human beings are often a terrible mess, but this tradition holds that none is fully and entirely bad: they are crossed up by life in some way. So you take note of the wrongdoing, you don't deny it, but you punish it less than you would have done if you had not seen into the human heart. Right away we think of Mozart: for he too portrays bad people (the Count, Elettra, even the Queen of the Night) as perverted by bad values, not as evil through and through.

That's how compassion is linked to mercy: through the imagination of the heart. Seeing a bad state of affairs, we might not know whether to have compassion for the offender or whether to wish him a horrible death. But seeing into the heart, we see a mixture of fortune and intention that makes us decide—often at least—that compassion is warranted by the nature of the person's predicament. (Even if we are orthodox Stoics and believe that all attachments to externals are unwise and should be avoided, we will also recognize that it is beyond the capacity of ordinary humans to attain this.) And that makes mercy in sentencing preferable to a rigid and merciless justice.

The orthodox Stoic believes that the sage does not feel the emotion of compassion: for such a person will have weaned him or herself successfully from the unwise attachments to externals that make chance events such large and significant blows, and the emotion of compassion requires the thought that the setback of the suffering person is large and serious. If the judge were really a sage, then, he or she might have mercy without compassion, thinking that the erring person is a "fool," that is, in the Stoic technical sense, someone who still has some wrong non-Stoic values. But since Stoics of Seneca's time believe that nobody living since the time of Chrysippus (third century BCE) has been a sage, they also recognize that erring with respect to values is ubiquitous, and that they themselves share the errors of the suffering person to at least some degree: so a space opens up in which mercy may be accompanied by compassion of a sort.

As for us, we should not accept the extreme Stoic view: we should say that at least some attachments to externals are wise and appropriate, for example, attachments to family and friends, and to the conditions of political activity. So we will then feel compassion in many cases, when people suffer damage with respect to these things in a way that is not entirely their fault. Nor, more pertinent to our topic, should we accept the extreme Stoic view that one's own moral agency is always immune to the blows of fortune: many cases of wrongdoing are cases in which moral agency was overwhelmed, or confused, or compromised by events or by customs beyond the person's control. If we feel that there is enough moral agency to blame the person for wrongdoing, we may yet recognize the role of circumstances sufficiently to feel the inclination to mercy of which Seneca speaks.

This Greco-Roman tradition is alive and well in the US tradition of the criminal law. At the penalty phase of a criminal trial, after guilt has been established, many jurisdictions in the United States give the defendant, by law, the opportunity to present a detailed life story in order to plead for mercy from the judge or jury. One state removed that opportunity from defendants in a range of cases, and the US Supreme Court held that they had violated a basic constitutional norm of "fundamental respect for humanity":

> A process that accords no significance to relevant facets of
> the character and record of the individual offender or the

circumstances of the particular offense excludes from consideration . . . the possibility of compassionate or mitigating factors stemming from the diverse frailties of humankind. It treats all persons convicted of a designated offense not as uniquely individual human beings, but as members of a faceless, undifferentiated mass to be subjected to the blind infliction of the penalty of death.[17]

Things don't always work this way in practice, for life histories soon become formulaic, and the likelihood that the narrative has been manipulated by a clever lawyer makes people skeptical. Still, seeing into the heart is honored in principle as a norm of judicial conduct.[18]

Seeing the Heart: Tito, Sesto, and Vitellia

First, a brief summary of the plot, since this opera is less well known than the others I have discussed. Set in the year 79 (the year of the eruption of Vesuvius), the libretto depicts intrigues connected to Tito's wish to marry. He is the son of the emperor Vespasian, the last of the four emperors in the famous "year of the four emperors," 69. As such he has deposed and put to death his predecessor Vitellius (Vitellio). The libretto provides Vitellio with a fictional daughter, Vitellia, who naturally feels hostile to Tito, and begins a plot against

---

[17] *Woodson v. North Carolina*, 428 U.S. 280, 304 (1976). See "Equity and Mercy" for discussion of other pertinent cases (1999).

[18] There is a very interesting debate about whether, if we extend sympathy in this way to the defendant, we are bound by consistency to extend it to victims, admitting "victim impact" statements at the penalty phase. I argue against this notion in *Anger and Forgiveness*, the John Locke Lectures in Philosophy (2016a). Briefly: all the legally pertinent evidence about what the defendant did to the victim has already been presented at trial; the victim impact statement is usually an occasion for friends and family of the victim to whip up vindictive sentiment by talking about indirect impact on them. There are two problems with this: first, it treats victims unequally, privileging those who have friends and family. Second, empirical evidence shows that it distracts the jury, giving them people to bond with who are likely to be more like them than the defendant is, in class and race.

him, pressuring the young Sesto, who is in love with her, to help her achieve vengeance. Then, however, she discovers that Tito has sent away the Jewish princess Berenice, on grounds that a foreign woman is unsuitable as empress. Vitellia now changes course and wishes to marry Tito instead of killing him. Tito, however, has his eye on Servilia, who is in love with Sesto's friend Annio. Servilia tells Tito honestly about her love, though she says she will marry the emperor if he commands her. Tito refuses to come between the two lovers, and leaves Servilia free. Meanwhile, Vitellia, hearing that Servilia has been preferred to her (and ignorant of the dissolution of that relationship) burns with anger once again. She commands Sesto to assassinate Tito. Sesto is extremely reluctant, but in the important aria "Parto, parto" agrees to carry out her wish. He goes to the Capitol and sets it on fire, in the general confusion stabbing someone whom he takes to be Tito.

In Act 2 it becomes known that Tito is still alive. Vitellia tells Sesto not to confess that he stabbed someone (who turns out to have been an ally of Sesto's dressed in Tito's clothes). (The friend, fortunately, survived.) Sesto is arrested, tried, and convicted. Annio begs Tito to show mercy. Tito summons Sesto, who asks Tito to imagine the confused emotions that were assailing him—but he takes all the guilt on himself (in the important aria "Deh, per questo istante solo"). Tito signs the death warrant, but then, in anguish, tears it up. He says he would rather be known as too lenient than as too harsh. Meanwhile Vitellia is feeling guilty about being the cause of her lover's death, so she decides to give up hope of an imperial marriage and to tell Tito the truth: she initiated the plot. She enters just as he is pardoning all the conspirators—and Tito, though shocked, includes her in the general mercy-granting. All praise Tito, and he asks the gods to cut his life short should he ever stop putting the good of Rome first.

We do not have to study this opera very long in order to conclude that the sort of mercy that interests Mozart and his librettist is the Greco-Roman, and not the hierarchical, sort. Tito does not portray his mercy as given out of a secure knowledge of a supra-human status. Indeed, his monologues are filled with struggle. Like Seneca in his nightly self-examination, Tito is constantly examining his own heart, and criticizing himself for all sorts of inappropriate passions. He is also full of doubt, and really doesn't know what to do. He depicts his mercy not at all as a mandate handed down from on high to humble erring mere mortals, but, rather, as a long-standing personal commitment that he finds in his own heart.

As I mentioned, Mozart signals connections to Freemasonry in the Overture, and the connections are deepened throughout—albeit without explicit further reference, since the opera was written for Leopold's coronation, and he was no friend of the order. The Roman Empire looks like a safe space for the triumphant autocrat. And yet, by selecting a story of an autocrat who rules with such moderation, allowing the Senate to operate with quasi-democratic freedom (as the opera depicts the situation), and who refuses tributes to himself in favor of welfare programs for the poor, Mozart depicts an enlightened monarch in the spirit of Joseph II on his better days. Leopold could not and would not object, since the libretto had been set so often and was widely admired; and of course he would want to be seen as a Tito, not a Nero, on his festive day. Under cover of orthodoxy, then, Mozart can and does allude to the key commitments of his order.

The real drama, however, concerns the other two leading characters: Sesto, who betrays his friend Tito under pressure of Vitellia's intemperate jealousy, and Vitellia, who undergoes a remarkable and wonderful transformation, present more in the music than in the words.

We don't approach this pair in a vacuum, for we know that Mozart is quite obsessed with the damage done to human relations by the morality of honor and status, which causes people—perhaps males especially—to see all human matters as matters of who is above and who below, who has insulted whom, how the insulted can avenge the insult. I argued in chapter 1 that *The Marriage of Figaro* depicts a struggle between this masculine honor-culture—exemplified not only by the Count but by Figaro as well—and a very different culture of reciprocity, imagination, and love that finds its home, in that opera, only in the women's world. Cherubino is quite a different sort of man from all the men who surround him, because he has been brought up in the women's world of music, laughter, and love. While both the Count and Figaro find themselves unable to talk about love, but only about insult and domination, Cherubino talks about love—and the opera sides with him, indicating that a new world of harmony can come into being only on the basis of substantial changes in the feudal order of masculinity. We won't get cultures of equal respect unless we learn reciprocity first in our intimate relations. The end of that opera is a cautious first step toward a radical reinvention of those relations (chapter 1).

This cautious first step requires both males and females to look into the heart. When the Countess says "Yes" at the opera's end, she inaugurates a regime of mercy based on understanding of human fallibility. The Count, zealous for punishment, says "no, no, no." But she says: "I am nicer, and I say yes" (*Più docile io sono e dico di si*)—yes to the imperfection and fallibility in human affairs which might be the object of hatred, but which might also be embraced with love.

Idomeneo, similarly, shows a transformation of a superstitious culture of fear into one of loving reciprocity—through the reinvention of the sentiments of leadership. A reciprocal and equal loving couple become the new model of rule.

Sesto is, we might say, Cherubino grown up and thrown into the middle of the real world—without any of Idamante's experience in leadership or war. That tender mezzo voice has now entered a world where the only music is the "concerto of trombones, of explosions, of cannons" for which Figaro prepared Cherubino[19]—and yet he is still singing in the same loving tones. What will become of

---

[19] Those words are from Figaro's aria "Non più andrai."

him there? What will become of tenderness and the wish for reciprocity, when greeted with the harsh reality of a violent and aggressive honor culture? At first, utter confusion. The diseased values in this case take the shape of a captivating woman, and he falls for her.[20] Vitellia, at first, is as utterly incapable of love as the Count in *Figaro*: all she wants is imperial status, and a man who can get it for her. Slighted by Tito, she seethes with a jealousy that has nothing to do with love. Worse still, she thinks of the young man who desperately loves her as a mere tool of her aim to establish her own superiority.

Sesto keeps trying to tell her that Tito is generous and kind and should not be harmed. But she has no interest in anything but her own status, and she goads him until he breaks. In the marvelous aria "Parto parto," the gentle young man, an utterly unsuitable assassin, tells her that he will go try to kill Tito only for her sake and for the sake of having a peaceful loving relationship with her in the future. "I'll go, I'll go," he says, with a moving combination of reluctance and determination. "But, my dearest, make peace with me again"—and Mozart makes this simple statement, "meco ritorna in pace," haunting, arcing upward in hope, and then gliding gently downward. His music, far more than his words, show that he is simply not going to fare well in the world of anger and revenge. The beautiful basset clarinet *obbligato* reminds us that we are dealing at all times with a loving heart, who is moved to action by heartfelt emotion but never loses sensitivity and the desire for peace.

Of course the assassination attempt is an utter disaster. A fire does break out, and for a while Sesto believes that Tito has died— but actually he hasn't been hurt at all. And now Sesto has to live with the fact that he has betrayed his friend, his values, and himself. As he stands before his fortunately still living friend Tito, he sees in

---

[20] It's worth noting that Cherubino already has an excellent model for male–female relations in his tender, adoring love for the Countess, not to mention his rather different sexual relationship with Barbarina. Sesto has lived, it seems, in an all-male culture that has not prepared him well for male–female relationships—so he makes a bad mistake.

him an utter rigidity that spells death. We recall that rigidity is the attitude of mind Seneca criticizes, because it involves a refusal of imagination, both to self and to another. In his utterly characteristic and utterly Senecan way of pleading for mercy, Sesto succeeds in reminding Tito of what reciprocity and love are all about—and also of the frailty in all human beings that both threatens love and makes it so beautiful when it rises above hate. (What would be beautiful about a love that had no struggle and no imperfection to contend with?)

The moral center of the opera, I contend, is thus Sesto's aria, "Deh, per questo istante solo" ("Ah, for just this one moment"). Sesto admits that he is a traitor and deserves to be regarded with horror. Still, he says, if you remember our earlier love, and look into my heart, you will not be so severe. Rigor and disgust kill the heart. Sympathetic understanding makes it come to life. Once again, the message is in the text up to a point, but the music deepens it: once again the long legato arcing phrases—and then, when we arrive at "Pur sareste men severo se vedessi questo cor" ("You would be less harsh if you could see this heart")—the delicate act of imagination, its pauses and hesitations, is depicted in the music, with its little pauses between small phrases. These little pauses for breath, or perhaps we might say suspensions of thought in mid-air, suggest that the breath of thought and humanity is being infused into Tito's harsh rigorism. Sesto has become himself again, and he reminds Tito of what love can look like—and sound like. If you would look into my heart you would see that I am a confused messed-up person who did a terrible thing under great pressure. And you would see in me the same person you used to love. Tito, of course, accepts the (musical more than verbal) invitation.

Sesto is right. We too often stand rigidly over the person who has done wrong, with a scary kind of firmness. But if we bend our thoughts just a little and try to see the world from their point of view, we will see that they are not demons, but full people capable of both good things and bad, and we will be more gentle with them.

But we have not finished with Mozart's surprises. Vitellia's emotional trajectory is underdetermined in the libretto. According to the libretto, she does at least come to a full appreciation of Sesto's unconditional and generous love, and she does decide to give up her hopes of power and glory to save him, by confessing to Tito that she has masterminded the conspiracy. Servilia has usefully reminded her that compassion has to be active: it's not enough to worry about Sesto without doing anything ("S'altro che lacrime"). So Vitellia decides to come forward and accuse herself. In the recitative "Ecco il punto" ("Now's the time") and the aria "Non più di fiori" she announces her decision. "No more will Hymen descend to weave delicate garlands."

However, think in how many ways that apparently sad text could be set. She is saying that she will not have the fancy wedding with Tito of which she has dreamed, and will not become the empress, but will face death to save Sesto. It would be most natural to set that text in a rather mournful or disappointed or at least conflicted way. After all, she is giving up everything that has defined her life hitherto. No more the glory and glamor of rule. Up to this point she has seen love only as ornament for her glory or an occasion for control. She might continue to struggle, hating the loss of power and glory that right action brings with it.

Mozart, however, doesn't see her that way. Vitellia sings the "no more wedding" text in soaring legato lines, in a gracious 3/8 rhythm and in the gentle key of F major—as if she has suddenly been relieved of a huge burden, as if it were actually a most wonderful, gracious, and gentle state of affairs not to have to care about power and status any longer, but to care only about love. And she announces firm resolve in the face of death, without fear or torment.

She has a moment of uncertainty and fear—"Unhappy, what will become of me?" (Indeed, several such moments, since the aria is a very long one.) But then she understands the essence of the matter so to speak: if someone could only see into her grief, there could actually be compassion. (*Chi vedesse il mio dolore, pur avria di me pietà.*) This new theme is introduced by the basset clarinet, which takes a very prominent part each time it recurs. And suddenly we realize that Vitellia is singing Sesto's music: the descending chromatic phrases of this section remind us rather forcefully of the ending of "Deh per questo istante solo," and are utterly unlike any music Vitellia has sung previously.[21] And the basset clarinet, Sesto's signature instrument, underlines the association. Empathetic imagination has shown her the way to the heart—of Sesto and his genuine and unconditional love.

And now, when the first theme ("Non più di fiori") returns, it soars up to F, as in the most happy triumph, because this strong and passionate woman has indeed triumphed—now, and not before—triumphed over her own jealousy and anger, into a future of reciprocity. Sesto's music sets the formerly haughty princess squarely on the terrain of love. After a few recapitulations of its various themes, the aria ends decisively, firmly, with the Sesto theme.

Clearly Mozart goes beyond the libretto here, expressing what we might call Mozartean ideas—of the triumph of love over narrow egoism and status-focused anger.

The opera takes up themes from the Greco-Roman mercy tradition. It is quasi-republican in its depiction of good leadership (thus honoring Seneca, who died in a conspiracy for republican freedom). But in its profound meditations on love, control, anger, gentleness, and the work of the imagination, these essential underpinnings of a durable republic, it is, surely, utterly Mozartean, and a most fitting final statement.

Mozart did bear his ills with a generous spirit, as Seneca advises. While he looked over his shoulder—death was upon him.

---

[21] I realized this because I learned both arias; having performed Vitellia's, I was then working on Sesto's (ultimately too low for my voice), and discovered the same vocal difficulties involved in singing the delicate chromatic lines. (Actually Vitellia's low A below middle C is too low for my voice as well, but one may hope to get by a single time.) Joan Sutherland's lowest recorded note was this one, according to internet sources, and in this aria. Needless to say, it is splendid.

PART II

5

Revenge and the Prison

Beethoven's *Fidelio*, Heggie's *Dead Man Walking*

> He tells me about how he organizes his cell. His life is lived twenty-three out of twenty-four hours a day in a space six feet wide and eight feet long. On one wall is a bunk, on the back wall a stainless steel toilet and washbasin, a stainless steel plate above the washbowl instead of a mirror. He keeps all of his stuff in a footlocker under his bunk. He uses the footlocker for weight lifting.
>
> —Sister Helen Prejean, *Dead Man Walking*, describing a letter from death row inmate Patrick Sonnier

Mozart's operas show people committing bad acts out of a desire for revenge. Usually, however, the revenge is merely threatened and not carried out. Sesto's plea moves Tito to mercy; Pamina is rescued from the schemes of the Queen and her servant Monostatos. Elettra (in *Idomeneo*) proves utterly impotent to take revenge on her enemies: she exhausts herself and collapses. Pascha Selim (in *Die Entführung aus dem Serail*) threatens Konstanze with "Martern aller Arten" ("tortures of all sorts"), giving the heroine an opportunity for a dazzling aria of defiance, but, in the end, he treats her generously, even allowing her to leave with her lover—who, he discovers, is the son of his greatest enemy—but, never mind, reason and mercy carry the day.

More generally, Mozart has distinct limits in understanding political evil. His paradigm of the *ancien régime* is the unfaithful Count in *Figaro*, a man not profoundly bad, but simply weak and confused. His allegedly tyrannical rulers, Pasha Selim and Emperor Tito, turn out to be arch-exemplars of moderation, mercy, and even respect for women. The Queen of the Night is closer to being villainous, but she is motivated by love of her daughter. The prison in *Entführung* is remarkably porous and gentle, giving the characters plenty of room to move around in the open and no reason to complain of hunger, thirst, or other unpleasant conditions. They even have (as usually and plausibly imagined) lovely clothes. In *The Magic Flute*, slavery exists, but it is but briefly glimpsed, and its brutality is not made evident.

Nor does revenge even *sound* bad: it remains firmly within the limits of good musical taste.[1] The arias of Elettra, Osmin (in *Entführung*), and the Queen are all musical utterances worthy of a stable personality—apart, perhaps, from a frenetic and slightly breathless quality in Elettra.

One might wonder whether these limits are the limits of opera itself, a genre that seeks to please its audiences, and whose audiences (and donors) are typically drawn from the leading classes of society. But such is not the case. From shortly after Mozart's time until the present day, operas have explored many ways in which the demand for revenge deforms human beings and their political institutions. Giacomo Puccini's *Tosca* (1899) contains a scene of political torture—offstage, but Cavaradossi's cries of agony are heard by the onstage characters (and the audience), causing Tosca to break down. Richard Strauss's *Elektra* (1909) delves into the inner world, showing how the desire for revenge, imagined as like a noose around the heroine's throat, impeding breath, distorts a person's entire life. Her music is famous, and scandalous, for its

---

[1] See Kivy (1999).

ugliness, as if parts of her humanity have been stifled—until, thoroughly suffocated, she collapses wordless at the opera's end. Leoš Janáček's *From the House of the Dead* (1930) depicts the cruelty and bleakness of a Siberian prison camp. Umberto Giordano's *Andrea Chenier* (1899) tells the true story of a poet guillotined during the Reign of Terror. And in another operatic account of the Terror, Francis Poulenc's *Dialogues des Carmelites* (1956), the nuns are guillotined at the end, one by one, as the completely unmusical sound of the blade (usually rendered by an amplified paper cutter, or even an actual guillotine) is heard above the orchestra. John Adams's *Dr. Atomic* (2005) depicts the invention and deployment of the atom bomb, ending with the first test at Los Alamos. There are many further examples that enrich our understanding of the inner and outer politics of revenge.

In this chapter I choose just two: the musical depiction of imprisonment and the hope for freedom in Beethoven's *Fidelio* (1814); and the depiction of a prison's death row and, at the end, of a convict's execution in Jake Heggie's *Dead Man Walking* (2000), an opera that, like Beethoven's, seeks to understand the roots of public dehumanization and cruelty, and also the capacity for love that gives human beings a dignity that makes every person more than their worst act.

The pairing of Beethoven with Heggie will raise some eyebrows. This book is not a musical ratings game, and I do not claim that Heggie is musically on a par with Beethoven. Such comparisons are irrelevant to my purpose. I select only operas with serious merit, but I also want to show opera as a living art form. I therefore have included two operas by living composers (Heggie and John Adams in chapter 8) that are both musically and dramatically impressive and also well established in the repertory. I pair Heggie with Beethoven only in the sense that Heggie has created a very effective musical-dramatic work that pursues the issues of *Fidelio* in our own troubled time.

Beethoven's *Fidelio*: Reaching for the Light

Fidelio, Beethoven's only opera, is an opera like no other. A drama of ideas that makes deeply moving theater out of abstractions, it never ceases to move audiences—especially, perhaps, in times of political tumult—with its vision of freedom secured through struggle, love, and hope. Originally titled *Leonore: or the Triumph of Conjugal Love*, it is ultimately based on a French libretto by Jean-Nicolas Bouilly, which had been set as an opera by three other composers before Beethoven;[2] it was prepared for his purposes by Joseph Sonnleithner. Its original premiere was in 1805, but revisions were made by Beethoven's friend Stephan von Breuning in 1806, shortening the opera from three to two acts. After further revisions to the libretto by Georg Friedrich Treitschke, along with many revisions to the musical score, the opera opened again in 1814.[3] Although the earlier versions exist and have their defenders, and are well worth listening to, it is almost always the 1814 version (by convention the only one called *Fidelio*[4]) that we hear today.[5]

Beethoven wrote four overtures for the opera. The one standardly played today is the brief overture known as the *Fidelio Overture.* The larger symphonic works known today as *Leonore no. 2* and *Leonore no. 3* are usually thought too lengthy for overture performance. However, Gustav Mahler, who greatly admired

---

[2] Bouilly based his libretto on a true story that took place during the Terror, but he revealed this only in his memoirs, published in 1836 (see Robinson 1996, p. 74), so all Beethoven would have known was that it was supposedly based on "historical fact." The first use of Bouilly's libretto was in Pierre Gaveaux's 1798 opera *Léonore, ou l'amour conjugal*; the second in Ferdinando Paer's *Leonora ossia L'amore conjugale*, 1804; both of these versions were known to Beethoven, and he had a copy of Paer's score. A third and slighter attempt was Simone Mayr's *L'amore conjugale*, 1805, which eliminates the political elements and turns the drama into a slender comedy. Nobody has suggested that Beethoven knew this work.

[3] See Robinson (1996).

[4] Beethoven always preferred *Leonore*, but his directors always overruled him in favor of *Fidelio*.

[5] For a detailed comparison of these versions, and also a discussion of the operas of Gaveaux and Paer, see Winton Dean, "Beethoven and Opera," in Robinson (1996, pp. 22–50). John Eliot Gardiner is a prominent defender of the 1805 version.

Leonore no. 3, conducted it between the end of the prison scene and the finale, and other conductors have sometimes followed this idea. Today the inclusion of the lengthy overture (about sixteen minutes) is generally considered either too long or too great a distraction from the drama's onward movement, or both, and so it is rarely performed in the middle of the opera, though symphony orchestras regularly program both that overture and no. 2. I like Mahler's idea, and surely *Fidelio* is a very short opera. The overture permits Beethoven to develop his musical material in a genuinely symphonic way, which opera typically does not allow. Its presence adds greatly to the weight of the work.

Beethoven found the whole business of opera difficult, particularly in light of his advancing deafness, which made teamwork a chore. Thus, though he never stopped looking for suitable opera libretti, he never completed another opera. The magnificent one he did complete must suffice. Let us turn, to its mysteries and complexities.

Fidelio poses three puzzles for its interpreters. The first, and the most hotly debated, is the relationship between its two acts, and whether the discontinuity we experience is a flaw or part of Beethoven's intention. The opera, it seems, begins as a romantic/domestic comedy and ends as a heroic drama of ideas. There is no doubt that the relationship between the acts gave Beethoven difficulty and was a major source of his revisions of 1814, which cut a lot of dialogue and slimmed down the psychology of the romantic comedy. Occasionally this has been offered as a reason to perform the 1805 or 1806 versions rather than the one we usually hear. The 1805 version is a worthy work in its own right and worth occasional performance. Usually, however, and I think rightly, the 1814 version is preferred. on grounds of its moving depiction of the struggle for freedom. This is the core of Beethoven, and he was never comfortable with the genre of domestic comedy, particularly when it involved erotic relationships. (He said that Mozart's *Don Giovanni* and even *The Marriage of Figaro* were ignoble works.) Although he was capable of idealistic passionate love, he frowned on eroticism, and if he had ever seen Mozart's scatological and sexually obscene letters he would have despised him completely.

The opera, however, is consistent in its discontinuities. What we ought to say, indeed, is that *Fidelio* is all about discontinuity: of mundane life as offering moments of breakthrough, in which ordinary people ascend to the sublime. Some of these moments are indeed in Act 2: Leonore's realization that she wants to help the prisoner, no matter who he is; the sacramental moment in which Rocco and Leonore offer the prisoner bread and wine; the famous trumpet call; the ecstatic duet; and the entirety of the finale, in which the entire people join in praising justice triumphant. But Act 1 already shows daily life as, so to speak, porous, offering moments of egress from the mundane world to some type of deeper or higher spirituality.

One of these is the four-part canon that begins with Marzelline's words, "Mir ist so wunderbar" ("I am struck with wonder"), in which the characters step aside from their daily activities into hushed reflections. We feel that something of a different nature is happening here: people are becoming thoughtful, even spiritual. Noting the parallel with the sacramental moment of Act 2, some interpreters hold, plausibly, that the Canon is also sacramental— its topic being marriage, a sacrament to which Beethoven attached great value.[6] The opera, after all, is about the triumph of marital love. In its moments of profound moral and spiritual commitment, daily life is penetrated by something more than daily. Another is Leonore's thrilling recitative and aria "Abscheulicher," with its ringing denunciation of political evil and its soaring vision of hope. This aria is surely the counterpart of Florestan's aria in Act 2, a fact that makes the alleged division between acts seem artificial and simplistic. Even evil is not merely domestic, but has a demonic intensity, in Pizzaro's thrilling revenge aria, that alerts us to

---

[6] See Joseph Kerman, "*Augenblicke* in *Fidelio*," in Robinson (1996, pp. 132–44).

the difficulty of the heroine's task, making us understand why real people so often think political revenge a worthy project.

Furthermore, the moral core of the entire work is in Act 1: the Prisoners' Chorus, which has no role in the plot and therefore must be there in order to express an idea of human freedom. We don't know who these prisoners are—whether they are all political prisoners like Florestan or whether many of them are common criminals. We do know that they are treated badly, ill nourished, not allowed fresh air and outdoor movement. As they feel the unaccustomed air on their faces and turn toward the sun, they sing, "Oh what joy! In the free air to breathe with ease! Only here, only here is life!" On the word "air" they move to their highest note, and the harmony shifts to what critic Paul Robinson rightly calls "an exalted subdominant—a move that becomes practically a harmonic code for the idea of freedom in the opera."[7] Beethoven impresses this phrase on each listener's mind. (And we can't help thinking about the connection between breath and singing: the conditions of opera itself involve a freedom that is all too often denied.) Next a single prisoner steps forward: "With trust we will build on God's help. Hope whispers gently to me: we shall be free, we shall find rest." Again the melodic line arcs upward, illustrating the idea of aspiration; and the word "free" occupies the highest note. All too soon, this brief window onto something wonderful begins to close: "Speak softly, restrain yourselves. We are observed by ears and eyes." The beauty of freedom is shown as much by the pathos of its denial as by the beauty of its momentary sighting. The discontinuity between freedom and the prison, between ordinary life and its hopeful transcendence, between going along as usual and moments of vertiginous ascent, is the real theme of *Fidelio*: doors opening and closing, surprising bursts of light.

There certainly are discontinuities in Act 1, between the mundane and a world of hope and aspiration: but even here we should

---

[7] Kerman (1996, p. 76).

not consider Beethoven's portrait of daily life trivial or dispensable. Beethoven's musical personality is famously double: the symphonies alternate between the grand (odd numbers) and the more relaxed and diurnal (even numbers): and yet nobody would say that (for example) the Sixth (Pastoral) Symphony is trivial, with its lovely depictions of relaxation in the countryside. Similarly, Marzelline's aria of longing for marriage, and even Rocco's wry aria about the need to make money, show Beethoven skillfully depicting aspects of the tapestry of daily life out of which high aspiration grows. In short, the first puzzle is really not a puzzle at all: it is Beethoven's portrait of our complex humanity.

Fidelio's second puzzle has been its politics: what idea of justice, or the just society, do its text and music embody? It is all so terribly abstract. Much has been written to little purpose about whether Beethoven liked or disliked the French Revolution. This is a pretty useless question, since one might easily love the Declaration of the Rights of Man and of the Citizen while detesting the Terror, and there were many stopping points along the way from the former to the latter—one of those being the point chosen by the leaders of the American Revolution, which of course was also part of Beethoven's mental context. What Beethoven puts into his opera is what he wanted us to know: that the arbitrary, lawless tyranny of some human beings over others is always wrong; that those who blow the whistle on crimes, as did Florestan, must be protected from the vengeance of those on whom they inform; that a prison system that deprives its inmates of fresh air and movement is horrible; and that the deliberate starvation of a prisoner is even more horrible. More generally, that human beings should be protected in their freedom to breathe and use their voices. (Enlightenment freedoms of expression, association, and of the press are essential supports for that idea.) In making Leonore the linchpin of the plot, the opera also insists strongly on the agency of ordinary people in bringing about political change. It thus has a democratic element.

Beyond this, the work is compatible—and is intended to be compatible—with many accounts of political authority, from constitutional monarchy to law-governed and not minority-oppressive democracy, and it is no surprise that it has been staged to great emotion at many different moments when the yoke of arbitrary power has been thrown off—notably at the reopening of many German opera houses after the defeat of the Nazis. One might object that *Fidelio* was also performed under the Nazi regime. Thomas Mann wrote from exile, "What obtuseness it took to listen to *Fidelio* in Himmler's Germany without covering one's face and fleeing the hall."[8] But conductor Wilhelm Furtwängler replied in a letter to Mann, "*Fidelio* never has been presented in the Germany of Himmler, only in a Germany raped by Himmler."[9] In other words, performing the opera was the ultimate anti-Nazi gesture, reminding everyone of the noblest values of German culture that the Nazis had suppressed. *Fidelio* is a call to conscience for audiences wherever it is performed, whether in pretty good or pretty horrible regimes.

The work's third puzzle is its sudden happy ending. The famous offstage trumpet call initiates an abrupt reversal in the fates of all the characters. Leonore has already foiled Pizzaro temporarily, but she succeeds only because of an event so unexpected, so almost random, that the characters would hardly be justified in relying on such an event for their future happiness. When Leonore and Florestan embrace in the duet "O namenlose Freude" ("Oh nameless joy"), their music is appropriately feverish, cascading upward with no secure basis, striving at the limits of their vocal range, without stable confidence, with words suggesting that words themselves have given out ("nameless" joy, "unnameable woes," "overlarge pleasure").

---

[8] Quoted in Robinson (1996, p. 158).
[9] Robinson (1996, p. 159).

The finale itself, it is true, sounds more sedate, in the confident key of C major. Everyone joins the final chorus. And the King's messenger seems to be all that could be wanted, although we have absolutely no idea who this king is or what his regime is like. Justice is apparently done, the villain punished, Florestan unchained.

And yet: what are we really to make of this fairy tale, this sudden exaltation? It is a moment, an *Augenblick*. And human lives do contain surprising moments of wonder and joy. But that very word, *Augenblick*, so often repeated in the opera (as Joseph Kerman reminds us in an insightful article) can't help reminding us that Pizzaro too has his *Augenblick*: his aria of sadistic revenge begins "Welch'ein Augenblick" ("What a moment"), and he repeats the word later, in the dungeon, when he is about to murder Florestan. When Leonore, asked to unchain Florestan, repeats the phrase, saying "O welch'ein Augenblick" ("What a moment"), what are we to make of this repetition?

Beethoven, like his audience, knew all too well that in real life politics is dizzyingly unstable. A promising beginning can all too quickly turn oppressive—as the early days of the French Revolution, with the Declaration of the Rights of Man and of the Citizen, was followed by the arbitrary cruelty of the Terror, and as the early days of Napoleon the liberal lawgiver, once the hero of Beethoven's Third Symphony, was followed by Napoleon the Emperor, at which point Beethoven is said to have withdrawn his dedication and titled the symphony simply "Eroica" with no real-life dedicatee. The play on the word *Augenblick* is surely a sign that we are meant to see the victory of the good as insecure and temporary, as in life it always must be.

At the end of the Bertolt Brecht/Kurt Weill *Threepenny Opera*, the hero is rescued by the King's order, delivered by a messenger on horseback—a satirical reference to *Fidelio*, I am certain— at which point Mrs. Peachum says, "Life would be so easy and peaceful, if King's messengers always came riding in." She means that we can't wait around for a happy deliverance: we must take the responsibility for freedom on ourselves. Surely Beethoven does not disagree.

A famous semi-staged version of the opera conducted by Daniel Barenboim in Chicago in May 1998 contained added narration written by Edward Said—spoken by Waltraut Meier, who played Leonore, as if Leonore is looking back from many years later, meditating on the fact that things did not work out as she wished.[10] This might initially seem like intrusive *Regietheater*, but in fact Said has written an excellent article on the opera arguing for just this sense of vulnerability and impermanence as built into its music,[11] and I believe he is right, though perhaps too pessimistic in the conclusion he suggests in his own summary, namely that "injustice continues to prevail"[12]—without qualification. Yes, power is unreliable, regimes are unreliable. We can't count on messengers who turn up at just the right moment. What we can nonetheless love and regard with awe is the struggle of courageous human beings who refuse the easy option of despair, who strive for the right against great odds, a struggle that is beautiful in itself, whether it ultimately prevails or not. Beethoven's music for Leonore and Florestan brilliantly depicts this difficult upward struggle.

What propels that struggle is hope, and *Fidelio* is opera's greatest musical depiction of that emotion. Hope is slippery. It does not track the probabilities: if your loved one is very ill, you can hope even when the situation is grave; you can also abandon hope when things are going somewhat better. Hope is a way of seeing a situation, as, so to speak, half-full rather than half-empty, and it is of crucial importance for action. People of hope will strive and struggle; without hope people will put up with the worst and do nothing. Immanuel Kant (1724–1804), a leading thinker of the Enlightenment and a philosopher whom Beethoven greatly admired, said that all human

---

[10] The speech is included in the materials with the Teldec recording.

[11] Said (1997, pp. 29–53).

[12] See "Chicago's *Fidelio*," in *Fidelio*, Barenboim, Daniel, cond. (1999).

beings had an obligation to cultivate hope in themselves, because we all ought to struggle for the good, and only hope can propel that struggle. That idea lies at the core of *Fidelio*.

The key arias of both Leonore and Florestan are musical embodiments of hope. They are different. Hers moves from denunciation of Pizzaro into a gentle meditative invocation of hope, the legato phrase arcing upward. Then, when hope arrives in response to her call, she is propelled into action, and the music becomes rapid, decisive, and heroic, her voice attempting the most difficult runs with seeming ease. In Florestan's case, his aria's meditative part is about his past, and he seems to have no path forward to action— and yet, suddenly, hope arrives in a fevered dream of Leonore, the vocal line leaping upward with unsteady and anxious thrusts. His hope, for the present, leads nowhere: he needs her actions to move himself forward.

The finale depicts justice arriving in response to the committed and courageous actions of good ordinary people. And it does not simply represent hope; it inspires it in its audiences, as unfailingly as its companion piece, Beethoven's Ninth Symphony. Asked by the King's messenger to free her husband from his chains, Leonore does so, exclaiming "O welch'ein Augenblick" ("What a moment")—quoting verbatim from Pizzaro but in the opposite moral—and musical—sense. At this point there is a naked oboe solo that arcs gently upward (another "exalted subdominant"), and then descends as if to touch the formerly imprisoned man. Gentle and serene, the melody was borrowed by Beethoven from his earlier never-performed cantata, written in 1790 to honor the death of the enlightened Emperor Joseph II, in which it is sung to the words, "Now mankind reaches toward the light." It has come to be called Beethoven's *Humanitätsmelodie*, "melody of Humanity."

Beethoven's ending is perilous and temporary—and, I believe, intended to be heard as such. And yet it tells us that the struggle for justice is not futile, that there are "moments"—openings for decent people to struggle for change, and sometimes for a while to succeed, propelled by hope and love. There are no solid reasons for hope, but hope is all we have to inspire us to fight for justice. And we must continue to fight because we can. We might call *Fidelio* Beethoven's—and our—*Humanitätsoper*, the opera of humanity, striving for the light.

Beethoven and Mozart are very different in their approaches to the idea of a "Republic of Love." Mozart attaches value to the erotic core of daily life—desire, love, jokes, craziness, all the things that made Beethoven spurn his works as base and immoral. While Beethoven does not repudiate all of daily life, he does dislike some parts of it that Mozart cherishes. I think that Mozart is right: we do need to love our bodies, their desires, and the craziness that people get up to—in order not to become cynical and despairing when lofty ideals don't always prevail. But Beethoven also brings an ingredient of aspirational spirituality, of morally earnest hope, that Mozart at least partly lacks, or achieves rarely (as at the end of *Idomeneo*).

Beethoven thus adds to humanity's arsenal of motives and ideas. It is difficult to imagine Putin's invasion of Ukraine being responded to by a performance of *The Marriage of Figaro*—at any rate the audience would have no idea what the connection was supposed to be. I think that there is one, lurking in the chapters of this book, but it's a long complicated somewhat Joycean story, going through a loving embrace of particular people in all their imperfection. Both Beethoven's Ninth Symphony and *Fidelio*, by contrast, clearly, powerfully, unequivocally gird us for the upward struggle, and it is perfectly clear that and how they underwrite earnest efforts against unjust aggression and in favor of justice. The fact that all this is achieved in music of the highest beauty and sublimity is what inspires a very special sort of hope.

Dead Man Walking: The Execution Chamber

Mozart and Beethoven imagine revenge as a personal project. Even if Don Pizzaro is somehow in charge of a prison, his vengeance is entirely personal; nor is there any ongoing state apparatus devoted to the maltreatment of prisoners. Modern societies have created political machines in which the state itself is the executioner—beginning already in Mozart's lifetime, with the guillotine, and continuing to the present day. The death penalty was controversial from its inception in Western thought, opposed already in antiquity by Plato and in Mozart's time by leading penologists Cesare Beccaria (1738–1794) and Jeremy Bentham (1748–1832). It remains controversial today, and many nations have ceased to use it.

Jake Heggie's 2000 opera *Dead Man Walking*, with libretto by Terrence McNally, is somewhat unusual in addressing explicitly, with no metaphorical cover-story, a current political issue in the composer's own country. As Heggie has often insisted and as we shall see, the opera is not a brief against the death penalty. It is concerned with foundational emotional and ethical questions, leaving it to the audience to make the connection between those issues and its graphic, indeed shocking, presentation of today's reality of death row incarceration and execution. Just before it ends, the audience is invited to join the rows of spectators and thus to become accomplices at an execution by lethal injection, which takes place, with considerable realism, during three and a half minutes of utter silence, save for the sound of the flatlining of the prisoner's EKG.[13]

---

[13] I have seen two productions, the one at Lyric Opera of Chicago in 2019, and the 2023 Metropolitan Opera production, which I saw on HD in a movie theater and later on my computer. Both were generally excellent. Ryan McKinny's performance as Joseph and Susan Graham's as Joseph's mother are common to the two, and both are superb. In Chicago Patricia Racette was somewhat lacking in emotional range as Sister Helen, whereas Joyce Di Donato, in New York, gave a performance of such subtlety and depth, as well as vocal excellence, that it must define the role for the future. The simpler Chicago production was, to me, somewhat more effective than Ivo van Hove's at the Met, with its excessive use of projections and its odd removal of prison bars and walls. But for those who want to see the opera, the Met HD version, easily available, will do just fine.

The opera's deeper investigation of motives and emotions is highly relevant to, but does not fully determine, our response to this harrowing scene.

Over the years, the death penalty has been justified in two different ways. The first justification, that it deters others from committing serious crimes, was criticized already by Bentham and Beccaria, and by now empirical studies contrasting jurisdictions with it and similar jurisdictions without it have shown that in fact the death penalty does not deter. Obviously enough, it deters the executed individual, but so does a life sentence without the possibility of parole. This point is taken as established in the opera and is not mentioned. Nor is it plausible to claim that the death penalty serves a second purpose of punishment, the offender's reform. The primary justification used these days is therefore retribution. Many people believe that in general the purpose of criminal law is retributive, and that the state is justified in taking vengeance on behalf of the victims of crime—and, often, on behalf of their grieving survivors. There are sophisticated philosophical forms of this idea that try to make retribution seem abstract and ethical.[14] But today's death penalty, and the views correctly characterized in the opera as allegedly justifying it, are far cruder: simply the familiar *lex talionis*, an eye for an eye, a life for a life. The prison guards actually recite these words, saying that the Bible demands retribution in kind. Similarly, the parents of the murdered teenagers feel justified in asking for the life of the man who took their children's lives, and the state agrees, even to the extent of inviting them to watch the execution. Even Joseph, about to die, says he hopes that his death will give them some relief, as if this is good and their right.

There are obvious flaws in this reasoning.[15] Taking the murderer's life evidently does nothing to restore the lost children. As Joseph's mother says, "Nothing can undo what's happened. Nothing." Like

[14] I discuss these in my *Anger and Forgiveness* (2016a, ch. 5).
[15] See ibid.

most forms of retributive fantasy (think of punitive divorce litigation) the idea of capital retribution typically makes survivors' lives
worse, encouraging bereaved people to obsess for years about the
convict's death rather than doing something productive to make
their lives and other lives better. One contrasting example of such a
productive "something" is the work of the group Mothers Against
Drunk Driving, whose members lobby for penalties that actually
do deter drunk driving (such as prompt suspensions of licenses
and sentences requiring the offender to blow into a breathalyzer
attached to the ignition before the car will start). The group's ac-
ronym is MADD, but in this case they have converted their retributive anger to a useful forward-looking purpose that saves lives,
thus sparing other parents the terrible agony they themselves have
experienced.

My own objection to the death penalty is, then, part of a very
general opposition to retributive punishment as based on an unreal
fantasy of proportionality and cosmic balance, and as leading to
unproductive actions. Taking a life does not balance out or restore
life. And bereaved survivors, despite being told again and again that
the murderer's execution will give them "relief" or "closure," rarely
have that happy experience—and even if they do, one might doubt
that such sadistic satisfactions deserved legal codification. Sister
Helen admits in the book that she made the mistake of ignoring
the parents' suffering, and she has since founded an organization,
SURVIVE, dedicated to helping families move into the future
rather than remaining stuck in the past; she has also played a significant role in the national organization Murder Victims' Families for
Reconciliation. Such work with victims' families is very important,
especially because American society is highly retributive and keeps
sending retributive messages their way.

The primary moral/political objections to the retributive death
penalty are, however, more specific. First and centrally, it can never
be the business of a decent state to replicate a terrible crime, in this
case taking a life with premeditation. This is Sister Helen Prejean's

primary argument in her excellent book *Dead Man Walking*, and, though made again and again for centuries, it has not been convincingly rebutted.[16] Even should one somehow get around that problem, which is prominently mentioned in the opera, there are others, which her book lays out with damning comprehensiveness. The death penalty is irrevocable, and by now, with DNA evidence, we know well that innocent people have been executed. (The opera brackets this issue by showing De Rocher's guilt clearly at the start.) Nor is the penalty fairly applied, because people who can afford a good lawyer never get the death penalty. The opera mentions this point briefly, showing that De Rocher's brother and co-murderer got a life sentence because he had a better lawyer—although the inadequacy of public defense law is emphasized far more in the book and film than in the opera. In effect the death penalty is for the poor (and often therefore for racial minorities). Another point the book makes is that people who kill Black victims rarely get the death penalty: the penalty typically selects for appealing victims whose lives society cherishes.[17] One might add that people with loving families who can testify at the sentencing hearing are favored over solitary victims. The opera dwells on the role of the victims' parents' advocacy in causing the rejection of Joseph's appeal to the Pardon Board.[18]

Nonetheless, twenty-seven states in the United States, plus American Samoa, still have the death penalty. Some have moratoria

---

[16] Prejean (1993).

[17] One distraction in the excellent Metropolitan Opera HD version of the opera is the casting, without any comment, of a Black couple as the parents of the murdered boy. Probably this is meant as color-blind casting, but it creates a question in the audience's mind. In the Louisiana of that time, a horror of mixed-race sex, especially of a Black man having sex with a white woman, was widespread, so we wonder whether the crime might have been in part a hate crime. That thought is utterly irrelevant to the libretto or the facts of the original Sonnier case.

[18] One non-starter is the idea that life imprisonment is very costly, and thus a waste of state resources. As Sister Helen shows in her book, the death penalty is far more expensive, given the need to go through numerous appeals and the huge expense of maintaining an execution chamber. She argues that it is a great diversion of public resources from ordinary crime-fighting activities.

on its use, or simply do not use it (Louisiana, the opera's setting, is now in this category), leaving only ten that actually use it. Much depends on the attitudes of the current governor of each state. There is also a federal death penalty, which is currently (2024) under a moratorium, but that depends on which party controls the presidency. (At the end of 2024, President Biden, preparing to leave office, commuted the sentences of all but three prisoners on federal death row to life imprisonment without the possibility of parole.[19]) The military also has a death penalty for certain offenses.

It is frequently said that the United States is the only "advanced democracy" with the death penalty, but the following countries, which I consider "advanced" democracies, have it: Japan, Taiwan, India, Indonesia, and Botswana. Most of these nations, however, circumscribe it narrowly and rarely practice it. Among non-democracies, China is the world's most active practitioner of the death penalty. (Russia has it on the books but has a moratorium currently.)

The opera wisely leaves the political/legal discussion of the death penalty to Sister Helen's book, where it is ably carried out with fierce advocacy and interwoven with the beautifully written account of her death row ministry as spiritual adviser to two specific convicts: Elmo Patrick Sonnier (executed April 5, 1984) and Robert Lee Willie (executed December 28, 1984). The opera is often said to follow the lead of the much-acclaimed 1995 movie based on the book and starring Susan Sarandon and Sean Penn. But this does Terrence McNally an injustice, because his libretto is much cleaner and also more compelling and profound than the film. The two have in common the condensation of the two stories into

---

[19] The three who are still under sentence of death are Dylan Roof, who murdered many people at a Black church in South Carolina; Robert Bowers, convicted of the Tree of Life Synagogue killings in Pittsburgh; and Dzhokhar Tsarnaev, the Boston Marathon bomber. The first and second committed hate crimes, the third a terrorist attack against Americans.

one, but the film focuses more on Robert Willie, whose outspoken Nazism and racism distract from the film's central issues and who seems to be manipulating Sister Helen rather than establishing a real relationship. Meanwhile Sarandon's Sister Helen comes across as girlish and inappropriately flirtatious, made up with shell-pink lips and Hollywood costumes that do not look like what even a relaxed order of nuns would permit. The convict character in the opera, Joseph De Rocher, is more like Sonnier, a serious and intermittently thoughtful man with no distracting hate politics; like Sonnier, he is a physically strong, sexy, and somewhat threatening individual who ultimately shows real inner depth. (The role is not easy to cast, since it requires the ability to do sixty pushups while singing very shortly thereafter. In my time baritone Ryan McKinny has virtually owned the role.)

As in Sonnier's case, Sister Helen's visits to the prison are initiated by a letter from De Rocher, which develops into a correspondence. Eventually he asks her to be his spiritual advisor up to his execution, and she agrees before even meeting him face to face. But at that point she must go to meet him, and in Act 1 she undertakes the long solitary drive to the prison, a place she has never visited, leaving the safe world of the convent behind.

The opera poses two questions, whose answers Heggie's music brilliantly braids together. First, why do basically decent people, bereaved survivors of crime, seek the death of the killer and create institutions that dehumanize people, denying their basic dignity and humanity? And second, what kind of people must we become, if we are to be able to have unconditional love for one another? The first question leads the opera to focus on the four parents, three of whom remain locked in the eye-for-an-eye mentality, while the fourth gradually opens himself to change. The second question leads the opera to cast the central narrative arc as a "journey" for Sister Helen, who needs to learn how to love the real world and Joseph in it; her journey toward emotional openness is paralleled by a corresponding journey made by Joseph, who gradually abandons his static fatalism, eventually becoming able to look into himself and to receive and give love.

The answers to both questions involve the idea of maternal love. The opera both begins and ends with Sister Helen singing *a cappella* the gospel song, "He will gather us around," a hymn depicting Christ as an embracing mother, just as the nuns spend their days as mothers to the children of the inner city, to whom they minister. The children soon enter and dance around Sister Helen and Sister Rose. Maternal love is musically and emotionally transparent, uncomplicated by the ills of the world—which have just been depicted in the prologue showing the murder, which uses a jarring, dissonant and rhythmically aggressive idiom that recurs later in the prison. The pure gospel motif recurs throughout the opera, along with soaring vocal lines that elaborate its basic idea. (Heggie began his career writing songs for [primarily] female singers, and he is a gifted melodist who writes beautifully for the female voice.) In the pardon board scene, Joseph's mother has a haunting aria about her love of her boy Joe, which develops the idea of an all-enfolding non-judgmental love. She pleads to the group, "Haven't we all suffered enough?"

What happens next, in the sextet "You don't know," one of the musical high points of the opera, is that the four bereaved parents, too, sing of their love of their children, their memories of times of caring—and their voices join with the voices of Joseph's mother and of Sister Helen's—all singing about parenthood as a great source of life and action. We feel, musically, the essential goodness of the parents' love and grief, and are inclined to sympathize with their demand. What we also see, however, is that this source, this spring of love, has been diverted and sullied: for the parents are calling on mother love for the purposes of hate. In effect, Heggie has constructed a musical demonstration of the Catholic idea (found with particular clarity in Dante) that all sins are forms of wrongly directed love.

This thread is picked up again in Act 2, when Owen, father of the murdered girl, tells Sister Helen that he is having doubts: "Nothing's gonna bring back my little girl. That's for certain. . . . I know my pain is about my child's death. Not his death." He and his wife have separated, and he is left with an unquenchable sadness, which he now sits with and accepts, rather than trying to convert it into retributive anger.

Musically, the opera is structured around a contrast between this maternal-love idiom, expressed in the Gospel song and in subsequent lyrical passages, and the cold idiom of the prison, with low instruments, low male voices (apart from the priest, sung by a tenor), and a general sense of menace and metallic inexorability. This aggressive, cold idiom refers back to the threatening music of the Prologue, depicting the crime—suggesting that the institutionalization of death expresses the same cruelty and brute indifference to human dignity that produced the original crimes.

But there is also a third musical idiom: that of popular rock music, in the teenage sex scene in the Prologue, where rock is playing on the car radio as the two teenagers prepare to make love; it recurs much later, when Joseph and Sister Helen acknowledge a shared love for Elvis and his music. This idiom is earthy and sexual, unlike the maternal-love music, but it is joyful and affirmative, unlike the idiom of the prison.

So far, we might be in vaguely Mozartean territory: society needs to learn from the women's world and adopt attitudes of unconditional love and forgiveness that derive from a mother's embrace of her child. We are all better than our worst acts. (For Mozart, of course, the women's world was erotic and playful more than maternal, and thus more in line with Heggie's eventual destination.) But if we accept maternal love as the opera's own norm, we would then have to conclude that Sister Helen is complete from the start and has no journey to make. And we have been given many indications that she does have a journey, one for which she is unprepared. Such a reading would also fail to make sense of the role in the opera of sensuous rock music.

I believe the opera's music conveys the idea that maternal love is beautiful, but insufficient when confronted with the complexities of the real world, with all of its dangers. Sister Helen has chosen a life that surrounds her with simplicity. She lives with other nuns with similar devotions; she ministers to children. She has deliberately shut herself off from the joyous but also sexually aggressive rock music of the Prologue, and from its moral dangers. For this reason she is utterly unprepared to meet and love a man for whom sex is a central part of life, and in whom sex lies very close to aggression. Her journey requires her to enter his world and to manage to love him.[20] Joseph spots this absence in her immediately, telling her of the joys of sex and deliberately shocking her—in earthy seductive music alluding to the idiom of the Prologue.

Joseph is also incomplete. He represents himself as a man of this world ("I believe in what's real"), but it becomes clear that he does not yet believe in the reality of maternal love and forgiveness. He will not permit his messed-up self to be seen and held by anybody, not even by himself.

Both characters, then, have a journey to make. Joseph has to accept his guilt and the possibility of being unconditionally loved. Sister Helen has to embrace not just innocence and maternal love of the innocent, but also sex, and even crime and guilt. Mothers have a difficult time seeing their children as sexual adults, and an even harder time seeing them as guilty of really bad acts. Joseph's mother keeps calling him Joe, even "little Joey" and talks about

---

[20] Throughout this chapter I speak of "love" more often than "forgiveness," a word the libretto often uses, because (see my *Anger and Forgiveness* [2016a]) institutionalized Christian forgiveness often requires a humiliating self-abasement before forgiveness can be granted. But Christ's forgiveness in the Gospels is (above all) unconditional, and it is really a freely given unconditional love. So is the love that Sister Helen ultimately expresses for Joseph. Even though she wants him to confess and repent *for his own sake*, that is not a precondition for her love, which precedes the confession and opens a way for it.

him as if he is still her little child. Sister Helen is unable at first to deal with the world outside the convent, and at the end of Act 1, when all the confusing influences of the convent-world and the prison-world surround her musically, in a powerful ensemble, she is overwhelmed, and faints. Heggie writes well for ensembles, and he exploits a possibility of opera that film and book lack, showing the conflicting internal pressures on Sister Helen's psyche.

Sister Helen's journey happens, musically, in two steps. Its first stage takes place in the duet between Sister Helen and Sister Rose at the start of Act 2, where the mother-love idiom, with its soaring soprano arcs, returns at a crucial juncture, as Sister Helen is finding herself unable to go to Joseph on Death Row just before his execution. Sister Rose asks her whether she has really forgiven him—meaning by this whether she can love him in the face of his guilt, love him unconditionally. Sister Helen says of course she has forgiven him, but Sister Rose doubts it. She reminds her that God can easily love anybody, but the human heart is less flexible. Sister Helen's job is to see Joseph as a mother sees her child. But since he is no child, but a sexually provocative and morally flawed adult man, who has committed a terrible crime, she must grow into a person who can love *that*, when she has been trying all her life to avoid both sex and aggression. She must work on the obduracy of her own heart. The duet, showing her what she needs to accomplish, prepares her for this task.

The second part of her journey, and a crucial turning point in the opera, is the scene in the prison right after that, where Joseph talks about the bright lights of Las Vegas and says she has probably never been there. Sister Helen says she actually has—her father took the kids there and they saw Elvis Presley, "the King." This is the first mention of her father, and it opens up a stream of memory of the delight of seeing the King. She admits that this was one of the most joyful moments of her life—even as Joseph says that he really wanted to *be* Elvis. Sister Helen's music changes, with sensuous bluesy rhythms and melodies, as she and Joseph list Elvis's song titles—ending with "Jailhouse Rock," at which they both laugh. The two have met in a shared space of worldly eroticism, as Helen lets out of hiding a sensuous earthy part of herself that "good girls" were supposed to suppress. Admitting her love for Elvis is admitting—above all, musically—to a complex humanity that she has not accessed in a long time. This is a necessary prelude to seeing Joseph/Elvis with love.

Only when Sister Helen opens herself to the possibility of loving Joseph as he is can she lead him to a true view of himself. Their shared bluesy music expresses the idea that movement and change, inspired by openness to the real world, are necessary prerequisites for love—of another or of oneself. Just as Christ asks us to view each person as dynamic, not frozen, as better than the person's worst act, so too the person who is capable of seeing another that way must also be open and dynamic within herself, not hiding in a fixed world of phobic piety that is a partial good but sorely incomplete. Here at last she attains this openness. And Joseph, feeling that he is genuinely seen, is eventually led by her to see himself as guilty but also as dynamic, capable of seeking and accepting forgiveness. (For similar reasons, Owen Hart's doubts and his openness to a new way of seeing the world brings him close to Sister Helen, while the other parents remain stuck.)

In the light of this scene, we now understand the musical idiom of the prison more fully. What seemed ominous about the prison music of Act 1 was its metallic rigidity, the sense it conveys of a world that boxes people into cells and refuses to look at them as people. This world is, in effect, the creation of the deformed love of these parents, and of so many other retributive bereaved families past and present. This love, instead of moving outward, has congealed over the decades into a fixed structure lacking the dynamism and openness that are essential to seeing others as human. Although officially Heggie takes no stand on the death penalty, he now develops further this idea of unyielding rigidity, showing how disturbing it is when a human being's life is in the balance. (Mozart made the same critique of conventional custom and religion at the end of *Idomeneo*.) The Guards, about to take Joseph out for execution, recite biblical commands as if they are unthinking puppets, mere instruments of a lifeless set of mechanical rules: "An eye for an eye. The Bible says it. The Bible tells us. A hand for a hand. The Bible demands it." The system demands a view of human beings as static, as fully defined by their one worst act. In short, it denies them their full humanity.

As midnight approaches, the Warden calls out (in nonmusical speech): "Dead Man Walking"—the conventional term alluding to a convict walking to his death. As the procession to the death chamber begins, everyone sings the Lord's Prayer—but it sounds growling and ominous, not like the message of Christ. It becomes increasingly discordant and confused. Sister Helen walks by Joseph, her hand on his shoulder (as the Warden has allowed), and reads from her Bible: "Do not be afraid. I have called you by your name. You are mine." Her Bible, unlike theirs, is loving and sees the particular. Helen and Joseph say their goodbyes, and each says "I love you" to the other.

At this point, music comes to a stop.

Joseph is strapped to the gurney—upright at first, as he apologizes to the parents. Then he is lowered to a flat position. "Proceed," says the Warden in nonmusical speech. "I love you," says Joseph looking at Sister Helen. Then come the 3.5 minutes of silence, as we, and the onstage spectators, see the drugs enter his system, one by one. We know that the first drug collapses his lungs, depriving him of breath. The second deprives him of movement. The third stops the heart.[21] The EKG flatlines, and we hear its beep.

Each key element of humanity has been assailed, one by one: breath, the carrier of expression, personality, and freedom;

---

[21] I follow Sister Helen's account, which corresponds in general outline to accounts of the process in news media, though there is variation depending on which drug is used in the first step. The actual time is much longer, since after the first step there has to be a pause of five minutes for a consciousness check.

movement, the dynamism that makes Joseph more than the sum of his acts; and, finally, life itself. Fittingly, this process has nothing at all to do with music, which is born of breath and is essentially dynamic. As in *Fidelio*, the prison has been defined as the enemy of breath and breathing humanity.

Music, however, has not been extinguished. Sister Helen walks to Joseph, touches his lifeless body, and begins to sing, softly, "He will gather us around." The same song as at the beginning, but transformed by the journey they both have traveled together, the women's world made Mozartean in its embrace of the body and this-worldly love. This combination of steadfast love with onward movement gives us a reason for this-worldly hope. There is a Republic of Love, because there is breath, even in the death chamber.

* * *

These two operas confront deformed people and institutions with what one might call radical hope: a hope not justified by any current facts, and not very likely to produce permanently just institutions, a hope that trusts in the possibilities of love within and between human beings. The operas are Mozartean, but they go beyond Mozart in confronting the worst and yet pursuing a struggle for the best. Perhaps *Dead Man Walking* is the more Mozartean, in its insistence that love of the body and its erotic desires is an essential part of complete love. Beethoven, however, seems the more hopeful, challenging audiences to resist the evils of their own time in this life and not simply by seeking inner emotional peace. But Sister Helen does not confine her efforts to Death Row. As the opera ends, she returns to her work with inner-city children. She will do that work better now, having gained knowledge of the world and of herself.

6

Liberty or the Inquisition?

Authority and Fear in Verdi's *Don Carlos*

> Teach that kingdoms rest on the foundation of the Catholic Faith; and that nothing is so deadly, so hastening to a fall, so exposed to all danger, (as that which exists) if, believing this alone to be sufficient for us that we receive free will at our birth, we seek nothing further from the Lord; that is, if forgetting our Creator we abjure his power that we may display our freedom.
>
> —Pope Pius IX, Encyclical *Quanta Cura* (to which the "Syllabus of Errors" is attached), 1864

The people of Spain throng the city square, cheering the King and Queen as they enter. The procession includes a group of monks leading arrested heretics; singing a dirge-like hymn as they march, they announce that this is a "day of wrath, of mourning, of terror." A group of deputies now present a petition for republican freedom and self-determination in Flanders—a cherished cause of Carlos, the King's son. The people initially cheer them on. When the King rejects their petition, Carlos challenges his father, drawing his sword. But Carlos is promptly disarmed by the King's trusted minister, Rodrigue, Marquis of Posa—at which point the crowd's support for republican liberty collapses, and they intervene no more—joining, instead, the musical jubilation as the heretics are burned at the stake. "Glory to God," they sing as the flames soar upward.

Republics sometimes die by conquest from without. But they also die by collapse from within. Unlike monarchies, which can maintain order simply through fear and obedience, republics need their people to be actively engaged, and this will not happen unless people love republican institutions and are willing to sacrifice—sometimes only their time, sometimes life itself—for the ideals that these institutions embody.

Can this headless form of government depend on people to do the job? Mozart suggests that it can—if people embrace the emotions of love and brotherhood that he so powerfully depicts. But he underestimates the strength of a powerful countervailing force: fear—especially the terror of damnation that makes people (and often even rulers) yield their autonomy to an authoritarian religion. A grave limitation in the optimistic Freemason Mozart is a failure to understand the power of religious authority, especially when linked to monarchical power. In *The Magic Flute*, the Queen of the Night, Freemasonry's enemy (probably representing the Catholic Church), is weak and ridiculous, albeit with some dazzling coloratura. Similarly, in *Idomeneo*, the cause of love wins the minute the voice from heaven speaks, with no further contest, because Idomeneo didn't really want to obey Neptune's command anyway, nor did his people want him to.

In the optimistic eighteenth century, many people imagined that Enlightenment values would gradually (but pretty quickly) win out over religious fear. Today we see that this has not happened. Every day, democracies are threatened by forces of repression and even terror that have religious/psychological origins. So those who seek the Republic of Love must grapple with the fear that saps strength from republican causes. This fear appears to be rooted in people's infantile neediness—which Mozart, again, underestimates. He typically imagines people as confident and mature in the face of oppression, energized and delighted by freedom. No room is made for the childlike need to be held and comforted that frequently leads people to seek an all-powerful parent, whether religious or secular. Later composers, seeing these issues more deeply, attempt to grapple with the problem of infantile dependency.

The *auto-da-fé* scene manifests, further, an ugly cousin of religious fear: religious hatred, understood here as a type of retributive anger targeting heretics and outsiders, seen as threats to the righteous. Mozart often underestimates the hydra-like power of revenge, which grows a new head as soon as one form is defeated. He believes that love, ally of freedom, reliably conquers the lust for revenge in people's hearts and minds—not seeing how often oppressors gain and maintain power through feeding and gratifying people's vindictive fantasies. Most successful autocrats portray themselves as defenders of their people against a variety of fear-inspiring real or (often) fictive enemies: heretics, immigrants, minorities, polluters of the nation. Religious autocrats have an especially easy time finding powerful motivators of this sort, since most religions portray themselves as locked in combat with forces of error and evil. The idea of getting power over enemies serves as an elixir to people who feel weak and needy, and religions are very good at depicting former foes suffering the tortures of the damned. Apropos of such religious texts, Nietzsche insightfully spoke of *ressentiment* as a type of retributive anger motivated by fear and weakness. He depicted this emotion as key to the cultural and political success of Christianity.

Chapter 5 studied the desire for revenge as a poison for both individuals and institutions. In *Don Carlos* (1867), Giuseppe Verdi (1813–1901) probes further, asking where this desire comes from, how it is linked to fear and neediness, and what gives it political power. The opera leads us to see that three anti-democratic factors in the personality—fear, neediness, and the lust for revenge—are interwoven and feed off of one another. Neediness feeds fear and retributive desires, which in turn render people weaker, more fearful and needier. As people sense their weakness increasing, their enemies loom larger, and their need to gain power over them becomes more urgent—and yet they cannot defeat their enemies on their own, since they are weak, but must entrust their fortunes to an autocrat, to a church, or both. Even the autocrat is human, and succumbs in the end to religious fear.

What is the solution to this problem, for those who love republican freedom? It seems straightforward: bring up people with mature independent personalities, capable of initiative and firmness. Verdi was such a personality if any there ever was, loving both life and freedom with all his heart and never succumbing to terror or vindictiveness despite living through the same difficulties that life brings to all human beings. And he had many allies. But he also saw that the alliance of determined mature individuals has powerful enemies and does not always carry the day. In *Don Carlos*, he probes these issues with neither optimism nor pessimism, but with realistic uncertainty, showing that even the opera's most appealing exemplar of enlightened maturity—Rodrigue, Marquis of Posa—is brought low by forces both outside and within himself.

Verdi's questions were much debated in the eighteenth century, when Friedrich Schiller (1759–1805) made them central to his drama *Don Carlos* (1787), and they were still debated when Verdi wrote his *Don Carlos*, basing its ideas not only on Schiller but also on his own experience and passionate involvement in Italian politics.

In grappling with these questions, opera has a potential advantage over straight drama. (Consider, in *Julius Caesar*, how hard it is even for Shakespeare to depict the key role of the people, as they waver in their loyalties.) In opera, the chorus can be a key actor, and can be divided, plural, wavering, ecstatic—whatever the composer needs. Verdi is opera's greatest master of choral writing. In *Don Carlos* he uses his mastery of choral composition to represent political emotions that Schiller has no way of depicting.

Verdi's Italian Republicanism

Verdi, among the composers this book considers, was the most politically involved in a practical way, a leading participant in the Italian Risorgimento, which sought to form a unified Republican Italy, dethroning neo-feudal power. Perpetually in trouble with the censors—as for example when *Un Ballo in Maschera* (*A Masked Ball*) was blocked because it represented the assassination of a king, albeit long ago and Swedish[1]—he displaced his real-life struggles onto many different times and places. Always, however, like Mozart, he explores republican aspirations with a keen eye for the emotions that propel or, in some cases, doom them. He understands brotherly love like nobody else, and understands, too, how the whole project of a Republic of Love is threatened continually by clerical authority and the human weaknesses on which it feeds. Because he was a leading political participant as well as an artist, his opera needs to be interpreted in the context of the political struggle of his time.

Verdi became involved in the Risorgimento early in his career. He was not a radical republican like (Giuseppe) Garibaldi and (Giuseppe) Mazzini, but more of a pragmatist like Cavour (Camillo Benso)—willing to accept a constitutional monarchy under Vittorio Emanuele II. Throughout his life he remained utterly devoted to Italian unification and self-determination—a gradual process that achieved substantial consolidation in 1861 and eventually culminated in the declaration, in 1871, of a united kingdom of Italy, free from both Austrian and papal domination.

---

[1] As is well known, Verdi ultimately transferred the action to colonial Boston and made the murdered man a British governor. The real-life assassination of Gustav III of Sweden in 1792 was the original subject; an intermediate rewrite in which the victim was a fictional Duke of Pomerania was also refused, leading Verdi to break his contract, with ensuing suit and countersuit. The revised opera eventually had its premiere in February 1859. (The original setting is often restored today.) So the opera was itself a masked performance—and in another respect as well, since the well-known homosexuality of Gustav III was suppressed and yet gestured at, in the character of the page Oscar, a rare "trouser role" in Verdi. See Hexter (2002).

From an early date, Verdi's operas allude to the liberation movement—or use charged language that was understood to allude to it. Because his music touched ordinary Italian people so deeply, he became identified with their hopes and fears. As conductor Riccardo Muti writes, "[H]is music was popular in the true sense of the term: it was a language that went straight to people's hearts, spreading its message."[2] Verdi's music was political not in spite of but because of his immense skill in portraying profound individual emotions and conflicts. That is how it got through to people and seemed to be about them, and this is still a source of its power for us today.

For this reason, many aspects of his operas were taken to have meaning for immersed political people whether or not Verdi planned things that way. Whatever disagreements may exist about the meaning of this or that reference, it is clear that throughout his works certain words, such as *patria* and *libertà*, and certain scenarios, particularly that of longing for one's *patria*, were sites of profound emotion, and were received by Italian audiences as expressing their more specific longing for an Italian nation of their own.[3] The most famous such passage, and one that even today never fails to stir varied audiences (who often applaud and demand an encore), is the chorus "Va pensiero" from *Nabucco* (1842), in which the exiled, enslaved Jews imagine their homeland:

> Va pensiero sull'ali dorate
> Va, ti posa sui clivi, sui colli
> Ove olezzano tepide e molli
> L'aure dolci del suolo natal! . . .
>
> O mia patria sì bella e perduta!
> O membranza sì cara e fatal! . . . etc.

---

[2] Muti (2022, p. 132).
[3] See Gossett (2007, ch. 11).

Go, thoughts, on golden wings,
Go, place yourself on your slopes, your hills,
Where the sweet breezes of our native land
Smell warm and gentle . . .

O homeland, so beautiful, and lost,
O memory so dear and fatal . . . etc.

That Verdi's audience could see their own plight in that of the Jews may seem strange, but in fact the Risorgimento supported full civil rights for Jews and an end to the ghetto, one of their major points of contention with papal authority. More generally, the ancient Jews struck audiences as like them: people with a deep affection for a native land that they long to inhabit as free people. The solemn beauty of the choral setting, marked to be sung in hushed tones, has always made this a high point of the opera.

There are similar moments in other operas: the chorus "Patria oppressa" in *Macbeth* (1847, sung by Scottish refugees in England, longing to return to their homeland, now dominated by the tyrant Macbeth); the recitative "O patria terra" from *Oberto* (1839), in which the Count, returning to his homeland after a long absence, proclaims his joy and love: "Oh patria terra, alfine io ti rivedo, terra sì cara e desiata" ("Oh fatherland, at last I see you again, land so beloved and longed-for").

One entire opera was clearly conceived to express and further stir such patriotic thoughts: *The Battle of Legnano* (*La Battaglia di Legnano*, 1849), composed shortly after the historic "Five Days" rebellion in Milan (March 1848) that left the republican cause in doubt, but made Verdi exhilarated and hopeful.[4] The librettist Cammarano proposed that they use the long-ago struggle of the Lombards against Frederick Barbarossa as an analogue of the struggle of their compatriots against the Austrians. By early 1849 a

---

[4] See, on all this, Phillips-Matz (1992, pp. 234–40).

nationalist rebellion in Rome was temporarily successful, and the Pope, who had previously been a reformer but had changed his views, was being held prisoner in the Vatican by the revolutionaries (though he later escaped). The sold-out premiere of the opera in Rome on January 27, 1849, was a celebratory event. Spectators pressed into the theater wearing revolutionary symbols on their hats and carrying tricolor flags.[5] The men's opening chorus declared, "Long live Italy! A sacred pact unites all its children!" (*Viva l'Italia! Sacro un patto tutti stringe i figli suoi!*). In the house a "veritable pandemonium" ensued.[6] And the triumphant final act aroused such emotion that the public demanded that the entire act be repeated. The final Chorus embodied the hopes of all: "Italia risorge vestita di gloria, invitta e regina qual'era sarà." ("Italy rises again, clothed in glory, unconquered and a queen she will be as she has been.) As if Verdi were the movement's prophet, a Roman republic was proclaimed on February 9, elections were held for a constituent assembly, and Mazzini, arriving in Rome in early March, was proclaimed Chief Minister.

The Risorgimento did not favor a competitive me-first type of nationalism. Instead, Mazzini, its chief theorist, held that passionate love of a *patria* was a kind of "fulcrum" on which one could eventually leverage sentiments of brotherhood among all human beings. Typically, he thought, people's imaginations are narrow, immured in selfish personal projects. Love of country calls the mind outward to noble ideals of freedom and self-determination, which should ultimately be realized for all peoples. Nor was love of country seen as in tension with individual freedom. As Bernard Williams writes: Verdi's was a liberal Romantic nationalism, "dedicated to ideals of individual as well as of national liberty." Although elsewhere in Europe nationalism took a "reactionary, medievalising, or paternalist" form, there was "not much room in

---

[5] Phillips-Matz (1992, p. 240).
[6] Ibid.

the Italian scene" for such views.[7] He and Mazzini should be classified with Romantic nationalists such as Herder and Abraham Lincoln, not with those who thought the goal ought to be for one's own nation to dominate others—or for the nation to deprive individuals of their freedom.[8]

Verdi's nationalism was always connected to a passionate anti-clericalism that he linked to his own personal sense of individual integrity and dignity. He wrote in 1870, "I cannot reconcile Parliament and the College of Cardinals, freedom of the press and Inquisition, the Civil Code and the Syllabus."[9]

By this time, Verdi was thoroughly identified with the revolutionary cause, and his music, with its powerful outreach to people of all sorts, served as a password for revolutionary ideals. As Phillips-Matz and others point out, at a time when signing a manifesto or circulating a pamphlet could be risky, whistling an air from a Verdi opera courted no risk, and yet could signal a person's politics to others. "Viva Verdi" was used as an acronymic code for Viva Vittorio Emanuele Re D'Italia (Vittorio Emanuele II being the liberal king who sought, and eventually headed, a constitutional monarchy).

In 1859, Verdi was elected as a member of the new provincial council, but he declined the office. In 1861, he was finally convinced to stand for office in the Chamber of Deputies, agreeing on the condition that he would be permitted to resign shortly after. He never enjoyed the role and was pleased when he was permitted to give it up. He remained political, however, to the bottom of his heart.

---

[7] Williams (1988a, p. 51).

[8] The topic of liberal Romantic nationalism in the nineteenth century in both Europe and the United States is studied with insight in James T. Kloppenberg, *Toward Democracy: The Struggle for Self-Rule in European and American Thought* (2016), especially ch. 14, which links Mazzini to Herder, Constant, Guizot, Wordsworth, and Lincoln.

[9] Letter quoted in B. Williams (1988a, pp. 52–53). By "Syllabus" he refers to Pius IX's "Syllabus of Errors," of which more below.

"Fire and Flames": The Birth of *Don Carlos*

"This opera was born in fire and flames," wrote Verdi to his French publisher.[10] And indeed its time was a dark one in Italian politics, one in which the future of republican self-government was on the line and the menacing hand of church authority felt everywhere.

Self-government had powerful enemies. Among the greatest was Pope Pius IX (1792–1878), who became pope in 1848, and was seventy-five years old when *Don Carlos* premiered. Initially sympathetic to the Risorgimento, he changed course after the revolution of 1848–1849 and adopted an extreme conservative and church-authoritarian posture. In 1864 he issued a "Syllabus of Errors," published as an addendum to his encyclical *Quantum Cura*, which was a no-holds-barred attack on all forms of liberalism, religious toleration, personal autonomy, and national self-determination. It still makes chilling reading. He reversed the religious toleration laws of the Roman Republic and reinstituted the Jewish ghetto, which he himself had previously opened. Pius IX also masterminded the notorious kidnapping of Edgardo Mortara, a boy taken by force from his Jewish home at the age of six, when a former servant said that she had baptized him during a time of illness. This kidnapping has been defended only recently by conservative legal scholar Adrian Vermeule of Harvard Law School, proponent of a new form of constitutional interpretation for the United States in which Catholic ideas play a central if somewhat veiled role.[11] So Pius IX is very much with us as we struggle with opponents of the very idea of self-rule.

Verdi clearly saw the Catholic Church as a, or even the, major foe of republican freedom, including his own freedom. In 1866 he wrote to his friend Giuseppe Piroli that if war broke out he would

---

[10] Letter to Léon Escudier, quoted in Phillips-Matz (1992, p. 514).

[11] Adrian Vermeule, *Common Good Constitutionalism* (2022). His approval of the Mortara kidnapping, energetically announced on (the former) Twitter in 2018, is highly controversial on the Catholic right.

be "the first target—not of the Germans but of the priests."[12] And war indeed threatened. His thoughts about Pius IX were at least one part of the inspiration for the chilling characterization of the Grand Inquisitor in *Don Carlos*.

It was at the beginning of this fraught pre-war period, in 1864, that Émile Perrin of the Paris Opéra approached Verdi about writing a new opera for them. Verdi was initially reluctant because of the notorious volatility of Paris audiences, from which he had suffered on a prior occasion,[13] but he was attracted both by the money and by Perrin's competent management. He agreed, and after considering several other ideas—including *King Lear*, which he rejected as lacking spectacle, and *Antony and Cleopatra*, for whose characters he felt little sympathy—he considered Perrin's scenario of Schiller's *Don Carlos*, conveyed to him through his French publisher Escudier, who visited Verdi's home in Sant'Agata. The scenario caught his imagination, and he agreed.[14] This marked the fourth time—after *Giovanna D'Arco* (1845), *I Masnadieri* (1847, from Schiller's *Die Räuber*), and *Luisa Miller* (1849)—that he had turned to the German poet.

Going to Paris, he worked closely with librettists Camille Du Locle and Joseph Méry (who, however, died in 1865). Verdi insisted on keeping two scenes from Schiller to which he was especially attached: the scene between Philippe and Rodrigue, with its passionate argument for freedom of speech and belief, and the pivotal scene between Philippe and the Grand Inquisitor. (The librettists complied in a masterfully compressed manner.) Verdi explicitly stipulated that the Inquisitor be "blind and very, very old." He also asked for additions, especially the *auto-da-fé* scene, whose central importance I have already underlined, but which could not be well

---

[12] Quoted in Phillips-Matz (1992, p. 512).
[13] The reception of *I Vespri Siciliani*, first presented in French in 1855, was very uneven.
[14] See letters quoted in Phillips-Matz (1992, pp. 499–500).

represented in the non-musical theater and took place offstage in the Schiller drama.

Meanwhile, war broke out: Prussia and Italy on one side, Austria and France on the other. Verdi returned briefly to his home in Italy, but prepared, reluctantly, to return to Paris, both because of his contractual obligations there and because he was worried that his home was right in the likely line of fire. He felt great guilt at leaving Italy at this time. He wrote to Piroli on June 9: "It is absolutely true that I am neither young enough nor strong enough to go to war; I am not good at giving advice; and I really am not good for anything. But [if not for his contractual commitments] I still would have stayed here, I would have tried hard, I would have done whatever small good I could, and I would have enjoyed it and suffered with my own people."[15] After his return to Paris, he tried to get out of his contract twice, and was refused; eventually he decided that he must stay in order to avoid costly litigation.

The war, as it turned out, was over quickly, and Italy was on the winning side, gaining control over Venice and Venetia under the Treaty of Vienna—thus the Austro-Prussian War is also known as the Third Italian War of Independence.

Rehearsals began, although Verdi said to Escudier he was "ashamed to keep myself busy with notes in these difficult and anguish-laden moments."[16] Once again, he tried to get out of his contract but was refused. His mood, briefly lightened by political events, darkened again with the death of his father, Carlo Verdi (b. 1785), in January 1867. Verdi had cared for him during a prior illness in 1852, and his death now, at a time when Verdi had chosen to be far away from Italy and was not able to be at his father's death bed, provoked a prolonged depression. This father–son relationship was quite different from the fraught relationship between Leopold Mozart and his son, which I discussed in chapter 3. Carlo had been

---

[15] Phillips-Matz (1992, p. 512).
[16] Phillips-Matz (1992, p. 514).

a humble innkeeper, who recognized his son's gifts and sacrificed a lot to give him a first-rate education, and Verdi remained devoted and grateful. Verdi was already feeling guilty about leaving Italy in her time of trouble in order to make money in France, and his father's death occasioned not only deep grief but also further guilt. To a friend back home he wrote, "Oh certainly certainly I would have wanted to close that old man's eyes, and it would have been a comfort for him and for me!"[17]

However, after avoiding rehearsals for a month, Verdi returned to work, preparing the opera for its much-delayed premiere, which took place on March 11, 1867. Because of the rigid Paris schedule (operas could start no earlier than 7 pm and must end no later than midnight because of the last train to the suburbs), he had to make last-minute cuts of fifteen minutes, including an opening scene in which Elisabeth is asked for help by suffering woodcutters, and a duet between Philippe and Carlos after the death of Rodrigue. (These scenes exist and are occasionally performed, but the wood-cutter scene is not very interesting musically and one needs a very strong reason to include it, given the opera's length.)

Throughout the opera's multinational history, Verdi made many changes and cuts, so there are many authentic versions, one of which—the five-act revision created for Modena in 1886—has become a favorite in today's opera houses. One thing Verdi never did, however, was write Italian words or compose for an Italian text. Others translated the French libretto into Italian, and he did not protest, but it is clear that the music is written for the French text and is best performed in that language. The primary reason that it was performed in Italian for much of the twentieth century in most opera houses was the preferences of singers for the Italian language. Any detailed comparison, however, will convince the comparer (singers included) that the Italian text often sits oddly with the emphases of the music. Verdi is second to nobody in his love for

---

[17] Phillips-Matz (1992, p. 518).

the Italian language; but in this case, having accepted a French commission and worked with two excellent French librettists, he created music of surpassing dramatic power for a French text.[18]

Verdi and Schiller

Fredrich Schiller (1759–1805) was one of the greatest artists and thinkers of the German Enlightenment. He was first and foremost a poetic dramatist, but his passion for philosophical thought was deep, and his dramas are typically full of long speeches in which characters articulate the reasons for their actions. Unlike Shakespeare and Goethe, who invite philosophical analysis but do not stop the action for explicit theorizing, Schiller tends to be a bit prolix and static—not only for modern audiences but even for Goethe, who objected to his tendentiousness. But Verdi was drawn to Schiller's passionate idealism, and had the good sense to make sure his libretti were sleek and well-pruned. *Don Carlos* (1787) had long been a beloved monument of Enlightenment humanism, and it gave Verdi a chance to approach themes that were dear to his heart, especially political self-determination and the need to curb the power of the Catholic Church.

The drama is set in Spain in 1567–1568, during the reign of Philip II and the dominance of the Inquisition. The historical events behind it involve a revolt in the Netherlands in 1568, over religious liberty, which eventually led to the creation of the (Protestant) Dutch Republic in 1581, though war with Spain continued until 1648, ending with the Treaty of Westphalia, which famously allowed each sovereign state to determine its own religion: *cuius regio, eius religio*. (This of course is far from a doctrine

---

[18] For an exhaustive account of the process of composition of these different versions, their assembly and reassembly into different performance texts, see Julian Budden's magisterial *The Operas of Verdi: Volume 3, from "Don Carlos" to "Falstaff"* (1981, p. 4–157).

of internal religious toleration, which took longer to attain.) The Dutch leader was the Protestant "William the Silent" (1533–1584), who was assassinated in 1584, though he does not figure at all in Schiller's drama.

The drama focuses on the King, his unhappy marriage to the much younger French princess Elisabeth of Valois, his guilt over his illicit affair with the Princess of Eboli, and his fraught relationships with his son Carlos and his advisor Rodrigue, Marquis of Posa. All the major characters are heavily fictionalized. Carlos in history was neither heroic nor in love with Elisabeth; he probably suffered from mental illness, which Schiller suppresses in order to romanticize him. The Marquis of Posa (Rodrigue) is a minor figure in history, whom Schiller elevates in order to have a spokesperson for his own Enlightenment views.[19]

To summarize the plot as Verdi's libretto presents it: Philippe has agreed to marry the much younger Elisabeth in order to settle a dispute between Spain and France. But before their marriage contract is known to her, she and Carlos meet and fall in love. Henceforth, separated by the marriage (and Elisabeth's refusal to enter into a guilty affair), they are unhappy. Philippe, meanwhile, has been having an affair with the Princess Eboli, although he is really in love with his wife and unhappy that she does not love him. (This aspect is emphasized by Verdi, and not so much by Schiller, who has different ideas about the King's affections, as we shall see.) Carlos's friend, the Marquis of Posa, Rodrigue, encourages him to console himself by working for a noble cause, the freedom of the Flemish people. He also encourages the King to permit Carlos to go to Flanders. This is the occasion of the great debate between the two about freedom of thought, of which more shortly. Rodrigue sees that the King needs a friend he can trust, and volunteers to be

---

[19] There are three spellings of the King's name: Philipp in Schiller's German, Philip in English histories of the period and English translations of Schiller, and Philippe in Verdi's French libretto. To avoid confusion I shall henceforth call him Philippe.

that friend, in the hope of making Philippe's rule more enlightened. Philippe reveals his unhappiness about his wife and his belief that she is having an affair with Carlos. Rodrigue insists that the two are innocent, and he offers to watch the Queen. The King warns Rodrigue to beware of the Grand Inquisitor.

Eboli, in love with Carlos, believes that he has come to meet her, but realizes that he is really in love with the Queen. Inflamed by jealousy, she threatens to go to the King—until she is dissuaded by Rodrigue.

A public ceremony for the burning of heretics is scheduled, and the King and Queen enter to preside. Carlos enters with a group of Flemish envoys who plead for their country's freedom. Although onlookers are initially sympathetic, the King is scornful and dismissive. Carlos, enraged, draws his sword against his father. The King asks for someone who will disarm the Prince, and when nobody else comes forward Rodrigue asks Carlos for his sword, and Carlos agrees. Carlos is arrested, and the King raises Rodrigue to the rank of Duke. The fire is kindled, the heretics are thrust into the flames, and a heavenly voice asks for peace for their souls. (This scene is drawn out with much spectacle.)

The King laments his loneliness and Elisabeth's lack of love. The Inquisitor then enters. Preying on the King's guilt and fear, he gives Philippe permission to kill Carlos, saying that even God allowed his son to be killed. Insisting that the Inquisition has the power to take down any king, he demands that Philippe turn over Rodrigue to the Inquisition to be killed. The King assents.

The Queen enters, upset at the theft of her jewel casket. Pointing to Carlos's picture there, the King accuses her of adultery, and she faints. As Posa and Eboli enter, he realizes his error and expresses regret. Left alone with the Queen, Eboli confesses her affair with the King, saying that she herself is guilty of what she accused the Queen of (falsely). Alone, she vows to enter a convent.

Rodrigue visits Carlos in prison, saying he has allowed himself to be incriminated to save his friend. An assassin from the Inquisition shoots him. The King arrives, frees Carlos, and mourns his friend's death. The people demand Carlos but are quickly cowed by the Inquisitors. In the confusion, Carlos escapes.

Elisabeth meets Carlos, who is about to leave for Flanders. She announces her plan to enter a convent. They vow to meet in Heaven. Then the King enters with the Inquisitor. Since Verdi's ending differs from Schiller's, I shall stop there, returning to the endings later.

Verdi's libretto is already complicated enough, but Schiller's play is stuffed with minor characters, courtiers and their intrigues. One difference between play and opera is the stripping away of these distracting extra characters and scenes in favor of an intense focus on the principals. Another is the element of choral expression added throughout, especially in the *auto-da-fé* scene, which is moved onstage. (Schiller does show Carlos drawing his sword against his father—but in Act 5 scene 4, Carlos is moved by Rodrigue's death, not the plea of the Flemish envoys.)

A crucial third difference is the opera's emphasis on the role of the Inquisitor. In Schiller the scene between the Inquisitor and the King happens in Act 5 (scene 10), after Rodrigue is already dead. In the opera it is right at the heart of the drama; it determines the fate of both Carlos and Rodrigue.

A further major difference lies in Philippe's loves and motivations. In Verdi, Philippe's passion is for his wife. The relationship between Philippe and Posa is one of trust and friendship. In Schiller, by contrast, his feelings for Elisabeth are cooler, and there is a strong homoerotic element in the Philippe–Posa relationship. (This is sometimes played up in productions of the opera, but Philippe's intense love of his wife, absent from Schiller, would have to remain.) In Schiller, when Philippe learns that Posa has apparently betrayed him to befriend Carlos (papers belonging to Carlos being found on him), he weeps—which he doesn't do for Elisabeth. (Thomas Mann puts the climax of Schiller's drama at this moment, in Act 4, scene 22, when the king is reported as weeping.) And later, when Posa dies at his hand, Philippe says, "I loved him, loved him a lot. He was my first love."[20]

Philosophically, the two works are similar in their emphasis on freedom and self-determination, although Schiller places the accent on freedom of thought and religious belief (*Gedankenfreiheit*), rather than nationhood and political self-rule as in Verdi. Still, the Enlightenment message of the Philippe–Posa scene attracted Verdi deeply, and he insisted on keeping its most famous lines in some form. In Schiller, Rodrigue says that the general principle of the entire universe, and God's in it, is freedom. The King insists that his absolute rule has created peace, but Rodrigue says, "The peace of a graveyard" (*la paix du cimitière*). And then he implores:

> Devote to your own people's bliss
> The kingly power, which has too long enriched
> The greatness of the throne alone. Restore
> The prostrate dignity of human nature,
> And let the subject be what he once was,
> The end and object of the monarch's care,
> Bound by no duty save a brother's love.
> And when mankind is to itself restored,
> Roused to a sense of its own innate worth
> When freedom's lofty virtues proudly flourish,
> Then, sire, when you have made your own wide realms
> The happiest in the world, then it may be your duty
> To subdue the universe.[21]

All this, in suitably condensed form, is in the admirably clear libretto. But there is one large difference. Schiller writes from a position of confidence: the Enlightenment has taken place, and we are

---

[20] My own translation from the German.

[21] Translation by R. D. Boylan, Project Gutenberg (Schiller [1787] 2004, Act 3 scene 10).

looking back at the errors of the past. Often characters, especially Rodrigue, talk of better times to come, and Schiller expects his audience to pat themselves on the back. Verdi removes these (rather naïve) expressions of self-satisfaction, as befits his own more pessimistic view of his times and of human beings.

Emotions, Personal and Political

Now let us return to the problem of republican politics and its musical depiction. What emotions must headless regimes based on brotherhood rely on, and what do they sound like? Schiller's drama contains many long speeches on this theme, but Verdi's opera, with its remarkable compression of ideas, gets to the heart of the issue. Carlos and Rodrigue share a passionate love of *liberté* that burns, they both say, like a flame in their hearts: "God, you sow in our souls a ray of the same fire, the same exalted love, the love of *liberté*."[22] But the joyful music, far more than the words, shows us what Verdi thinks and feels about the emotions motivating the creative love of a free nation. The two friends sing in close harmony, in the open key of C major. The rhythm is 4/4, so one could march to it, and yet it is light and buoyant, full of triplets, their voices expressing the happy emotions and the close cooperation and fraternal love that freedom inspires. So far, there seem no obstacles to freedom's progress.[23] The music of freedom moves outward with a joy untainted by either fear or retributive anger, seeking not pain for enemies but simply liberation from a painful yoke of repression. Right away we are drawn to this joy and want it to sustain itself. As Bernard Williams observes, this music "creates in the audience a feeling of liberation, a sense of committed and energetic individual

---

[22] My translation.
[23] See Budden (1981, p. 65): the passage "represents the world of straightforward loyalties in which Carlos seeks relief from the torments of conflict in which his love for Elisabeth has plunged him."

action, which is deeply invigorating." And he is speaking not of this passage alone, in which passionate action dedicated to liberty is explicitly discussed, but also of a thread running throughout the opera, and other Verdi operas as well. Indeed, this "experience is the basic, central response to Verdi's art. . . . Verdi's work sometimes directly expresses the values he believed in; in its entire conception it embodies them."[24]

If republics are to survive, however, they also need to ponder the emotions of individuals and their relationship to the public cause—a problem as old as the civil wars depicted in Greek tragedies[25] and one that opera, with its deep probing of the inner world, is also well equipped to depict. Sometimes personal relationships support the public cause, as in that early ecstatic scene of friendship, but often they are in tension with it. Later, when Rodrigue, doing Philippe's bidding in the *auto-da-fé* scene, asks Carlos to surrender his sword, drawn for the sake of that same republican cause, we hear the liberty theme recurring ironically in the background, reminding us that Rodrigue's new alliance and deep friendship with the king has forced him, at least temporarily, to betray the cause of freedom.[26] Verdi's music can in this way depict emotional conflict—even, in this instance, a conflict not fully acknowledged by Rodrigue himself.

Every major character in the opera save one faces a tragic conflict between personal love and political duties, and Verdi illuminates these conflicts with unparalleled subtlety, as Philippe (much more complicated and genuinely tragic than in Schiller) wavers between love of his wife and the needs of state, between guilt at his affair with Eboli and his public role, and between love of Rodrigue, the

---

[24] B. Williams (1988a, pp. 55–56).

[25] Not to mention the roughly contemporaneous ancient Indian (Sanskrit) epics *Mahabharata* and *Ramayana*.

[26] See Budden (1981, pp. 118–19), who quotes a letter from Verdi about the performance of this passage in which he says that after Rodrigue's request to Carlos to give him the sword "I would like a very long silence and when the clarinets take up the tune of the duet I would like a very soft, veiled sound—almost as if behind the scenes . . . ."

one man he trusts, and the Inquisitor's command to surrender him. Carlos, Rodrigue, Eboli, and Elisabeth all, similarly, grapple with conflicts between public duty and private passion and between multiple loves. Carlos is torn between his love and the cause of Flanders; Eboli between her frustrated and jealous love of Carlos and her loyalty to her Queen; the Queen between her public duty and her hidden love of Carlos. For all of them, these conflicts prove enervating, leading them to fail in their public roles—or, in the case of Carlos, to act recklessly, inspired by jealousy of his father, in a manner that does a disservice to the cause of Flanders. Elisabeth and Eboli are led by guilt and exhaustion into the cloister. The King is led by sexual guilt and lonely exhaustion to yield to the Inquisitor's demands, as we shall see. Rodrigue's motives are the most complex. Although his love of Carlos is real, and although he never abandons it in his heart, he forms a fatal alliance with Philippe. Initially Rodrigue sees the King's loneliness and his newfound openness toward Rodrigue as a great opportunity for the republican cause, and he therefore allows himself to be led into a bond of trust that will prove fatal for Carlos. In the end, he can only repent by giving his own life for his friend.

Three of the opera's most memorable emotional—and musical—moments are such moments of internal conflict. If Verdi is a master of choral writing, he also rivals Mozart in writing arias for solo voice. The aria from its inception was conceived as a vehicle for exploring contrasting and often conflicting emotional states. But the rigid form of the baroque *da capo* aria allowed just two states, with the first reasserting itself, albeit with some variations. Mozart used the aria far more flexibly and expressively, as did Verdi from the very beginning of his career, creating unforgettable moments of conflict and contrast—for example the sequence "Ah forsè lui" ("Ah, perhaps it is he") and "Sempre libera" ("Always free") in *La Traviata*, in which Violetta's defiant assertion of her freedom appears to displace her acknowledgment of love, but listeners are convinced that the two remain in conflict in her heart. By the time of *Don Carlos* and *Aida*, he uses the aria as a free-form monologue in which emotions and their dilemmas are exposed in all their confusion.

In *Don Carlos*, the three characters in question find no escape from their dilemmas, and all three slip into a despairing withdrawal from life itself. The first such scene of conflict is Philippe's scene and aria, "Elle ne m'aime pas . . . Je dormirai" ("She does not love me . . . I shall sleep"), on which I shall shortly focus. That scene ends with his imagination of his own death, which alone will put an end to turmoil. The second is Eboli's aria "O don fatal" ("Oh fatal gift"), in which she confesses that she has betrayed her Queen (in her affair with the King). It begins with a storm of passion, as she curses the beauty that led to her error. Then, in a gentler vein she professes her love for her queen, and vows to enter a convent. Only a quasi-death offers a solution. But she then thinks of Carlos and realizes that she alone has the power to save him from death—so her grim resolve leads to hope that someone she loves can be saved, if not she. The third is Elisabeth's fifth-act aria, "Toi qui sus le néant" ("You who knew the emptiness"), sung at the tomb of Charles V. Invoking the (supposedly) dead King, Elisabeth says that he understood the emptiness of all earthly attachments. But then the music shifts to a different, more lyrical register as she recalls her love of her homeland and her brief happiness with Carlos. Wishing Carlos success and happiness, she concludes that for her, nonetheless, there is no alternative to death. In all three cases the ravaged characters conclude that there is no exit from their moral and emotional torment—depicted in some of Verdi's most eloquent solo music as each alternates between passionate love of this world and an inability to find a way to live in it.

The only character who is free from conflict is the Inquisitor, who insists (in Schiller, though the same absence of human recognition is in the music Verdi writes for him) that people do not matter as individuals—"Mankind is numbers, Nothing but numbers"—and whose only goal is increasing the power of the

Inquisition. Verdi moves this scene up to the very center of the opera and gives it enormous emphasis. The scene begins with the King's lonely reflections about his wife's lack of love for him and his own advancing age, leading into the beautiful and profoundly sad aria in which he imagines his own death and burial: "I shall sleep in my royal mantle / when the last hour has struck for me, / I shall sleep in the stone vaults / of the Escurial."[27] The slow solemn rhythm suggests a funeral march. Philippe's despair is the underpinning, we now see, for his repudiation of individual liberty and his defense of absolutism. What Williams calls a "cloud of hopelessness"[28] has spread over his public concerns so that he can no longer understand the appeal of values such as personal agency, vigor, or self-assertion. This emptiness of soul is something new in Verdi, closely akin, as we shall see in chapter 9, to the sources of antiliberalism in Wagner. And Verdi's subtle portrait even suggests that authoritarian domination of others is a type of revenge monarchy takes upon happier and more independent souls. (Accordingly, the Inquisitor, who has the emptiest soul and is barely a person at all, is the most vindictive of rulers.)

The Inquisitor now enters—blind, led by a helper—to the accompaniment of a sinister snaky contrabassoon (the only time Verdi makes major use of this instrument). The following scene is virtually unique in opera: a ten-minute scene between two deep bassos, and an orchestral focus on deep winds and strings. The entire musical texture of the scene is expressive of the link Verdi is proposing between inner emptiness and susceptibility to tyranny (whether succumbing to it or imposing it on others). During its course, the Inquisitor, both blind and "very, very old," as Verdi specifies, wheedles, manipulates, threatens—and ultimately gets Philippe to agree in principle to put Carlos to death (saying that

---

[27] *Je dormirai dans mon manteau royal / Quand aura lui pour moi l'heure dernière, / Je dormirai sous les voûtes de pierre / Des caveaux de l'Escurial.*
[28] B. Williams (1988a, p. 55).

after all, God himself chose to allow his son to be killed). Next, and even more threatening to the King's fragile psyche, he gets him to turn over Rodrigue, who is blameless and whom the King loves, to the judgment of the Inquisition. In Schiller, Rodrigue has already been killed with the King's reluctant permission, because treasonous documents that really belong to Carlos are found on him, so the Inquisitor's discussion of Rodrigue is ex post. In Verdi, by contrast, it is a crucial moment of choice, ultimately of betrayal.

How does this happen? The Inquisitor first preys on Philippe's pride, saying that if he admits his need of Rodrigue then he is really one of the "innovators" (*novateurs*)—a republican who thinks there is no need of absolute monarchs. The Inquisitor then preys on fear: "Sire, if I were not here in this palace today, by the living God, tomorrow you yourself would be before us at the supreme tribunal." So far Philippe is not defeated: using the familiar "tu," he attacks the Inquisitor's "criminal pride" (*ton orgueil criminel*). The Inquisitor then says, "Why have you invoked the spirit of Samuel?"—an apparent reference to the biblical story of Saul consulting the witch of Endor. Accusing the King of destroying his life's work, he then prepares to depart.

It is then that Philippe yields, calling him back and asking for peace. The sinister character of the music convinces us that something profoundly threatening has been said, and that Philippe yields to this threat. But what has been said? Why the reference to Saul and the Witch of Endor? It seems to be a charge that Philippe has been consorting with demons, and especially with women who summon demons. Obscure though the remark is (no doubt deliberately so, since guilt is summoned more powerfully through insinuation than straightforward accusation), it seems to allude to Philippe's sexual immorality with Eboli. Sexual guilt has always been a potent device of subordination used by a religion bent on securing its own temporal authority, and perhaps by Catholic Christianity above all (as Verdi would know well, living, defiantly and with a lot of obstreperous public bullying, with Giuseppina

Strepponi outside of marriage from about 1847 to 1859—though once they did marry in 1859, that marriage lasted until her death in 1897, and Verdi never returned to the Church, despite many pleas from his pious wife).[29]

Philippe yields (as Verdi never yielded). He sues for peace, betraying both his son and his friend. "The pride of the King bends before the pride of the priest." We sense that he yields so easily because his life has lost meaning in his own eyes. It takes only a small weight of guilt to defeat a man already hollowed out within.

The scene shows how religion plays on guilt and despair to secure its own supremacy. More generally, it knows how to find the chink in any person's armor to secure fearful submission. Because the Inquisitor is not a full human being, he experiences neither guilt nor depression, though he understands all too well how to exploit both. (Empathy is not sufficient for compassion, without good will and decency.)

And what of the people, who have already, by this time in the opera, collaborated in the ghastly burning of heretics in the public square? Let us now return to that pivotal scene. It was inserted in part to give an occasion for spectacle. But Verdi resisted the suggestion of his librettists of a procession of the entire court, insisting that the focus must be on the cruelty of the Inquisition: "If you want some spectacle there's only one way of achieving it: a chorus of the Inquisition, a kind of judgment scene, but rapid and violent."[30]

At first, as the procession enters, the people joyfully proclaim the glory of Philip, while it is only the monks who say that it is a day "of anger, of mourning, of terror." Later in the scene, when the Flemish deputies make their plea, backed by the Queen and

---

[29] A brief first marriage was ended by his young wife's death. Right around the time of *Don Carlos*, Verdi was rumored to be having an affair with the singer Teresa Stolz, whom he evidently greatly admired, and who became his companion after Strepponi's much later death. But all discussions of a possible liaison are mere conjecture.

[30] Quoted in Andrew Porter, "Verdi's *Don Carlos*: An Introduction," in the materials accompanying the libretto in the Deutsche Grammophon recording (Orchestra and Chorus of the Teatro alla Scala, conducted by Claudio Abbado) (1983, pp. 33–43, at 36).

Carlos, the people even initially support their plea. And yet they are perfectly aware that this King's ceremony is being celebrated by the burning of (Protestant) heretics, and they appear to take this ghastly spectacle in their stride, even as the Flemish deputies rail against it, saying "God allows these crimes! God does not extinguish these flames." Nor do they persist in their support of the deputies: once they are arrested and Carlos is disarmed, that's that, and they cheerfully go over to the other side. As the flames light up the sky, Philippe and the monks sing "Glory to God," and the people join in: "Glory to God." Their weakness and fear produce a slide into retributive hatred. Since their efforts on behalf of the deputies have been futile, at least they can have the satisfaction of revenge.

In short: the people are labile and utterly unreliable. (Later they quickly back off from an abortive attempt to rescue Carlos.) Whether they have a strong antecedent desire for revenge on the Church's enemies is unclear. But they are ruled far more by fear and weakness than by the flame of liberty. They go along with the celebratory music of revenge and hatred, because they feel themselves impotent and do not love freedom enough for risky dissent.

What is special about religion? Political authority also evokes fear and groveling. It too preys on weakness to stir up retributive anger. But for Verdi at this time, religion has a special power to undermine republican projects, because of its ability to manipulate through fear of eternal damnation and through widespread guilt about sexuality. This may be a contingent fact, although certainly in our time, too, religion has been a powerful opponent of cherished freedoms over people's own bodies.

It is now time to look back to Mozart. In chapter 4 we saw Tito rejecting government through fear and retribution, in favor of a merciful and inclusive politics. He arrived at that destination through the participatory imagination, accepting Sesto's offer to "see this heart"—not just understanding what Sesto feels, but also seeing Sesto as a person worthy of concern, and as rather like himself. As in Seneca, so in Mozart: understanding the many obstacles to goodness makes the ruler lenient, remembering that he too is fallible. Why doesn't this happen in the Inquisitor scene? The Inquisitor, representative of the Church eternal, is committed, it seems, to being non-human and non-fallible—even though that very posture is a profound betrayal of Christ's teaching, since Christ was fully human and suffered fear and pain as a human. The Inquisitor, however, is determined to refuse himself all compassion with Philippe's suffering and to maintain a posture of rigid judgmental externality—because that's how the Church has ruled sinners for ages. He shows that one can manipulate through a kind of empathy—namely, understanding clearly how someone so placed thinks and feels—but without a sympathy that feels that the sinner might be oneself, and a self worth caring about. In that sense, empathy (seeing the other's perspective) is not sufficient for compassion.

The scene reminds one of the way the series of sermons about sexual sin terrorized the young Stephen Dedalus at the student retreat in *Portrait of the Artist as a Young Man*—in which normal adolescence is made to seem the blackest crime, dooming the soul for all eternity. Thinking of this comparison we see too, however, the role of the point of view of the artist in the work. Just as Joyce sets things up so that we already sympathize with Stephen and are outraged at the cruelty of the sermons, so too Verdi, omnipresent in his work, sets things up so that, unlike the Inquisitor, we take a Mozartean internal view of Philippe, and are outraged by the Inquisitor's cruel domination. Could there be an opera written from the point of view of the Inquisitor, seeing only what that mind sees? Perhaps, but it would be deeply repellant and off-putting as a work of art. However, unlike Mozart, Verdi allows us to see the Inquisitor as a character in his work and to appreciate his power over millions of Mozartean and Verdian people. He lets us see, then, that terror and retribution are not easily eliminated from our political lives, and can be kept at bay only by the most determined efforts of both politics and art.

Given its history, it is no surprise that *Don Carlos* contains trenchant and unforgettable depictions of religious imperialism and human weakness, as the crowd prefers religious terror to the call of liberty, and as Philippe surrenders Rodrigue to the Inquisitor out of personal guilt and fear. But, equally characteristic of its composer, it also contains sympathetic and even merciful depictions of human torment and frailty, in Philippe, Rodrigue, Eboli, and Elisabeth. Only the Inquisitor receives no mercy from Verdi's capacious humanism, because he is the only character unmoved by human love.

Schiller's play ends abruptly, as Philippe, turning Carlos over to the Inquisitor, says, "Cardinal, I have done my part. Now do yours." Verdi's ending is far more mysterious: A monk who may or may not be Charles V (who is supposed to have died years earlier) appears and apparently saves Carlos from the Inquisition—but only by drawing him into the monastery. This ending does incorporate some of the spectacle that Verdi so loved, but it has been found deeply unsatisfactory by many: Is it darker or less dark? What really becomes of Carlos and his cause? The audience is invited to ponder this puzzle. I myself find Verdi's invitation to ponder liberating rather than unsatisfactory.

In one way, Verdi's ending is darker than Schiller's: Schiller, as I noted, repeatedly signposts the Enlightenment to come, telling his audience that they can look back on these grim events from the position of victors in the struggle for republican freedom. In the opera, Carlos does make a desperate guess that the power of the Inquisition will be broken by God, but the murky ending undermines the authority of his prediction. Here, I think, Verdi sees more deeply than Schiller and is more in harmony with the uncertainties of Beethoven's *Fidelio*: The struggle for free speech and freedom of action is perpetual, and must be fought actively, energetically, without succumbing to personal fear or guilt, by every person who loves self-government, in every generation—as love of liberty contends with superstition and needy fear. Just as Leonore's triumph is uncertain, a challenge to the future rather than a stable reality, so too the ending of *Don Carlos* is as "dark" or "light" as people make it in their lives.

The opera, I said, is skeptical about freedom's future. But there is one aspect of it that gives us reason for optimism about the world, and republican projects in it—the personality of its creator, which suffuses the entire work with his zeal for liberty, his compassion, his unquenchable joy. "To the world, as to the nation he helped to found, he left an enduring legacy of music, charity, patriotism, honour, grace, and reason," concludes biographer Mary Jane Phillips-Matz. "He was and remains a mighty force for continuing good."[31]

---

[31] Phillips-Matz (1992, p. 766).

7

Internal Exiles

Oppression and Reconciliation in Britten and Janáček

Him who despises us, we'll destroy.
　　—The people of the Borough, in Britten's *Peter Grimes*

What does the world matter, if we are together?
　　　　　　　　　　—Laca, in Janáček's *Jenůfa*

Every known society contains "internal exiles." By this term I mean people who are nominally citizens or at least subject to the legal jurisdiction of a particular nation, but who are cut off from legal protection of their rights and from meaningful participation in the political community. They are oppressed by the community and alienated from it, without legitimate cause. Mozart's operas sometimes contain such characters, but typically portray them in a cartoonish and even offensive way: Osmin the Moorish eunuch in *Entführung*, the dark-skinned and enslaved Monostatos in *The Magic Flute*. There is neither realism nor sympathy with the plights of these characters; here Mozart displays a great flaw.

Later composers have done far better. Indeed this is a very productive category in post-Mozart opera. One could write a book about this alone. Verdi is preoccupied with exiles, as I've shown in chapter 6. Some of these exiles (the Scots in *Macbeth*, the Jews in *Nabucco*) are literal (external) exiles, far from their homeland. But some of his characters are internal exiles: the Roma characters Azucena and Manrico in *Il Trovatore* are despised and persecuted, in Spain, for their racial identity. (Manrico turns out to be biologically Spanish, not Roma, but he thoroughly identifies as his mother's child.) The jester Rigoletto is mocked and stigmatized, in sixteenth-century Mantua, for his physical disability, a curvature of the spine. In both cases the opera thoroughly sympathizes with the suffering caused by exclusion and explores its consequences. Equally subtle, and superbly crafted, is Verdi's portrait of the "fallen woman" in *La Traviata,* who is shown to be morally superior to all the prejudiced people who spurn her. And as I'll argue in chapter 10, Verdi's final opera, *Falstaff,* daringly tackles the exclusion and denigration of aging people, with wit, panache, and zestful humor.

Verdi is not alone in his focus on internal exiles. One of the most popular operas of all time is Georges Bizet's *Carmen* (1875), a work of consummate musical genius by a composer who was always a rebel and always sympathized with the subordinated. Bizet's heroine is a Roma woman, who, with all her people, was stigmatized and ostracized, both in the Spain of the opera's setting and in the France of its production. But she is a rebel, determined to seek her own freedom. Throughout the opera she engages in a series of subversive acts, tricking the police, masterminding a smuggling operation, and in general successfully asserting her will against a society that treats her as a mere object. That she dies at the end is only to be expected, given the forces arrayed against her; but she dies triumphant, without compromising her values. Bizet was continually pressured to change the plot and make her less heroic, but he too refused to compromise. His one concession to social pressures was to introduce the character of Micaëla, a "good woman": but he then turns the tables on his critics by making her her own sort of rebel, traveling alone to the Pyrenees and bravely confronting male aggression both there and, earlier, in Seville. The opera was a failure at its opening, and the composer died before the opera itself triumphed, as it soon did, though its deeper challenge is often avoided.[1]

We could multiply examples. This category is especially productive today, with the topic of racial exclusion prominent in new works, some of which will no doubt become established in the repertory. In this book I have chosen to deal with operas by living composers only when these works are established and frequently produced, so that readers will have chances to see them—as is the case with Heggie's *Dead Man Walking* (chapter 5) and Adams's *Nixon in China* (chapter 8). Perhaps another book, whether by me or by someone else, will investigate other new works further!

In this chapter, therefore, I choose to illustrate the idea of internal exile with just three established operas, revolutionary in their time: *Jenůfa* (1904) by Leoš Janáček (1854–1928), the story of rural society's persecution of a young woman who has a child out of wedlock, and two operas by Benjamin Britten (1913–1976). First, *Peter Grimes* (1945), a horrifying depiction of a rural community's stigmatization and eventual destruction of a man who strikes them as different—for no reason at all. This opera is so dark, offering no hope of escape or transcendence either for the protagonist or for his tormentors, that I continue the chapter with an analysis of Britten's almost contemporaneous *Albert Herring* (1947), a gentle comedy that explores its protagonist's escape from oppression and the possible regeneration of the whole community through human sympathy. I then turn to Janáček, since his *Jenůfa*, like *Albert Herring*, but with great seriousness, shows a hopeful path of escape from the blind tyranny of the crowd.

Having recently published a book focused on Britten's 1962 masterpiece *War Requiem*,[2] but also giving detailed analyses of many

---

[1] See my "Carmen's Freedom," Program of Lyric Opera of Chicago (2022) and online. I explore the opera's relationship not only to its well-known source, Prosper Mérimée's *Carmen* (1845), but also to another important source often ignored, Alexander Pushkin's *The Gypsies* (1827), a far more favorable and non-stigmatizing treatment of the Roma people.

[2] Nussbaum (2024).

of his earlier works that bear on its themes of love, sexuality, and aggression, presenting in the process a great deal of context about British society of the time in relationship to those themes, I shall not repeat myself here. I shall focus on the operas themselves, and only briefly allude to their wider social surroundings. I hope readers who want to know more will turn to my 2024 book.

Peter Grimes: The Crowd's Destructive Power

Peter Grimes is a musical tour de force, in which music and drama are inseparable at every stage, and in which Britten boldly deploys all the resources of the orchestra, as well as the singers, both chorus and soloists, to probe human emotions. Because four of the five orchestral Interludes that precede and then suffuse each scene ("Dawn," "The Storm," "Sunday Morning," and "Moonlight"—the fifth Interlude, the Passacaglia before Act 2 scene 2, being omitted) are often performed, with Britten's approval, as the orchestral suite titled *Four Sea Interludes*, it is easy to conclude (a) that the music is about the sea, not people, and (b) that it is in principle comprehensible without its dramatic context and purpose. This conclusion would be profoundly mistaken: these Interludes explore emotions of anxiety and aggression that are projected onto the outer world by human reactions to a natural setting. They are no more separable from the people than are the winds and storms on Emily Brontë's moors from the inner world of Heathcliff.

The opera is preoccupied with two emotions: anxiety and an aggressive rage that reacts to anxiety by deflecting it back against some target. Britten understands that people do not like to sit helplessly with fear and the possibility or certainty of loss. All too often, they prefer to pin their discomfort on a fictive target whom they then persecute with all the rage at their disposal. The two emotions lie very close to one another in the music. "Dawn" is no calm lovely sunrise: though initially serene, it is marked by tendrils of shooting fear that gradually acquire a marked aggressive character. "The Storm"'s powerfully jagged rhythms are minds fearfully propelling themselves forward to ward off disaster, but at the same time, paradoxically, surges of aggression targeting helpless scapegoats—as we increasingly see when these themes recur in the ensuing scene, during which Grimes's alienation becomes complete and the community's attitudes lethally hostile. By the time we get to "Sunday Morning." we are prepared to see that the music's very orderliness and unanimity is aggressive, directed at a feared outsider. "Moonlight" is not really serene: its light shines ominously over the now-hopeless protagonist's future grave. In every case, as I have said, these tentacles of orchestral expression penetrate the scenes to follow.[3]

Peter Grimes is extremely painful to experience—not only for the present author, who spent many days watching/listening to different productions of the work (definitely not recommended for mental well-being), but also for audiences, as reviewers and even sober analysts repeatedly observe. Unlike most operatic tragedies, and certainly unlike *Jenůfa*'s treatment of a similarly bleak theme, it offers no hope at all—no room even for the Aristotelian thought that despite misfortune, "the noble shines through," and integrity will survive the world's onslaughts. The work somehow creates for audiences the impression that those creeping tentacles and, eventually, sharp weapons of emotion are directed at them, as if each becomes the outcast Grimes, to be driven mad and both psychologically and physically destroyed. This effect is often enhanced in production when the Chorus directly faces the audience, especially at the climactic end of Act 2, singing "Now is gossip put on trial," before they march off to Grimes's cabin. The relentless assault on the listener creates a devastating experience of claustrophobia and

---

[3] See the insightful analysis by Hans Keller, "*Peter Grimes*: The Story, the Music Not Excluded" (1983, pp. 105–20).

desolation analogous to Grimes's own.[4] The entire work is thus a powerful exercise in empathy, in which compassion for the outcast is not a calm and lovely positive emotion but an attitude won from great, and similar, pain.

The topic of the community and its persecutory tendencies was not a new one for Britten, even so early in his career. Like the opera's protagonist, Benjamin Britten was born in Suffolk, the opera's setting, and like Grimes in the opera, who tells Balstrode that he doesn't leave the Borough because "I am a native, rooted here," Britten repeatedly expressed love for his rural home on the seacoast, lived there for most of his adult life (taking daily morning swims in the frigid sea), and eventually founded there the Aldeburgh Festival, which continues to this day, a major music festival all of whose settings are buildings of that town. Britten's childhood was happy. He was by all accounts liked by other boys and not bullied at school. In spite of a heart defect caused by pneumonia, which eventually shortened his life, he became a keen cricketer and tennis player and was happy in his age-group, even being selected as "Victor Ludorum," the champion of games. All through his life he was basically loved and embraced, and was as happy as anyone could reasonably expect to be: tremendous public and critical success; a thirty-nine-year happy domestic, sexual, and creative relationship with the singer Peter Pears, the first and still best singer of the opera's leading role; even honors from the Crown, as Baron Britten of Aldeburgh.

And yet from his childhood he had huge imaginative empathy for the underdog and the marginalized, and he sought to understand the reasons for society's manifold oppressions. Cruelty to non-human animals was a cause from early on, and he was even forced to leave school over an essay attacking the cherished British

[4] One eloquent assessment is by Edmund Wilson in "An account of *Peter Grimes*," in Brett (1983, pp. 159–62) ("You feel, during the final scenes, . . . that you are in the same boat as Grimes").

practice of fox-hunting.[5] In one of his earliest works, the song cycle *Our Hunting Fathers*, written with the poet W. H. Auden, the two men explore the roots of anti-animal behavior, linking it (in 1939) with antisemitism and warlike aggression, and suggesting that the root of the problem is an anxiety about embodiment and mortality, which leads the dominant group to project negativity outward as aggression.[6] The target of persecution might be almost anybody that could, by some difference, remind the dominant class of what it fears (dirt, death, the body).

Meanwhile Britten, like Auden, had become an outsider in three distinct ways (in addition to his concern for animal welfare): he was an artist in a philistine culture; he was a pacifist in a culture heading for war; and he desired—and by the time of *Grimes* had—sexual relations with men.[7] In terms of difficulty for his life, pacifism loomed largest and was the main cause of his emigration to the United States, during which time he began his long and happy partnership with Pears.[8] During a visit to California—after he and Pears left the Auden circle, which both men found uncomfortably bohemian—he conceived the plan of an opera based on poems in *The Borough* (1810) by George Crabbe (1754–1832). By this time,

---

[5] Britten never stopped eating meat, but his concern for animal treatment continued, and he and Pears loved the two dachshunds with whom they lived; Pears even wrote a book about dogs. A plan for an opera for children titled *Tyco the Vegan* was never realized, and no sense of its content survives (see my *The Tenderness of Silent Minds* [2024]).

[6] I explore the cycle in detail in my book, especially the remarkable song "Rats Away!," a song of exorcism in which a terrified subject tries to rid his dwelling of vile dirty creepy things. Much later Lady Billows, in *Albert Herring*, speaks of women's sexual impurity in just such terms.

[7] See my *The Tenderness of Silent Minds* at ch. 4 (2024). Despite Auden's urgings, Britten probably never had sex with anyone until around the time of his departure for the United States in 1939 and shortly after his mother's death. His sexual relationship with Pears began on a visit to Grand Rapids, Michigan, a fact the two recall with some humor. Again despite Auden's urgings, he preferred settled domestic monogamy to a more bohemian lifestyle, and felt that this disciplined lifestyle supported his creativity.

[8] Indeed, in an interview where Britten asserted that the general theme was "the individual against the crowd," he mentions "ironic overtones for our own situation"—as conscientious objectors, and the "tremendous tension" that this caused them to experience (Brett 1983, p. 190).

his thoughts were already turning homeward; his longing for his Suffolk roots, perhaps intensified by reading Crabbe, made him feel that facing the military service tribunal was preferable to remaining in exile. In 1942, he and Pears returned to Britain—with a commission for the opera already in hand.[9] Both men succeeded in winning conscientious objector status; they continued their artistic careers uninterrupted, although their pacifism caused lengthy visa problems every time they wanted to visit the United States.

Outsiders, then, were of very general interest to Britten, and he had long abhorred the way crowds behaved. In *Peter Grimes* he continues and deepens the inquiry begun in *Our Hunting Fathers*. Even in 1945, early in his long career, Britten is a master of choral writing, and the true "hero" or villain of the opera is the crowd. Britten equals (and is greatly influenced by) Verdi in his versatile use of the chorus. But in *Grimes* he does something Verdi never did: he creates memorable individual types within the group, each with their own personality and story, yet all joining together in the general persecution. In this way he is also able to explore different degrees of partial independence from the group.

The opera concerns a fisherman, Peter Grimes, who is suspected of behaving cruelly to his apprentices. It opens with a judicial inquiry into the death of a previous apprentice out at sea. Grimes, plainly innocent, defends himself with calm and clarity: the conditions out at sea, lack of water and harsh climate, caused the boy's death, and no neglect by him was involved. He is acquitted, but with the advice not to take another apprentice: a woman's help would be better. Grimes and the schoolteacher Ellen Orford then discuss their love and their plans for the future. It becomes clear that Grimes wants to marry Ellen but feels that he can do so successfully only if he makes more money, since that is the value the Borough understands. For

---

[9] It was not his first opera. The first, *Paul Bunyan* (1941), was a failure in New York, largely because of Auden's horrible libretto (see my *The Tenderness of Silent Minds*, ch. 3 [2024]); Britten did create some lovely music for the opera, and promoted a revival of it shortly before his death.

that he needs another apprentice, despite his awareness that the Borough will view this choice with skepticism.

Meanwhile, various inhabitants of the Borough are already turned against Grimes, refusing to believe in his innocence. When he remains determined to get another apprentice from the workhouse, they immediately suspect that Grimes will behave harshly to him. Peter tells the retired sea-captain Balstrode that the people listen to money, so he will win them over by making money with another apprentice. Balstrode, sympathetic, asks Peter why he doesn't move away to try his fortunes elsewhere, but Peter replies, "I am a native, rooted here." The Borough's suspicion is compounded by alarming external conditions: Balstrode warns that a fierce storm is approaching, and the music makes the danger evident. Peter sings the haunting aria, "What harbor shelters peace," imagining a peaceful life with Ellen.

During the frenzy of anxiety precipitated by the storm, in the next scene, suspicion mounts and mounts. Grimes enters from the storm, wild and disheveled. At this point utterly disconnected from others, he sings the visionary aria, "Now the Great Bear and the Pleiades where earth moves / Are drawing up the clouds of human grief." Boles, an evangelical, exclaims that Grimes has sold his soul to the devil and that "His exercise / Is not with men but with killing boys"—the source, later, of the chorus's persecutory chant, "Grimes is at his exercise." The crowd diverts Boles from violence by starting up the ditty "Old Joe has gone fishing." At this point Ellen and Hobson, the constable, enter with the new workhouse apprentice (a boy in a nonspeaking role). Grimes takes his new apprentice home. Thus ends Act 1.

However, by now Grimes's psychology is affected and it emerges he has treated the boy roughly, though not with deliberate sadism. On Sunday morning, after the storm, Ellen, sitting with her knitting by the sea, while hymns and prayers from the church are heard in the background, sees a bruise on the boy's neck. She confronts Peter, who insists that he must go to sea with the boy and earn money to fulfill their dreams. Ellen tells him that they should admit failure: even money will not stop the Borough's gossip and aggression. Peter then strikes Ellen and leaves with the boy.

Fresh from church,[10] worked up into a frenzy of righteous aggression, the people of the town assail the absent Grimes with the repeated refrain, "Grimes is at his exercise." The cry of persecution mounts, despite dissuasion from Balstrode and Ellen. They all decide to charge over to Grimes's home en masse, singing the terrifying chorus, "Now is gossip put on trial, / We shall strike and strike to kill / At the slander or the sin"—and of course it is plain by this time that they will not "strike" their own "slander." Balstrode follows slowly and reluctantly. Only Ellen, and Auntie and the Nieces (of whom more later) are left on stage, to sing of maternal love and sympathy. So ends Act 2 scene 1.

Scene 2 takes place at Grimes's cottage. The crowd's impending arrival causes Grimes, by now agitated and losing emotional control, to press the boy to descend the staircase to the ship too rapidly. The boy falls and is drowned. Now Grimes has no hope of realizing his dreams.

In Act 3, several days later, Grimes has gone mad. Alone by his boat, he sings an aria in which his earlier dreams turn to disconnected nightmares. Ellen and Balstrode try to speak to him and bring him home, but he can no longer hear them. Balstrode tells him that the only thing left for him to do is to sail his boat out to sea and sink it. After ironically recapitulating his aria "What harbor shelters peace," Peter does so.

Both Britten and Pears insisted (though they have not always been believed) that the opera concerns the very general problem of "the individual against the crowd."[11] In Crabbe's poem Grimes

---

[10] The local church is Anglican—Crabbe (1754–1832) was an Anglican clergyman—but its religious attitudes are severe and repressive like the rest of the Borough's inhabitants. It is not the tolerant sort of Anglican church for which Britten wrote so much wonderful music.

[11] Britten in an interview quoted in Brett (1983, p. 190).

is a rough and sadistic character, apparently made so by his own father's harsh treatment of him. So the crowd has good reason for its hostile attitude. During the process of composition Britten and his librettist, Montagu Slater, changed the character completely, removing the roughness and making him something of a dreamer, and also removing any signs of sexual interest between Grimes and his boys. There is no hint of bad behavior or of any chronic psychological flaw. Indeed, despite Slater's Marxist desire to bring in issues of class conflict, Britten insisted on removing every particular cause of persecution that might make the behavior of the Borough plausible and quasi-rational. Grimes is not different in race, class, or sexuality. He is not even an interesting romantic hero. Pears sums it up: "He is not a sadist or a demonic character, and the music quite clearly shows that. He is very much of an ordinary, weak person, who, being at odds with the society in which he finds himself, tries to overcome it and, in so doing, offends against the conventional code, is classed by society as a criminal, and destroyed as such. There are plenty of Grimeses around still, I think!"[12] Musicologist Hans Keller believes this claim should be extended: there is something of Grimes in every one of us.[13] I am sure he is correct.

How, then, is Grimes singled out from the group? We can only say that he sings in different keys and rhythms. He prefers E, A, and D major,[14] while the Borough prefers E-flat and B-flat. And from the very beginning of the opera he is rhythmically different: Judge Swallow sings in bouncy staccato phrases that sound like folk tunes, while Grimes defends himself in a steady legato. Throughout the opera the people of the Borough sing tunes, often rhythmically marked, that remind one of folk song—and also, as Ashby shows in his powerful article, use dance-rhythms.[15] The chorus that I have called "terrifying" intensifies this tendency, with its simple trochaic

---

[12] Pears, "Neither a Hero Nor a Villain," in Brett (1983, pp. 150–52).
[13] Hans Keller (1983, p. 111).
[14] See Brett, "Britten and Grimes" (1983, p. 184).
[15] Arved Ashby, "*Peter Grimes* and the 'Tuneful Air,'" in Rupprecht (2013, pp. 63–85).

rhythms that assail the audience. Britten loved English folk songs, studied them, and arranged them masterfully for piano-voice recitals with Pears, so the association of the Borough with these idioms does not mark the Borough people as bad or crude. Nor is Peter marked as educated or a Byronic hero by his characteristic modes of song—legato with long phrases, with a yearning ninth in "What harbor shelters peace," or dreamily sitting on the same pitch in "Now the Great Bear." He is just different, and that is his doom. Even when he first joins the round "Old Joe has gone fishing," he sings it differently, legato and rather lyrically.[16]

Peter is indeed something of a dreamer, but that is not the cause of his persecution, except indirectly: it is just a manifestation of a difference, of the fact that despite pressures to conform he has managed to form a distinct individual self. It is just that distinctness that the Borough hates and wishes to extirpate.

Britten understood what modern sociology has proven again and again: stigma and persecution don't need reasons. As Erving Goffman trenchantly points out in his classic book *Stigma*,[17] everyone has vulnerabilities, everyone is hiding them. So picking out someone for stigmatization is nothing more than a deflection onto the other of people's anxieties about themselves. Eyes of a different color, or red hair, just any difference at all, can serve as an occasion for the operations of stigma. Those who pick on the "other" are all hypocrites, hiding something about themselves. So the inhabitants of the Borough emphasize collective/traditional forms of rhythmic utterance all the more when their vulnerabilities are most threatened with exposure. Mrs. Sedley, hiding her addiction to laudanum, is (as Ashby shows) the most rhythmically folksy of all.

---

[16] Britten had definite views about how the role should be sung: the voice should be "not too heavy, which makes the character simply a sadist, nor … too lyric, which makes it a boring opera about a sentimental poet-manqué" in Brett (1983, p. 104).

[17] Goffman (1963).

The completely general and causeless nature of the persecution of Grimes is crucial to the opera's emotional effect. Opera audiences are likely to have no specific traits in common with this rough fisherman. But because he is a kind of blank slate, all can see themselves in his place and feel themselves receiving the anger of the crowd.

Nor do the people of the Borough have a comprehensible collective flaw. It's just that they are human, therefore weak, and they band together in predictable ways to protect their weakness. Insecurity leads them to rely on the collective, and through the collective they convert their fear into aggression. Britten insisted that their behavior is not about living near the sea: When director Tyrone Guthrie wanted to emphasize the role of the sea in his production, Britten said, "No, it's got nothing to do with the sea. It has to do with the people of the village." Guthrie said, "But Ben, the sea made these people what they were." To which Britten replied, "No, these people would be the same wherever they were."[18] (Similarly, the people in *Our Hunting Fathers* didn't persecute animals because they lived in proximity to dangerous foxes: the reflex to persecute, there too, antecedes any specific danger, though it stems from general human vulnerability.) Here, it's not about "rural people" or "sea people" or even "English people." Just people, people vulnerable to whatever dangers their particular circumstances afford. And people do not like the one who is unlike them, because difference looks like a denial of the crowd's authority. "Who holds himself apart / Lets his pride rise / Him who despises us / We'll destroy."

What happens to the persecuted Grimes is that the aggression of the crowd digs into him and grows inside, producing contradictory tendencies. On the one hand he wants to be like them, to fit in. Grimes's dreams, though initially visionary ("Now the Great Bear and Pleiades") turn out to be conventional when given concrete form: money, marriage with Ellen, children, ergo a need for even

---

[18] Brett, "Peter Grimes on Stage," in Brett (1983, pp. 88–104, at 97).

more money. "They listen to money, These Borough gossips . . . I'll win them over, . . . I'll marry Ellen." These external demands, internalized, crowd out the real love he may once have felt for Ellen and eventually drive her away. At the same time his sense of failing those demands makes him lash out in self-hatred, ergo his roughness to both Ellen and the boy. Jenůfa, as we shall see, is lucky: she has an inner citadel of love that has not been poisoned by the townspeople, and Laca can access that. Grimes has nobody to be. He can't be what they admire, and he can't be anybody else, has no personality left that has not been co-opted and poisoned by them. As the opera goes on, his distinctive musical idiom increasingly gives way to Borough-sing, until he is even singing the ditty "Old Joe has gone fishing," the way the Borough sings it, as far from Grimes-sing as any Borough tune could be. By the opera's end, he has no musical self.

What could have helped him? In what harbor might he have found peace? Balstrode suggests that he should move somewhere else (just as Peter Pears suggests that Grimes would have done better in a city). But Grimes's heart is tied to his home.

The opera does contain other characters who have managed to form some tentative measure of individuality, resisting the crowd's pressure. Most obvious among these is Ellen, whose genuine, if wavering, love for Grimes sets her apart from the others. Her aria "Embroidery in childhood" late in the opera—after the suit she made for Peter's apprentice washes up on the shore—shows a depth of introspection and genuine sorrow that other Borough inhabitants do not attain:

> Embroidery in childhood was a luxury of idleness
> A coil of silken thread giving dreams of a silk and satin life
> Now my broidery affords the clue whose meaning we avoid!
> My hands remembered its old skill
> Those stitches tell a curious tale
> I remember I was brooding

> On the fantasies of children
> And dreamt that only by wishing
> I could bring some silk into their lives
> Now my broidery affords the clue whose meaning we avoid

Here Ellen reflects about her childhood, her wishes and dreams, in a way the Borough sternly discourages. In the end, however, she proves well-intentioned but weak, accountable to the Borough, and ultimately unreliable. Perhaps Balstrode, too, shows signs of having something of a definite self: he tries to understand Grimes's plight, and his final advice to commit suicide, not sadistic but merciful, derives from his understanding that Grimes has no life anywhere else. But, when pressured, he follows the persecutory procession to Grimes's cottage, albeit slowly and reluctantly. The rest are colorful distinct cartoon types, with no discernible inner cores, thoroughly parts of the Borough and under its sway.

This leave us with three characters who are defined as outside of the Borough because they are exiles, quasi-outsiders, who for that reason are unable to help Grimes: Auntie the bar-owner and her two "nieces," barmaids who may or may not be prostitutes. (They cleverly deter the repugnant Boles but appear more welcoming to others.) To me these characters, never discussed as interesting and treated as merely comic baggage, are a key part of Britten's construction. The Borough allows alcohol and extramarital (heterosexual) sex to exist: it needs and indulges these "vices." But the purveyors of "vice," though allowed to live, are stigmatized internal exiles and are thus able to attain a semi-detached perspective on Borough hypocrisy.

At the end of the second act, after the crowd has left to exact its terrible penalty, the Nieces, Auntie, and Ellen are left alone on the stage. The Nieces sing, "From the gutter, why should we trouble at their ribaldries?" Auntie: "And shall we be ashamed because we comfort men from ugliness?" Both, then, in contradistinction to the Borough, simply accept the body and its needs. The three then join with Ellen, singing: "Shall we smile or shall we weep, / Or wait quietly till they sleep?" In a quartet of a wonderful purity, they ascend serenely to a realm in which men are comforted by women ("They are children when they weep, / We are mothers when they strive") and women have no shame before vulnerable bodies. These women are all powerless, and thus unable to save Peter. But they exist as reminders of what human love could be if people simply trusted and comforted—rather than demonizing—one another. (Britten's female relatives, his mother and his two sisters, were powerful loving support figures throughout his life, and he always favored the careers of women in the arts.[19]) Not surprisingly, the quartet has a Mozartean sound. This scene above any other gives a hint of what a community life might be if based on maternal love rather than stifling conformity.

As we have seen, the accidental death of the new apprentice seals Peter's doom and ends his sanity. In his extended "mad scene" (Act 3 scene 2) he has mere fragments of music to offer, mere shreds of a self. Peter does not even recognize Ellen. In this final scene, music itself dies out—in the words of Joseph Kerman, "is reduced successively to zero." Balstrode gives his command to Peter in nonmusical speech. He then accompanies Peter to the boat and his fatal voyage. Music is done for—Britten's devastating way of showing the death of the self, Peter's yielding to a despair beyond tragedy.[20]

The opera's descent into silence develops a tradition of connecting personality and possibility to musical breath. In *Fidelio* the loss of breath is temporary: after the prisoners go back to their airless prison, Leonore's hope is kindled in music of thrilling ambition—and ultimately prevails. The silence of the death chamber in *Dead Man Walking* does represent the extinction of one life and its hope,

---

[19] See my *The Tenderness of Silent Minds* (2024, ch. 6), especially on Isobel Holst and Marion Stein. At the Aldeburgh Festival, Britten's sisters helped Britten and Pears host the public in their home.

[20] See Kerman (1949, pp. 277–84), as quoted in Brett (1983, p. 99): "the dead hopelessness, past tragedy, of Grimes's ultimate predicament."

but after that extraordinarily long silence, vocal breath reasserts itself in Sister Helen's soft yet insistent singing of "He shall gather us around." The only opera I can compare to *Grimes*'s total extinction of voice is Strauss's *Elektra*, whose heroine's personality has been similarly hollowed out, in that case by the obsessive idea of vengeance, which shreds her other concerns. She compares the desire for revenge to a cloth around her throat that chokes off breath—and so it does at the opera's end. Singing done for, Elektra performs a wordless dance and collapses, dead.

Elektra is stifled by a personal obsession, Grimes by society's persecution—but the two are more alike than that contrast suggests. Society's voices have long poisoned Grimes's inner song-world, and Elektra's internal poison is in origin social, not evolutionary: it is what her society teaches people to feel when wronged. Both works, then, see certain social myths and tendencies as stifling, hostile to music, which is the expression of personality and quite literally the breath of life.

Albert Herring: Reconciliation and Hope

Peter Grimes was followed, only a year later, by another very dark work, *The Rape of Lucretia*, a "chamber opera" that had its premiere in 1946 at the Glyndebourne Festival. Britten became fond of the chamber opera genre, one that he used brilliantly from then on. It permitted him to work with a leaner orchestra and less reliance on the whims of designer and stage director. He also loved the ease of reperformance by groups of many different kinds, from Glyndebourne stars to local amateurs. *Lucretia* has a marvelous score, but its libretto, by Britten's fellow pacifist Ronald Duncan, has generally been found wanting. For his next opera, Britten turned to a very different subject and a different librettist.

Britten had already begun to collaborate with librettist and director Eric Crozier (1914–1994), stage director for the first production of *Peter Grimes.* Crozier formed a fertile partnership and friendship with Pears and Britten that included cooperation in founding the English Opera Group in 1947 and, shortly thereafter, in 1948, the Aldeburgh Festival. Crozier wrote the libretti for *Albert Herring* (1947) and (along with E. M. Forster) for *Billy Budd* (1951). He often stayed (sometimes with his wife, mezzo-soprano Nancy Evans) at the Britten-Pears house, and they even assigned him a room of his own. (The one thing he disliked about the arrangement, he said, was Britten's expectation that guests would join him in an early morning plunge in the frigid North Sea!) The friendship suddenly ended in the mid-fifties, for reasons that remain unclear.

The English Opera Group was founded in 1947 by Britten, Pears, Crozier, and painter and set designer John Piper. Its purpose was to promote performances of British works (primarily). The Board included music publisher Ralph Hawkes, émigré conductor and editor Erwin Stein, theater director Tyrone Guthrie, and art historian Sir Kenneth Clark.[21] The first prospectus announced:

> The time has come when England...can create its own operas.... We believe the best way to achieve the beginnings of a repertory of English operas is through the creation of a form of opera requiring small resources. [*The Rape of Lucretia* is discussed as the first example of this approach.] The success of this experiment has encouraged the...persons chiefly involved...to continue their work as a group by establishing... THE ENGLISH OPERA GROUP, incorporated on a non-profit-making basis. The Group will give annual seasons of contemporary opera in English and suitable classical works including those of Purcell.[22]

---

[21] Clark became "Sir" in 1938, when his knighthood was conferred, but was not yet Baron Clark of Saltwood, as he became with a life peerage in 1969.

[22] Carpenter (1992, pp. 248–49).

The brochure announced Britten's *Albert Herring* (libretto by Crozier) as the Group's first project and made an appeal for 12,000 pounds, announcing that the first 2,000 had already been donated by a "private subscriber." (The donors were Dorothy and Leonard Elmhirst, founders of Dartington Hall, the famous progressive arts-oriented school.) They got some more money from the Arts Council, and appointed Anne Wood, who had worked with Pears at the BBC, as general manager. (This choice begins what I would call an Aldeburgh tradition of promoting women to high positions in opera administration, to be followed by similar choices in the Festival. Composer and conductor Isobel Holst, daughter of composer Gustav Holst, was director of the Festival for many years.) *Albert Herring* had its premiere at Glyndebourne in June 1947, with Britten taking up the unaccustomed role of conductor.

Albert Herring, one of the repertory's most endearing and musically rich comic operas, is a highly significant work in the evolution of Britten's thinking about crowds, exclusion, and hope. Although it does not negate the dark insights of *Grimes*, it opens a path for reconciliation. The libretto is based on Guy de Maupassant's 1887 novella *Le Rosier de Madame Husson*, but Crozier and Britten, though retaining the turn-of-the-century date, transpose the setting to Loxford, a fictional Suffolk town very like Britten's own Aldeburgh. The opera had a mixed reception at its Glyndebourne opening, but quickly established itself in the repertory, and a demand for performances from other nations swelled. Because of its small scale, vocally and orchestrally, it is not performed in major opera houses, but it is a staple of chamber opera all over the world, and also of conservatory and university productions. Although it was first performed at Glyndebourne, it quickly became associated with the first Aldeburgh Festival (June 1948), with Nancy Evans singing the key role of Nancy (named, of course, for her).

Here's how the Festival began: Britten, Pears, Crozier, and Evans had traveled together to performances in Amsterdam and the Hague, and were on their way by car to Lucerne when, according to Crozier's memoir, Pears said, "Why not make our own festival? A modest festival with a few concerts given by friends? Why not have an Aldeburgh festival?" Or, in Pears's version, "Why don't we have a festival in Aldeburgh? Why do we have to go abroad to Switzerland to perform *Albert Herring*? Why can't we perform it at Aldeburgh?"[23] That was the start of the Aldeburgh Festival, a hybrid arts festival that endures, and thrives.

Britten and Pears chose to open the first festival with the second performance of Britten's *Canticle* I "My beloved is mine."[24] Its text is by Francis Quarles (1592–1644). According to the official account given by the Britten-Pears Library, "Although ostensibly a text celebrating the poet's ecstatic communion with God, Britten clearly meant the work also to be interpreted as a declaration of the personal and professional relationship that now existed between himself and Pears." The ecstatic words of love and reciprocal partnership needed no gloss, and were sung by Pears with Britten at the piano—a bold statement of presence and inclusion, in that conservative community.[25] Their second bold statement was to choose *Albert Herring* as the festival's operatic centerpiece. The opera was, of course, new, a good reason to present it. But it was also all about a small Suffolk town, its sexual prejudices and repressions, and their joyful overcoming by a formerly repressed young man (performed by Pears)—a rather risky topic in the circumstances. And yet *Albert Herring* is so endearing, so gentle in its satire, that it won and still wins the day. The opera must be interpreted in this context, as a statement that qualifies the bleakness of *Grimes* and challenges the community to accept people who are "different"—even while Britten and Pears received the public into their own home.

The opera should also be seen as part of Britten's program to bring music to the community. Throughout his career, Britten

<hr>

[23] Carpenter (1992, p. 252).

[24] The first performance had been at a memorial concert in 1947 for Dick Sheppard, one of the founders of the Peace Pledge Union.

[25] See my *The Tenderness of Silent Minds* (2024, ch. 6), which quotes the entire text.

loved writing for amateurs—local choruses, local orchestras. He demanded a lot of them, but he also respected them and let them in. (His monumental *War Requiem* was performed by professional soloists with an amateur chorus.) He also loved to write for young people, as in his marvelous "A Young Person's Guide to the Orchestra." There is probably no distinguished composer since Bach whose compositional life has been more community-focused. *Albert Herring* is a musically intricate opera, with wonderful orchestral and vocal ensemble writing. And yet it is performable by high-level amateurs because of its small scale, its even division of vocal labor among many interesting and rewarding roles, and its vocal demands, which can be wonderfully realized by the best professionals, such as Pears, the first Albert, but which can also be enjoyably and admirably performed by conservatory and university students. It even includes a group of children. Not only the opera's content, then, but also the type of work it is, offers an invitation to the community: join us in making music and laughing at human folly—including yours, including ours.

The setting is Loxford, in 1900. Albert Herring, a young grocer, lives under his mother's control, unable to enjoy a sexual life out of sheer fear of her disapproval—though he envies the happiness of the young couple Sid and Nancy, whose displays of affection show him how rewarding sexual life can be. It's not a stretch to see this as a gentle self-satire: the prissy Britten, who (apparently) never had sex with anyone as long as his mother was alive, but yearned for both freedom and acceptance. Albert shows his rule-bound and repressed nature in his treatment of the three children who visit the grocer's shop in the hope of stealing some apples but are not allowed to take any. (This Edenic theme continues as Sid shows himself a skilled apple thief and greedy apple-eater.)

Meanwhile the town has its annual task of choosing a May Queen, an old local tradition. A group of leading citizens meets at the home of the formidable Lady Billows, whose vocal characterization, as she swoops up and down, establishing her authority over several octaves, is satirical without being at all repugnant. The guests include the Mayor, the Vicar, the schoolteacher Miss Wordsworth, and Superintendent Budd, the chief of police. They deliberate, considering a whole list of young women. Being a chamber opera, the work has no chorus, but this set of citizens takes its place. Each has a distinctive musical idiom that in each case satirizes some aspect of village life and yet allows the people to seem potentially kind and good. Each one has appealing traits—including Miss Wordsworth's affection for her students, Lady Billows's love of the town and its traditions.

In Act 1, however, they reveal the negative side of village norms. Lady Billows offers a financial reward for the May Queen: "Must make virtue attractive, exciting, *desirable* for young people." (She mentions a rise in out-of-wedlock births, and expresses disgust in her marvelously swooping way.) Going through a long list of candidates for the May Queen role, they sternly find fault with the sexual conduct of all: nobody is pure enough for the job. (Assessment is based on gossip gathered and recorded by Lady Billows's assistant Florence, and of course nobody debates the veracity of her innuendoes.) Lady Billows becomes more and more indignant, singing a remarkable dramatic-soprano aria of denunciation: "Is this all you can bring? Each single name reeking impurities. Not one thing but stinks of sensual shame. . . . Is this the town where I have lived and toiled? . . . Shame to Loxford: sty the female sex has soiled." Her long hysterical catalogue of types of filth echoes the tone of the speaker in Britten's early "Rats Away!," a song of exorcism that is one of the high points of *Our Hunting Fathers*.[26]

It's hard to say what opera aria this slightly mad utterance resembles—perhaps Elettra's mad denunciation at the end of *Idomeneo*, but with a greater emphasis on bodily disgust. In any case it is so over the top that it is not scary in the way that *Grimes*

---

[26] See above, n. 6.

is scary. Lady B does once mention a whip, but in reality all she proposes is not giving any of the girls a large financial reward.

Then someone suggests that there could be a May King, so why not Albert? All agree that he meets the purity test, and the group visits the grocer's to announce that he will be crowned May King. Albert is embarrassed, but accepts.

Throughout this Act the ensemble writing is intricate and polyphonically expressive, as is the orchestral writing (perhaps especially for woodwinds).

Act 2 is the ceremony itself, with all the ridiculous fauxpatriotism of such a local village ceremony. The hymn of glorification sounds like a miniature coronation anthem. Meanwhile the children mess up their song, despite Miss W's best efforts, and all are focused on the food and drink more than on moral pieties. Lady Billows swoops triumphantly. Superintendent Budd discourses on Empire: "It's chaps like young Albert keep the British Empire on top of the world where it has always been."

The musical achievement of Act 2 is remarkable: it is very funny and a devastating satire of a certain sort of stuffy British solemnity—and yet, musically it is not boring. The clever and intricate music tells the audience that there is more to this place than its surface tedium—and perhaps more to the people than their ridiculous behavior.

At the ceremony Albert is tricked by Sid, who puts rum into his drink. Albert gets drunk, and returns home in a rebellious mood, eager to break free. As the act ends, he takes his cash prize and goes on an extended spree, just as Sid whistles to Nancy and they begin their tryst.

As in *Grimes*, each act is followed by an expressive orchestral interlude.

Act 3 begins the following afternoon. Albert has not returned, and people fear for his safety. His mother begins mourning, convinced that he is dead. When his wreath from the ceremony is found on the road, people's worst fears are apparently confirmed. The various inhabitants sing an intricate Passacaglia, each uttering their own sentiments: "In the midst of life is death." The solemn and intricate music is slightly absurd (since the audience is convinced that Albert is not dead), and yet the people all reveal genuine emotion and real affection for Albert, thus showing themselves capable of better and less exclusionary behavior. Even Lady Billows expresses genuine grief: "O weep for him, whose simple fame shone clearly like a candle-flame blown bright by the wind, then out again." Just as the musical climax of *Grimes* is the terrifying confrontational chorus "Now is gossip put on trial," so the musical climax of *Albert Herring* is this compassionate embrace of the threatened and vulnerable Albert in all his strangeness.

Just then, Albert returns, none the worse for his experiences, which clearly included more drinking, brawling, and some type of unspecified sexual activity. Albert feels liberated from his mother's heavy hand and announces new-found freedom and happiness. Lady Billows is shocked ("You will pay for your night's holiday, . . . you will creep in the shade of a profligate's grave"), and his mother says she will never forgive him (though the love she has already expressed makes it clear that the threat is empty). But Albert is not frightened at all. He goes right back to work: "Good day, your Ladyship, please let me get on, for I'm all behind." Our sense is that he will continue to lead a peaceful life among them. At the conclusion, he invites the three children into the shop, offers them "a nice peach," and urges them to help themselves. Sid picks up the wreath, but Albert tosses it away.

This satire on British sexual mores is not caustic or devastatingly negative. It is loving, and it ends in some sort of reconciliation. Albert doesn't leave, and he doesn't suffer. The opera's emotional center is Nancy, both sexual and moral: she doesn't like the way her lover has tricked Albert, and has genuine sympathy for him, but, unlike Albert, she cautiously leads a free sexual life. At the end, the town welcomes Albert, and appears to relax its stern demands, albeit grumpily.

What did Albert do, and with whom? It is perfectly clear that all sexual activity has come under suspicion, so in a sense it doesn't really matter whether Albert's sexual debut is heterosexual or homosexual. The libretto gives no clue, though in one recent Glyndebourne production the director has Albert pull some women's underclothes out of his pocket. No doubt this is what most of the audience would have imagined, and would imagine even today, since in 1900, the opera's dramatic date, a gay coming-out was not in the cards. But Peter Pears is playing the role, and in Aldeburgh, so the question is gently raised. (Pears disliked playing heterosexual love scenes: the role of Essex in *Gloriana* was not a favorite.) And the whole plot is so suggestive of Britten's own life and his own move away from prissy purity that it can certainly be read (as suggested above) as a gentle self-portrait, particularly when performed in Aldeburgh. In a marvelous production by Chicago Opera Theater in 2023, as Albert returns to work at the very end and says to Lady Billows, "Let me get on, for I'm all behind," the hero smiles subversively, tapping his backside. Such rear-end jokes are not foreign to the Britten-Pears correspondence—including Britten addressing Pears as "my darling *Pyge*" (ancient Greek for "rear end").[27]

Instead of avoiding all questions about the relationship between his sexual life with Pears and society's norms, in short, Britten and Pears foregrounded these questions—with humor, and with an inclusive message: No matter what Albert's sexuality is, audiences should agree that repression is damaging and that the whole town can live in peace together by relaxing its severity. The most interesting thing about the ending, given the era of its performance, is that the audience is told nothing about Albert's orientation. The work's message is that all Alberts are entitled to seek happiness and

---

[27] Letter 180 in *My Beloved Man: The Letters of Benjamin Britten and Peter Pears* (2016). In letter 11, Pears addresses Britten (whom he often calls "pussy-cat") as "my most beautiful of all little blue-grey, mouse-catching, pearly-bottomed, creamy-thighed, soft-waisted, mewing rat-pursuers."

to live at peace with their Suffolk neighbors. All of this is done in some of Britten's most inventive and delightful music. Britten and Pears were never narrowly focused on the plight of same-sex lovers. (Don't forget that long list of women who are rejected for alleged impurity at the opera's start.) They were concerned with shame about the body and sexual repression more generally, as damaging to women and men, whatever their orientation. Nothing in Britten, I believe, is "all about" homosexuality. He is concerned with human embodiment, human sexuality, and human freedom, all very badly treated in the England of his time.

One crucial question: Why doesn't Albert disintegrate under pressure the way Peter Grimes disintegrates? Well, this is a comedy. But there are significant hints of a deeper answer, which *Jenůfa* will develop at greater length. Despite his naïveté and gullibility, Albert has a core of inner good sense that carries him through the storm. He also has a mother who loves him, whatever her flaws, and two excellent friends in Nancy and Sid, who show him how a life outside rigid conventions might be lived successfully. In short, he resembles the young Britten, whose inner integrity never wavered despite the crowd's assaults.

Does this opera show that crowds can be generous and compassionate? Only with a lot of qualification. If the "different" one is a major artist who proposes to do great good for the entire community, meanwhile behaving with discreet politeness, then the answer is a tentative yes (though we should not forget the persecution of Alan Turing, the great mathematician and computer scientist, sentenced to chemical castration for same-sex acts in 1954). Such a conclusion seems not so positive. But Britten clearly was a gradualist about social acceptance. He and Pears said they detested the growing gay rights movement for its rude in-your-face tactics. And they really did love the traditional rural town they depicted and lived in. They wanted to loosen it up a bit, but not to jettison valuable traditions. Once "loosening" had begun, spaces would emerge in the community in many different places and ways. This in fact happened in Britain, and same-sex acts were legal by 1967, after a Royal Commission recommended decriminalization in 1959 and a lengthy public debate ensued.[28] He and Pears bequeathed their love letters to the museum in Aldeburgh so that people could learn of the reality of their love and the dignity with which they lived it. Before his death he became Baron Britten of Aldeburgh. When he died in 1976, Queen Elizabeth wrote Pears a letter of consolation, as to any grieving spouse. Even Lady Billows can experience the tug of compassion. Or at least she can learn to behave as if she does. And from Albert's point of view, that is just good enough.

Jenůfa: Oppression and Radical Love

Albert finds a qualified escape only in a fanciful comedy, though one that points to the real-life escape of Britten and Pears. Janáček's *Jenůfa* shows us a serious path toward escape from the crowd's relentless persecution—through mutual love and a radical reinvention of religious paradigms of love—not unlike the escape Britten and Pears actually found in life and music.

Jenůfa was Leoš Janáček's third opera, but the first to show his daring mature style, and the first regularly performed today. It was completed in 1903, relatively late in his long life (1854–1928). The opera combines musical originality with stunning insight into concrete characters who are forced to grapple with difficult ethical and emotional dilemmas. Also called *Její pastorkyňa* (*Her Stepdaughter*, from the title of a stage play by Gabriela Preissová, produced in 1890, that was the composer's basis for his libretto), *Jenůfa* had its premiere in January 1904—in Brno, because the schemes of a personal enemy had denied the composer a premiere in Prague. At first only a local success, it eventually became an international triumph in 1916 with its Prague premiere, which took place when

---

[28] See *The Tenderness of Silent Minds* (Nussbaum 2024, ch. 4).

the composer was over 60 years old (in an inferior revised version made by a fashionable conductor, now never performed).[29]

Jenůfa took its composer nine years to write, and it was completed during a time of great personal tragedy; his daughter, Olga, age twenty, died of typhoid fever in 1903. (His only other child, a son, had died young in 1890.) Olga, always frail, took a passionate interest in the opera during its composition, imploring her father to play it for her on the piano because, she said, "I won't live to hear it." It is dedicated to her memory.

Born in the small Moravian town of Hukvaldy, Janáček is one of three distinguished Czech composers of this period, the other two being Dvořák (1841–1904) and Smetana (1824–1884).[30] He is the only one who was Moravian rather than Bohemian, and the customs and people of Moravia were dear to him throughout his life. Like the other two, he took great interest in folk songs and their expression of national identity. But his primary interest was always in individual people and the dilemmas they faced in rigid societies. Three of his greatest operas (*Jenůfa*, *Káťa Kabanová* [1921], and *The Makropulos Affair* [1926]) all focus on the plights of women, and *The Cunning Little Vixen* (1923) focuses on the life and death of a female fox. Its ending was chosen by Janáček for performance at his own funeral.

Janáček focused obsessively on the music of everyday speech. He notated "speech melodies" wherever he went. Even while sitting by his daughter's sickbed, he musically notated her sighs as she was breathing her last—not out of hard-heartedness, but in the belief that the music of speech was at the heart of a person's humanity. He therefore disliked poetic libretti, and is probably the first composer of opera to use prose. In place of poetry, he often

[29] See Tyrell (1992), collecting pertinent letters and other documents about Janáček's struggles to get the opera performed.

[30] The outstanding biography is by Jaroslav Vogel, *Leoš Janáček: a Biography* (1981). Also valuable is the memoir by Janáček's wife of over fifty years: Zdenka Janáčková, *My Life with Janáček*, translated John Tyrell (1998).

uses repetition of short phrases, and *Jenůfa* is full of many such repetitions. Unfortunately, audiences who read the supertitles of a production are frequently unaware of this, because supertitles standardly omit them.

Above all, Janáček's interest is in the individual trying to achieve ethical freedom and a meaningful life in a world in which many choices are taken from her by social constraints. In *Jenůfa* he grapples with two weighty ethical issues: infanticide and the nature of forgiveness. On both issues the opera offers subtle and original insights, focusing, always, on the individual and her freedom, or lack of freedom, and on the creative potential of reciprocal unconditional love.

Jenůfa is set in a small, highly conventional, mill town, where most inhabitants are either employers or employees of the mill.[31] Musically Act 1 is dominated by two ideas working against one another. At the outset, and repeatedly throughout the Act, we hear the rhythmic beat of a xylophone on a single note; this motif suggests the rhythmic dripping of the water over the mill-wheel, but also the ticking of a clock. It signifies time and nature, constraining the characters. Against this relentless beating are surging strings, suggesting human striving, as the characters try to achieve something within time's constraints. Jenůfa is introduced by a particularly sweet and vulnerable phrase from a solo violin. And from the start she is extremely vulnerable to the constraints of time, because she is pregnant and unmarried, and her lover, Števa, may be called away to the military. In any case he has not married her.

Two aspects of Jenůfa emerge early in the Act. The first is her tenderness and the vulnerability of that tenderness: she cares for her little plant, which Laca, petulant and jealous of his brother Števa's romantic success, has kept damaging. But we also see something

---

[31] The most valuable musical/dramatic interpretation is Michael Ewans, *Janáček's Tragic Operas* (1977). I disagree with some of his emphasis on tragic inevitability, but his suggestions are always worth pondering and his musical analysis is compelling.

else: she is known for her *razum,* her manly good sense, as the villagers see manliness. This quality in a woman, associated also with her stepmother, seems to mean some type of daring independence and command. She is literate and teaches other girls to read: she would be a good schoolteacher, they say. The stress of her situation, she says to her grandmother, has made her *razum* flow away like the water over the mill-wheel. We soon see, however, that it is not really gone. When Števa enters, drunk, celebrating his non-induction into the army, she lectures him sternly on his drunkenness—annoying him and dooming her own marital prospects. Musically we hear her inner firmness as well as her vulnerability. That vulnerability makes her care all too much about the attitudes of the village, which are those of an unreflective type of Roman Catholic piety and an attachment to conformity and social norms.[32]

The opera will ultimately be a story of profound love and mutual attunement, and Act 1 also introduces us to Laca, who, like Jenůfa, has both adolescent vulnerability and a core of inner firmness. The music depicts his childish aggressiveness toward Jenůfa, whom he teases out of jealousy and spite on account of her preference for his good-looking but ultimately worthless half-brother. The climactic episode of the Act is Laca's half-accidental slashing of Jenůfa's cheek with his knife (after he has pointedly said that, unlike him, Števa cares only for her cheeks). He clearly intends the injury at least subconsciously, and yet is also clearly not a malicious person. We hear from the Miller that his impulsive and childish behavior to Jenůfa is not at all typical of him; others treat him as a reliable worker and a man of substance, and everyone knows that he loves Jenůfa. Both Jenůfa and Laca, then, become confused and unreliable under the ticking clock of time; but both, unlike Števa—who cares only for

---

[32] The composer, who grew up in an Augustinian abbey, was officially Catholic throughout his life, but he did not have a warm relationship with the Church.

short-term pleasure—have an inner core that will ultimately carry them through life's pressures.

Act 1 takes place outdoors, in the autumn sun. Despite its characters' anxieties, the town is exuberant, and the Act is filled with joyful choral dancing, showing us the united good cheer of the people. Act 2, by contrast, is set in the winter, indoors, and it has no role for the Chorus, because Jenůfa has been hidden away from the shaming gaze of the crowd to give birth to her child. (Her stepmother, the Kostelnička, has told everyone that she is traveling abroad.) The musical texture of the Act is thin, dark, and brooding (bassoons play a major role). This Act is dominated by the Kostelnička, the stern highly respectable Church-Wardeness (that's what the name means, from her former marriage), who must figure out a way to deal with the illegitimate birth in such a way as to allow room for a happy life for Jenůfa. The music associated with her shocking decision becomes increasingly harsh and dissonant—by contrast to Jenůfa's calm stability.

We must now pause to consider the Kostelnička's options, because they are often misunderstood. The Kostelnička's decision to kill Jenůfa's infant is often seen as simply monstrous, a sign that she has lost her sanity. Critics, however, rarely consider her choice as that of a real person in a concrete historical and social context, and we must now do so.

Infanticide is forbidden by Christianity, Judaism, and Islam (though it was a respectable practice among the ancient Greeks, where "exposure" of an infant was a common practice). In the eighteenth and nineteenth centuries, the Christian cultures of Europe treated both the unwed mother and her illegitimate child with immense harshness, even when the mother could show that she was seduced by false promises, or even raped, often by a man of greater wealth or higher social station. A lot of infanticide was probably covered up by the fact that stillbirths did not have to be registered.

But when infanticide could be proven, much sympathy was shown—not by society as a whole, but by a whole chorus of eminent writers, who treated the act as wrong but urged mercy on account of the untenable social situation of the unwed mother in a rigidly moralistic society. The most famous such case in literature, and surely well known to Janáček, is Marguerite in Goethe's *Faust*, who kills her baby and is sentenced to die, but whose penitent soul ascends to heaven with the help of an army of angelic intercessors. Goethe's earlier *Urfaust* ended with a harsh judgment: "Sie ist gerichtet." ("She is judged.") But by the time he published *Faust* Part One in 1808, he had altered this to "Sie ist gerettet"—"She is saved."

Even the highly moralistic George Eliot, in *Adam Bede* (1859, based on a real legal case), allows Hetty Sorrel (who abandons her illegitimate child to die of exposure, and is initially sentenced to death) to be transported, instead, to Australia, where she can begin a new life.

Here Eliot, well-read in philosophy, echoes the view of none other than the most rigid defender of capital punishment in the history of philosophy, Immanuel Kant—again a thinker clearly in the background of this opera. For even Kant—a prime contender otherwise for first place in philosophy's misogyny sweepstakes—insists in his *Doctrine of Right* (1797) that indulgence should be shown to the woman who commits infanticide in harsh social circumstances. It is the one case where, in his view, capital punishment for murder is not required. Penal law "finds itself in a quandary," so that law must be "either cruel or indulgent." The act is bad and should be punished, and yet the unwed mother is a victim of social circumstances that put her outside legal justice in a "state of nature." The passage is so unlike Kant that commentators have found it surprising, but it is clear that he treats the woman as not a monster but a rational agent choosing a bad act out of lack of alternatives.

Literature also shows us clearly that the alternative of keeping and raising the child was an ugly one. Society bore down harshly both upon the woman who, while still unmarried, kept the baby and on her illegitimate offspring. The heroine of Mrs. Gaskell's *Ruth* (1853), seduced by an aristocrat with false promises of marriage, is urged by a sympathetic dissenting cleric to move elsewhere and pass herself off as a widow. She does so successfully for many years, and is about to get married, when her seducer turns up in town and the truth is somehow revealed. Ruth loses her employment, her fiancé, and even the love of her righteous now-adult son (who repents only at her graveside).

As for illegitimate children, they did better in some places than in others. Pierre, in Tolstoy's *War and Peace* (1867), even inherits his father's estate. In the more puritanical Britain, illegitimacy was freighted with severe social and financial disadvantages—although Anthony Trollope, in *Doctor Thorne* (1858), put in a plea for acceptance, and Wilkie Collins, in *No Name* (1862), issued an eloquent call for reform of punitive inheritance laws.

The Moravian town where *Jenůfa* takes place is even more puritanical than Victorian Britain. Its Protestant faith is enforced by severe and rigid social codes. Had Jenůfa kept her child, she might possibly have been socially forgiven if Števa had quickly married her. The Kostelnička therefore broaches the possibility with him while Jenůfa and the child are asleep. But he refuses to take responsibility, considering her beauty to be ruined—he really does care only for her cheeks. With the possibility of marriage to Števa off the table, the life that looms ahead is extremely bleak, both for her and for the little child. The Kostelnička knows this well, and she loves her stepdaughter. Next she interviews Laca, and discovers that, although he loves Jenůfa very deeply, the presence of his brother's child would be disqualifying for marriage. With the baby, then, there will be no marriage and no happy future. Nor will Jenůfa herself entertain the thought of infanticide—and if she did she would be punished, probably with death.

On the far side of infanticide the Kostelnička can see a happy future for Jenůfa—and of course she sees rightly, as the opera's hopeful ending shows. But for this future to exist the infanticide must be done, and done by her alone, with Jenůfa utterly ignorant of what is happening. In short, the Kostelnička must sacrifice her own moral purity and inner peace to save her beloved stepdaughter. (She notes that the infant has been baptized and thus will not be outside God's salvation.)

The Kostelnička knows that she will be committing a terrible crime, and yet if she does not commit it she will be ensuring lifelong misery for the person she loves most. Her dilemma is tragic—the clash of "right with right" characteristic of Greek tragedy (to which the opera has usefully been compared). She is truly in Kant's "state of nature," where the usual boundaries of law and morality fail to fit the situation. Her choice is both rational and horrible, and it is dictated above all by love. It is an altruistic sacrifice of her own future life. As the music of the Act becomes more and more dissonant, she becomes increasingly deranged by guilt: not because she is a moral monster, but because, having made a choice for the sake of love, she must bear the moral weight of the choice she has made, rather like Orestes pursued by the Furies. Janáček shows us her torment with devastating dramatic and musical clarity. If she were not a highly moral and sensitive woman, she would not suffer as she does. The opera's compelling and original twist to Goethe's well-known Marguerite scenario thus lies in the presence of a third party who chooses to bear the weight of guilt in order to spare another.

Meanwhile Jenůfa, in complete ignorance of what her stepmother has done, accepts the news of the baby's death as a profound tragedy, but also with a growing inner strength and stability, expressed in her beautiful prayer to the Virgin Mary, to be discussed later. She accepts Laca's offer of marriage.

Now to forgiveness, and Act 3. Act 3 is set in the springtime and again outdoors, and the townspeople return to the stage. The atmosphere appears auspicious, and the celebration of the wedding vows of Jenůfa and Laca lead the townspeople to want gaiety, although Jenůfa prefers a solemn simplicity. (After all, she knows of the birth and death of her child, so she cannot see herself as a virginal bride.) But spring is also a time of thawing ice. Before long, the corpse of the little child is discovered in the river, its identity clear from its clothing. Immediately the people start to accuse Jenůfa. However, the Kostelnička quickly comes forward to accept responsibility, assuring everyone that Jenůfa had absolutely nothing to do with the murder. She asks Jenůfa to forgive her and surrenders herself to the authorities. Jenůfa and Laca express their steadfast love for one another, and set out to make a life for themselves far away from the town.

The opera is always described as a story of forgiveness, and this is not wrong. But because interpreters do not examine different accounts of forgiveness known to religion and philosophy, they do not clarify the radical nature of Jenůfa's and Laca's moral achievement.[33] Christian forgiveness comes in several varieties, and the most usual type, which I shall call "transactional forgiveness," is not a pure good, but, very often, an ally of punitive attitudes of humiliation and domination. As defined for centuries by the Church, it is a practice involving the waiving of angry attitudes—but only if the sinner confesses, abases him or herself before the wronged party, and vows to be different in the future. It may ultimately be before an imagined angry God that the penitent must plead for forgiveness, but agents of the Church or of social authority are all too eager to assume this role. The practices of confession and contrition are suffused with shame and humiliation, as the penitent grovels in fear.

The Gospels contain some examples of transactional forgiveness, but Jesus more often commends two other attitudes: unconditional forgiveness, and unconditional love. Unconditional forgiveness looks a lot more morally attractive, in its respect for the sinner's autonomy, but the organized Church, not surprisingly, had little use for it because the Church lacked a central role in the

---

[33] See my *Anger and Forgiveness* (2016a, ch. 3), with further references to the philosophical and religious literature.

process. Furthermore, even unconditional forgiveness is at times suspect. St. Paul, for example, urges people to treat an enemy well, "for in so doing you will heap coals of fire upon his head" (*Romans* 12:20). This gloating attitude of superiority is all too common in social life, where people seek to demonstrate their own superiority by behavior that is "holier than thou."

From the very beginning, Jenůfa's understanding of Christianity is utterly different. In her Act 2 prayer to the Virgin Mary, she addresses Mary and Jesus as loving and merciful patrons of all exiles and sinners. The music is soaring and serene—similar in many ways to the women's quartet at the end of Act 2 of *Peter Grimes*. No groveling is required here: the Virgin Mary is a source of pure unconditional love, a sheltering unjudgmental maternal love. (This attitude too is found in the Gospels, in Christ's simple injunction to "love your enemies," and especially in the parable of the Prodigal Son, in which the father runs out to receive his son without any demand of confession or abasement, motivated solely by intense love. But such generosity tends to get short shrift in organized religion and in hierarchical societies.)

Jenůfa models her conduct, in this Act, on a radical and (in her context) heterodox idea of unconditional love (certainly with a scriptural foundation but foreign to the ideas of these local Catholics) that has long shaped her inner world and given her strength. Thus, she never asks Laca to beg forgiveness for his earlier act of aggression. She dismisses the very idea: "I forgave you long ago." (We might call this true unconditional forgiveness, purified of its assumption of moral superiority.) And she refuses her stepmother's attempt to kneel and beg forgiveness: "Do not kneel, dear mother. There's already been enough humiliation and torment." Like the Prodigal Son's father, she simply leaves the moral work to her: "We should not curse her, and we should not condemn her: give her time to atone."

This mature understanding of love has early roots in her Act 1 tenderness for the plant, combined with her inner core of *razum*.

But she has also progressed, losing the unsteadiness of her early self, and learning to distinguish real love from mere glamor. We feel that during the long months of isolation she has not been morally idle, but has rethought and reshaped her relationship to others and to herself.

Laca too has evolved. In Act 1 he was petulant and childish, lacking self-understanding of his own jealousy. In Act 2 he has evolved toward an open admission of his deep love, and a generous willingness to disregard social stigma. His love, however, is still not fully unconditional, since he is unwilling to marry her if his brother's child is to be part of the picture. By Act 3—although of course, given the child's death, there is no way of testing this proposition—we feel that his love has evolved yet further, and that when he says the world doesn't matter if they are together, he really means that his devotion is in no way transactional or conditional. One of this opera's great strengths is in its portrayal of moral evolution through, we feel, constant self-control and moral effort guided by the eyes of love. Peter Grimes utterly lacked this dimension of moral effort, allowing the Borough's norms to determine his life's course. And really, no Borough inhabitant makes an effort to grow and change. Albert Herring is different, more like Laca, though as yet with nobody to love.

The love of Jenůfa and Laca is emotionally convincing and deep because it is founded on a shared view of unconditional love. Jenůfa has noticed "the generous way in which you behaved to me while I was kept in hiding"—not condescending, not assuming moral superiority—and already in Act 2, her love acknowledging his own unconditional love, she sees that he is the man for her. (Thus Janáček is able to eliminate a long scene in Preissová's play in which Laca convinces Jenůfa of his love.) At the end of Act 2, seeing already that he is willing to take her with all her sorrow and hardship, she says, "Then I'll gladly share the good as well as the ill that may befall us."

When they are left alone, at the end of Act 3, she gives him one last chance to leave her, saying, "You were always the best and finest man of all." Laca passes the test, saying: "What does the world matter, if we are together." Joined in a love as radical as it is rare, they transcend society's conceptions of sin and forgiveness. Each of them has a deep and steady inner world, and this enables them to move beyond the crowd.

The libretto gives us all this, but what words cannot convey is the depth of Janáček's music, as he finds daring musical expression for ideas of surging love, unconditionality, and the transcendence of mere social forms. Among comparable composers of his time, only Mahler (who, invited by Janáček in 1904 to attend a performance of *Jenůfa*, replied asking for a German-language vocal score, but never got a response, since no such score was available) has a similar musical affinity for these ideas, and Mahler never wrote an opera. Like Mahler (especially in his Second Symphony), Janáček expresses an unconventional religious vision in ecstatically passionate music. Unlike Mahler, he embodies the vision in vibrant individual lives.

So, as the final music swells upward, with Jenůfa's "Oh Laca, dearest Laca! Oh come! Come!," they go forth into the new universe of inner freedom that their love has created.

Janáček and Britten are kindred spirits, understanding the soul-crushing potentiality of unyielding conventions and rigid un-Christlike Christianity. Britten expressed his vision in many works, including his *War Requiem*, with its portrayal of unconditional human love embodied in a fully human Christ. But this same cast of mind inhabits (by its absence) *Peter Grimes* and (by its incipient presence) *Albert Herring*. For both, the solution to the evils of internal exile lies ultimately in each human soul, and, potentially, in a reformed community animated by respect and love for the souls of all.

The crowd has a terrible power, and we are all weak. But republican self-government requires citizens who can think for themselves and stand up against group pressure. Otherwise democracies will collapse into autocracy, as so many have and as others may in the near or distant future. Mozart has little to say about this impediment to the creation and sustenance of a Republic of Love. These three operas illustrate the contribution that opera as a genre can make to political thought on this topic. Because they depict the persecutory power of groups, and yet describe people who, partly or wholly, manage to become and be themselves, they show how communities might resist that power—by nourishing the core of integrity within each person through education (Jenůfa's *razum*), by supporting people's continued efforts to evolve and improve, and, above all, through love.

They also show the disaster for both individuals and communities if these efforts should fail.

8

War and the Search for Peace

John Adams's *Nixon in China*

This trip should not be one which would create very great optimism or very great pessimism. It is one in which we must recognize that twenty years of hostility and virtually no communication will not be swept away by one week of discussion. However, it will mark a watershed in the relations between the two governments; the post-war era . . . now comes to an end from the time that I set foot on the soil of Mainland China, and a new chapter begins.

—Richard M. Nixon, press conference before the 1972 trip to China

[S]oon our words won't be recalled / While what we do can change the world. / We have at times been enemies, / We still have differences, God knows. / But let us, in these next five days / Start a long march on new highways, / In different lanes, but parallel / And heading for a single goal. / The world watches and listens. We / Must seize the hour and seize the day.

—Nixon in *Nixon in China*, closely based on his actual speech at the banquet

Mozart on War: Evasion and One Profound Insight

What can operas tell us about war and peace? Surely this is a crucial topic for the Republic of Love. Mozart is evasive. In *Così fan tutte* the young men head off to war in a company of soldiers to the tune of a cheerful march, and the ensemble as a whole informs us that the life of the soldier is a great life (*bella vita militar*) with lots of travel, every day a new place, both on land and sea. Even the sounds of shells and guns are listed just after trumpets and fifes as things that strengthen both "arms" and "spirits." Nor does the music contain anything ominous—although stage directors have at times added the missing elements in production, showing the men returning wounded from the front.

In *The Marriage of Figaro*, however, Mozart contributes a profound insight that does no work in the opera itself, but points the way to future honest confrontations by others. At the end of Act 1 the young Cherubino, about to leave the female world of amorous sighs, courtly dances, and, crucially, music, is taunted by Figaro, who describes the world of war as the antithesis of that gentle world. Instead of dancing the fandango, he says, you will march through mud, *il fango*. And this world is also a world of anti-music: Cherubino will march "to a concerto of blunderbusses, / shells, and cannons / whose shots, on all pitches, / make your ears whistle."[1] Figaro sees what the ensemble in *Così* does not: war is not a jolly business, a kind of genial world tour. Instead of cheerfully complementing fifes and brass, shells and gunshots are profoundly anti-musical. They hurt your ears. And worse.

---

[1] "Al concerto di trombone, / Di bombardi, di cannone / Che le palle In tutti i tuoni/ All'orecchio fan fischiar." The words *concerto* and *tuoni* are musical words used, ironically, for the anti-musical noises of war. The word *trombone* is frequently translated as "trumpets" or "bugles." But it is also the word for "blunderbuss," and I think Da Ponte is clearly having fun with its double meaning, both musical and anti-musical. "Fischiar" can mean either "ring" or "whistle." For further discussion, see ch. 2 of my *The Tenderness of Silent Minds* (2024).

In *Figaro*, not surprisingly, Cherubino never does go to war; the action remains confined to a world in which music is audible.

If we follow Figaro's idea, we might suppose that the idea of writing an opera about war is a self-defeating task: it means turning into music something that subverts the very being of music. Either the opera will be evasive, like *Così*, or it will depart from its very nature. However, there is a great deal more to be said, and sung.

Operas Approaching War and Peace-Making

Many composers have written music on war-related themes, and there are reasons to think we can gain special insight from their efforts. Opera can investigate the character and psychology of war and peacemaking and the emotions involved in each, with a depth that is rare in other arts—especially because, unlike non-musical drama, it includes both individual figures and a chorus (see also chapter 6).

To summarize the options simplistically: An opera concerned with war can take one of three forms. First, it can be zealously and simplistically nationalistic, pursuing or celebrating a nation's victory as if it is perfectly successful. A lot of symphonic music is of this sort, from the marches of John Philip Sousa to Tchaikovsky's 1812 Overture, written in 1880 to celebrate Russia's victory repelling the French invasion. As if taking a cue from *Così*, the overture uses real cannons as musical instruments. This sort of celebration is not always foolish: celebrating, as Tchaikovsky did, the liberation of one's own people from a brutal conqueror seems rational and good. Many national anthems are of this exultant my-nation-has-prevailed sort, and some of these, especially *La Marseillaise* in its setting by Berlioz, have been high-quality music. But the one-sidedness of such triumphalism is not likely to provide material for opera, since opera is always concerned with complex characters of varied types. I think Prokofiev's version of *War and*

Peace approaches simple triumphal nationalism, but in so doing it falls greatly short of the human complexity of Tolstoy's novel.

Second, an opera about war can be pessimistic in the sense made familiar by Schopenhauer (see further in chapter 9), depicting both war's projects and its people as doomed to failure and hence worthless, caught in a web of illusion. Since Schopenhauer thinks no project worthwhile if it does not achieve stable success, peace-making, too, would seem doomed. And in fact, in all of human history nobody has really put a lasting end to war, whether by conquest or diplomacy, though some peace agreements last longer than others.

It is difficult to make a successful opera out of such doomed projects and futile people, but Mussorgsky's *Boris Godunov* (1874) comes close. The opera shows the Russian people as perpetual victims and dupes of a sequence of self-serving would-be rulers: Boris himself, the false Dimitri, the Polish princess Marina and her Jesuit advisor Rangoni—so that in the end the holy fool seems to speak for the opera when he sings, "Darkest darkness, endless darkness. Woe to Russia. Weep, weep, Russian people, starving people."[2] The opera has non-Schopenhauerian emotional weight only through the Shakespearean character of Boris, and it holds the audience's interest largely through his complex emotions of guilt and aspiration, his mixture of good and bad traits.

Between the superficiality of triumphalist nationalism and the nihilism of Schopenhauer there is a lot of space within which operas about war can offer insight. Human beings can be shown as worthy and lovable even though their context dooms them to be victims of an endless sequence of wars. Verdi's *Aida* (1871) is a

---

[2] This particular nihilistic ending is not in Pushkin's play, where the Fool is a character but plays a reduced role. However the actual ending of the play is pessimistic enough: Boris dies, his children are murdered by agents of the false Dmitri, the boyars proclaim the death of the children (calling it a suicide) and proclaim Tsar Dmitri Ivanovich, asking the crowd to cheer for him. The crowd remains silent. Presumably this suggests that any government that prevails by force is likely to be unaccountable to the people—and that is similar to Mussorgsky. But it also signals the ongoing instability of political authority.

wonderful example of such an opera.[3] All the major characters are decent—even the jealous Amneris—but they are trapped by a politics fixated on reciprocal retribution with no interest in diplomacy and peace-making. Right from the beginning we are thrust into an unending sequence of tit-for-tat wars between two powerful and roughly equal kingdoms. In the opera's very first sentence, the high priest Ramfis says: "Yes, reports say that the Ethiopians dare to try once again ('*ancora*'), and to menace the valley of the Nile and Thebes." The invaders are said to have burned crops and laid waste to the fields, and the Egyptians fear death and captivity for their own people. Later the Ethiopian king Amonasro tells his daughter Aida that the Egyptians have done the very same thing: "They have desecrated our houses, our temples, our altars, carried our maidens off in chains, slain mothers, the aged, the young." The only reason the Ethiopians have not done the same this time is that their invasion is not successful. The opera shows the terrible pain and also the profound moral conflicts these wars cause for decent people, and the opera, though known for its spectacle, is above all a superb intimate study of these conflicts. Memorably it ends with its protagonists literally suffocated in a subterranean tomb. But—although the opera's final word is Amneris's "pace, pace," none of the major power-holders are doing anything about this pernicious and seemingly endless cycle.

Wars do end, however. Sometimes, too, they don't even start. Operas can in principle portray the constructive diplomacy that ends or prevents wars. When wars are averted beforehand, and a measure of international cooperation is produced, it is typically through laborious transnational efforts at understanding and deal-making. These topics seem boring and non-operatic, but there is reason to think again. Efforts toward peace are executed by flawed individual people, often very strange people, doing their

---

[3] See my program essay on *Aida*, "War, Enemy of Love," Program of the Lyric Opera of Chicago (2024a, pp. 24–26).

best: getting an idea, taking risks, feeling anxiety, losing sleep, and delving deep into themselves. This search has something heroic about it and is of profound human interest. John Adams's *Nixon in China* (1987) is a bold attempt to depict this sort of realistic heroism, making opera out of real people's imperfect search for understanding and for at least some human progress.

Nixon in China: An Opera
Searching for Peace

John Adams (a great admirer of both Mozart and Verdi, as is evident from his many interviews) has written a Mozartean/Verdian grand opera about the search for détente—in partnership with librettist Alice Goodman and director Peter Sellars. How he managed to do this, creating a work that captivates audiences and plunges them into a complicated search for international reciprocity or even rapprochement, is one of the most electrifying stories in the history of the genre. Librettist Alice Goodman and composer John Adams have continually insisted that the opera should be seen as a "heroic opera," which it weirdly but indubitably is—one of their most astute points being that heroic projects in real life are undertaken, if they are, not by blameless figures of legend, but by profoundly flawed and yet energetic and visionary men and women.

Adams belongs to a generation that came of age in the shadow of the Vietnam War and efforts to avoid it. He graduated from Harvard in 1969, the year of the takeover of Harvard's University Hall by antiwar activists and the decision of President Nathan Pusey to call in the city police. All this he describes vividly in his appealing autobiography, *Hallelujah Junction*,[4] though he does not mention that the spring of 1970, when he was a first-year graduate student, still at Harvard, was even worse: the tumult unleashed

---

[4] Adams (2008).

by student reactions to Nixon's carpet bombing of Cambodia led to the cancellation of final exams. Adams was antiwar, but not a radical or an activist, and indeed seems to have been focused above all on avoiding military service. He vividly and correctly conveys the way in which the lives of an entire generation were dominated by the war and fear of perishing in what virtually everyone our age, at least at most universities, saw as a useless and unjust conflict.[5] Being a man, Adams got a draft notice, and he describes his elaborate stratagems to raise his blood pressure through medication, until his draft board finally gave up on him.[6] Women faced no direct peril, but cared about those who did. For an entire generation, the emotional stress of personal peril was exhausting, and usually very self-focused, even if there were also objections to the war's injustice. Adams never remarks on the war's class and race bias, but it was there to be seen, if one began to consider who actually did the fighting. (Nor did people think much about Vietnamese lives, and to this day they are not mentioned on the wall of the Vietnam Veterans Memorial.)

That was how things were then. Adams's generation typically saw Nixon as a major cause of the war's moral horror, despite his campaign promise to end it, because he and Kissinger escalated it first in a useless and horrible fashion. (Sworn in in January 1969, he planned and presided over the invasion of Cambodia.) The Watergate break-in that eventually led to Nixon's resignation in August 1974 came in June, 1972, a few months after the China trip in February; but well before that time our generation on college campuses were confirmed anti-Nixonites. And even staunch Republicans were already turning against Nixon by 1972, because his corruption was gradually becoming evident: the key memo in

---

[5] I say "our" because Adams and I were born just a few months apart, and I was also at Harvard during this time, arriving as a graduate student the year he began his graduate studies.

[6] Adams (2008, pp. 42–46). The draft lottery, which ended student deferments, began in December 1969.

the quid pro quo ITT affair—in which the Nixon administration agreed to settle an antitrust suit against ITT in return for a large donation to a fund for the 1972 Republican National Convention—was published by a journalist one day after the China trip.[7] Only two years later, Nixon was forced to resign.

And yet: at the very same time—between February 21 and 28, 1972—this flawed President undertook a bold initiative in China designed to pierce through years of suspicion and ignorance and at least to open the door to peaceful cooperation.

Meanwhile, John Adams was developing his gifts as both composer and conductor. From the beginning, Mozart played a central role. He tells us that he was entranced, as a boy, by Mozart's life story, which made him imagine a possible life for himself as a composer. He listened to many Mozart recordings, along with Beethoven, Bach, Duke Ellington, Benny Goodman, and many others. At Harvard his first big undertaking as a conductor was a production of *The Marriage of Figaro* at Leverett House at Harvard, with stage direction by fellow undergraduate John Lithgow. Much later, his opera *A Flowering Tree* is based on *The Magic Flute*.[8] As I shall suggest, *Nixon in China* exhibits a Mozartean sensibility (along with specific allusions to Mozart)—accepting flawed human beings and honoring their efforts, while favoring a politics of dialogue and peaceful exchange.

But how could a composer from that background, who felt himself scarred by Vietnam, agree to write an opera on Nixon's visit

---

[7] The memo, sent by ITT lobbyist Dita Beard, disclosing the quid pro quo, was written in June 1971 but published by columnist Jack Anderson on February 29, 1972—the very day after Nixon's return from China. Beard testified before the Senate Judiciary Committee in March 1972, initially lying about the memo and her role, as she later admitted, and feigning a heart attack to terminate the interrogation. (Two cardiologists examined her and found no problem.) She retired to a horse farm in Colorado and died in 1992, two years before Nixon. Rumors of the quid pro quo were already current before her memo was leaked: I remember discussing them with my father, hospitalized for cancer surgery in late 1971. (A determined Republican, he nonetheless stopped supporting Nixon then and there. He died in early 1972.)

[8] Adams (2008, pp. 15–16, 36, 296–98).

to China? Clearly director Peter Sellars, who proposed the idea in 1983, was very persuasive and, ten years younger than Adams, less focused on Vietnam. But for Adams, doubts remained: "My own antipathy toward that president who'd tried to draft me and send me to fight in Vietnam had not even begun to reach equanimity,"[9] he reminisces. Adams was no China buff: in the trio of creators it was Sellars who had the detailed knowledge of Chinese history and politics. But Adams had watched with fascination the TV footage of the Nixon visit back in 1972, and he knew that Nixon had written a lot about it since. He began to think that poetry and music could lift the historical characters onto a mythic plane, presenting their efforts as more general forms of human aspiration to détente and understanding. (Adams knows Schopenhauer and alludes to his view of musical representation in this context, though certainly without the pessimism.[10]) Moreover, he welcomed "the opportunity to move, over the course of three acts, from the plastic cartoon versions of people that the media is always presenting us with, to the real uncertain, vulnerable human beings who stand behind those cardboard cutouts."[11]

By now, followers of Adams's career can see that trying to prevent war's horrors is a major theme in his work (*The Death of Klinghoffer*, *Doctor Atomic*), and that he takes that task to require arduous if always incomplete efforts to understand another group's history and point of view (the Jews and Palestinians in *Klinghoffer*).[12]

The opera is thoroughly collaborative. Sellars (b. 1957), an enfant terrible of operatic staging, had the idea first and has been continuously involved in major productions, but during the work's

[9] Adams (2008, p. 135). That remark shows the self-focus common among privileged young people in that era. His Vietnam "scars" were minor inconveniences.

[10] See Adams in Andrew Porter interview (note below), p. 30. Adams often alludes to myth as a key, for him, in approaching the characters: see, for example, Daines (1996, p. 43) and Adams (2008, p. 13).

[11] Porter (1988, pp. 25–30 at 26).

[12] In his commentary on this chapter at Brown University, David Armitage made very insightful comments on these two operas, especially the latter. I hope they will form part of his own forthcoming book on opera.

creation the intimate partnership between Adams and young poet Alice Goodman determined most of the work's key features. Goodman (b. 1958), eleven years younger than Adams, wrote the libretto for *Klinghoffer* too, but then—having converted from Judaism to Christianity in 1989—dropped out of the arts world to become an Anglican priest. She now serves as Rector of a group of parishes in Cambridgeshire, England. In 1987, the year that the opera premiered, she married the distinguished poet Geoffrey Hill (1932–2016) and is therefore Lady Hill. She describes her conversion as a repudiation of ideas of retribution she heard from her childhood rabbi.[13] (It is most surprising, though a common error, that a person so insightful would equate one rabbi's retributive views with the entirety of Judaism.) She and Adams rarely met, but corresponded back and forth with a fruitful if not always harmonious reciprocity.

What was happening at the opera's dramatic date, February 1972? The Vietnam War was dragging on, long after the carpet-bombing of Cambodia; it ended only with the fall of Saigon in 1975. Back in the United States, the Watergate break-in, key exhibit of Nixon's criminal paranoia, was being secretly planned. China was in the middle of the Cultural Revolution (1966–1976), a brutal purge of both ideas and people in which both Mao and Mme. Mao (Jiang Qing) were leading participants, she as part of the ultra-revolutionary "gang of four." Zhou Enlai, the Premier, increasingly at odds with Mme. Mao behind the scenes, was already ill with the bladder cancer that killed him in 1976, and Mao had already refused him medical treatment that would have saved his life if administered promptly, although this refusal was not known at the time of the opera's composition. By the time the opera had its premiere in 1987, Mao and Zhou were both dead (both in 1976), and the Cultural Revolution, declared a failure, had been replaced by a somewhat more relaxed regime led by Deng Xiaoping, a protégé of

---

[13] See Rahim (2017).

Zhou. It appeared that the nation was tending toward greater openness and democratization—until the Tiananmen Square massacre in 1989. Jiang Qing, arrested shortly after Mao's death, was imprisoned, and eventually (released for medical treatment) committed suicide in 1991. The Nixons were both still living (she died in 1993, he in 1994), and he had written a great deal, attempting to rehabilitate himself but also shedding a lot of light on his dealings with China. Henry Kissinger lived to see his 100th birthday in 2023, at which time he was fêted by a lavish celebration at the New York Public Library, attended by all sorts of famous people who had condemned his actions in Vietnam.[14] Before the opera was restaged at the Metropolitan Opera in New York in 2011, new revelations in a book by Mao's personal physician darkened American views of Mao's personal conduct and showed clearly his role in, effectively, killing Zhou.[15]

Each time the opera is produced it looks different in the light of new events and information—underlining its message of the instability and uncertainty of efforts toward peace and détente— a theme much emphasized by Nixon in his writings about 1972. But on one point the 1972 trip has proven irreversible. Before 1972, China was a black box, rather like North Korea today. No American could visit there; scholars were forbidden to do research there. In 1954, at the Geneva Conference, US Secretary of State John Foster Dulles refused to shake the hand of Zhou Enlai. The prevailing idea was that Communists were so evil that one could not even speak to them or try to coexist with them peacefully. By 1987, by contrast, China was wide open. (Even I visited in that year, to give lectures on feminism and liberal theories of justice, and I saw the traditional murals at the Summer Palace—painted out during the Cultural Revolution—being repainted.) This basic openness

---

[14] See Jonathan Guyer's hilarious "I Crashed Henry Kissinger's 100th Birthday Party" (2023).

[15] Li Zhisui (1994).

to the world has never been reversed, despite the greater repression of citizens that is in place today. Even Xi Jinping, though no moderate, does not really wish to extinguish profitable trade relations or the thriving tourist economy—which inevitably gives rise to human contacts and a reciprocal flow of information that cannot be fully managed. (Xi's catastrophic attempt to close the nation down during Covid did not win support for such policies, which he quickly abandoned, and the lucrative tourist trade is back in operation.) On the US side, Nixon reversed decades of shunning—which grew out of the same McCarthyite Cold War behavior in which he himself participated, so he is absolutely correct (as he says in Act 1) that his trip involves admitting that he had been wrong. In 1972 he urged Americans to conclude, as he had, that disapproval does not mean non-communication; and he tempered his disapproval with an invitation to seek peace together—at that time a remarkable volte-face.

Even though the prospects for peaceful détente have ebbed and flowed over the period since Nixon's trip, then, there was something big that his bold step created, and even today, with suspicion and fear relatively high, we can all see this achievement. At first the opera was wrongly understood as a satire, a reaction that greatly annoyed all three of its creators. Adams and Alice Goodman have been consistently emphatic about this error and insisted that they never would have gotten involved had it been a satire. The term "heroic opera," probably coined by Goodman, stuck, and all three creators have endorsed it.[16] What is heroic about it is to take a bold risk for peace and understanding, when a continuation of suspicion and hostility would have been so much easier. And though the Americans' efforts to understand the thought and culture of China were halting and full of blind spots, they were also fueled by much study and genuine desire to see the other. That is what I would call anti-retributive heroism, the type of heroism sorely lacking in the

---

[16] See Porter (1988, p. 27).

world of *Aida*. (*Aida* was playing in repertory with the new opera in Houston at the time of its premiere, and Sellars claims that the work is full of small allusions to the Verdi opera.[17])

Adams made an initial decision of great importance: he would not write pseudo-Chinese music or even music filled with Americans' idea of Chinese sounds (as in Puccini's *Turandot*). He had no interest in that: he is an American composer, and the music, he insists, is American music through and through. Besides, his idea of the opera is that it is "an American opera, an opera that is rooted in our peculiarly skewed image of ourselves, an opera that aims to be both theatrically entertaining and psychologically acute."[18] His partial allegiance to the minimalism of Steve Reich and Philip Glass gives the work a kind of out-in-space universal flavor, with its repeated arpeggios that Adams compares to a ukulele under the vocal lines.[19] This style, certainly not that of classical Western orchestral music, makes it capable of embracing contrasting cultural ideas (a purpose for which Glass effectively uses a more extreme minimalism in *Satyagraha*, about Gandhi, and *Akhnaten*, about ancient Egypt).[20] But the opera is also filled with allusions to big band music and to jazz, and the very brass-heavy orchestra also has four saxophones. Adams's parents were contemporaries of the Nixons, and Adams thinks of the white big band sound of Glenn Miller and Benny Goodman (Adams is an excellent clarinetist, as was his father) as what the Nixons would have heard in their heads when they fell in love, and thus as conveying, "with its admixture of sentimentality and reminiscence, . . . the ideal of Nixon's

---

[17] See Daines and Sellars (1996).

[18] Adams (2008, p. 141).

[19] Porter (1988, p. 28). The musical language of the work is given an exhaustive and superb study by Timothy A. Johnson in *John Adams's Nixon in China: Musical Analysis, Historical and Political Perspectives* (2011).

[20] Adams acknowledges the influence of Glass's *Satyagraha*, and Armitage, in his comments on this chapter, convincingly finds that influence in the first two acts, "particularly his arpeggiation, strong beat and use of electronic instruments, the pulsing harmonics communicating the hectic stress of Nixon's brief, four-day, visit to Beijing."

imagined Middle America."[21] (Although Adams does not state this, Nixon also admired jazz, and he was an avid and fluent pianist; a recording exists of him serenading Duke Ellington impromptu at the piano with "Happy Birthday," when Ellington was awarded the Presidential Medal of Freedom in 1969.) Mao was inter alia a fan of jazz, and the scene in Act 3 in which he and Jiang Qing recall their torrid love affair is very jazzy. As for the ballet in Act 2: the actual ballets choreographed by Jiang Qing used a kind of pastiche Russian-ballet-like music, but Adams, rather than doing a knock-off of a knock-off, does his own minimalist thing.

Above all, Adams has a gift for melody and rhythm, and also for the musical creation of character.[22] He uses these gifts expressively and with increasing independence and variety as the work goes on—by Act 3 discarding the minimalist repetitive undercurrent altogether and allowing the instruments, as well as the voices, to disengage and go their own way.[23]

The great distinction of the Adams-Goodman partnership is empathy. Adams remarks that he sees parts of himself in all the main characters except for Mao and Kissinger, and he can find acquaintances of his to help him relate to those characters. Alice Goodman found Mao accessible because he seemed like her husband: brilliant, a poet, irascible, aggressive, given to withering repartee. But the pair hardly relied just on their own experience: they read extensively, including Mao's poems, letters between Nixon and Pat during the war, and much more. Most of the libretto, though

---

[21] Adams (2008, p. 141): "Thus a big band became the nucleus of the orchestral sound for *Nixon in China*," a sound heavy on brass and winds and further padded by the addition of four saxophones. See Daines (1996, pp. 37–54, at 46), where Adams rejects the idea that the opera is satirical and asserting its Americanness: "At no point in this opera did I want to write fake Chinese music; the music is inexorably American, no matter who is singing."

[22] See Adams (2008, pp. 140–41): "I found I loved creating character through harmony and rhythm."

[23] See Porter (1988, p. 28): "the instruments somehow emerge out of the orchestra and begin to develop their own personality, they intertwine and interlock, and, as the Indians say about sitar music, they create a garland with the voices."

artfully crafted in semi-rhyming couplets, is based on things the protagonists actually said, even in the intimate exchanges of Act 3.

Act 1 depicts Nixon's arrival and the initial greetings between the two groups; then, in a separate scene, the meeting between Nixon and Mao in Mao's study; and finally the state banquet with its hopeful toasts by Zhou and Nixon. The first scene of Act 2 shows Pat's tour of the city conducted by some highly guarded Chinese women; and then the presentation of Jiang Qing's ballet "The Red Detachment of Women" before the group, leading to Mme. Mao's blistering aria denouncing all deviations from political orthodoxy. Act 3 shows the two couples, the Nixons and the Maos, reminiscing (in complexly interweaving vocal lines) about their earlier lives. Finally, Zhou, unable to sleep, delivers the opera's final statement.

Mozart's guidance (often and amply acknowledged by Adams) is omnipresent throughout. There are specific borrowings: the three secretaries of Mao (who have come to be known as the Maoettes) clearly allude to the three Ladies of *Magic Flute*, while Mme. Mao's ferocious aria reminds us of the Queen of the Night in its implacable and vindictive spirit as well as its daring high notes. But there are more pervasive influences. As David Armitage eloquently says, Adams owes to Mozart "his characteristic mood shifts within the bar . . . the singular importance of dance—fandangos and contradanse for Mozart, the foxtrot for *Nixon*; and above all the creative use of ensemble singing as the enactment of equality and reciprocity."[24] I would go further: the entire ethos of the opera is Mozartean, in its merciful approach to human frailty, its concern for overcoming fear and revenge with a search for connection and understanding.

On the whole, as I shall show, the opera succeeds admirably in its aims. But I must begin by expressing my view that it has two big flaws. The first is that the ballet scene of Act 2 is a disaster. Peter Sellars was greatly attached to doing a version of this actual

---

[24] Armitage, comments presented at Brown University, March 2025.

historical ballet, based on recordings that exist, and was already working on it, so he decided to include it in the opera. And he remains convinced that this scene is the very heart of the opera.[25] But Adams himself says that it didn't interest him as much as the other scenes because it was satiric.[26] And truly, what is the point of satirizing what was in reality already a piece of revolutionary kitsch? What is that scene accomplishing? And since the audience knows nothing of the original ballet, and most will not know that such ballets really existed, they can hardly know what is real and what is satire.

Furthermore, the idea of Pat Nixon being so shocked by the brutal treatment of the heroine by the landowner that she intervenes in the artwork is utterly unconvincing, especially when, otherwise, stoicism and polite composure are her hallmarks. This scene utterly confuses the audience, messing up the consistent picture of Pat that emerges both before and after.

A third problem is the political statement Sellars wants the ballet scene to make. He sees in his version of the ballet all sorts of subtleties about the politics of the Cultural Revolution and specific participants in it, but these points would be and are utterly lost on American audiences. The aria of Jiang Qing after the ballet, by contrast, is very dramatic, appropriate, and to the point, dramatizing effectively her form of totalitarianism. So what was needed was something else leading up to it, and following the very moving aria by Pat at the end of the first scene of Act 2.

The other huge flaw in the opera is the character of Kissinger. It is a character-driven opera, and the creators have nothing to say about Kissinger or his inner life, so he is included, in effect, only because he was historically present. In Act 2, Sellars weirdly makes that actor play the capitalist landlord in the ballet, but this only adds to the confusion. In Act 3, Kissinger is hustled offstage with a

---

[25] Daines and Sellars (1996, pp. 1–19).
[26] Daines (1996, p. 48).

lame excuse about having to go to the bathroom, and he is seen no more. It would be better to have had him present in Act 1 as a minor character and simply omitted him later.[27]

However: let us put these problems to one side. *Nixon in China* is a heroic opera, and its weight and force come above all from its five heroes. The people of the two nations are also heroes, of course, as indeed we are told in the opening chorus, "The people are the heroes now." But the Chinese people are muzzled—they can barely say anything to Pat's gentle questions. And the American people are present only by implication, in Nixon's constant concern with the TV news and their likely reactions. Adams and Goodman are above all psychologists, and they focus on the in-depth portrayal of five complicated figures, and it is through them that we come to know, as well, the character of their respective regimes and peoples.

Central among these is Richard Nixon, whose daring decision set the whole project in motion. At the time of the opera's premiere, Nixon had become, as Adams remarks, a cliché of late-night TV comedy. The challenge therefore was to burrow into him and give him weight. Adams says he imagines him as like Verdi's Simon Boccanegra, a politician who strives for the good but is troubled by cabals and suspicions.[28] Adams had the great good fortune to work from the beginning, even while writing the score, with one

---

[27] David Armitage makes a heroic effort to rescue this character (in his commentary on this chapter at Brown University). Kissinger, he argues, represents the sort of stealthy, silent, behind-the-scenes maneuvering that is often central to foreign affairs. The very fact that we do not see him doing anything openly is precisely the point. I find this imaginative but unconvincing. First of all, it does not fit perfectly with Kissinger's historical role. He did make a secret trip to China at Nixon's behest, before the official trip was planned. But once the trip was under way, his role was openly that of advisor and planner: after all, he is present and highly visible. Perhaps more decisive, it makes a mess of Kissinger's role in the ballet, where he is supposed to represent not a person of stealth but a brutal and violent landlord. Finally, we see nothing that suggests the role of stealthy agent, and surely one cannot expect an opera audience to conclude from the utter absence of visible action that he is actually acting in secret. I think that Armitage could be right that Sellars had some such idea, but if so, Adams and Goodman simply didn't do anything with it.

[28] Adams in Elena Park, "The Myth of History: John Adams and Peter Sellars Talk *Nixon in China*," *Playbill*, February 1, 2011, p. 4. The description of the character is mine.

of opera's greatest singer-actors, baritone James Maddelena, who played the role of Nixon from 1987 until at least the Met performance of 2011, which anyone can see on Met HD On Demand. The score is already remarkable, but Maddelena makes it indelible. Nixon is seen as genuinely idealistic, and yet also given to petty vanity and over-confidence, and always to mercurial shifts of mood that veer into a dark paranoia.

Adams deploys three musical devices to etch this quixotic character: a lot of staccato, so that Nixon's utterances are assertive but not serene and confident (like those of Zhou); a wavering unsteady vocal line, often going up and wildly down on the same syllable; and, finally, music that is often doing something different from what the text is doing. In Act 1 Nixon enters with bravura: Air Force One actually lands on the stage, "to the accompaniment of my stuttering brass tattoos and fractured version of 'The Star-Spangled Banner.'"[29] He and Pat walk down the stairs, and he shakes hands with Zhou. After a little small talk about the trip, Nixon bursts out with staccato self-assertive excitement in his aria "News Has a Kind of Mystery." Although he is clearly delighted with the fact that his words are being broadcast live in prime time in the United States, the staccato repetitions of "News! News! News!" and "Made history!," together with the swooping of the vocal line makes his pride sound uncertain, jittery. He then describes his reaction looking down at China from above: "the countryside / Looked drab and gray, "Brueghel," Pat said. / "We came in peace for all mankind" / I said, and I was put in mind/Of our Apollo astronauts . . . ." Here Nixon's pride and genuine idealism burst forth, but with his repetitions of "I said" (the repetitions are not in the printed libretto, therefore Adams's solo creation), also a characteristic Nixonian vanity and self-assertion.

And it is all unstable: he immediately turns to inner anxiety about whether the mission will succeed. In staccato bursts, "We live in an

---

[29] Adams (2008, p. 145).

unsettled time. / Who are our enemies? Who are / Our friends?" This uncertainty is rational and even admirable, given the risks and the stakes, but it must not be permitted to ruin the effort. So Nixon then calms himself down, describing how they have flown "across a sea of distrust / Filled with the bodies of our lost; / The earth's Sea of Tranquility" (naming the area on the moon where the astronauts landed). This second moon/astronaut reference pleases him, and the music grows calmer, but it can hardly remain so, given the reference to his service in the Pacific in World War II, much on his mind throughout the opera, given that this is the meaning of the Pacific Ocean in his mind. And sure enough, as he asserts, "I know America is good at heart," the D minor chord undercuts his optimism.

After a scene change, back in his hotel room, paranoia takes over in full Watergate mode, in a low guttural staccato: "The rats begin to chew the sheets, / There's murmuring below. / Now there's ingratitude!" And then, pulling himself out of his nightmare, Nixon asserts, "My hand / Is steady as a rock"—although the rushed compressed music is anything but steady.

Adams and Goodman have distilled from the things that really were said and a few that were not a masterful musical character portrait, and it says a lot about war and peace. The good thing about the search for peace is that real people dream of it and strive and create imaginative schemes. The bad thing about the search for peace is that real people are what we are stuck with, and real politicians at that, with the vanity and insecurity characteristic of that species. Both Adams and Goodman insist repeatedly that Nixon was not a totally mendacious and evil person.[30] Despite his evident flaws, Nixon had the boldness of mind to think up this trip and do it, when perhaps no other politician would or could have. But he is also Nixon, and mistrust and suspicion gnaw at him at every moment, making the vision flicker unstably before his eyes.

---

[30] Porter (1988); Rahim (2017).

In the meeting with Mao, Nixon more or less holds his own, though outfoxed by Mao's superior wit and historical/philosophical depth. Finally Nixon recovers his bearings, insisting, "my feet / Are firmly planted on the ground, like yours, like you I take my stand / Among poor people. We can talk." At this point Mao pays him a grudging tribute: "*Six Crises* isn't a bad book."

The state banquet is a grand and auspicious occasion. Both Nixon and Zhou deliver admirable toasts that approximate what was actually said. Zhou speaks of the desire of both nations to find common ground and the desire of the younger generation for peace. Nixon replies in a very gracious speech, complimenting the dinner, the way the band plays American dance music, and Zhou's eloquence. He then says that their words won't be remembered, but their actions "can change the world. / We have at times been enemies, / We still have differences, God knows. / But let us, in these next five days, / Start a long march on new highways, / In different lanes, but parallel / And heading for a single goal." Shortly thereafter, when they are about to toast Washington's birthday, as suggested by Pat, he breaks in: "Everyone / Listen, just let me say one thing. / I opposed China. I was wrong."

Broadcast to the world on live TV, this is a message to the American people: look at things differently. It is also a daring departure from his own McCarthyite past and his previous posture of self-defensiveness. Indeed, from much of his character. Making peace means ceasing to be entirely Nixonian.

Nixon is a labile and unsteady peacemaker, but here he uses his very humanness and vulnerability to good effect. His flaw of unsteady attention now becomes a strength. Showing the US public that he has been wrong is a very American, and democratic, way of exercising strong leadership for peace—which would have to win support at home—and a way that in other areas Nixon pursued all too little.

Let us now turn to the Maos, before returning to Pat Nixon and, at the end, to the two couples and Zhou. Both Mao and

Mme. Mao are totally unlike Nixon in being utterly dogmatic and unswerving in their allegiance to their ideology and goals. If there is doubt within, it is not permitted to find voice without. In part that is a style of leadership; but we eventually get the impression that the two, especially Mme. Mao, have formed themselves so as to extinguish inner doubt and perhaps even introspection. The Maos' style of leadership is suited to autocracy rather than to democracy, where leaders are accountable to people's voices and need to hear many points of view. Adams says that he sees Mao as a *heldentenor* (a Wagnerian heroic tenor), and in the office scene the physically frail Mao, who can hardly stand, surprises everyone with his heroic self-assertion, his iron will, his wide range of references to world literature and philosophy (including Plato and the Bible), and his wily wit. The role is set in a very high tessitura and is musically heldentenorish indeed, and very aggressive—a kind of witty learned Siegfried, if there can be such a thing (and Goodman says her famous poet-husband was such a person).

In her Act 2 aria, Mme. Mao displays a parallel radicalism and strength of will, with even more ferocious dogmatism and less knowledge of literature and philosophy. Adams and others describe her as a "coloratura," but this is inexact, since the aria contains no ornamentation and requires little flexibility. Indeed, in the open declarative key of B-flat major (though with various later modulations), her aria is one of the opera's simplest musical statements—soaring, heroic, implacable. "I am the wife of Mao Tse-Tung / Who raised the weak above the strong." She is actually a dramatic soprano with a strong high D. Having learned this aria—but never performed it in public because I could not consistently achieve consistent vibrato on that note—I can say with confidence that it is an expression of iron will and unswerving dogmatism, as she keeps repeating "I speak according to the book." And though she presents herself as subservient to her husband, Adams's blazing statement leaves us in no doubt: she is, now, the fully equal co-leader of the revolution—as, of course, at that time she was. She even briefly equals his wit: "I cut my teeth upon the land, / And when I walked my feet were bound / On revolution." The pun on foot-binding is pure Mao, but she turns it into a deadly serious, indeed murderous statement. (I wanted to learn the aria out of emotional curiosity, to explore the alien world of this violent certainty.) In the heroic music Adams writes for this pair, he shows deep insight into the emotional substructure of violent revolution, and its ensuing autocracy, and he shows how hard it will be for Americans to relate to it.

Adams not only creates vivid characters with distinctive musical personalities, he also creates portraits of political regimes. He shows the audience why these two regimes must cooperate, but also how difficult it will be to do so. Revolutionary autocracy thrives on iron will and never admitting to weakness or a change of view. Democracy thrives on leaders who can relate to people's insecurities and longings and admit to vulnerability and a possible change of course. Nixon shows both bold decisiveness and human-all-too-human Americanness, and that makes it hard for him to equal the Maos in debate and strategy. Musically Nixon is a kind of sour unhappy Mozartean, Mao a Wagner hero: can they inhabit the same opera? Will they be able to find a basis for reciprocity?

Let us now turn to Pat Nixon, the most Mozartean of all the characters, meaning the most inclined to a politics of compassion and reciprocity. At first she seems to be playing the stereotypical role of the American wife, standing by her man and suggesting nothing daring (only the toast to Washington's birthday). But in Act 2 we get inside her, as she pauses on her tour (after she demonstrates great grace and curiosity in her interactions with the guarded Chinese women), in an aria about progress and understanding that is visionary but quintessentially American and of the heartland. Adams has said that this aria, with its inner reflections, belongs after the ballet and is more in keeping with the inwardness of Act 3.[31] I totally agree, and wish it were possible to do a whole-sale rewrite of Act 2 without Sellars and his ballet, but at this point, with Goodman disengaged from opera and Sellars very much on the scene, there seems little chance of this happening.

> This is prophetic! I foresee
> A time will come when luxury
> Dissolves into the atmosphere
> Like a perfume, and everywhere
> The simple virtues root and branch
> And leaf and flower. On that bench
> There we'll relax and taste the fruit
> Of all our actions. Why regret
> Life which is so much like a dream?
> Let the eternal plan resume.
> In the bedroom communities
> Let us be taken by surprise.
> Yes! Let the band play on and on,
> Let the stand-up comedian
> Finish his act, let Gypsy Rose
> Kick off her high-heeled party shoes;
> Let interested businessmen
> Speculate further, let routine
> Dull the edge of mortality.
> Let days grow imperceptibly
> Longer, let the sun set in cloud;
> Let lonely drivers on the road
> Pull over for a bite to eat,
> Let the farmer switch on the light
> Over the porch, let passersby
> Look in at the large family

[31] Daines (1996, p. 42). He sees the opera as a whole as moving from outward assertion "toward a more inward reflective state."

> Around the table, let them pass.
> Let the expression on the face
> Of the Statue of Liberty
> Change just a little, let her see
> What lies inland: across the plain
> One man is marching—the Unknown
> Soldier has risen from his tomb,
> Let him be recognized at home.
> The Prodigal. Give him his share:
> The eagle nailed to the barn door.
> Let him be quick. The sirens wail as bride
> and groom kiss through the veil.
> Bless this union with all its might,
> Let it remain inviolate.

This aria is as close as anything in the opera to being a pure work of the imagination. It is a superb poem. With great imaginative insight, Goodman depicts the inner hopes and yearnings of a thoroughly American woman who has considerable insight into the longings of her fellow Americans. It is a huge contrast with the world of Mme. Mao, with its violent certainties, its decisiveness, its insistence on total and constant revolution. Pat's world is one of small, gradual changes that make the nation a little more equal (until luxury is just a perfume), the lives of individuals and families just a little bit more relaxed, the American world more tolerant and inclusive. The Statue of Liberty will look at the heartland, not just New York. Veterans will be welcomed at home (as at that anti-war time they surely were not): they will receive the unconditional love the Prodigal Son receives from his father. People don't have to struggle quite so hard. It is the message of the War on Poverty (whose programs Nixon largely supported), combined with the peace message of this trip—but peace at home too. It is a Protestant Utopian fantasy, but not without a sense of the current American reality. Only Pat in the opera acknowledges the deep divisions in America created by the Vietnam War. There is anxiety in her vision: sirens wail because the nation is still at war. But it may turn out well, the riven nation may yet remain "inviolate." In her America the way things get better is not by total revolution, it is by gradual change and internal healing, propelled not by ideology but by the simple virtues of America's people.

Adams's music for the aria expresses its spirit. Pat is a lyric, not a dramatic soprano. The aria is to be sung tenderly, reflectively. Virtually every phrase arcs upward and ends on a high note (though only twice does it reach B-flat, her highest note), expressing aspiration and hope, in a serene and meditative legato. It is very reminiscent of "The Lark Ascending" by Ralph Vaughan Williams (1920), a wordless musical expression of aspiration (though inspired by a Meredith poem) that was seen by many as an expression of hope for national recovery after the First World War. Pat's hope is American wishful thinking: for simple virtues, for pleasant and non-abrasive diversity (veterans, Gypsy Rose Lee, the family at dinner all relaxing together, but no immigrants or Black people—although in fact Nixon himself was a key supporter of civil rights legislation), for rest after hard work. It is a conception of happiness the Maos would never aspire to. One obstacle to détente lies in the differing conceptions of hope and progress on the part of the leaders and their people. (Needless to say, this is a portrayal of American fantasy, not reality, though it does say something about America; we learn nothing in the opera about the hopes and wishes of the Chinese people, because they are afraid to speak and, indeed, warn Pat that speaking is dangerous.)

Act 3 explores these issues of desire and difference further, tentatively suggesting a basis for reconciliation. The five heroes are all on stage throughout (Kissinger having left for the bathroom, never to return!), and their vocal lines intertwine, in some of Adams's most intricate and lyrical music. As he points out, the orchestra is now used more flexibly, as the instruments throw off their minimalist repetitiveness. Flavors of both jazz and big band music weave in and out.

The most common staging has the two couples sitting on two beds side by side, and one couple side by side with the other, while Zhou is apart. I have also seen the act staged in a way that represents three separate bedrooms, and frankly I find that staging more effective.

It is nighttime, and both couples turn back to the past. Nixon recalls his war service in the Pacific: the trauma of being bombed by the Japanese—but also the longing for real food, and his delight at eventually being able to open a hamburger stand when he was able somehow to swap Spam for ground beef ("I found / The smell of burgers on the grill / Made strong men cry"). He also found pleasure in winning at poker. Pat remembers her anxiety back home and her habit of dressing up for him, even though he was so far away, as if he might walk in at any moment, and her anxious scrimping and saving to make a real home on what was left from his military salary. (All this is closely based on their wartime letters, though Goodman does not mention that Pat was not merely a housewife: she also worked for the Office of Price Administration while her husband was away.)

Actors have considerable leeway here. Maddalena portrays Nixon as newly attentive to Pat, having taken her for granted before. As for Pat, in the Met production Janis Kelly is bored and frosty until late in the scene, though I would say that is not what the tenderness of the music suggests.

Meanwhile the Maos relive the days when they met and fell passionately in love, and Mao is suddenly able to dance with her in fantasy, a sexy jazzy number that makes their relationship feel very different from the Nixons', electric and erotic, with no tenderness. (She says, "We'll show these motherfuckers how to dance.") Mao, always guarded, reveals nothing of his inner life, apart from sexual desire, but Jiang Qing remembers sensuous experiences—the taste of wild apricots, of chicken and peppers, lizards warming themselves in the sun. And with this is mingled the drama of the revolution marching onward. Zhou joins some of these memories, both the hope for revolution and the taste of apricots.

In his superb book on the opera, Timothy A. Johnson remarks that what all the characters have in common is their memory of simple pleasures, food in particular.[32] Remember that Nixon insisted to Mao that he comes from a poor family, and gave this as a reason why they can talk. Here he shows the audience that he has known great physical hardship and some hunger.

Both "sides," then, have a basis for communication and, perhaps, détente in their vivid awareness of mortality and the needs of the body. Both understand, from their own experience, the similar needs of their people. Just as "Nick's Snack Shack" was a success because Nixon understood how much the men hated Spam and longed for burgers, just as Pat took pride in creating a home out of meager savings from his thin paycheck, so the Maos knew the agonizing hunger of their people. (The opera, however, omits the disastrous Great Chinese Famine of 1959–1961, in which Mao's authoritarianism played a horrible role: his rural subordinates were so afraid to give him bad news that he himself actually did not know about the famine until the death toll was enormous—a point in favor of a style of leadership that is willing to admit being wrong. In 1972 these facts were not understood in the West, but by 1981 they were the subject of Amartya Sen's *Poverty and Famines*, part of the basis for his 1998 Nobel Prize.[33])

As for Nixon, when we think of his politics we must not forget that he was the first US President since Truman in 1945 to make a proposal for universal health insurance. He did so in 1974, though his resignation that same year aborted the project.[34] And although the food stamp program began under Lyndon Johnson, it was greatly expanded under Nixon.

The two couples also share memories of love, though of different sorts, the Maos focused on sex, the Nixons on mutual support and

---

[32] Johnson (2011, ch. 15), a masterful discussion of the theme of détente in the opera.
[33] Sen (1981).
[34] See Nixon ([1974] 2009).

tenderness. And eventually they give way to the universal human need for sleep. Only Zhou remains awake.

Zhou Enlai is an important figure throughout the opera. Because of Mao's failing health, it is he, as Premier, who greets the Nixons at the plane and who gives the toast at the state dinner. It is likely that he played a major role in agreeing to and arranging the entire visit. The Americans knew him as a leader to reckon with at least since the Geneva Conference of 1954, when Dulles famously refused to shake his hand. He is a towering figure, who inspired Nixon (and Kissinger) with great admiration and respect. Nixon speaks of his "vitality and mental vigor," his quickness and his "fine sense of humor"—concluding that no world leader he has met exceeds him "in terms of the ability to conduct conversations at the highest level in an effective way."[35]

To Americans, Zhou was, and still is, a person easily misunderstood. He was so suave, so gracious in manner, that it was easy to believe that he was, so to speak, the "good Communist," opposed to harsh or violent tactics. However, he was Mao's right-hand person for decades, and at the date of the opera he is still alive and Premier, right in the middle of the Cultural Revolution, when leading reformers had been killed or banished. It is now clear that in order to survive the Cultural Revolution he had to endure the persecution and humiliation of numerous friends, and even the torture, rape, and murder of his own adoptive daughter in 1968 at the hands of Mao's Red Guards. He survived, clearly, not only by stoical endurance of loss but also by persecuting others, solidifying his bond with Mao.

This apparently paradoxical juxtaposition of traits is described vividly by biographer Dick Wilson:

He personified the old-world Chinese virtues of gentleness, politeness, and humility, yet put them to work for a political

---

[35] Price (1977, p. 5), quoted in Johnson (2011, p. 145).

ideology that invoked violence and destruction as a necessary part of its programme. . . . He spoke so softly, moved so meekly, and yet some of the things he said and did in order to give his country a swift passage from feudalism to modernity in one lifetime were cruel, militant, unforgiving.[36]

Nixon, while not emphasizing cruelty and violence, fully understood that beneath their civil rapport were profound and unalterable differences:

Chou is a total, dedicated Communist. He believes deeply, and he never let me forget it. Not every hour on the hour—it was beneath the surface—we didn't let it color our conversation so as to become belligerent. There was firmness, but never belligerence. Whenever he said something really tough, he became much cooler, and spoke more softly.[37]

Zhou, both in the opera and in life, was Mao's ally and right hand, and he always supported violent tactics where necessary. Far more subtle and pragmatic than Mme. Mao, he saw the good of his country as requiring dialogue. He was more or less convinced by 1972 that the Cultural Revolution was a disaster, and he was increasingly at odds with the Gang of Four. But he remained at Mao's side. The opera does not address these specific points, but it does accurately portray a man wedded to the ideals of the revolution, utterly subservient to Mao, yet with an open mind about how to advance Mao's ideas in a modernizing world.

Zhou is present throughout Act 3 and involved somewhat in the dialogue, joining the Maos in their memories of the early days of the revolution. But at the opera's end he is the only one still awake, and his monologue ends the opera, in what Adams calls "the most

---

[36] Wilson (1984, p. 17), quoted in Johnson (2011, p. 154).
[37] Price (1977, p. 6), quoted in Johnson (2011, p. 146).

intensely personal, introverted, and elegiac moment in the whole opera" (1996, 42).

> I am old and I cannot sleep
> Forever, like the young, nor hope
> That death will be a novelty
> But endless wakefulness when I
> Put down my work and go to bed.
> How much of what we did was good?
> Everything seems to move beyond
> Our remedy. Come, heal this wound.
> At this hour nothing can be done.
> Just before dawn the birds begin,
> The warblers who prefer the dark,
> The cage-birds answering. To work!
> Outside this room the chill of grace
> Lies heavy on the morning grass.

This aria is both cautious and infused with doubt and self-doubt. Musically it proceeds, often, from note to neighbor note—in pointed contrast to Mme. Mao's heroic leaps and Nixon's staccato jumping. And as it progresses the harmonies grow more dense and dissonant—again in contrast to Mme. Mao's wide-open major chords. Zhou's doubt, however, is not egocentric like Nixon's in the "rats" aria: it is detached, reflecting on the revolution and on history in the longest sense. Although at the time of the opera's composition Zhou's fatal cancer was not known to Americans, he speaks as if he knows that death stares him in the face, sooner rather than later. Unlike the Maos, he expresses real uncertainty about their acts during the revolution, though Goodman gives no specific examples. She made a fundamental choice to have him voice no deep personal guilt but only collective uncertainty, perhaps because relevant facts were not available to her, perhaps because she wanted the opera to end with an assessment of the nations' progress toward détente, not a Boris-like soliloquy of personal anguish. So she gives him vague unease and a sense of an unhealed "wound," rather than the highly specific images that are likely to haunt someone guilty of the murder of friends in the middle of the night.

The aria is moving, but its ending is problematic—a rare poetic error on Goodman's part, I think. The final line "the chill of grace / Lies heavy on the morning grass" is, to me, mysterious and not evocative. Why is grace heavy rather than light, chilly rather than warm (frost melting as the sun rises)? And why grace? We learn from interviews with the creators that they were aware that the given name Enlai actually means "grace," and that Zhou's father had given him that name because, just as the child was born, he himself received an important promotion from the emperor. Nixon was aware of the etymology, if not the story, and writes in his 1982 memoir that it "succinctly captures his presence and disposition."[38] But surely Zhou himself would not like to allude to that pre-revolutionary sense of "grace" as "emperor's bonus." Nor would he more generally be alluding egocentrically to his own character traits: such self-focus is utterly alien to the character. In any case the audience knows nothing about the etymology and, in the absence of explanation, would be likely to hear it in a Christian sense, as I initially did, and think it is something that Alice Goodman the Anglican priest likes to think about, and not her character Zhou. It sounds like a cultural misstep. So the last sentence of the opera leaves us confused.

Fortunately, however, Adams's music makes no such error, and the audience can derive from the music a suitable sense of uncertain introspection, and yet at the same time stature, perspective, and a determination to face uncertainty with work. As I said, the early part of the aria emphasizes hesitancy and anxiety. As the sun rises and the birds sing, the harmonies become more complex but remain dissonant. However, the addition of gradually ascending

---

[38] See quotation from Nixon's 1982 memoir in Johnson (2011, p. 154–55).

lines in the strings suggests a kind of new hope. "Morning grass" concludes without a cadence, hanging in the air. And after the singer concludes, the violins continue their upward movement— but still on dissonant chords—and eventually end, very softly hanging in space. The suggestion is of unfinished and clouded, yet genuine, aspiration. The audience is left, with Zhou, to face the as yet empty canvas of the future. As he turns to his work, so we are left with a void that we are invited to fill with our own work and thought.

The opera makes a unique contribution to reflection about peace-making by showing its human prerequisites—imperfect people with intermittent insights, propelled by differing combinations of idealism, vanity, and good judgment, taking a risk of determined work and diplomacy that never fully concludes, that always hangs in the air awaiting the next day's work. The Schopenhauerian would say: because it is all unstable and unfinished, it is worthless. And of course that sort of utopian/apocalyptic thinking is a major impediment to any search for peace in today's world. *Nixon in China* says: here is the real daily work of peace, and it involves ego-centrism, paranoia, people talking about hamburgers in the middle of the night, people dreaming of sex, a lonely man unable to sleep and yet facing the new day's work with resolution. All this is the re-ality of peacemaking, and it is not disgusting or worthless. It is what real human efforts are like—and we may embrace them, and try to embody them, if we choose.

9

Ahasuerus "Redeemed"

Wagner from Despair to the Closed Community

[F]or all their wonders and power there is an all-consuming assertiveness in Wagner's works which can be disgusting.

—Bernard Williams, *On Opera*

The man had so much ability, talent and interpretive skill—more than words can say. Yet so much affectation with it, such lordly pretension, self-aggrandizement, and mystagogical self-dramatization—again, more than words can say or patience can bear.... There is in Wagner's bragging, his endless holding-forth, his passion for monologue, his insistence on having a say in everything, an unspeakable arrogance that prefigures Hitler.

—Thomas Mann, letter to Emil Preetorius, 1949
(from California)

At the end of Richard Wagner's *Die Meistersinger* (1868), cobbler-poet Hans Sachs, celebrating the victory of young Walther and the successful marriage of tradition and innovation that has enabled him to win over the conservative Masters, concludes with a warning:

> Habt acht! Uns dräuen üble Streich':
> zerfällt erst deutsches Volk und Reich,

in falscher wälscher Majestät
kein Fürst bald mehr sein Volk versteht;
und wälschem Dunst mit wälschem Tand
sie pflanzen uns in deutsches Land;
was deutsch und echt, wüsst' keiner mehr,
lebt's nicht in deutscher Meister Ehr'.

Drum sag' ich Euch:
ehrt Eure deutsche Meister!
Dann bannt Ihr gute Geister;
und gebt Ihr ihrem Wirken Gunst,
zerging' in Dunst
das heil'ge röm'sche Reich,
und bliebe gleich
die heil'ge deutsche Kunst!

Beware! Evil tricks threaten us:
If the German people and kingdom should one day decay,
under a false foreign (French-Italian)[1] rule,
soon no prince will understand his people any more;
if foreign (French-Italian) mists with foreign vanities
should infiltrate our German land,
then none would know what's German and true,
if it did not live in the honor of the German masters.

Therefore I say to you:
honor your German masters,
then you will conjure up good spirits!
And if you favor their endeavors,
even should the
Holy Roman Empire dissolve in mist,

---

[1] The German word *welsch* can mean "foreign" in general, but refers in particular to the French and Italians.

for us there would yet remain
holy German art![2]

Sachs's monologue puts words to a spirit present in Wagner's music from the confident C major Prelude onward—a spirit of assertive nationalism utterly at odds with Mozart's Republic of Love, with its delicate reciprocities, and equally at odds with Verdi's Risorgimento politics, so sympathetic to all outsiders who struggle against oppressive power. *Die Meistersinger* has no institutional politics, because the city it represents seems to have no institutional structure. But in its negation of all that is other and different it becomes something rather worse: a closed community whose people have no desire and no aptitude for the political negotiation of differences, and no possibility of even becoming different (except perhaps by renewing a Germanness that has become stale). Hans Sachs seems to be the kindest, gentlest avuncular figure, bringing the two lovers together and ensuring that the true musical genius, Walther (a new arrival in Nürnberg but a German through and through, just exactly as German as the composer) wins the prize. But the atmosphere of jollity and communal celebration should not distract us from the chilling message in his words.

How did we get there? Wagner is, within opera, the great antagonist of the Republic of Love. In this chapter I shall trace a development of thought and music-drama that explains the arrival at a closed society as stemming from a profound fascination with despair and Schopenhauerian world-weariness that long precedes his encounter with Schopenhauer's writings in 1854. This fascination leads Wagner not to Schopenhauer's compassionate renunciation, but to a peculiar idea of redemption through "holy German art"

---

[2] The translation, by Peter Branscombe, is from the edition of the libretto accompanying the 1995 Chicago Symphony Orchestra production (1995), with several suggestions borrowed from the useful version by Thomas S. Grey in his valuable article "Wagner's *Die Meistersinger as National Opera*," in *Music and German National Identity (1868–1945)*, ed. Celia Applegate and Pamela Potter (2002, pp. 78–104).

that is in the end inseparable from his antisemitism, his xenophobic paranoia (no French influences, please!!), and related fantasies of cultural purity. I shall claim that for Wagner alienation and despair leave the truly great poet-composer nowhere to find solace and expression but in what *Jewishness in Music* calls a "like-endeavoring community," whose prophetic voice he becomes. And that means a community that he designs and whose boundaries he polices. All outsiders must be banished.

Several caveats must be entered, and weighed, at this point. First, it is clearly a mistake to read Wagner's operas simplistically in the light of the endless flow of strident, often virulently antisemitic prose works that issued from his pen. However: it is just as mistaken to treat the operas as if Wagner's mind did not permeate every aspect of them, and as if that were not the same mind that created the prose works. Music in Wagner is inseparable from text and meaning. We should ground our interpretations in the works, but we may cautiously consult the prose works, especially works about music, for clues to his underlying preoccupations. Second, it is clearly a mistake to read Wagner simply in the light of what the Nazis later made of him. However: it is just as mistaken to avoid or deny elements of the work that prefigure Nazism—as Mann acknowledged only after the war, and from the safe distance of California. Third, as Nietzsche repeatedly says: Wagner is a consummate actor. We must ask, then, whether there are really views in his works at all, or only poses. However, it is just as mistaken to treat the works as mere aesthetic games and to deny their utter seriousness and their endless monological assertiveness.

A warning: I am no lover of Wagner, not even an ambivalent one. Many people, including great interpreters such as my teacher and friend Bernard Williams, are torn, experiencing profound emotional responses to Wagner's works, but also at times the response of disgust that he mentions in his very insightful critique. In chapter 3 I described Patricia Williams's memory of an early date with Bernard at a performance of *Tristan und Isolde*, which she later understood as a "test" of their budding relationship—the test presumably being whether one was deeply enthralled and transformed. She passed the test. I would have failed miserably. I think *Tristan* is a tedious opera and that the view of love in it—all unsatisfied longing and no reciprocity—is adolescent and boring. I do think that Wagner is a supremely talented composer, and I can admire from a distance what he does. I also learn about life from the (to me sick) view of life on exhibit there. But I am not moved or transformed. I do prefer the *Ring* to Wagner's other works, and find there less of what I object to than elsewhere (see further below). But I am still not a fan.

By now readers will find this no surprise. Anyone who chooses to spend half of a book on opera talking about Mozart and much of the rest talking about Verdi is no Wagnerite. But readers should still be warned, since people I admire react very differently. My angle, such as it is, can be but one path through the work; furthermore I will be dealing with just two works, briefly with *The Flying Dutchman* (*Der fliegende Holländer*), and, more extensively with *Die Meistersinger*. However, my purpose in Part II of this book is to confront antagonists of the Republic of Love that Mozart did not envisage. I have explored most of these antagonists by examining how subsequent opera composers who are themselves sympathetic to Mozart's outlook confront them. But the very existence of a great composer who was himself an antagonist ought to be confronted as well.

Wagner and the Jews: Persecution Complex and Political Project

There can be no doubt that Wagner hated Jews.[3] As he wrote to Liszt (his father-in-law) on April 18, 1851, his "resentment" of

---

[3] Three excellent treatments of this issue are: Hans Vaget, "Antisemitism," in *The Cambridge Wagner Encyclopedia*, ed. Nicolas Vaszonyi (2013, pp. 16–20); Dieter

Jews is "as necessary to my nature as gall is to the blood."[4] There can also be no doubt that Wagner expressed this hatred repeatedly, indeed obsessively, in prose works, from *Jewishness in Music* (1850, new edition 1867) to the late "Regeneration" essays that link antisemitism to Wagner's artistic-regeneration project. There is much doubt about whether and how this hatred expresses itself in the operas, partly because critics tend to look in the wrong place—for specific characters and passages that caricature Jews, rather than what I think the real issue: a general hatred of difference and dialogue that clearly lies at the heart of much of his creative output and that has, as music critic Eduard Hanslick writes of the Prelude to *Meistersinger*, a "brutal effect" (*brutaler Wirkung*).[5]

However, we must begin by studying *Jewishness in Music* to see what Wagner said there and how it bears on his view of music culture.[6] The pamphlet was published in 1850 in the *Neue Zeitschrift für Musik* under the pseudonym K. Freigedank (K. Freethinker), though Wagner was generally known to be the author. It begins from an allegedly shared starting point: "we" dislike Jews, find them repugnant, and dislike associating with them. Wagner notes that, as a liberal, he favored Jewish emancipation, but—the social result, now that they are exerting great cultural power, is unmistakably bad.

What is bad about the influence of Jews in society? Jews, he insists, are always foreigners within the German nation. Even

Borchmeyer, "The Question of Anti-Semitism," in *Wagner Handbook*, ed. Ulrich Müller and Peter Wapnewski, translation edited by John Deathridge (1992, pp. 166–85); and Thomas S. Grey, "The Jewish Question, in *The Cambridge Companion to Wagner*, ed. Thomas S. Grey (2008, pp. 203–18).

[4] Quoted in Vaget (2013, p. 19).

[5] Quoted in Grey (2002, p. 88). The full quote explains the dative: "*ein* Musikstück von...brutaler Wirkung."

[6] I cite the translation of William Ashton Ellis in *Richard Wagner: Judaism in Music and Other Essays* (1995, pp. 75–122), though at times I correct the translation, as with the title itself: *Das Judentum* is much better rendered as "Jewishness," since it is the status and cultural practices of Jews, not their religion, that the essay targets.

though they have gained some political rights, they speak the language as aliens do, and their "creaking, squeaking, buzzing snuffle" is so "outlandish and unpleasant" that we can hardly pay attention to what they are saying. Jews never exchange emotions with us, except as a parrot would imitate human expression. Their only dealings with us are in matters of exchange and profit.

What, then, of Jews in music? If we listen to the music of an actual Jewish service in the synagogue, says Wagner, we will be "seized with a feeling of the greatest revulsion, of horror mingled with the absurd, at hearing that sense-and-sound-confounding gurgle, yodel, and cackle, which no intentional caricature can make more repugnant than as offered here in full, naïve seriousness." Should Jews then attempt musical composition in the world of high music-culture, they are bound, as aliens, to fail miserably. Wagner now considers two cases: first Felix Mendelssohn (1809–1847), whom he treats as a Jew, neglecting his family's renunciation of Judaism, their adoption of a Christian surname (Bartholdy), their decision not to have their son circumcised, and Felix's completely non-religious German upbringing including Christian baptism at age seven. In this case at least, assuming he was aware of these well-known facts, Wagner's criterion is clearly racial. He treats Mendelssohn as a tragic case: a man of talent, doomed by his Jewishness to produce merely derivative and second-rate works. The second, unnamed, is Wagner's great enemy Giacomo Meyerbeer (1791–1864, Jakob Liebmann Meyer Beer), the highly successful German Jewish opera composer who dominated the Paris opera world. Wagner's hatred for Meyerbeer was deeply personal: in his years in Paris, despite constant groveling sycophancy on Wagner's part, he had failed to gain the great man's support, and he returned to Germany licking his wounds. In the present essay he treats him with unreserved contempt and blames everything he dislikes on Meyerbeer's Jewishness. After remarking that German culture itself is dead, and the Jews are but the maggots devouring its corpse, he then more briefly discusses two Jewish poets, Ludwig

Börne and Heinrich Heine, who, says Wagner, converted to Christianity in order to find "redemption."[7] But, he concludes, it did no good: despite his considerable gifts, Heine's poetry is "arid."

The pamphlet ends with a rhetorical flourish, as Wagner pivots to address Jews. German music-culture must be regenerated, and Jews should "take part in this bloody, self-annihilating struggle." His final sentence is a warning: "Only one thing can redeem you from the burden of your curse—the redemption of Ahasuerus—going under (*Untergang*)." (Ahasuerus, the mythical Wandering Jew, is always seeking an end to his wanderings, and the death that eludes him.)

This ominous conclusion remains vague. *Untergang*, literally "going under," can mean "death," and it does mean that in the myth of Ahasuerus. But it can also be used of the setting of the sun. Nietzsche uses it to describe Zarathustra's descent from his mountaintop. It needn't connote violence, and in the 1867 edition Wagner removed the words "bloody struggle." It must mean ceasing to be Jewish, but if Felix Mendelssohn, uncircumcised and with no Jewish education, didn't escape the "curse" it is difficult to know what still-living person would, or how.

I think what Wagner must mean is that escaping Jewishness is not something individuals can do, whether by conversion or by secular education and assimilation. The entire Jewish community must cease. Right now, he has said, German culture has become stagnant, like a corpse, which is why "maggots" can feed on it. For that reason Germans have turned elsewhere, to France and to the Jews, for artistic models. But German culture must be revived—and then kept away from contamination by the Jews. So long as Jewish culture remains in the midst of the healthy German culture of the future, that culture will also be at risk. This idea surely is ominous.

---

[7] This is an extremely implausible account of the conversion of these two worldly and satirical writers, who plainly sought to avoid the social disabilities Jewishness brought with it.

The 1867 preface, which accuses the Jewish community of ganging up on Wagner in the press, confirms that reading: Jewishness is a powerful social counterforce that must be stopped.

Why did Wagner hate Jews? One factor was probably anxiety about his own origins, since he discovered letters suggesting that his real biological father may have been actor and playwright Ludwig Geyer, who became his mother's second husband after the death of Carl Friedrich Wagner six months after Richard's birth. (Wagner grew up bearing the name Geyer and believed until age fourteen that Geyer was his biological father.) Wagner later speculated that Geyer was Jewish. Another cause is clearly envy and resentment directed at Meyerbeer, who failed to recognize his talent despite years of the most servile sycophancy. But the paranoid and egomaniacal personality of Wagner needed no specific occasion or person—if he isn't recognized as supreme and given the whole world, then enemies are to blame. Throughout the history of Western thought, after all, Jews have been a handy name for the "other," for all enemies of what is fair and good.[8]

In Wagner's later prose writings his paranoia about Jewish cultural influences knows no bounds, although he vacillates between a race-science account of Jewishness, in his correspondence with the race-theorist Gobineau, and a cultural account of the "problem." Always, though, the "solution" is the same: regeneration of German culture through "holy German art," meaning: Wagnerian music-dramas, with Wagner calling the tune. Never does he urge violence against Jews, or even physical deportation. However, their entire community must "go under."

Is there antisemitism in Wagner's operas? In opera scholarship we find two extremes. One position is that we find numerous specific characters who are anti-Jewish stereotypes, including Beckmesser in *Meistersinger*, Alberich in the *Ring*, and Mime in part of the *Ring*, namely in *Siegfried*, though not in *Das Rheingold*.

[8] See Nirenberg (2013).

Theodor Adorno famously said that all of Wagner's losers are Jews,[9] and many agree. They point to Beckmesser's clumsiness with language and melody, to Alberich's greed, and (perhaps most convincingly) to Mime's small stature, wheedling sing-song speech, and greedy heart. To others, prominently including Dieter Borchmeyer and Thomas Grey, there is not a trace of antisemitism in the operas. They point to the fact that Wagner, who never concealed his antisemitic thoughts when he had them, never mentions any such aspects of the operas, nor do Cosima's copious diaries of their personal conversations. (She suggests, indeed, that the small size of the Nibelungen is meant as a reference to east Asian races.) In the sensible middle is Hans Vaget, who says that, given the intensity and obsessiveness of Wagner's fixation on Jews, it would be surprising if none of this seeped into the work one way or another; in addition, the connection of Beckmesser with Wagner's enemy the music critic Edouard Hanslick, whose mother was Jewish, makes that reference more plausible than the others. (Hanslick is singled out for paranoid critique in the 1867 Preface.)[10]

Wagner clearly wrote for eternity, creating myths to sustain and regenerate German culture. In that project any very specific allusion to today's politics would be a distraction. Therefore he would not create obvious antisemitic stereotypes, particularly when investigating the tragic consequences of universal human tendencies, such as greed and failure to love. Beckmesser, being a comic figure as the others are not, can perhaps bear the weight of greater particularity, but in the end of the day he is still a stereotype of the learned pedant. To this extent the Borchmeyer faction is on strong ground. Nonetheless, Vaget is clearly right about Wagner's preoccupations and the likelihood that they would shape the works in one way or another. Thus Mime's ugliness does appear so close

---

[9] Adorno, *In Search of Wagner*, trans. Rodney Livingstone (2009, original German publication 1952).

[10] See Borchmeyer (1992), Vaget (2013), and Grey (2008).

to the ugliness depicted in *Jewishness in Music* that a likely account is that when Wagner set out to imagine ugly fawning venality, the physical and vocal traits he had already associated with Jews came naturally to mind.

There is, however, a different point to be made. The Borchmeyer faction clearly wants to reclaim the operas for our enjoyment, and they think that if they show there are no specific stereotypes there, they have shown that there is nothing sinister there that we may connect to Wagner's antisemitism. Mann, Williams, and I think that there is a different and, in a sense, a deeper sinister something, and that it assumes prominence in *Die Meistersinger*: a picture of the healthy community as a closed community from which all difference and dissent have been banished, so that it speaks only in Wagner's voice. Regeneration through art means accepting Wagner as one's savior. It means a generic attitude to difference of which cultural antisemitism is one species.

The Flying Dutchman: Pessimism, Alienation, Redemption

In the summer of 1839, Wagner embarked on a sea voyage along the Baltic coast. Burdened by debts and, even more, by humiliation, having been fired from his position as director of the opera house in Riga, he fled with his wife Minna across the Prussian border without passports and boarded a small trading vessel headed ultimately for London. At this stage his project was still ultimately to conquer Paris through the success of his great opera *Rienzi*—a plan doomed to fail, because he never won the support of the leading Parisian luminaries, especially Giacomo Meyerbeer, whom Wagner had flattered and addressed with fawning letters until it became clear that Meyerbeer was never going to recognize Wagner's greatness. Later, however, as Wagner mythologized his own life in later essays and letters—especially the long *A Communication to*

My Friends, published in 1851—the voyage became the seed for a wholly different project focused on a new aim: becoming the prophet of the German art of the future.[11]

The voyage was rough and terrible, lasting three and a half weeks, and at one point the seas were so tumultuous that the captain found a temporary safe harbor along the Norwegian coast. During this painful experience, however, Wagner said that he heard in his head themes that later became parts of *The Flying Dutchman* (1843). In retrospect at least, the voyage focused his mind on the figure of the eternal Jew Ahasuerus, who longs for "peace amid the storms of life." *Ex post*, Wagner felt in himself a deep identification with Ahasuerus's longing for peace and redemption, and also with the idea that he can be delivered from his wandering only by a noble and selfless woman, just as the Dutchman is redeemed by Senta's selfless devotion.

Thus, according to the Wagner of 1852, the voyage was the origin of his opera *The Flying Dutchman*. And that opera—though not very successful at the time, and not very central, then, to Wagner's sense of self—was later reinterpreted by Wagner as the start of his true life's journey as composer of the German music-drama of the future. Furthermore, the voyage, though at the time part of a project ultimately aimed at Parisian success, was reimagined as a voyage away from the false lures of Paris and the humiliation he suffered there, toward his true *Heimat*, Germany, and toward his true vocation as Germany's prophet.

In the *Communication*, Wagner points out that the idea of the Wanderer is very old, indeed a "primeval trait of human nature,"

---

[11] See the excellent treatment in Thomas S. Grey, "The Return of the Prodigal Son: Wagner and *Der fliegende Holländer*," the introductory essay in Grey, ed., *Richard Wagner, Der fliegende Holländer*, Cambridge Opera Handbooks (2000, pp. 1–24). Large sections of *A Communication to My Friends* and pertinent letters are reproduced in Appendix B, and my quotations are taken from there. See also the excellent treatment of this period in Wagner's life in Martin Gregor-Dellin, *Richard Wagner: His Life, His Work, His Century*, trans. J. Maxwell Brownjohn (1983, pp. 108–28).

which can also be seen in Homer's Odysseus, who longs to return home to Penelope. However, in his own opera—and in its larger significance in his life—we see, he announces, something both deeply mythic and utterly new. The woman is no longer Penelope, "the domestic paragon." In the figure of Senta, she is "the woman of the future." And Odysseus's longing for home has been replaced by "a longing for something new and unknown, something never before experienced and yet heralded by a sense of anticipation." These obscure remarks Wagner now connects with the new "emotional, longing sense of patriotism" that he feels toward Germany: his wandering was his "homelessness in Paris," and his longed-for home, the "redeeming woman," is Germany itself, "that is to say, the sensation of being embraced by some intimately familiar community." One might wonder why this is supposed to be something new and unknown: but it is no ordinary sort of patriotism that Wagner expresses. What he is gradually disclosing to his supporters is the idea that Wagner, returning to the woman Germany, and being embraced by her, will be the prophet of that community, leading it to a hitherto unknown type of redemption through artistic self-transcendence.

In this chapter I am not particularly concerned with *The Flying Dutchman* itself, though musically it is an admirable opera, if not as original as what was to follow it. I am concerned with the mental path from *The Flying Dutchman*—or its later reimagination— to *Die Meistersinger* and Sachs's final speech. In fact we can see two rather different paths that lead from *The Flying Dutchman* to Wagner's future. One follows the idea of redeeming personal love, thinking of passionate erotic love between individuals as what gives meaning to human life. This path, suggested by Senta's sacrifice, leads to the *Ring*, which I think the part of Wagner least tainted by his peculiar cultural narcissism. In the end the *Ring* is about the growth of Brünnhilde's understanding of love and the way in which her ultimate capacity for love despite love's imperfection gives meaning to human life.[12] But that is not the path emphasized in the 1852 *Communication*. Wagner also saw his early opera as the start of his vocation as German composer, and thus of the search of the German people for cultural redemption through German Art, with Wagner as their prophet. He read this meaning into the opera after the fact, connecting it to his return to Germany and his rejection—and overcoming—of French and Italian music. In this reading Senta is not an individual at all: she is the embracing and adoring German public. This path leads to Wagner's later essays on art as cultural self-purification. It also leads to *Die Meistersinger*.

Die Meistersinger: Cheerfulness, Self-Satisfaction

The C major Prelude to *Die Meistersinger* is a wonderfully joyful and buoyant introduction to Wagner's comedy. This musically masterful introduction, with its dazzling polyphony and its subtle weaving-in of motifs later associated with the major characters, places the listener in an emotional landscape that appears totally different from that of the immediately preceding *Tristan* (1867), with its agonizingly unrelieved longing. It expresses good cheer and is likely to induce it in the listener, who would not expect at this point that the drama to come would be so deeply imbued with the spirit of Schopenhauer. Even Nietzsche, by this time Wagner's harsh critic, speaks of its "current of well-being, the most manifold well-being, of old and new happiness."[13] It is a joy expressing solid confidence, and Nietzsche is not wrong to suggest that it is a

---

[12] Here I agree with Philip Kitcher and Richard Schacht, *Finding an Ending: Reflections on Wagner's Ring* (2004). My program essay "Philosophy and the *Ring*," on the Lyric Opera of Chicago website for the never completed Ring cycle of 2020–2021, argues for a similar conclusion (2020).

[13] Nietzsche (Walter Kaufmann trans.) ([1886] 1966, section 240).

confidence "very much including the artist's happiness with himself, which he has no wish to hide."

Writers repeatedly describe the Prelude as "heavy" (Nietzsche, Mann); Hanslick, we saw, even described its effect as "brutal." The Prelude introduces a comedy—and yet it is so unlike, say, a Mozart overture, in which laughter can be heard from the orchestra. It is the music of a solemn occasion, such as an academic graduation ceremony—in an unreal university with no protests, no drunken students, no surprising moments of dissonance and humor. We think of people dressed in the medieval regalia of a graduation (and of course the regalia omnipresent at such graduations stems directly from the customs of the medieval university, literally represented in the Nürnberg of Wagner's fantasy). When Brahms, accepting an honorary degree from the university of Breslau (now Wroclaw in Poland), decided to deliver a musical gift of thanks, he wrote his "Academic Festival Overture" (1881), a work bubbling with quirky joy and warmth, with the tunes of student drinking songs, the delight of slightly rebellious and certainly boisterous young people ready to challenge authority. It suggests an openness to change and difference—as if it would not be so surprising or terrible if Breslau became Wroclaw and both Germany and Poland joined the EU. Wagner's Prelude is nothing of this sort. Assertive and monological, it already settles all questions: this is how things are and must be, namely the way that I, the artist, decide.

If there is any past work that the Prelude suggests, it is the Coronation March from Meyerbeer's *Le Prophète* (1849), which introduced the coronation of the false prophet as Emperor; and in fact our Prelude is not so much a graduation prelude as a coronation prelude. It has the same triumphant spirit of solemn reverence—but it is just so much better musically, so much more varied and complex, as if Wagner is saying, "Don't crown that false Messiah Meyerbeer. Crown me!" In his companion to the opera, John Warrack tentatively suggests another similar anything-you-can-do reference to Meyerbeer later in the opera, but this one seems to me both certain and utterly predictable.[14] Crown me, the true prophet of Holy German Art.

Wagner hoodwinks people all the time—not all people at all times, but this Prelude is so scintillating that it has had the oddest effects. On February 20, 2001, the New School in New York installed a new President—former Nebraska senator Bob Kerrey, who was hoping to establish a base in New York for a future presidential run—a hope derailed only two months later by belated revelations about war crimes he had committed in Vietnam, crimes that involved killing women and children at point blank range and later claiming they were enemy guerrillas (a lie easily believed in part because of the racism with which that war was suffused). The New School—that famous home of European Jews and other dissidents seeking a place to breathe freely—had assembled a ceremonial group to honor the occasion, consisting of the late Senator Joseph Lieberman as emcee, and various recipients of honorary doctorates, a racially and nationally diverse group, including me (a convert Jew), one other person I knew (Jewish economist Joseph Stiglitz, who won the Nobel Prize later that same year), and five or six others of different geographies and ethnicities. Kerrey spoke of "the extraordinary ethnic, religious, racial and political diversity of New York City" as befitting the New School and its founding.[15] "We are a genuine multicultural metropolis, a true city of the world," he concluded. Then the student orchestra began to play—the Prelude to *Die Meistersinger*. I remember exchanging raised-eyebrow looks with Stiglitz at this point. If Wagner duped these welcoming open-arms New Yorkers (and one soon-to-be-unmasked Nebraskan), he could get away with a lot more. And has.

And what is the triumph in Wagner's Prelude about? It is the triumph of German Art. Think how Mozart represents the working of

---

[14] Warrack (1994, p. 112). He compares Sachs's contemplation of his beloved Nuremberg with a similar moment in Meyerbeer's *Les Huguenots*. (Warrack wrote most of the chapters in this handbook; others will be cited under the author's name.)

[15] New School University (2001).

art on a population, as he does in *Figaro*. Art, for Mozart, is about an antinomian craziness that opens out into many types of love, subverting authority and dead conventions. *Tutti contenti saremo così*: we will all be happy in *that* way. Wagner's Prelude wants none of that craziness. Its heaviness is precisely the refusal of craziness. "We will all be happy—in *my* way."

Sachs's Monologue: Schopenhauer in Search of a Happy Ending

Die Meistersinger is a comedy; but a central place in it is given to pessimistic Schopenhauerian reflections, in Sachs's famous *Wahn* monologue. The speech's importance is underlined by Wagner in a letter to King Ludwig (November 22, 1866):

> The theme of the third act on which I am now working is: *Wahn! Wahn! Überall Wahn!*; this theme is brought out everywhere. . . . It is theme that rules my own life and the lives of all noble hearts; would we have to struggle, suffer, and make sacrifices if the world were not ruled by *Wahn*? . . . If Hans Sachs did not know a way of using *Wahn* to some nobler end, . . . oh how sad would my theme sound today! But the music I hear is: *Wach' auf, es nahet gen den Tag* [Wake up, daybreak is near.][16]

Wagner announces several important things in this letter. First, that *Wahn* is the theme not just of one speech but of the whole third act. Second, that it is a theme central to human existence and the suffering it involves. And third, that Hans Sachs will find a way to use *Wahn* to a "nobler end"—an end clearly connected to the triumph of German art, since the music he hears in his head is the opening line of a poem written by the historical Hans Sachs in praise of

---

[16] Warrack (1994, p. 111).

Luther, and sung in Act 3 by "the entire *Volk*" as they greet Hans Sachs at the start of the singing competition. (We should note at this point that Luther was a famous antisemite.) Having been profoundly disunified the night before, when rioting broke out in the streets of Nürnberg, the Volk now sing as one, a chorale in praise of Sachs and his leadership. So the noble end is connected both to art and to the unity of the entire people.

Wahn is best left untranslated. It can mean "illusion" or "delusion," and sometimes is rendered "madness," but "illusion" is probably closest to Schopenhauer's meaning. In 1854, Wagner's pessimistic reflections, long with him in his personal identification with Ahasuerus, took on a new theoretical concreteness when he read Arthur Schopenhauer's *The World as Will and Representation*—though he no doubt knew the general idea already, given Schopenhauer's tremendous fame and influence. It is abundantly clear that Schopenhauer impressed him profoundly, and that this influence can be felt at least in *Tristan und Isolde*, *Meistersinger*, and *Parsifal*, perhaps also in the *Ring*.

What did Wagner find in Schopenhauer's famous book that gave new shape to his thoughts?[17] According to Schopenhauer, there are two great forces or tendencies in the world: "representation," a faculty of cognition through which we grasp the world (or rather our own representations of it), and *Wille*, a dynamic force of striving (felt subjectively as erotic desire)[18] that animates all of nature and causes the perpetuation of life. *Wille* causes us to act in ways that are ultimately futile and productive only of suffering: when we try to become happy, we either fail to get the object we seek, or,

---

[17] I give a much more detailed account of Schopenhauer's views in ch. 2 of *The Tenderness of Silent Minds: Benjamin Britten and His War Requiem* (2024), with extensive references. An excellent summary is in Bryan Magee, *The Tristan Chord: Wagner and Philosophy* (2000), ch. 9, and ch. 14 on *Meistersinger*. I use the following edition of Schopenhauer: Arthur Schopenhauer (1818–1844), *The World as Will and Representation*, trans. E. F. J. Payne (1958).

[18] *Wille* operates in inanimate nature as well as in animals and humans, so "erotic desire" is too narrow; but that is the form it characteristically takes subjectively in our lives.

attaining it, become bored with it. Thus the human quest for happiness is all illusion, and this illusion happens to all people because *Wille* is using us for its own ends, primarily the preservation of the species. To Wagner's existing thoughts about endless wandering and the impossibility of peace, Schopenhauer adds a powerful metaphysical analysis.

For Schopenhauer, art can help us see the futility of our lives; it cannot offer us anything better. Through art we can stand back and grasp the manifold forms of *Wille*'s operations, but the most we can get out of that is a lesson not to engage in doomed projects. This limitation Wagner will not accept: it remains his position, from *The Flying Dutchman* onward, that a rescue beckons, through some type of self-sacrifice and transcendence, typically involving a true and loving woman. As time went on, he increasingly conceived of this transcendence as possible only through art, indeed only through "holy German Art"—and the "woman" increasingly becomes the adoring public that embraces the artist's vision.

For Schopenhauer, enlightened people who understand how the world works will seek to detach themselves from their own illusion-driven projects and turn with noble compassion to the sufferings of others.[19] Up to a point, that part of Schopenhauer evidently appealed to Wagner, and it seems likely that he thought of Hans Sachs as such a person.[20]

Let us approach Sachs's *Wahn* monologue in that spirit. Sachs is motivated, first, by his futile love for Eva, who loves him in a way, but loves Walther far more deeply and passionately. Then, too, he is inspired by the riot that has just taken place in Nürnberg, with its real and alarming violence. Perusing a large book of "city-and-world history," he finds in it again and again the same story: *Wahn* everywhere, doomed projects one after another, and as Schopenhauer explicitly says, violence breaking out because of the demands of

---

[19] See Schopenhauer (vol. I, sections 68 to 70).
[20] See Lucy Beckett, "Sachs and Schopenhauer," in Warrack (1994, pp. 68–82).

conflicting grasping egos.[21] The monologue is drawn closely from Schopenhauer in its description of the origins of violence and the delusions of pleasure that give rise to conflict.

With a solemn and noble sadness, Sachs renounces all hope of winning Eva as his own wife and decides to devote his efforts to ensuring that Walther wins her. Magee says that Sachs is "thus ensuring that he himself will spend the rest of his life alone and childless" (252–53). This seems to me a step too far, since both Wagner and the audience know that the historical Hans Sachs did in fact take a second wife at age sixty-six, only a little more than a year after the death of his first wife—a twenty-nine-year-old widow, who brought with her six children from her first marriage.[22] So Sachs was surely not alone. Furthermore, Wagner actually planned a drama on this topic![23] All we really know is that there is genuine and deep sadness here, and a renunciation of a selfish wish in favor of supporting the happiness of Eva and Walther. The sound-world of the speech shifts from the happy mood of the genial C major Prelude to a more tragic tonality, involving the C–F-sharp tritone.[24] However: even if we are supposed to think of Sachs as making, sadly, a noble sacrifice, the project of fostering the young couple's passionate erotic love is hardly one that Schopenhauer's noble man ought to approve.

And what is supposed to be the upshot of Sachs's ruminations for the drama as a whole, and for its audience? Magee says that "the resignation achieved within the work is authentic, so that one could go into a performance of it with all the troubles of the world on one's shoulders, and come out truly reconciled to life with all its folly and grief" (253). This—as Magee concedes—is a "kind of

---

[21] See the discussion in Magee (2000, p. 251).

[22] With his first wife he had seven children, all of whom died in childhood; I find no record of children with the second wife, but her own six would have prevented loneliness! Sachs lived fifteen more years after that marriage.

[23] See Warrack, "Sachs, Beckmesser, and Mastersong," in Warrack (1994, pp. 49–65, at 55).

[24] See Magee (2000); and the excellent detailed analysis in Warrack (1994, pp. 111–34).

life-assertion," and is thus not fully Schopenhauerian. But the real problem with Magee's conclusion is that it omits the role of art and its role in the community.

Wagner told Ludwig that what he himself hears in his head at the end of Sachs's speech is the poem of the historical Sachs, which the Chorus will shortly sing to honor Sachs, German art, and the master-song competition. So Sachs's announcement that he will "guide the *Wahn* subtly to perform a nobler task" must be about not only the Eva-Walther marriage but also the task of art in unifying the entire community and leading it to self-transcendence.

By this time we have already heard Walther's Prize Song, and we already know how good it is. So we know that Walther is not just passionately loved by Eva, but also artistically worthy of her and of the Prize. We are prepared for his subsequent triumph: he is the hero who will regenerate German art. Through Sachs's tutelage he has learned to moderate his excesses—but of course he has been tutored by a German, not a Frenchman or a Jew. And although he is a newcomer to Nürnberg, he is thoroughly German geographically and artistically: he comes from Franconia, and he has formed his artistic imagination by studying the works of Walther von der Vogelweide, the great German lyric poet (c. 1170–1230), known for his passionate love lyrics. So Walther brings to Nürnberg something that is in a sense new, a freshness and passion that have become lost in their rather stagnant culture—but something that is also very old, drawn from the deep true sources of German art. In no sense is he the foreign element that Sachs will decry.

And, of course, Walther is Wagner.

Sachs's Final Speech: Evolution and Political Meaning

Sachs's final speech might at first reading seem strange, coming after the *Wahn* monologue. Why on earth would its Schopenhauerian meditation lead to a stern warning against foreign influences? Sachs is a man of delicate sentiments and moving compassion. The *Wahn* monologue shows him as a person who genuinely acts for the good of others, rather than permitting himself to pursue selfish ends. The result of his soul-baring speech is that we honor Sachs and are inclined to believe what he says to us at the opera's end. He seems the nicest, kindest man in the world.

The connection between pessimistic reflections and the idea of redemption through a closed community and its holy art is an old one in Wagner's meditations. We've seen that it goes straight back to his misery in Paris and his idea of rescue from his storm-tossed agony through the embrace of Germanness—indeed by *becoming* Germanness himself and finding communal solace as the prophet of German redemption. Now that Sachs has become a trustworthy prophet within the opera, and, in effect, the agent of German redemption from civic strife, it is only fitting that he be the one to deliver the concluding message as Germany's anointed prophet: Pessimism will meet defeat and communal happiness will be attained, if only the people follow the Sachsian/Wagnerian path to happiness. Walther, I have said, is Wagner, but so is Sachs: one represents Wagner's musical genius, the other the discursive insight that accompanies and suffuses it.

Already in 1845, not long after the premiere of *Flying Dutchman*, Wagner wrote a sketch for *Meistersinger*, and that sketch was already full of patriotic nationalism.[25] Even the *Wahn* monologue showed Sachs meditating about the preservation of German culture. An 1861 draft retained the emphasis of the last speech on "holy German Art." But between 1845 and 1861 something gets lost: a note of irony. Sachs, who had been detached and ironic, now becomes dead earnest in his concluding speech. In the first full libretto, in 1862, he makes a very long speech with pacifistic sentiments. By 1867, while composing the music for Act 3, Wagner

---

[25] See Grey (2002).

considered leaving out the speech entirely. Then, however, Cosima apparently persuaded him that a speech was crucial, and that Wagner should write a shorter speech for Sachs in which he puts forward ideas about art that Wagner had been publishing in his prose essays (usually known as "Regeneration" essays). The result is a speech without irony, without pacifism, and with dead-serious insistence on the removal of all foreign influences. Wagner identified with many of his characters and made them into what he wanted to be and say. Now he first (in the *Wahn* monologue) makes Sachs a Schopenhauerian and a man of refined compassion—and then, in the conclusion, shows him finding the Wagnerian solution to pessimism (not at all Schopenhauerian): redemption and regeneration of the entire community through Wagnerian music. The compassionate Sachs is still compassionate, and he sees the illness that menaces the community. Out of disinterested sympathy he offers his medical prescription.

In short: the only healthy community is a community of Wagnerites who think alike and who venerate their community's prophet, taking their marching orders from him. Wagner's utopian redemption-fantasy is not just antisemitic—Jews are only one species of a genus of foreign peoples in need of aesthetic redemption, and indeed the French get the worst of it in this particular version—it is egomaniacal and monological. Germans may remain German—because Wagner's project is the creation of "holy German art." But this does not mean that they may remain Germans in the sense that Goethe was a German—curious, exploratory, embracing humanity in all its diversity, loving individuals as ends in themselves.

The people laud Sachs's speech with unanimity and joy. They look like the nicest people in the world, not interested in harming anybody. We can hardly forget, however, that one manifestation of *Wahn* prominent in Sachs's thoughts was a propensity to violence. If real foreigners should try to sully the purity of holy German art, Wagner offers no guarantee that *Wahn* would not again break out. My own reflections in chapter 7 about the behavior of closed communities tell the same story: wherever groups hold to a group norm and troublesome outsiders—or insiders—do things differently, violent behavior cannot be ruled out. Violence, as both Jenůfa and Peter Grimes learned all too well, need not be physical to cause enduring, even lethal, harms.

* * *

What did Wagner think would happen next? Didn't he worry that the cult of Wagner would itself become stale and frozen, in need of new challenges? Apparently not: he seems to have thought that truly great art defies this bad fate and retains a freshness that can be accessed again and again without satiety. There is of course much truth in that. And should the surrounding culture start to go stale, some mini-Wagner could arise to recall it to its noble roots in Wagner's art, just as Walther in the opera drew inspiration from Walther von der Vogelweide. But this would be truly a mini-Walther, because Wagner is unable to imagine anyone going beyond him. So the mini-Wagner would likely have to be a conductor or producer, not a composer of original German music. Bayreuth was Wagner's way of remaining relevant for centuries into the future, frozen yet alive—but numerous talented directors and producers of varying talents and ideas have interpreted Wagner there. If someone had insisted that some true Walther of the future, some new composer, would need to be performed there—and note that, despite all the squabbles in the Wagner family over the future of the Festival, this has not yet happened[26]—Wagner might at the limit possibly have conceded that some bright young German composer just might turn up some day. Just as he took his place

---

[26] The exception is the period of American occupation from 1945 until the Festival's official reopening in 1951, when all sorts of foreign music could be heard—including Verdi and Puccini. All along, however, the roster of artists has been highly diverse, including Jews, openly homosexual artists, and even the anti-fascist Arturo Toscanini.

alongside Beethoven (and Beethoven orchestral works have occasionally been performed at Bayreuth), so this new composer might enter Bayreuth at Wagner's side. But of course that person would have to be as German as Beethoven and Wagner, no admixture of Frenchness or Italianness or Jewishness allowed.[27] And that person would have to acknowledge the same debt to Wagner that Wagner did to Beethoven. That is how German art would remain holy and German and true.

Does the conclusion of *Meistersinger* prefigure Nazism? Not in so many words, clearly. It is an aesthetic project with no definite political application, and even the aesthetic project imposes the task of self-transcendence on everyone, not only on Jews and Frenchmen. But—as both Mann and Williams see—its monological spirit surely prefigures some sort of fascism, and its intolerance cries out for some authority to police the boundaries of the regenerated community. (After all, the Nazis went after many groups who did not fit their image of the healthy German: liberals, gays and lesbians, religious minorities, Roma people, and many others who refused to get with the program.) The French might be kept out by strong national border-enforcement, since they are not internal infiltrators; Jews and domestic other out-groups must be combatted from within, as poisons to the healthy community. Surely the Nazi project of persecuting "degenerate art" is prefigured here, if not its specific applications.

---

[27] Who might that be? Wagner would have detested serialism or even partial serialism, so he would sternly veto Alban Berg, perhaps the greatest post-Wagner Germanic opera composer so far. Berg has three strikes against him: he is a modernist, he is Viennese rather than German, and he studied with (the Jew and serialist) Arnold Schoenberg. Wagner would probably have found Richard Strauss sentimental and second-rate, I think not wrongly (at any rate after *Elektra* and *Salome*). As for Hans Werner Henze and Karlheinz Stockhausen, their experimentalism would have appalled him. Paul Hindemith was, I believe, a very fine composer, and was defended by Wilhelm Furtwängler as the new German composer of the future; but he never found a way to marry drama and his best music. And he had the bad taste to marry a Jewish wife, which led to his exile from Germany. All in all, Wagner would say, we are still awaiting a worthy successor, just as the world awaits the second coming of Christ.

We should agree with Hanslick: the cheerful Prelude is actually "brutal," and it goes with the apotheosis of Wagner, at the opera's close, as Walther/Sachs. The problem is in the confidence and assertiveness, which arrived on the scene early in Wagner's life, as soon as he found himself unwilling to suffer. His tempest-tossed voyage led him to refuse the reality of others, consequently to refuse all vulnerability and doubt. These traits lie at the heart of anti-liberalism, and they have a real political significance.

Cultural antisemitism of Wagner's sort is not about Jews as real people with real practices. It is more deeply about Jews as other, as those who go their own way and won't join the general chorus. The culture of those Others must "go under," as Wagner has already decreed.

Wagner is the arch-enemy of Mozart's Republic of Love not because he hates Jews, though he certainly does hate them. He is Mozart's arch-enemy because he hates craziness, doubt, playfulness, difference, and reciprocity, aspects of humanity that the Republic of Love cherishes and cannot do without. Even when Wagner follows what I think his better path to a thought (in the *Ring*) about overcoming selfishness through personal erotic love, it is not Mozartean love: it has too little reciprocity, playfulness, and humor. But that better path is surely not the path he chooses in ending *Die Meistersinger*. Whatever people may say about Wagner's antisemitism, a profoundly narcissistic abhorrence of all difference, which entails antisemitism, is most certainly in the operas, especially this one.

10

A "Pandemonium as Bright as the Sun and as Crazy as a Madhouse"

Verdi's *Falstaff*

What joy! To be able to say to the Public: "WE ARE BACK AGAIN!! COME AND SEE US!!"

—Letter from Verdi to Arrigo Boito, July 7, 1889

All your life you have wanted a good subject for a comic opera. This is a sign that the nobly merry vein of art exists potentially in your brain.... There is only one way to finish better than with *Otello* and that is to end victoriously with *Falstaff*. After having made all the cries and lamentation of the human heart resound, to end with an immense outburst of hilarity! It's dazzling!

—Letter from Boito to Verdi, July 9, 1889

The Aging Opera Composer in a Society that Makes No Room for the Aging

Mozart never grew old. Death was omnipresent in his psyche, and he certainly had many periods of illness, especially toward the end. Still, he did not experience, or even contemplate, some specific trials reserved for those artists—and, really, workers at any trade or profession—who do live and work into old age—including daily worries about bodily aches and pains, struggles with fatigue, a heightened looming awareness of time's brevity, an increasing sense of social isolation and stigma, and, perhaps most depressing, for someone who ages in reasonably good health, the illnesses and deaths of so many friends and contemporaries.

Philosophy and art have said little about how to access sources of joy and creativity during this sometimes vexing, sometimes delightful time of life. Cicero's marvelous dialogue *De Senectute* (c. 45 BCE) depicts its main interlocutor, the eighty-three-year-old Cato, writing a new book, learning new languages, and having pleasant dinner parties with his social circle. In the process Cato does effectively confront the social stereotyping and denigration that the aging person encounters every day: imputed physical incapacity, imputed mental and creative decline, all without specific evidence about the individual. These unpleasant experiences happen today as they happened in Republican Rome, for our society is rife with ageist prejudice. Indeed ageism is what we might call "the hate that dares not speak its name," a prejudice so ubiquitous that it is not fully recognized as a societal problem. Cicero's Cato sees all this, but because this fictional hero is rich and independent, the work fails to describe fully the aging person's needs for social support, both material and human, and for recognition as a fully equal and creative human being. Aging is a complex set of problems for the Republic of Love, as yet imperfectly explored.

Among great artists, Shakespeare is rare in a boundless empathy that extends generously into this stage of life, as yet unknown to him, and, as it turned out, never known—not only in *King Lear*, whose protagonist, increasingly isolated, loses all joy, and conforms to social stereotypes by losing both physical and mental competence, but also in the three plays dealing with the character Falstaff, who surmounts so many obstacles with zest—until his greatest friend, Prince Hal, drives him away, and he dies, in effect, of the loss of love. Opera in particular has had little to say about or to aging people, even though its very survival as an art form depends on such people, who comprise an increasingly large fraction of its audience. There are many questions an opera about aging might address: Is aging always tragic and a source of isolation and diminution? Can societies effectively confront their sources of stigma against aging people, rooted no doubt in fear? Are there no ways of fashioning aging as, potentially, a source of new connections, new sources of inspiration and invention, and new beauties—if one is prepared to laugh at the ridiculous limitations one also encounters?

Today the classical music world knows an increasing number of composers still creating significant works in very advanced age.[1] Among these, Philip Glass (b. 1937), John Corigliano (b. 1938), Aulis Sallinen (b. 1936), and John Adams (b. 1947) still write for the operatic stage, a more stressful form of creation than symphonic writing, involving rehearsals and work with numerous collaborators. And yet—apart from Sallinen's *King Lear*, written in his sixties, and the *Lear* of Aribert Reimann (1936–2024), written in his forties—they have not so far approached the theme of aging in their work.[2] In part of course this is due to a difference between opera and stage drama: we have, and increasingly will have, first-rate aging actors, still active, to act the roles of aging protagonists—Chicago's famed Mike Nussbaum (1923–2023, who performed

---

[1] These include (among those who have composed at least one opera) Philip Glass (88), John Corigliano (87), Aulis Sallinen (90), John Adams (78), Elliott Carter (who died at 103, still composing every day, and his one opera, *What Next*, premiered when he was 90), Einojuhani Rautavaara (who died at 87), Hans Werner Henze (died at 86), Aribert Reimann (who died in 2024 at 88), and Aaron Copland (who died at 90). (Ages are as of October, 2025.)

[2] I confess that I have never heard Rautavaara's six operas, only some of the twenty-five operas so far by Glass, and none of Henze's seventeen operas, so I base this claim on plot summaries. Glass has new works regularly premiered every year: in 2023, his "Triumph of the Octagon," a symphonic tone-poem, was given its premiere by Riccardo Muti and the Chicago Symphony Orchestra, and was so successful that it formed part of the CSO's international tour; his most recent opera was *Circus Days and Nights* in 2021; Corigliano's latest opera, *The Lord of Cries*, based on Euripides's *Bacchae*, with a libretto by his husband Mark Adamo, premiered in Santa Fe in 2021, and the CD recording has recently been released in 2023. (Adamo is currently 63, and also a composer of operas, so in those ways the couple and their mutual support parallel the Verdi-Boito relationship.) Adams's most recent opera is *Antony and Cleopatra* (2022).

with distinction until his recent death at 99), James Earl Jones (93, d. 2024), Rita Moreno (93), Jane Fonda (87), Morgan Freeman (88), Betty White (d. 2021 at 99), Anthony Hopkins (87), and so many others. And of course we also know superb living aging singers: Leontyne Price (98), Sherrill Milnes (90), Marilyn Horne (91), Fiorenza Cossotto (90), and may they all live in good health until this book is published.[3,4] But they are not still singing in public. Placido Domingo (84) is a rare outlier, able to perform on the opera stage in old age.[5] But opera singing is a very demanding athletic performance, and very few voices last that long (unlike, say, the popular music performances of Tony Bennett, which continued in top form until shortly before his death at 96).[6] So in an opera dealing with aging, the aging people must typically be portrayed by people under sixty, as a kind of masquerade, which is often made to seem grotesque and condescending by composers and librettists, gratifying popular prejudice—but consequently irritating to those in the audience who dislike cheap shots at their own dignity. (We all object to blackface and yellowface, but rarely are protests heard against similar denigrating portrayals of aging people. Thus we no longer see a blackface Otello, but we are constantly asked to laugh at the incompetence and indignity of Don Pasquale, Dr. Bartolo, and their like, typically performed by singers decades younger.[7])

---

[3] These ages are current as of October, 2025.

[4] We should also honor the amazing long careers of Magda Olivero (1910–2014) and Licia Albanese (1909–2014). I heard Albanese give a master class in around 2000. Although her singing was grainy, her advice to young singers about phrasing, nuance, and character was wonderful.

[5] I have a marvelous 1969 recording of Verdi's *Il Trovatore* starring Price, Cossotto, Domingo (in the year of his Met debut), and Milnes. How amazing and delightful that all are still living fifty-five years later. Among aging singers still on the opera stage we can include comic bel canto bass-baritone Alessandro Corbelli (b. 1952) and the great Renee Fleming (b. 1959). As time goes on there will be more, because study of the aging voice is advancing.

[6] There are many more, including Bob Dylan (83) and Mick Jagger (81), the latter all the more remarkable for his charismatic movement.

[7] One of the greatest buffo basses, John Del Carlo, died in 2016 at the age of sixty-five, still performing at the top of his form. He humanized these characters and gave them a dignity they are typically denied.

Giuseppe Verdi (1813–1901) lived to be eighty-seven, most of those years in vigorous good health, despite his frequent complaints about transient and non-threatening health problems. His wife, Giuseppina Strepponi (1815–1897), predeceased him by four years, and also had chronic arthritis that at times inhibited her mobility. Not Verdi: although he liked trips to health spas, he didn't really need them. He was often seen striding vigorously around the town, and he presented an imposing, if kindly, figure to new acquaintances and visitors. His main impediments to creativity were psychological. As we saw in chapter 6, intense emotional involvement in the political situation of Italy caused him an anguish that sometimes interfered with composition—as did the death of his father. Later on, episodes of depression—especially over the deaths of long-term friends—left him unable to create for months at a time.

Verdi was a man full of joy, whose work—however tragic its plot content—always seems to spring from deep love of human beings and delight in life itself. Even arias apparently about a furious desire for revenge express this joy. My daughter at age three especially loved the effervescent father-daughter duet from *Rigoletto*, "Si vendetta, tremenda vendetta," and would request it repeatedly by the name "vendetta," not understanding the word at all, and then dance or jump for joy at the music, which seems to me a very natural response to what Verdi wrote, since the music expresses the joy of the father and the (kidnapped and raped) daughter at having found one another again, and the father's (fatally deluded) idea that he will make everything right by retaliation. Even Manrico's famous so-called revenge aria from *Il Trovatore*, "Di quella pira" is all affirmation—he intensely loves his mother, unjustly persecuted for her Roma identity and about to be executed, and he is going off to save her (*Madre infelice, corro a salvarti*, "Unhappy mother, I run to save you"), violence being mentioned only as a fallback if her tormentors should try to stop him. The aria is not about anger—it is an outburst of risk-taking love: he explains to Leonora, whom he is leaving behind, "I was already a son before I loved you" (*era già figlio prima d'amarti*), not necessarily what a girlfriend wants to hear, but the truth about him.

As Verdi aged, sometimes this joy temporarily ran out of steam. And even he, famous and relatively well off as he was, suffered from society's denigration of aging people, as if they were no longer good for anything. Luckily a remarkable friendship came to his aid. His two late collaborations with poet and composer Arrigo Boito (1842–1918)—*Otello* (1887) and *Falstaff* (1893)—restored and nourished his compositional joy, giving him the psychological wherewithal to tackle these huge operatic projects. In fact, as we'll see, it isn't as though Verdi needed to be pampered in order to create—he loved composing and composed fluently and easily. But he needed a well-put suggestion and a responsive friend to interact with. (Notice that Verdi's letter expressing delight at the idea of a new opera precedes Boito's letter trying to talk him into the idea.) These prerequisites provided, he rushed at the projects and their problems, creating *Falstaff* in what Boito justly calls (before the fact) "an immense outburst of hilarity" that is "dazzling"—musically utterly new and adventurous, possibly the best thing he ever wrote.

In this chapter I'll study the evolution of *Falstaff*—the choice of subject, the friendship that nourished it, the genius of the libretto, and finally the truly dazzling music that Verdi came up with— asking what statements about life and aging the work makes, and where Verdi is in the work. Once again, as is typical of Verdi, the work is inspired and nourished by a specific context, so we must study it that way before analyzing the remarkable music.

One might ask how this question is political, in the way that most of this book's questions are political. An obvious answer is that aging citizens are "internal exiles" (in the sense of chapter 7) if anyone is, condescended to, discriminated against, and not even considered chic and fascinating the way Roma people have often been found chic.[8] Doing justice to the worth and dignity of aging people is a major task for the Republic of Love. But aging people are not only victims and sources of embarrassment: they are a rich resource for the Republic of Love, whose wisdom and creativity, properly supported by friendship free of stigmatizing condescension, can offer bold new insights. That is what *Falstaff* shows us, in the process of mapping out a political approach to the depressions and pains of life that is the antithesis of Wagner's.

The Choice of Falstaff: Challenges of the Character

Verdi had long toyed with the idea of writing a comic opera.[9] His early attempt, *Un giorno di regno* (usually translated as *King for a Day*, 1840, his second staged opera after *Oberto*, 1839), was generally accounted an utter failure. It was written at a hard time: he lost two children in 1838 and 1839, and then his young wife in 1840. The libretto was clumsy and chosen in haste, the cast apparently unsuited to comic performance. Opening night was a disaster, and the rest of the scheduled performances were canceled by La Scala. The work has occasionally been revived in recent years, but it is safe to say that it will never become a standard repertory item. So, given that early failure, Verdi had something to prove to himself and to others. Over the years, various critics, and even the great composer Rossini, said that Verdi was incapable of writing a comic opera. Occasional comic elements in serious operas—for example *Un Ballo in Maschera* and *La Forza del Destino*—showed that he

---

[8] A recent peeve: in our university all faculty are required to complete a sequence of highly time-consuming trainings: one on sexual harassment, one on protecting children, and one on fire safety and evacuation. They are always the same. We have to repeat them every two years, apparently because it is assumed that "normal" people forget things they have learned every two years. But if an aging person forgets an event that occurred decades ago, he/she is held to be feeble and over the hill.

[9] See Phillips-Matz (1992, p. 700).

had a sense of humor; but his friends all knew that. What he needed was the right time and the right subject.

Over the years he considered *Don Quixote*, comedies by Goldoni and Molière—but nothing came of those musings. In the end it was Boito who tempted him—with an appealing sketch for *Falstaff*. Both the theme and its lead character amused him, and we'll see how (in no simple manner) he fit his own identity into the work as a whole.

To make an opera of Shakespeare's character Falstaff is a challenging task. The character in *Henry IV*, Parts I and II, has long fascinated both audiences and critics. But there would be no good way to turn these chronicle plays into opera. On the other hand, the character in the late slight comedy *The Merry Wives of Windsor*—allegedly written because Queen Elizabeth asked Shakespeare to show her "the fat knight in love"—lacks substance and interest: distinguished critic Harold Bloom rightly describes him as "a nameless imposter masquerading as the great Sir John Falstaff."[10] He henceforth calls him "pseudo-Falstaff" and "the False Falstaff." Pseudo-Falstaff has no interesting views, no substance: he is treated as the butt of a long series of fat jokes. As Bloom says: "Shakespeare's immortal Falstaff suffers the terrible final humiliation of public rejection but retains pathos, dignity, even a kind of nobility as he goes down. . . . All the False Falstaff retains is his tormented rump" (317). So the challenge is somehow to use the basic frame of the comedy but insert into it the great character.

Why and how, then, is the Falstaff of the history plays a compelling character? There are many accounts of him, but here is one, based largely on that of Harold Bloom, whom I find convincing.

First, he is, as Bloom says, "vastly intelligent and witty beyond all measure" (324). As he himself says: he is witty himself

---

[10] Harold Bloom, *Shakespeare: the Invention of the Human* (1998, p. 315). (Henceforth Bloom, *Shakespeare*, and, within the text, page numbers without a title refer to this book.)

and the cause of wit in others. A poet like his creator, he creates a boundless freedom for himself out of words. As A. C. Bradley summarizes: "The bliss of freedom gained in humour is the essence of Falstaff" (296). His humor is satirical: he reduces authority, pomp, and convention to nothingness with his wit. Bradley again: "They are to him absurd, and to reduce a thing *ad absurdum* is to reduce it to nothing and to walk about free and rejoicing" (296). He has rightly been compared often to Socrates—but Socrates was not creative with language, nor was he funny. People who treat Falstaff as primarily about appetites forget his boundless creativity: he is, in effect, Shakespeare's genius in the mode of humor. Bloom again: "When we listen to Falstaff, we are inundated by abundance and resonance and are seduced by the beauty of his laughter and his vitalizing diction (*Falstaff*, 13).

Falstaff is also all for *living*: his irreverence is anti-state and anti-war but life-enhancing, and his wit harms no one. He turns his Socratic intellect to the goals of life, what Bloom calls his "vitalization of the intellect" (283).[11] Falstaff sees no point in acquisitive war's alleged glory. He wants to continue living (that's the context in which he says "give me life"), but more generally he wants people to flourish and be merry. He just doesn't get with the acquisitive-colonial goals of the British monarchy (whether of Hal's day or of the Elizabethan era in and for which Shakespeare wrote). No imperial domination for him, no defeated Armada, no plundered booty. Falstaff would never say "Once more unto the breach, dear friends, once more, / or close the wall up with our English dead." It is for that career as an imperialist warmonger that Hal deserts him. Hal as Henry V was the orthodox British hero for the long era of British colonialism. He also played well in the embattled time of a newly threatened Britain, as the popularity of Laurence Olivier's 1944 performance showed, although one could support a program

---

[11] Bloom's later separate book about the character is aptly entitled *Falstaff: Give Me Life* (2017, hereafter Bloom, *Falstaff*).

of national self-defense while repudiating empire. (Falstaff would have been no friend of Hitler and would not have supported pacifism in that war.) In our different era, and for a Britain ashamed of the destructions of empire, Kenneth Branagh portrayed the ugly costs of war in his excellent *Henry V* (1989), taking, so to speak, Falstaff's side and even inserting flashbacks from the history plays to give Falstaff (a well-cast Robbie Coltrane, later the Hagrid of the Harry Potter films) a cameo appearance.

Falstaff is also for love. He really loves Hal, and, as Bloom points out, he dies for love as much as any Romeo. So if we think of him as a great vitalist, it is a vitalist with deep emotions and boundless intellect: it's all of that that he wants when he says "Give me life."

It is easy to think he is just an old drunk and self-indulgent: I used to have that view myself, and didn't care to study him more closely. I was wrong: he values both the bodily appetites and the poetic intellect, and never lets the former dim the latter. The appearance of dissipation comes from the contrast with his pseudo-noble surroundings: people who make war on others for glory do not value the body; indeed their aim is to destroy bodies. They would say that they have high values and aims, and he is low. He would say that they are empty and his pursuits are real life.

How on earth could one put this immensely complicated poet of freedom into an opera built around a slender farcical plot? Other composers had tried, including Antonio Salieri in his *Falstaff* (1799). Otto Nicolai's *The Merry Wives of Windsor* (*Die lustigen Weiber von Windsor*, 1849) achieves something not altogether awful; but it is very thin stuff, and the well-known overture is thought to be by far the best part.[12] To do Falstaff justice, one would have to have a libretto that inserted large chunks of the "real" Falstaff into that plot, and how would one do that? His fantastical

---

[12] On other attempts, see Budden (198, pp. 419–20, at 419). Budden gives Nicolai more credit than I do, but that is in part because he gives Falstaff less, calling him the "prototype of all likeable fat scoundrels."

rhetorical and verbal creativity is not easily at home in an opera libretto. One would need a selection of those words, together with a lot of musical invention and musical creativity. Throughout, underlying even the most ridiculous farcical plot twists, one would have to rely on the capacious artistry of a great composer to bring the noble-comic spirit of Falstaff to life. In effect that spirit—defiant, boisterous, life-affirming, loving—would have to be in the opera as a whole, not just in a single character. This, in turn, might best be achieved by writing an opera not just *with* music but also *about* music. We shall see how Verdi and Boito accomplished this.

Verdi and Boito: A Work of Joyful Friendship

Arrigo Boito (1842–1918) was twenty-nine years younger than Verdi. He was a brilliant librettist—I would say the best ever, with such fertile command of language, source material, comic invention, and deeper meaning that I would rank him ahead of Da Ponte, who had the wit and the poetry, but (as we saw in chapter 3) not always deep human insight. Boito was not just a librettist; he was also a rather tormented composer. He had great gifts, but composition was a struggle for him, and he both destroyed and put aside many efforts. His one finished opera, *Mefistofele*, based on Part Two of Goethe's *Faust*, was initially a failure in 1868, but a revised version did much better in 1875. The work is profoundly impressive and is still a part of the regular operatic repertory. Boito also worked on and off for years on an opera about the emperor Nero and his struggles with Christianity. The unfinished work was finished by Arturo Toscanini after Boito's death, and performed in 1924, but *Nerone* has never caught on, although the libretto is acclaimed, and the work itself has some passionate admirers. A performance at the Bregenz Festival in 2021 was warmly received, and online extracts suggest that renewed attention is overdue. Meanwhile, he wrote the libretto for Ponchielli's *La Gioconda* (1876)—and then for Verdi's

Otello (1887) and *Falstaff*. Between 1887 and 1894, Boito was involved in a passionate secret love affair with the actress Eleonora Duse; they remained on good terms after the end of the affair, and their letters over the years survive. Both in this case and in the case of Verdi, Boito turns out to have had a remarkable genius for loving friendship.

As a young poet, Boito had provided the text that Verdi set in *L'inno delle nazione* ("The Hymn of the Nations"), a choral work written on commission for the International Exhibition in London in 1860, but this occasion did not lead to a close association.[13] Indeed, around this time Verdi somehow took offense at something Boito said in an ode he composed to his good friend Franco Faccio (composer and conductor), so Verdi kept the younger man at arm's length for some time. It was the publisher Ricordi who brought Boito and Verdi together. Ricordi wanted the two to work together on *Otello*, and in 1879, after Boito was already at work on the libretto, Ricordi wrote Verdi urging him to let bygones be bygones and trust the younger man: "If my memory does not fail me, I know that Boito did you some wrong [with his ode]; but I am sure that he did not know that he was doing it, with his nervous, odd character.... I find Boito an honest, loyal sort, indeed a perfect gentleman."[14]

Verdi gave Boito a tryout by allowing him to make a revised version of the libretto to *Simon Boccanegra* (original 1857, revival 1881), and Verdi was delighted with Boito's work, which he called "divinely well done."[15] He allowed himself to be tempted by the evolving *Otello* libretto, and from then on the collaboration bloomed. Apart from the evidence of the work they did together, we have two hundred ninety letters back and forth, which show an increasingly deep mutual reliance and relaxation.[16] Boito always

---

[13] See Phillips-Matz (1992, pp. 447–50).

[14] Phillips-Matz (1992, p. 650).

[15] Phillips-Matz (1992, p. 657).

[16] See Marcello Conati and Mario Medici, eds., *The Verdi–Boito Correspondence*, English edition prepared by William Weaver (1994). I often cite the English of this

begins his letters with the salutation "Dear Maestro," and addresses Verdi with the formal "Lei," while Verdi addresses him as "Dear Boito" and addresses him with the equally formal "Voi." This was the norm in these times. (Even Verdi's wife addresses her letters to him with "Dear Verdi.") The content of the correspondence shows considerable equality and increasing intimacy. I think Budden is correct in saying that the relationship reads less like father and son than like two brothers, and he concludes, "To Boito falls much of the credit for rejuvenating Verdi in his old age."[17]

What were the obstacles? I have mentioned depression at the deaths of friends, so rather than merely interweave these into the narrative of *Falstaff*, which can be confusing, let me describe the friends up front. Three deaths troubled him (and Boito too). First (in order of the onset of grave illness) was the long slide into dementia, due to tertiary syphilis, of conductor Franco Faccio (1840–July 1891). His agonizing decline is described in detail to Verdi by Boito in various letters, as he visits him and attempts to get him into treatment (not that there was any real treatment at that time). Meanwhile, by doing Faccio's teaching for him, Boito makes sure he continues to get a salary.

Second was the death of Verdi's lifelong friend Giuseppe Piroli (1815–November 14, 1890), a very close companion in the Risorgimento, who served with Verdi on the Council. Verdi was very fond of him and exchanged hundreds of letters with him over the years that are precious sources for biographers.[18] He died after a short illness and hospitalization, apparently of age-related causes.

Third was the illness and death of conductor Emanuele Muzio (1821–November 26, 1890), one of Verdi's few students (though he was not much younger), and a lifelong associate and friend,

---

edition, but sometimes the versions by Phillips-Matz are more idiomatic English, so my versions are eclectic.

[17] Budden (1981, p. 420).
[18] La Scala keeps an archive of this correspondence. Istituto Nazionale di Studi Verdiani (2017).

who helped prepare scores and conducted many performances of Verdi's works. He died of a liver ailment that some ascribe to chemicals in a hair dye he had used for years.[19] His final letter to Verdi (which Verdi received only in January 1891, since it was attached to Muzio's will, which he received on that date) is heart-rending and must have been so to Verdi:

> I will soon go on to the other world, filled with love and friendship for you and your good, dear wife. I have loved you both, and remember that my faithful friendship never flagged from 1844 until now. Remember me sometime, and goodbye, until we meet—as late as possible—in the other world. Kisses and kisses from your faithful loving friend E. Muzio.[20]

Now let us double back to set these losses in the unfolding narrative of *Falstaff*. Verdi had been aware for some time that Boito was working on a sketch for an opera based on the character Falstaff and the basic plot of *Merry Wives*. He himself was toying with other ideas—including *King Lear* (for which a sketch survives). But in July 1889, when Boito sent him his sketch for *Falstaff*, he was delighted, praising Boito's work in a letter of July 7, and saying that, when he compares the libretto with *Merry Wives*, "it would be impossible to do better than you have done." He wrote again on July 7, with huge enthusiasm—as the passage in the epigraph, from the end of his letter, shows. However, the letter as a whole was more cautious, mentioning "doubts and discouragement." What about "the enormous number of my years"? He says he knows Boito will reply saying his health is excellent, but still: what if he proved unable to finish the work and Boito spent his time in vain—meanwhile being distracted from his own opera *Nerone*? How to overcome these obstacles? "Can you offer good answers to my objections? I wish

---

[19] Phillips-Matz (1992, p. 704).
[20] Phillips-Matz (1992, p. 706).

you could, but don't think it possible." But then, if you could—
"What joy . . . ," etc as in the epigraph. In short, Verdi heard in his
head the usual social voices whispering of incapacity, but he didn't
truly want to believe them. He needed, and found, a counter-voice.

Verdi's eagerness could not have been more evident, and on July
9 Boito replied, with great delicacy and care, addressing himself
to Verdi's doubts. First, he is confident that he could still finish his
own opera in addition to doing *Falstaff.* (That never happened, but
it was hardly Verdi's fault.[21]) Second, "I do not believe that writing a
comic opera would fatigue you. Tragedy makes the person writing
it actually *suffer.* . . . But the joking and laughter of comedy exhila-
rate mind and body." You, he continues, are full of desire to work,
and you have long wanted to write a comedy. And then follows the
passage quoted in my epigraph, portraying the comedy as a victorious capstone to Verdi's career. He proposes that they get to work
in secrecy, so nobody will pry or bother them.

Verdi wanted to be won over, and Boito's letter hit just the right
notes. On July 10, Verdi replied: "Amen: so be it. Let us do *Falstaff*
then. We won't think for the moment about the obstacles, age,
illnesses."

The two men got right to work, exchanging many letters about
the details of the libretto. Basically happy with the words of Acts
1 and 2, Verdi began to compose the music. He finished Act 1 by
March 1890—despite the worries of both men about Faccio's health
and the burden on Boito. Verdi spent a relaxed summer with his
wife and other visitors, including soprano and friend Teresa Stoltz,
and when she returned to Milan he sent her two pork shoulders,
one for her and one for Ricordi, together with his personal recipe
for cooking them, with great detail and high good humor.[22] Later

---

[21] Boito had deep psychological impediments to writing music, and sometimes a
graphophobia so extreme that he was unable even to write letters.

[22] Phillips-Matz (1992, p. 704) gives the recipe in full if you want it. I have no idea
how pork could be shipped without spoilage in those days, but in the end nobody was
poisoned.

in the summer, news of the illnesses of Muzio and Piroli began to burden Verdi; he consulted with Muzio's doctors and at Muzio's request found him a nursing home in Pisa. Boito visited with bad news about Faccio, and Boito himself was exhausted by his additional duties doing Faccio's job teaching at the conservatory; also, his long affair with Duse was nearing its end. Nonetheless, exhilarated by Boito's visit, Verdi managed to map out most of Act 2, by beginning with a part in the middle that he had clearly in his head and then gradually filling in the rest—despite grumbling melodramatically in a letter to Stolz that life has no meaning and old age is terrible. Piroli died on November 14, but visitors to a dinner party at the Verdis' home around that time (with Boito present) found Verdi, nonetheless, in excellent form. A local news report said that Verdi "has never seemed younger or in better spirits."[23] It was on this occasion that Verdi and Boito went public with news of their opera. Boito suddenly proposed a toast: "'I drink to the health of Big Belly!'" Everyone was puzzled, but then he went on: "'I drink to the health of *Falstaff*.'" ("Big Belly" was the name the two men gave to their opera; as we'll see, they talked about it as a kind of obstreperous child.) Immediately the news was in all the local newspapers.

However, when Verdi received news of Muzio's death on November 26, he really did become depressed. To singer and friend Maria Waldmann he wrote, "In about fifteen days I have lost my two oldest friends. *Dead*! And both were younger than I!! Everything ends! Life is a sad thing!!" This rhetoric is characteristic of Verdi, but this time he really did stop writing. Although Boito gently nudged him to begin the new year "smiling," Verdi wrote Ricordi that the opera would not be finished in 1891: he was simply unable to work the long hours that used to be easy for him. In the spring he told some visitors to his home that he was working on an opera but didn't know what would come of it or if it would ever be finished.

---

[23] Phillips-Matz (1992, p. 705).

A visit from Boito made things take a turn for the better—although Verdi reported on May 1 that Big Belly was weak and needed more food. "Big Belly? Poor thing! After that illness of four months he is skinny, so skinny! Let's hope to find some fat capon to swell his belly again! Everything depends on the doctor! Who knows? Who knows?"

Then in June came a decisive turning point. Like one parent reporting to another about a toddler's misbehavior, Verdi wrote to Boito on June 12:

Big Belly is on the road to madness. Some days he does not move, he sleeps, and is in bad humor. At other times he shouts, runs, jumps, tears the place apart. I let him act up a bit, but if he goes on like this I will put him in a muzzle and straitjacket.

Boito understood right away that this was a reference to progress on Act 3, and replied with delight:

Great! Let him do it; let him run; he will smash all the glass and furniture in your room; it doesn't matter much; you will buy more; he will break up the piano; it doesn't matter much; you will buy another one. Let everything be wrecked, so long as the *great scene* gets done. Hurrah!

> *Hit him! Hit him! Hit him! Hit him!!*
> *What pandemonium!*

But it is a pandemonium that is as bright as the sun and as crazy as a madhouse!!

I already know what you are going to do. Hurrah.

This exchange gives us a window into the heart of a friendship. From the very beginning, Verdi had a problem with Act 3 of the opera, the scene in the forest, which always struck him as undramatic. His plunge into depression prevented any solution to this problem, and perhaps a creative impasse was part of the depression. But now he has discovered that the right solution is for everything to go crazy—as it does, in the most delightful and artistically masterful way, a pandemonium truly as bright as the sun. (The references to "hit him" are to the way the "fairies" torment, prick, and pummel Falstaff in jest, doing no real damage.) The two men share a fantasy of the opera as their unpredictable and ill-mannered child (straitjacket) or possibly dog (muzzle). Unlike the couple's fantasy of a child in Edward Albee's *Who's Afraid of Virginia Woolf*, this fantasy cements a loving friendship rather than tearing one apart. And unlike the Albee couple's fantasy of their child's death, it is essentially a fantasy of birth and growth, of the manic disruption caused by an outburst of creativity. The intimate love and understanding involved in this exchange cannot be overestimated. (Meanwhile Faccio finally died in an asylum on July 21, and Verdi consoles Boito and praises his devotion; Boito poignantly states that once Faccio was a lifeless corpse, "the noble expression of human reason reappeared.")

There were no further setbacks, and after the usual time for casting and rehearsals, the opera had its premiere at La Scala on February 9, 1893. It was a huge success.

Boito's Libretto: To "Mediterraneanize Music"

Nothing is more obvious than that *Falstaff* is a brilliantly unified work, with no tension I can find between music and words. Still, since we know that Boito wrote the words first—subject always to Verdi's critique and modification—and since its marvelous achievement as a work of art in its own right has often been passed over, I want to pause here.[24] Both Verdi and Boito were passionate

---

[24] In this section I am much indebted to a fine chapter in James A. Hepokoski, *Giuseppe Verdi: Falstaff*, Cambridge Opera Handbooks (1983, pp. 19–34).

Italians. Both had long expressed (in letters to friends) concern that the spirit of Italian opera was being hijacked by a heavier German spirit, and Verdi shared this concern. Wagner of course had fought this battle from the other side, attempting to free opera from the grip of the Italians and the French, not to mention the Jews (see ch. 9). And Verdi worried that Wagner's heaviness was having a bad influence on Puccini and young Italian composers in the *verismo* school. He did not directly criticize Wagner: he simply said that Germans have a different spirit "inside of them," and that therefore, "We cannot—rather, I will say we ought not to—write like the Germans, nor the Germans like us."[25] In a late 1891 letter to Boito he makes a pointed joke against Wagner's cultish pomposity. Suggesting that in one scene there might be a violin playing from the balcony of the auditorium, he jokes: "If now they put orchestras in the cellar [an allusion to Wagner's placement of the orchestra beneath the stage at Bayreuth], why couldn't we put a violin in the attic?!! If I were a prophet my apostles would say, '*Oh what a sublime idea.' Ha ha ha ha!* What a beautiful world this is!" Poking fun at the way Wagner sets himself up as a prophetic leader of an otherworldly cult, he makes it clear that the actual world is far more fun.

Boito was more judgmental: to his good friend Bellaigue, he wrote, apropos of *Falstaff*: "The human spirit must be 'Mediterraneanized'; only there is there true progress." When Bellaigue failed to get his meaning, he points out in another letter that the phrase "to Mediterraneanize music" is taken from Nietzsche.[26] There are two sources for this in Nietzsche: one is a fragment of 1887: "die Musik 'mediterranisiren': das ist meine Losung" ("to 'mediterraneanize' music: that is my watchword"). The second, with a fuller context, is in the 1888 *The Case of Wagner* (*Der Fall Wagner*). Discussing Bizet's *Carmen* as a contra-Wagnerian paradigm, he emphasizes

[25] Letter quoted in Hepokoski (1983, p. 33).
[26] Letters quoted in Hepokoski (1983, p. 34).

the need for music to be lighter, more dance-like, more worldly, and with a more this-worldly conception of love as tragic fatality. He then says in French: "il faut méditerraniser la musique" (section 3).[27] It is clear, then, that to "Mediterraneanize" does not necessarily refer to cheerfulness, but to a general manner of engagement with both happiness and unhappiness: this-worldly, honest, with no fog of hagiography or other-worldly spirituality.[28]

The libretto pursues this goal in three ways: concision, versatility of poetic language and meter, and the brilliant creation of a worthy central character.

First of all, then, the clunky plot of *Merry Wives*, with its superfluous characters and plot twists, is stripped to its bare essentials, creating a work lasting barely two hours. Boito keeps Bardolph and Pistol, but cuts out the forgettable Nym—as well as George Page, his son William, Sir Hugh Evans, John Rugby, and Peter Simple. Several other minor characters have no lines. Doctor Caius is a mixture of Robert Shallow and his nephew Slender; little of the original Caius remains, since his humor, such as it was, came from a mangled French accent. Mistress Quickly becomes a friend of the wives rather than Caius's servant; Anne Page becomes, instead, Ford's daughter Nanetta—a change that intensifies the motives for Ford's anger; Fenton is all love, and his pecuniary motives for the courtship are omitted. All sorts of superfluous incidents are cut, and Falstaff's three humiliations reduced to two.

In creating the libretto's poetry, Boito fully exploits the resources of the Italian literary tradition. Critic James Hepakoski describes in detail the huge variety of traditional meters he employs, the versatile ways he mixes them, and their range of literary reference. The rhythms of the text are rapid, fleeting,

---

[27] Nietzsche, *The Case of Wagner*, in Friedrich Nietzsche, *The Birth of Tragedy and The Case of Wagner*, trans. Walter Kaufmann (1967).

[28] Boito's struggle with Wagner was complex and ongoing; *Nerone* has been characterized as Wagnerian rather than Italian. (I'll decide when I've heard it.)

constantly shifting. The sparring of the young lovers and their signature-phrase *Bocca baciata* ("a mouth that has been kissed") are drawn from Boccaccio, and Boito draws attention to this in another letter to Bellaigue just before the premiere: "Come, come, dear friend, come and hear this masterpiece; come and live for two hours in the gardens of the *Decameron* and breathe flowers that are notes and breezes that are timbres."[29] (Note his emphasis on the musical self-referentiality of the text, which we will explore later.) Boito completely invents Nanetta's Act 3 aria and most of Fenton's. Throughout, too, are scattered archaic and poetic words, often rhythmic and onomatopoetic, most taken from Boccaccio or other earlier Italian poets.[30] Boito clearly wants to emphasize the libretto's Italian roots, and he often pointed out that the plot of *Merry Wives* itself derives from an Italian source, the stories of Ser Giovanni Fiorentino.

Next and most central: the character of Falstaff regains his dignity. He loses most of his ruffianly thievish behavior. What Boito triumphantly succeeds in keeping is his satirical assault on warlike honor: the great honor monologue is grafted into *Merry Wives* intact, its poetry amplified by the music, whose comic effects help the satire along. His statement "Go, old John" (*Va, vecchio John*) has weight and dignity. Falstaff's monologue about the restorative effects of hot wine, his reminiscence of his slender youth, and at least a dozen other key lines from the Henry plays[31] add to the portrait, so that we get a Falstaff who is, once again, a poet, a champion of freedom, and a self-creator out of language. The key line "I am not only witty in myself, but the cause that wit is in other men" (*Henry IV* Pt 2, I.ii, 6–10) is given a pivotal place at the end of Act 3, where Falstaff rises from his apparent humiliation, converting it to a coronation. If directors sometimes encourage an undignified

---

[29] Letter quoted in Hepokoski (1983, p. 29).
[30] See Andrew Porter, summarized in Hepokoski (1983).
[31] See the list in Hepokoski (1983, pp. 27–28).

clownish performance, that is their mistake. Michael Volle's 2023 performance at the Metropolitan Opera (preserved in the Met HD series) shows how the role should be played. Volle is a leading Wotan in Wagner's *Ring*, and his Falstaff is Wotan's comic cousin—with more humanity and self-knowledge. No clown makeup: Volle (age 63 at the time) shows his own noble slightly jowly and sunken face, and we can see in him the dignity and the poetry of the character as well as the way vanity and greed lead Falstaff into ridiculous situations. And beautiful undistorted singing throughout, as if to show that the soul of the man is youthful beneath the paunch.

There is one crucial new thing about Boito's Falstaff: he is not just a poet, he is also a composer. He alludes at crucial junctures to the effects of music on him and inside him—and, through him, on others. We need now to study this more closely. Lest, however, we be tempted to say that Falstaff represents Verdi, let us remember that "Big Belly" is the entire Verdi-Boito artwork, and that Verdi is everywhere in it.

The Music: Innovation, Rapidity, Complexity

The music of *Falstaff* is bursting with innovation—with rapid movement, complex structures, and orchestral laughter. From its beginning on an accented upbeat to its end in a fugue, it is unlike anything else Verdi ever wrote, and unlike anything anyone else was writing. It has no overture (already with *Aida*, Verdi had been freeing himself from that convention[32]). Instead, after a mere seven bars of boisterous music, we are plunged right into hurtling movement and comic action.[33] The work's complicated fleet-footed ensembles are notoriously difficult to perform, particularly with

---

[32] Indeed he never adhered to it formulaically: for example, the early *La Traviata* has a short prelude rather than an overture.
[33] See Hepokoski (1983, p. 1).

singers who are also moving and acting. (Riccardo Muti has even said that a concert version is better for doing justice to the music, but surely Verdi would not have agreed.) And throughout there are various Mozartean imitations of laughter in the orchestra,[34] as if the music itself is having wonderful fun, bursting with delight.

Verdi rebuts baneful stereotypes of aging in many ways inside the opera, but also, and above all, in the very writing of it. It is a commonplace that aging people are stuck in a groove and cannot take us to a new future. *Falstaff* takes opera to a new future without Wagnerian sermonizing, just by its endless musical inventiveness and forward-looking imagination. And of course the stereotype was always stupid. An aging composer doesn't have to be anyone's acolyte or to worry about public norms. Age frees the creator to do whatever he or she pleases, and a long career also imparts a wealth of experience that enables the creation of new forms. As to the stereotype that aging people are tired and lack energy, there is no opera in the repertory more bursting with joy and vitality.

I suggested above that we should not think of Verdi as identifying with the character Falstaff alone: instead, in a work stuffed full of self-quotations from other Verdi operas, as if making a friendly joke of them,[35] Verdi is clearly everywhere in the text. Riccardo Muti writes perceptively that *Falstaff* is in that sense an autobiography. Its protagonist is "the aged Verdi who thinks about his path as a man and composer."[36] Everything is part of Verdi's life: young love, Falstaff's youth, married life, the comedy of aging.

Let us now examine four examples of this playful musical self-referentiality, in which we encounter music about music, and creativity about a history of creativity:

---

[34] See Hepokoski (1983, pp. 5, 7).
[35] See Muti (2022, p. 165). There are allusions in particular to *Traviata* and *Il Trovatore*.
[36] Ibid.

The Young Lovers

Verdi and Boito do something very original with the two young lovers: they never have an extended scene, but pop up here and there throughout the work, as if they are always somewhere behind the scenes[37]—exchanging brief endearments, always with the Boccaccio line "Bocca baciata," etc., describing how love does not exhaust itself, but, instead, renews itself like the moon. The music is sweet and pure, untarnished by life's pains, constructing a bright thread through the whole opera. And now we can mention that the poetry is somewhat archaic, as if it came from a long-ago memory. It is as if the aging Verdi, with a long history of life and love, recalls in gusts of beautiful memory the pure love of youth that is still inside of him—for of course it is still inside him, since he has just written this music. Muti puts it well: "For what concerns love, I think that one of the greatest achievements of Verdi was that of writing with the soul of a young innocent while being 80 years old and after 50 years of putting troubled and violent passions into music."[38] In the musically dazzling portrait of Ford's jealousy, Verdi shows that love can sometimes have a tragic conclusion (after all, he has just written *Otello*), but he ends the work with the happiness of the young couple (and the repentance of Ford).

"Quand'ero paggio"

In Act 2, beginning his courtship of Alice Ford, Falstaff reminisces about his life as a man and a courtier. Borrowing lines from two separate passages in Shakespeare (*Henry IV* pt 1, II.iv, 325–28 and *Henry IV* pt. 2, III.2, 25–27), Boito assembles the following text:

---

[37] Boito draws attention to this plan in a letter of July 12, 1889: "I would like to sprinkle the whole comedy with that light-hearted love, like powdered sugar on a cake, without collecting it in one point" (Letter 125).

[38] Muti (2022, p. 167).

FALSTAFF

Quand'ero paggio
Del Duca di Norfolk ero sottile,
Ero un miraggio
Vago, leggero, gentile, gentile.
Quello era il tempo
Del mio verde Aprile,
Quello era il tempo
Del mio lieto Maggio,
Tant'ero smilzo, flessibile e snello
Che avrei guizzato attraverso un anello.

When I was a page
of the Duke of Norfolk I was thin,
I was a mirage
delicate, light, charming, charming.
That was the time
of my green April,
That was the time
of my happy May,
I was so lean, flexible and slender
that I could have slipped through a ring.

The character Falstaff is gently mocking himself and showing himself to Alice not as a buffoon devoid of self-awareness, but as an ironic commentator on his own life. The rapidity of the poetry creates an effect of grace and self-awareness beyond anything in Shakespeare. But the music is yet more remarkable. The entire aria is fleet of foot; it takes a mere thirty to thirty-two seconds to sing (those who try to draw it out are to be chastised!). It ought to be sung, and often is, with impeccable grace (Bryn Terfel's occasional squeaks and burps are an artistic error, Fischer-Dieskau's simplicity the right approach), showing a Falstaff who knows and still is that slender grace, even if externally he has become larger. He is a character of dignity whom a woman actually might fall for, and when the role is played that way, with the grace of the voice and its music enlivening the whole persona (as by Michael Volle), we see what Verdi and Boito were after. The aging Falstaff has self-respect and even delicacy, and though Verdi is present throughout the opera, his own wit and grace shine through with special clarity in this aria. In the Met staging Volle is carving a chicken while he sings it, giving Alice a few slices and putting the rest on his own plate—thus creating a pointed contrast between his youthful self, still present in the aria, hence in him, and his current outwardly gluttonous self. Muti calls the aria "an ironic vision of all his life as a man and composer" (167). It all goes by so quickly—like life—but the heart and the mind are still young. The comedy of aging sexuality requires this delicate balance in performance—otherwise the scene is merely pathetic.

And of course the aria's grace is not just Falstaff's—it is Verdi's: he is saying to the audience, "This grace, this mental fleetness of foot, is still in me." He proves his point by the music he composes.

The Trill Scene

At the opening of Act 3, Falstaff has just emerged, sodden, from the Thames, to a bright descending passage in the violins that follows a compressed staccato introduction. But he is in a sour mood, and his music is dark: only grumbling bassoons, C clarinets, horns, and trombones accompany his complaints, with a descending theme. Having summoned the landlady, he ruminates: "Nasty world, villainous world, vile world." He orders some wine. Then more growling from the bassoons etc., and he joins them: that he, a noble knight who has lived a life of adventure, would be dumped in the river with a load of dirty laundry! Only his paunch saved him, as it swelled and pulled him up: "a base death (*brutta morte*), water inflated me (*mi gonfia*)" (and a crescendo from the strings depicts the swelling!).[39] "Vile world, there's no more virtue, everything is going downhill," and again the descending growling theme. Now, accompanied by low strings, he sings his old song, "Go, old John" (*Va, vecchio John*)—but now in a minor key, and with muted dynamics, without any of the old bravado and joy. "Go on until you die. True manliness has disappeared from the world." And again: "What a nightmare of a day." Next he begins to reflect on his age: "I grow too stout, my hair is turning gray." A reader of Verdi's letters cannot help noticing a characteristic Verdian way of melodramatically grousing and complaining.

But then the landlady brings him some wine, and he drinks it, accompanied by a reappearance of the bright descending motif from the violins. Immediately he begins to feel its restorative effects. Boito now draws on a speech of Falstaff about the effects of sherris-sack from *Henry IV* pt 2, IV.iii. Here's the original speech:

> A good sherris sack hath a two-fold
> operation in it. It ascends me into the brain;
> dries me there all the foolish and dull and curdy
> vapours which environ it; makes it apprehensive,
> quick, forgetive, full of nimble fiery and
> delectable shapes, which, delivered o'er to the
> voice, the tongue, which is the birth, becomes
> excellent wit. The second property of your
> excellent sherris is, the warming of the blood;
> which, before cold and settled, left the liver
> white and pale, which is the badge of pusillanimity
> and cowardice; but the sherris warms it and makes
> it course from the inwards to the parts extreme:
> it illumineth the face, which as a beacon gives
> warning to all the rest of this little kingdom,

---

[39] Boito is more scientific than Shakespeare, who has Falstaff saying that his bulk nearly sank him, but for the fact that the water was shallow.

man, to arm; and then the vital commoners and
inland petty spirits muster me all to their captain,
the heart, who, great and puffed up with this
retinue, doth any deed of courage; and this valour
comes of sherris.

The speech is wonderful in itself, and it gains greatly from its trans-position to a context in which Falstaff is about to give up hope and is brought back to life and energy. But Boito does not simply lift the speech from Shakespeare; he marvelously transmutes it so that it is all about the creation of music. As wine's effects mount to the brain:

> Il buon vino sperde le tetre fole
> Dello sconforto, accende
> l'occhio e il pensier, dal labbro
> Sale al cervel e quivi
> risveglia il picciol fabbro
> Dei trilli; un negro grillo
> che vibra entro l'uom brillo
> Trilla ogni fibra in cor, l'allegro etera al trillo
> Guizza e il giocondo globo squilibra una demenza
> Trillante! E il trillo invade il mondo!!

> Good wine dispels the grim madness of despair,
> kindles the eyes and the thoughts.
> From the lips it rises to the brain,
> and there it awakens the small blacksmith of trills,
> a black cricket (grillo) inside the tipsy man (brillo).
> Every fiber in the heart trills; the merry sky itself quivers
> with the trill, and a trilling madness unbalances
> The joyous globe! And the trill invades the world!!

What has happened is that the wine makes Falstaff make music: the internal *fabbro* (blacksmith) of trills is the composer's musical imagination (as well as a reference to percussion and brass instruments), and this is now associated with a "cricket," perhaps a reference to the string instruments! And an entire symphony of trills begins inside the man, spreading out to the air—and then, to the whole world. Victoriously, the trill takes over the universe.

Of course as Falstaff sings this the orchestra is trilling. Beginning with the flutes, the trill spreads to the whole wind section, then to the strings, and finally to the brass and the tympani—until it has indeed invaded the whole world of the work!! Wine makes music (or removes psychological impediments to music), and music makes the world. Both text and music show the way in which a creative fire inside the artist (which might be temporarily eclipsed but is always there inside, a small *fabbro* in the mind and heart) makes something that then kindles a spark of joy in the audience, bringing us all to creative life together.

This scene more than any other shows Verdi's face in the work and marks its core theme as the aging composer's continued creativity, which magically creates a universe. Who brings the wine? I suggest it is his friend Boito.

The Final Scene and Fugue

Act 3 has all the opera's ingredients mixed together, and tossed up in the air in the bright pandemonium Boito mentions. There is great lyrical beauty in Nanetta's aria to the fairies and her exchanges with Fenton. That lyrical grace is Verdi. Next door to the beauty is manic comedy, as the townspeople dressed as goblins roll Falstaff around, making him dizzy (*ruzzola ruzzola*), and children playing fairies prick and pinch him: *pizzica pizzica stuzzica spizzica*, etc. This manic comedy is also Verdi. The alliterative, onomatopoetic, and increasingly crazy libretto is great fun in itself, but as set for these light voices, even more fun, punctuated by Falstaff's cries of "Ahi, ahi, ahi." What could be merely sadistic becomes a kind of madhouse dance of increasingly crazy fizzy words and music: because it is as bright as the sun, the madhouse is a delight.

Falstaff's deflation harms nobody because, as we eventually see, he is in on the joke: everyone, he says, makes fun of him, but "without me they would lack a pinch of salt. It is I who make you witty. My wit creates wit in others." In effect Falstaff now takes center stage as the knowing creator of the work, and—after the false wedding has been unmasked and Ford has become reconciled to the (now married) young lovers—he leads the entire company in a final fugue that includes the audience as well:

> Tutto nel mondo è burla
> L'uom è nato burlone.
> Nel sua cervello
> Ciurla sempre la sua ragione.
> Tutti gabbati! Irride
> L'un l'altro ogni mortal
> Ma ride ben chi ride
> La risata final.

> Everything in the world is a comedy.
> Human beings are born comics.
> Their reasons sway this way and that
> In their brain.
> Everyone is crazy. All mortals
> Laugh at one another.
> But the person laughs best
> Who has the last laugh.

Fugues are relatively rare in nineteenth-century music, and hard to find in Romantic opera, apart from those in the orchestral Prelude to Wagner's *Die Meistersinger* and the later street brawl scene.[40]

---

[40] One can add the opening chorus of Saint-Saens's *Samson and Delilah* (1877). Verdi also used a fugue in the battle scene of *Macbeth*, and alluded to this with humor in contemporaneous letters.

(They become more common again in the twentieth century, but still more often in symphonic music than in opera.) Verdi's formal choice refers, once again, to the technical tools of the composer's art. It also alludes to the baroque and classical tradition of which Verdi is the heir—perhaps especially to Mozart, whose comic spirit can be felt throughout this opera.[41] Verdi's use of choral fugues in his *Requiem* is dead serious, nothing at all like this. And what we might call this "pandemonium fugue" sets up a fertile tension between the craziness of which the words speak and the tremendously complicated ordering that the music creates. The fugue finale is so technically complex and involves so many people that it is almost unperformable. (Fortunately it is usually staged so that the cast faces the audience, including them in the pandemonium—and thus the singers can watch the conductor.) No part of the work is more deserving of Boito's epithet, "a pandemonium as bright as the sun and as crazy as a madhouse."

One more nineteenth-century fugue must now be mentioned: the *fuga infernale* in the Witches' Sabbath scene in Boito's own *Mefistofele* (1868). Could Verdi (*inter alia*) be paying a compliment to his friend, librettist, and fellow composer?[42] In that scene, the Devil proclaims the worthlessness of the world and human beings. Here Boito and Verdi, as anti-devils, proclaim the joy and delightfulness of human life.

In this joyful masterpiece, Verdi says to the world: You may think that at my age I am just a joke, but the joke is on you. It is I (not you) who create this delight, this laughter. You say I am tired and decrepit, but see what I just did!

---

[41] Haydn uses fugues in *The Creation* and *The Seasons*, Mozart in several choral works, including the *Requiem*, and also in the overture to *Die Zauberflöte*.

[42] Verdi's initial impression of *Mefistofele* was positive though mixed (Istituto Nazionale di Studi Verdiani (2017), editor's introduction, lii–liv). The extant letters do not comment on this possible reference, but they don't discuss the final fugue at all, or only its pre-composition libretto.

Life is a comedy, and it leaves us, at times, with little dignity. And yet the craziness of these mad people is subtle, artistic, an orderly dance—in fact, an opera—that fills minds and bodies with the most interesting and enlivening musical ideas, and with love of the world's flawed people in all of their comic efforts to live well. The conclusion is that these efforts will often turn into pratfalls, but those of us who are in on the joke, able to accept our own vulnerability, will prevail, attaining and expressing joy.

The politics of this opera are not shouted from the rooftops, but it is surely Mozartean in a wish for all of us to have what might be called a "facilitating environment"—spaces to play, to laugh at ourselves, and to enjoy life's pleasures, with mercy toward self and others when we go wrong. It is opposed in every way to the authoritarian and theocratic politics of Pius IX, who put our flaws on his list of Errors and endeavored to suppress them all, with no mercy. The world of *Falstaff* is one of free bourgeois families, enterprising women, and husbands who learn not to rule with a jealous hand. The world, as Verdi saw it, of the new republican Italy. It shows people who meet pain and depression not with a closed-off and intolerant sense of self, but with openness, effervescence, and humor—thus repudiating the thoughts that led to Wagnerian politics.

As for the politics of aging, the work offers us a lot, on two distinct levels. First, the history of its genesis reveals the importance of supportive human connections and collaborations, cultural and personal, for a time of life that might otherwise produce isolation and unhappiness—a Winnicottian "facilitating environment." Think of the trill scene: societies should find more ways to promote that trill of joyful creativity, springing from one person to another. Policies of many kinds, including to a worldwide assault on compulsory retirement, can assist inclusion and undermine stigma.

There are also political ideas offered in the work itself. I've mentioned the general ideas, but there are also ideas related specifically to aging: the need to respect aging bodies, even when they seem unlovely or lacking in grace; the importance of understanding that such Falstaffian people may offer illumination, wisdom, and creativity, a wit that creates wit in others, if they are respected, included, and permitted to exist in society's midst rather than relegated to its shadows. Falstaff's challenge is profound: I am ungainly, and yet I deserve love. The root cause of prejudice against aging people is fear for oneself, inspired by aging bodies that remind people of their mortality. A work that makes the audience love its aging protagonist and his ungainly body, thence their own vulnerable bodies, addresses this fear directly, and turns it into knowing laughter.

Aftermath

Initially Verdi felt sad after the opening. When he sent the score to Ricordi to print, he enclosed a melodramatic note, "The last notes of *Falstaff*. Everything is over. Go, go old John, go on down your road as far as you can. Entertaining sort of rascal, eternally true, under different masks, in all times, in all places. Go, go on, go on. Addio!" And from Genoa he sent Ricordi a letter saying that he would like to fly back to Milan in a balloon (!!) to begin rehearsing again. "Everything ends!! Alas, alas! too sad!! This thought is too sad!! It is all Big Belly's fault! What madmen!! Everyone. He, You, You, You, You. Everything on earth is a joke."[43]

Boito, emotionally responsive as always, told Verdi that he really needed to be involved with further productions, particularly one coming up soon in Rome: the work was a big hit, and had importance for culture generally.

From this transfusion of happiness, strength, truth, light [and] intellectual health shall come a great good for art and for the public. . . . A very new art form such as *Falstaff* must not be

---

[43] Quoted in Phillips-Matz (1992, p. 719). Letter of March 3, 1893. Throughout I do not transcribe Verdi's own ellipses, three dots that he uses as liberally as he also uses exclamation points—because they will be misread as my own ellipses, indicating omitted material. So I use them only for that latter purpose.

abandoned by its creator after the first experiment, even though this produced prodigious results.[44]

So Verdi went to Rome, where he was celebrated by King Umberto I[45] and made an honorary citizen of the city. For a long time after this, returning home, he was in terrifically good spirits, joking with everyone, his letters bursting with humor.

Verdi lived another eight years. He did not write another opera, but he wrote a series of choral works to sacred texts (the *Quattro pezzi sacri*) and corresponded with Boito about these. His wife's health began to decline, and he urged Boito to visit to cheer them up. Her cough turned into pneumonia, and she died on November 14, 1897. Boito was similarly afflicted: his wife died in June 1898. Verdi's heartfelt letter of consolation (written while she was still living but soon to die) is the only one in which he addresses his friend by his Christian name.

After his own loss, Verdi did not go back to his home but spent time in Milan, in order to have more people around, including Boito and other friends. Boito described him to a friend as "marvelously well . . . as merry as a lark," walking, playing the piano, visiting with friends. Then on January 21, 1901, he suffered a massive stroke. Basically unconscious from that time on, he died on January 27, with Boito at his side. His one brief return to consciousness came when the doctor put Verdi's gold watch, which struck the hours with a musical phrase, to his ear: he opened his eyes, smiled, then lost consciousness again.[46] There can be no better commentary on that sad day than Boito's own in a lengthy letter to Bellaigue,

---

[44] Ibid. Written March 19.

[45] Umberto I (1844–1900) was the son of Vittorio Emanuele II. As a young man he fought for Italy's independence from France and Austria, but as a king he was more conservative and militaristic than his father, and focused on colonial expansion; eventually he was assassinated by an anarchist. This honor paid to Verdi the old republican shows that the ideas of the Risorgimento were still somewhere in his somewhat eclectic political mind.

[46] See Walker (1982, p. 508).

written on Easter Day (April 7) —because, he says, he has been unable to write about Verdi until then:

> This is the first time that I have dared to write of him in a letter.…
> I threw myself into my work, as if into the sea, to save myself…
>
> Verdi is dead. He has carried away with him an enormous measure of light and vital warmth. We had all basked in the sunshine of that Olympian old age.
>
> He died magnificently, like a fighter, formidable and mute.… [A detailed description of Verdi's last days follows.]
>
> My dear friend, in the course of my life I have lost those I have idolized, and grief has outlasted resignation. But never have I experienced such a feeling of hatred against death, of contempt for that mysterious, blind, stupid, triumphant and craven power. It needed the death of this octogenarian to arouse those feelings in me.
>
> He too hated it. For he was the most powerful expression of life that it is possible to imagine. He hated it, as he hated laziness, enigmas, and doubt.
>
> Now all is over. He sleeps like a King of Spain in his Escurial,[47] under a bronze slab that completely covers him.

Boito then proposes a collaborative work about Verdi—as soon as he finishes "my cruel labor" (i.e., *Nerone*). Bellaigue published a book on Verdi on his own in 1912, in time for Verdi's centenary in 1913.[48] It is dedicated to Boito, "In memory of the teacher we loved."[49]

It is this love that sustains all inhabitants of the Republic of Love, like a trill running through the great somewhat disorderly orchestra of our political and personal lives.

---

[47] Referring to King Philippe's aria about his own future death in Verdi's *Don Carlos*; see chapter 6.

[48] Bellaigue (1912).

[49] *En souvenir du maître que nous avons aimé.*

Conclusion

Operas engage in political thought—not only through their plots and the details of their libretti, but also and especially through the paths mapped out for listeners by their music, and the emotions and thoughts that this music summons into being.

There are many types of political thought, just as operas too exhibit endless variety. This book has not been a survey of the many different contributions operas make to political thought, a project that would quickly turn diffuse and unilluminating. Instead, I have focused on one picture of a republican political community bound together by brotherhood and love, as realized in a remarkable way in the operas of Mozart, an optimistic Freemason and a spirit of unsurpassed grace and vision. Feudal arrogance above and groveling fear below are replaced by reciprocity, equality, and compassion. The product is the new free individual—a core ideal of the liberal Enlightenment, and one that still beckons to us even when our age is full of doubt about the fate of liberalism. In an era when men always called the tune, Mozart had the daring to seek new paradigms of political emotion in the women's world, and his operas show repeatedly that a reform of class relations will prove impotent without a deeper reform of the gendered sentiments with which men and women encounter one another.

Mozart's music expresses in glorious and subtle detail the highest Freemasonic aspirations of his era, but Mozart also understands that a successful Republic of Love cannot be forever solemn. It must have been fun inhabiting real life as it is and embracing real people as they are. It can venture serious flights of idealism, but it must also include jokes, masquerades, and quirky outbursts of craziness. A spirit of hope and joy pervades the Republic of Love, not in spite of its humor but because of it: the serious business of Mozartean comedy is its ability to laugh at the absurd (including the absurd in oneself) while aiming for the sublime. This ability is rooted in an acceptance of people and their bodies as basically good and not disgusting—the opposite attitude from the Schopenhauerian pessimism that gives rise to Wagner's totalitarian dramas of despair.

In the Mozartean republic, individuals and institutions support one another. We don't need to begin *in vacuo*, first engineering people with the right sentiments who will then proceed to the creation of political institutions, since we can strive, at the same time, to create institutions that perpetuate and sustain republican ways of thinking and feeling, making sympathy and reciprocity more easily available. We are always beginning with something flawed, both individuals and institutions, but as we strive to reform both they increasingly support one another.

* * *

Mozart was naïve, and he died young. His project is a paradigm that we can consult in our own daily efforts, and his operas remind us of the delightful fun of real-life striving. But the paradigm itself remains incomplete. The Mozartean Republic of Love is ignorant of some serious obstacles in the way of its own success. A clear-eyed confrontation with these challenges is essential to building a more adequate paradigm in our hearts and minds, fortified against these dangers. As Part II has shown, other composers of opera who share Mozart's goals and his general sensibility have confronted the dangers in their own times, and this book has explored a selection of these operas, including two by living composers.

The first danger is the institutionalization of revenge in the form of penal institutions and draconian penalties that express a retributive spirit, rather than one of deterrence and reform. Both Beethoven's *Fidelio* and Jake Heggie's *Dead Man Walking* conduct a searing critique of the breath-denying penal institutions of their very different times, in a spirit of love for human dignity and uncertain hope for better times. Here striving individuals and flawed institutions conduct a productive dialogue.

Mozart believed that freedom-denying religions were already yielding to new religions of autonomy and love. He was naïve. Religions of the breath-denying variety continue to tyrannize over weak people and institutions, creating monarchies of fear where a Republic of Love might have grown. Verdi faced this problem courageously, both in his life and in music of enormous expressive power, creating an indelible musical warning against the Inquisition in our midst and showing, by the very existence of this free and glorious music, that the Inquisition does not always carry the day.

Religion is not the only societal force that creates tyrannies of fear. The very power of the crowd—so democratic in theory, but in practice a cruel tyrant like no other—can crush aspiring individuals with its weight. For both Benjamin Britten and Leoš Janáček, the problem of subordination by the crowd is a catalyst for operas of searing power. Peter Grimes's fate is grim: the crowd destroys him both externally, dooming his prospects, and internally, laying waste to his psyche. Janáček's Jenůfa, by contrast, escapes the cruelty of the villagers through generous mutual love and a move to a new place. Albert Herring, like Britten himself, discovers freedom while remaining in his beloved Suffolk home. What makes escape possible for Jenůfa and Albert? For both, a capacity for unconditional love and the inner cultivation of a citadel of inner integrity. Both composers also point to the possibility of societal cultures with greater openness and breathing space—such as the city for which Jenůfa and Láca leave their repressive town; such as real-life Suffolk in and for which Britten created his Aldeburgh Festival.

The grim torments of war lie beyond Mozart's sunny imagination. And it is indeed hard for opera to depict an experience whose very nature seems anti-musical. But musical works can warn against war and show paths of reconciliation and hope—as Britten did in his *War Requiem,* the subject of my previous book. In the present book, John Adams shows that opera can even depict the difficult effort of diplomacy, as flawed individuals open a space for communication and understanding.

Mozart's heirs are better understood if we face what they are arguing against. And the Mozartean opera tradition has a theoretical/musical antagonist: the spirit of Schopenhauerian nihilism, combined with overweening arrogance and Messianism, in the operas of Richard Wagner, which seek rescue for shipwrecked humanity in a closed community that listens obediently to a single voice.

No book about Mozart should end with Wagner. To more fittingly conclude this book, I have turned, or returned, to Verdi, and to one further challenge for the Republic of Love, the challenge of aging—met, in *Falstaff,* with an outburst of hilarity, an intricate and musically innovative pandemonium of joy, friendship, and delighted love of the world.

* * *

Opera is no longer the popular art form that it was in Verdi's time, when laborers walking down the street would greet one another and signal affiliations by whistling an opera tune. At the annual Grammy Awards, heralding the most popular American music, opera is present, but relegated, with all classical music, to a separate smaller ceremony, ignored in most major media writeups. But opera was not a truly popular art form in Mozart's time either, or, for that matter, in Wagner's: nineteenth-century Italy apart, it has remained a bourgeois entertainment. On account of its high production costs, it has rarely had substantial working-class audiences. Today, however, with the wide availability of recordings and streaming, it is far more accessible to a wide public than it ever has been. Schools and universities can and do take advantage of these possibilities. (For example, most colleges and universities subscribe to the Metropolitan Opera's HD On Demand, which offers a vast store of productions at the push of a button.)

Nor are live performances out of reach for the non-bourgeois, as they used to be when I was a (bourgeois) child in Philadelphia. The Met HD performances, shown live in movie theaters throughout the world, have vastly expanded opera's reach. Ticket policies, too, are creatively meeting our time's challenges, with Lyric Opera of Chicago, for example, offering student tickets at $20.00. Other companies have been even bolder in search of inclusion. In today's Philadelphia, Opera Philadelphia's new General Director and President Anthony Roth Costanzo has instituted a policy by which all seats are either $11 or any higher price a person chooses. The generosity of this "pick-your-price" policy has led to a great jump in attendance and also in donations, both large and small, putting the company on a sounder financial footing than ever. These new strategies are themselves an aspect of realizing a Republic of Love—making the institutions of opera themselves embody opera's best insights.

Opera is alive, and it will continue to evolve, producing new insights. Not just for elites, it is for anyone who wants to try it, a passionate and fascinatingly intricate art form that offers rich understanding of the world and of ourselves. It is surely not the only route to the political insights of this book. But it remains vibrant and vital. And I believe that no other route to this type of political understanding is more gloriously moving, more urgingly joyous, and simply more fun.

References

Adams, John. 2008. *Hallelujah Junction: Composing an American Life.* London: Faber and Faber; New York: Farrar, Straus and Giroux.

Adorno, Theodor W. (1952) 2009. *In Search of Wagner.* Translated by Rodney Livingstone. London: Verso Books.

Allanbrook, Wye Jamison. 1983. *Rhythmic Gesture in Mozart: "Le Nozze di Figaro" and "Don Giovanni."* Chicago: University- of Chicago Press.

Badol-Bertrand, Florence. 2006. "Introductory Essay." In *La Clemenza di Tito,* directed by René Jacobs.

Barenboim, Daniel, cond. 1999. *Beethoven: "Fidelio."* Teldec (2 CDs). Liner notes, p. 20 ("Chicago's Fidelio").

Barshack, Lior. 2008. "The Sovereignty of Pleasure: Sexual and Political Freedom in the Operas of Mozart and Da Ponte." *Law and Literature* 20:47–67.

Bartsch, Shadi, and David Wray, eds. *Seneca and the Self.* 1st ed. Cambridge: Cambridge University Press, 2009.

Bellaigue, Camille. 1912. *Verdi.* Paris: Librairie Renouard.

Bloom, Harold. 1998. *Shakespeare: The Invention of the Human.* New York: Riverhead Books.

Bloom, Harold. 2017. *Falstaff: Give Me Life.* New York: Scribner.

Borchmeyer, Dieter. 1992. "The Question of Anti-Semitism." In *Wagner Handbook,* edited by Ulrich Müller and Peter Wapnewski, translation edited by John Deathridge, 166–85. Cambridge, MA: Harvard University Press.

Brett, Philip, ed. 1983. *Benjamin Britten: "Peter Grimes."* Cambridge Opera Handbooks. Cambridge: Cambridge University Press.

Braunbehrens, Volkmar. (1986) 1991. *Mozart in Vienna: 1781–1791.* Translated by Timothy Bell. New York: HarperPerennial.

Brown, Bruce Alan. 1995. *W. A. Mozart, "Così fan tutte."* Cambridge: Cambridge University Press.

Budden, Julian. 1981. *The Operas of Verdi: Volume 3, from "Don Carlos" to "Falstaff."* New York: Oxford University Press.

Carpenter, Humphrey. 1992. *Benjamin Britten: A Biography.* New York: Charles Scribner's Sons.

Carter, Tim. 1987. *W. A. Mozart: "Le Nozze di Figaro."* Cambridge Opera Handbooks. New York and Cambridge: Cambridge University Press.

Cassius Dio. 1925. *Roman History,* Volume VIII: Books 61–70. Translated by Earnest Cary and Herbert B. Foster. Loeb Classical Library 176. Cambridge, MA: Harvard University Press.

Caston, Ruth R., and Robert A. Kaster, eds. 2016. *Hope, Joy, and Affection in the Classical World: Essays in Honor of David Konstan.* New York: Oxford University Press.

Conati, Marcello, and Mario Medici, eds. 1994. *The Verdi–Boito Correspondence.* English edition prepared by William Weaver. Chicago: University of Chicago Press.

Cook, Malcolm. 1992. *Beaumarchais: "Le Mariage de Figaro."* Bristol: Bristol Classical Press.

Cress, Donald A., ed. 1987. *Jean-Jacques Rousseau: The Basic Political Writings.* Indianapolis: Hackett.

Daines, Matthew. 1996. "An Interview with John Adams." *Opera Quarterly* 13:37–54.

Daines, Matthew, and Peter Sellars. 1996. "*Nixon in China*: An Interview with Peter Sellars." *Tempo* 197:12–19.

Darabont, Frank, dir. 1994. *The Shawshank Redemption.* Burbank, CA: Warner Bros. Pictures.

Da Ponte, Lorenzo. (1961) 1993. *Three Mozart Libretti: "The Marriage of Figaro," "Don Giovanni," and "Così fan tutte."* Translated and edited by Robert Pack and Marjorie Lelash. New York: Dover Publications.

Da Ponte, Lorenzo. 1979. *Three Mozart Libretti: "The Marriage of Figaro," "Don Giovanni," and "Così fan tutte."* Translated by Robert Pack and Marjorie Lelash. Reprint of *Mozart's Librettos.* London: C.F. Peters, 1941; reprinted by Meridian Books, 1961. New York: Dover Publications.

Da Ponte, Lorenzo. 2000. *Memoirs.* Translated by Elizabeth Abbott. With an introduction by Charles Rosen. New York: New York Review of Books.

Darnton, Robert. 1996. *The Forbidden Best-Sellers of Pre-Revolutionary France.* New York: W. W. Norton.

Dent, Edward J. 1913. *Mozart's Operas: A Critical Study.* London: Chatto & Windus.

Ellis, William Ashton, trans. 1995. *Richard Wagner: Judaism in Music and Other Essays.* By Richard Wagner. Lincoln: University of Nebraska Press.

Ewans, Michael. 1977. *Janáček's Tragic Operas.* London: Faber and Faber.

Goffman, Erving. 1963. *Stigma: Notes on the Management of Spoiled Identity.* New York: Simon & Schuster.

Gossett, Philip. 2007. *Divas and Scholars: Performing Italian Opera.* Chicago: University of Chicago Press.

Gregor-Dellin, Martin. 1983. *Richard Wagner: His Life, His Work, His Century.* Translated by J. Maxwell Brownjohn. London: Collins.

Grey, Thomas S. 2000. "The Return of the Prodigal Son: Wagner and *Der fliegende Holländer.*" In *Richard Wagner: "Der fliegende Holländer,"* edited by Thomas S. Grey, 1–24. Cambridge Opera Handbooks. Cambridge: Cambridge University Press.

Grey, Thomas S. 2002. "Wagner's *Die Meistersinger* as National Opera." In *Music and German National Identity (1868–1945),* edited by Celia Applegate and Pamela Potter, 78–104. Chicago: University of Chicago Press.

Grey, Thomas S. 2008. "The Jewish Question." In *The Cambridge Companion to Wagner,* edited by Thomas S. Grey, 203–18. Cambridge: Cambridge University Press.

Guyer, Jonathan. 2023. "I Crashed Henry Kissinger's 100th-Birthday Party: The Elite Love Him but for Some Reason Won't Say Why." *Intelligencer* (New York Magazine), June 8, 2023.

Hepokoski, James A. 1983. *Giuseppe Verdi: "Falstaff."* Cambridge Opera Handbooks. Cambridge: Cambridge University Press.

Herder, Johann Gottfried. 2002. *Herder: Philosophical Writings.* Edited and translated by Michael N. Forster. Cambridge: Cambridge University Press.

Hexter, Ralph. 2002. "Masked Balls." *Cambridge Opera Journal* 14:93–108.

Hunt, Lynn, ed. 1993. *The Invention of Pornography: Obscenity and the Origins of Modernity, 1500–1800.* Cambridge: Zone Books.

Israel, Jeffrey. 2019. *Living with Hate in American Politics and Religion.* Foreword by Martha C. Nussbaum. New York: Columbia University Press.

Istituto Nazionale di Studi Verdiani. 2017. *The Correspondence between Verdi and Piroli.* Curated by Giuseppe Martini. Parma: Istituto Nazionale di Studi Verdiani. https://www.museoscala.org/en/media-library/podcast/the-corresp ondence-between-verdi-and-piroli-curated-by-giuseppe-martini.html.

Janáčková, Zdenka. 1998. *My Life with Janáček: The Memoirs of Zdenka Janáčková.* Edited and translated by John Tyrrell. London: Faber and Faber.

Johnson, Timothy A. 2011. *John Adams's "Nixon in China": Musical Analysis, Historical and Political Perspectives.* Abingdon and New York: Ashgate.

Joyce, James. (1934) 1992. *Ulysses.* Reprinted in 1961. New York: Random House.

Keller, Hans. 1983. "*Peter Grimes*: The Story, the Music Not Excluded." In *Benjamin Britten: Peter Grimes,* edited by Philip Brett, 105–20. Cambridge Opera Handbooks. Cambridge: Cambridge University Press.

Kerman, Joseph. 1949. "Grimes and Lucretia." *The Hudson Review* 2 (2) (Summer): 277–84.

Kerman, Joseph. 1988. *Opera as Drama.* New and revised ed. Berkeley and Los Angeles: University of California Press.

Kerman, Joseph. 1990. "Reading Don Giovanni." In *"Don Giovanni": Myth of Seduction and Betrayal,* edited by Jonathan Miller, 108–25. Baltimore: Johns Hopkins University Press.

Kitcher, Philip, and Richard Schacht. 2004. *Finding an Ending: Reflections on Wagner's "Ring."* New York: Oxford University Press.

Kivy, Peter. 1999. *Osmin's Rage: Philosophical Reflections on Opera, Drama, and Text.* Ithaca, NY: Cornell University Press.

Kloppenberg, James T. 2016. *Toward Democracy: The Struggle for Self-Rule in European and American Thought.* Oxford: Oxford University Press.

Landon, H. C. Robbins. 1982. *Mozart and the Masons.* New York: Thames and Hudson.

Li Zhisui. 1994. *The Private Life of Chairman Mao.* New York: Random House.

Mackie, Patrick. 2023. *Mozart in Motion.* London: Granta.

Magee, Bryan. 2000. *The Tristan Chord: Wagner and Philosophy.* New York: Henry Holt.

Mörike, Eduard. 1997. *Mozart auf der Reise nach Prag.* Translated by Michael Fleming, in *Eight German Novellas,* 164–220. Oxford and New York: Oxford University Press, 1997.

Müller, Gerhard. 1997. "Die Stadt als Schauplatz." Program essay.

Muti, Riccardo. 2022. *Verdi, the Italian: In Music, Our Roots.* Translated by Fulvia Di Pasquale. Ravenna: RMMusic.

Nettl, Paul. 1952. *Mozart and Masonry.* New York: Philosophical Library.

New School University. 2001. "Bob Kerrey Installed as New School University's 7th President: Former Senator and Governor of Nebraska to Guide University's Seven-School Constellation into New Century." Press release, February 20.

Nietzsche, Friedrich. (1886) 1966. *Beyond Good and Evil: Prelude to a Philosophy of the Future.* Translated by Walter Kaufmann. New York: Vintage Books.

Nietzsche, Friedrich. (1886) 1996. *The Wanderer and His Shadow* in *Human All Too Human.* Translated by R.J. Hollingdale. Cambridge: Cambridge University Press, sec. 160.

Nietzsche, Friedrich. 1967. "The Case of Wagner." In *The Birth of Tragedy and The Case of Wagner,* translated by Walter Kaufmann, 155–92. New York: Vintage.

Nirenberg, David. 2013. *Anti-Judaism: The Western Tradition.* New York: W. W. Norton.

Nixon, Richard. (1974) 2009. "President Richard Nixon's Special Message to the Congress Proposing a Comprehensive Health Insurance Plan, February 6, 1974." In "Nixon's Plan for Health Reform, in His Own Words," *KFF Health News,* September 3.

Nussbaum, Charles O. 2007. *The Musical Representation: Meaning, Ontology, and Emotion.* Cambridge, MA: MIT Press.

Nussbaum, Martha C. 1994. *The Therapy of Desire: Theory and Practice in Hellenistic Ethics.* Princeton, NJ: Princeton University Press.

Nussbaum, Martha C. 1999. "Equity and Mercy." In *Sex and Social Justice,* 134–83. New York: Oxford University Press.

Nussbaum, Martha C. 2001. *Upheavals of Thought: The Intelligence of Emotions.* New York: Cambridge University Press.

Nussbaum, Martha C. 2013. *Political Emotions: Why Love Matters for Justice.* Cambridge, MA: Harvard University Press.

Nussbaum, Martha C. 2016a. *Anger and Forgiveness: Resentment, Generosity, Justice.* Oxford University Press.

Nussbaum, Martha C. 2016b. *Not for Profit: Why Democracy Needs the Humanities.* Updated edition. Princeton, NJ: Princeton University Press.

Nussbaum, Martha C. 2018. *The Monarchy of Fear: A Philosopher Looks at Our Political Crisis.* New York: Simon & Schuster.

Nussbaum, Martha C. 2020. "Philosophy and the Ring." *Program essay of the Lyric Opera of Chicago* for the never completed *Ring* cycle of 2020–21. https://www.lyricopera.org/lyric-lately/philosophy-and-the-ring/

Nussbaum, Martha C. 2022. "Carmen's Freedom." *Program of the Lyric Opera of Chicago.*

Nussbaum, Martha C. 2024. *The Tenderness of Silent Minds: Benjamin Britten and His "War Requiem."* New York: Oxford University Press.

Nussbaum, Martha C. 2024a. "Aida: 'War, Enemy of Love.'" *Program of the Lyric Opera of Chicago,* March 2024, 24–26.

Phillips-Matz, Mary Jane. 1992. *Verdi: A Biography.* Oxford and New York: Oxford University Press.

Porter, Andrew. 1983. "Verdi's *Don Carlos*: An Introduction." Liner notes for *Don Carlos.* Orchestra and Chorus of the Teatro alla Scala, conducted by Claudio Abbado. Deutsche Grammophon, 33–43, at 36.

Porter, Andrew. 1988. "*Nixon in China*: John Adams in Conversation with Andrew Porter." *Tempo* 167 (December): 25–30.

Prejean, Sister Helen. 1993. *Dead Man Walking*. New York: Random House. Updated edition with new preface by Archbishop Desmond Tutu. New York: Vintage Books, 1994.

Price, Raymond. 1977. *With Nixon*. New York: Viking Adult.

Rahim, Sameer. 2017. "Alice Goodman on Writing Political Operas—and Her Late Husband Geoffrey Hill." *Prospect*, August 17.

Rice, John. 2009. *Mozart on the Stage*. Cambridge: Cambridge University Press.

Robinson, Paul, ed. 1996. *Ludwig van Beethoven: Fidelio*. Cambridge Opera Handbooks. Cambridge, UK: Cambridge University Press.

Rosen, Charles. 1976. *The Classical Style*. New York: W. W. Norton.

Rupprecht, Philip, ed. 2013. *Rethinking Britten*. New York: Oxford University Press.

Rushton, Julian. 1993. *W. A. Mozart: "Idomeneo."* Cambridge Opera Handbooks. Cambridge: Cambridge University Press.

Said, Edward W. 1997. "On *Fidelio*." *London Review of Books*, October 30. Reprinted in a slightly different form in *Said on Opera*. New York: Columbia University Press, 2024, 29–53.

Saura, Carlos, dir. 2009. *Io Don Giovanni*. Madrid: Alfresco Films.

Schiller, Friedrich. (1787) 2004. *Don Carlos: A Play*. Translated by R. D. Boylan. Project Gutenberg. EBook 6789. Last updated July 20, 2014. https://www.gutenberg.org/ebooks/6789.

Schmidt, Eberhard. 1997. "Sinnspiel Zauberflöte." Program essay.

Schopenhauer, Arthur. (1818–1844) 1958. *The World as Will and Representation*. 2 vols. Translated by E. F. J. Payne. New York: Dover.

Sen, Amartya. 1981. *Poverty and Famines: An Essay on Entitlement and Deprivation*. New York and Oxford: Oxford University Press.

Seneca. 2012. *Anger, Mercy, Revenge*. Translated by Robert A. Kaster and Martha C. Nussbaum. Chicago: University of Chicago Press.

Solomon, Maynard. 1995. *Mozart: A Life*. New York: HarperCollins.

Sonnleithner, Leopold von. 1919–1920. "Über die Zauberflöte." *Mozarteums Mitteilungen* (Salzburg) 1(1–2).

Steinberg, Michael P. 2004. *Listening to Reason: Culture, Subjectivity, and Nineteenth-Century Music*. Princeton, NJ: Princeton University Press.

Stroeher, Vicki P., Nicholas Clark, and Jude Brimmer, eds. 2016. *My Beloved Man: The Letters of Benjamin Britten and Peter Pears*. Aldeburgh Studies in Music 10. Woodbridge, Suffolk: Boydell Press.

Thomson, Katharine. 1977. *The Masonic Thread in Mozart*. New York: Lawrence & Wishart.

Tyrrell, John. 1992. *Janáček's Operas: A Documentary Account*. Princeton, NJ: Princeton University Press.

Vaget, Hans. 2006. "Mörike's Mozart and the Scent of a Woman." In *The "Don Giovanni" Moment: Essays on the Legacy of the Opera*, edited by Lydia Goehr and Daniel Herwitz, 61–74. New York: Columbia University Press.

Vaget, Hans. 2013. "Antisemitism." In *The Cambridge Wagner Encyclopedia*, edited by Nicolas Vaszonyi, 16–20. Cambridge: Cambridge University Press.

Vermeule, Adrian. 2022. *Common Good Constitutionalism*. Boston and New York: Polity Press.

Vogel, Jaroslav. 1981. *Leoš Janáček: A Biography*. New York: W. W. Norton.

Waldoff, Jessica. 2019. "Mozart and Freemasonry." In *Mozart in Context*, edited by Simon P. Keefe, 50–58. Cambridge: Cambridge University Press.

Walker, Frank. (1962) 1982. *Verdi the Man*. Chicago: University of Chicago Press.

Warrack, John. 1994. *Richard Wagner: "Die Meistersinger von Nürnberg."* Cambridge Opera Handbooks. Cambridge: Cambridge University Press.

Williams, Bernard. 1988. "Don Giovanni as an Idea." In *On Opera*, edited by Patricia Williams, 31–42. New Haven, CT: Yale University Press, 2006.

Williams, Bernard. 1988a. "Rather Red than Black: Verdi, *Don Carlos*, and the Passion for Freedom." In *On Opera*, edited by Patricia Williams, 49–56. New Haven, CT: Yale University Press.

Williams, Craig A. 2010. *Roman Homosexuality*. 2nd ed. Oxford: Oxford University Press.

Wilson, Dick. 1984. *Zhou Enlai: A Biography*. New York: Viking.

Index

For the benefit of digital users, indexed terms that span two pages (e.g., 52–53) may, on occasion, appear on only one of those pages.

Page numbers followed by n indicate footnotes.